Mapping Christian Rhetorics

D0148803

The continued importance of Christian rhetorics in political, social, ped-agogical, and civic affairs suggests that such rhetorics not only belong on the map of rhetorical studies, but are indeed essential to the geography of rhetorical studies in the twenty-first century. This collection argues that concerning ourselves with religious rhetorics in general and Christian rhetorics in particular tells us something about rhetoric itself—its boundaries, its characteristics, its functionings. In assembling original research on the intersections of rhetoric and Christianity from prominent and emerging scholars, *Mapping Christian Rhetorics* seeks to locate religion more centrally within the geography of rhetorical studies in the twenty-first century. It does so by acknowledging work on Christian rhetorics that has been overlooked or ignored, connecting domains of knowledge and research areas pertaining to Christian rhetorics that may remain disconnected or under-connected, and charting new avenues of inquiry about Christian rhetorics that might invigorate theory-building, teaching, research, and civic engagement. In dividing the terrain of Christian rhetorics into four categories—theory, education, methodology, and civic engagement—*Mapping Christian Rhetorics* aims to foster connections among these areas of inquiry and spur future collaboration between scholars of religious rhetoric in a range of research areas.

Michael-John DePalma is an assistant professor of English in the Professional Writing Program at Baylor University, Waco, Texas, U.S.

Jeffrey M. Ringer is an assistant professor of English in the division of Rhetoric, Writing, and Linguistics at the University of Tennessee, Knoxville, U.S.

Routledge Studies in Rhetoric and Communication

Mapping Christian Rhetorics

Connecting Conversations,
Charting New Territories

Edited by
Michael-John DePalma and
Jeffrey M. Ringer

NEW YORK AND LONDON

First published 2015
by Routledge
711 Third Avenue, New York, NY 10017

and by Routledge
2 Park Square, Milton Park, Abingdon, Oxon OX14 4RN

First issued in paperback 2017

Routledge is an imprint of the Taylor & Francis Group, an informa business

Library of Congress Cataloging-in-Publication Data

Mapping Christian rhetorics : connecting conversations, charting new
   territories / edited by Michael-John DePalma and Jeffrey M. Ringer. —
   1 [edition].
      pages cm. — (Routledge studies in rhetoric and communication ; 21)
   Includes index.
   1. Rhetoric—Religious aspects—Christianity.   I. DePalma, Michael-John,
1977–, editor.
   BR115.R55M37 2014
   261.5'8—dc23
   2014022484

Typeset in Sabon
by Apex CoVantage, LLC

ISBN 13: 978-1-138-09778-0 (pbk)
ISBN 13: 978-1-138-78141-2 (hbk)

For our families

Contents

Acknowledgments

This project began to take shape in the pews and prayers and communities of faith that have had a significant place in our lives since childhood. Long before we discovered the excitement and challenges of writing about religious rhetorics, our experiences as Christians—be they wonder, dissonance, peace, or dissolutionment—demanded that we attend closely to the ways religious beliefs and traditions inform human experience. What was initially born out of those experiences found its form in a friendship. For nearly a decade, we have had the opportunity share our ideas, beliefs, and questions with one another. Over meals and beers, on planes and beaches, through comprehensive exams and the birth of our children, the thoughts that populate this volume emerged. We are thankful that what started as a passing discussion about Augustine in Durham, New Hampshire during the fall of 2005 has grown into a longstanding friendship and scholarly pursuit.

We are grateful to the authors in this collection for their thoughtful contributions to discussions of Christian rhetorics. We have learned much from the insights they share, and we are thankful for the opportunity to collaborate with such an outstanding group of scholars. We also appreciate the work of Liz Levine, Joshua Wells, Felisa Salvago-Keyes, and Andrew Weckenmann at Routledge, and we offer our gratitude to the anonymous reviewers for their valuable feedback and generative recommendations.

The support from our colleagues at Baylor University (Mike), the University of Tennessee (Jeff), and Lee University (Jeff) is also deeply appreciated. Mike especially thanks Lisa Shaver, Kara Poe Alexander, Coretta Pitman, Richard Russell, Maurice Hunt, Josh King, Dianna Vitanza, Tom Hibbs, Wes Null, Danielle Williams, Vicki Klaris, Barbara Saunders Jones, Mona Choucair, Emily Setina, the Waldens, the Ponds, the Trozzos, the Engebretsons, the Costons, and the Kings for their encouragement and support. Mike also thanks Dean Nordt and Dean Driskell of Baylor's College of Arts & Sciences for funding to support this project. Jeff is grateful for the support and encouragement from his colleagues at Tennessee—Janet Atwill, Russ Hirst, Mike Keene, Kirsten Benson, Lisa King, Tanita Saenkhum, Stan Garner, Dawn Coleman, Luke Harlow, and Jud Laughter—as well as his colleagues in the Department of Languages and Literatures at Lee University, his previous institution.

We are also thankful to the many others who had important influences in shaping this project: Tom Newkirk, Larry Prelli, Jess Enoch, Elizabeth Vander Lei, Pat Bizzell, Suzanne Bordelon, Jim Webber, David Gold, Catherine Hobbs, Jan Fernheimer, Michelle Payne, Cristy Beemer, Laurel Medhurst, and Martin Medhurst. We are also grateful to our students from whom each semester we gain a deeper appreciation for the challenges and excitement of using writing as a tool for engaging the intellectual, ethical, and spiritual complexity of human experience.

Mike: I want to thank my friends and family for their unwavering love and support. August, Brad, Brett, Mike, Karl, Dan, Andrew, Jimmy, and Alex are cherished friends who have cheered me on in success and built me up in failure. I am also grateful to my San Diego family, especially Donald and Lynn, and the Dulls, for their love and kindness. I am thankful, too, to my aunts, uncles, and cousins in New York, who have always loved me wholeheartedly. I, too, want to thank my grandparents for their legacy of care. I am grateful also to my sisters-in-law, Charmaine and Ashley, for the unique friendships we share. I am deeply appreciative, too, for my brother Thomas, whose love has sustained and encouraged me for thirty-one years, and for my nephew, Judah Michael, who has my name and my heart. I especially want to thank my parents for cultivating every dream that I've ever expressed, for sacrificing so that I would not have to, for believing in me when I could not. Finally, I want to thank the two for whom I live—Lily and Courtney. For you, my love and gratitude is boundless. Above all, I am thankful to Christ for my vocation, and I give Him praise for this endeavor.

Jeff: No small thanks goes to my family. To Mom and Dad, thanks for training me up in the way I should go and for teaching me to be a critical thinker. To Jen and Billy and Jonathan and Breanna, thanks for being there, for caring about what I do, and for letting me be an Uncle. To my in-laws, Will and Prudence and the whole Barker clan, thanks for being so enthusiastic about my work. To my beautiful wife, Sarah, thanks for your patience, kindness, enthusiasm, and grace as I finished this project. Thanks for your love and friendship, and for staying interested. Finally, to Zoe and Ben, thanks for embodying life and grace and blessedness—and to letting us all get a bit of sleep now and then. I love you all.

Introduction
Current Trends and Future Directions in Christian Rhetorics

Michael-John DePalma and
Jeffrey M. Ringer

> [W]e are today witnessing the return of religion. [. . .] This is why
> it is important—and perhaps why it is the duty of us academics and
> intellectuals—to find new ways of thinking about religion [. . .].
>
> —Laurent Pernot, "The Rhetoric of Religion"

In a 2012 story on National Public Radio's *Here & Now*, host Robin Young
interviewed Dave Imus, an independent cartographer who crafted "The
Essential Geography of the United States," a map that won best in show at
the prestigious Cartography and Geographic Information Society Competition in 2010. In the interview, Imus explains that his goal in making the
map was to bring "into focus the principle elements of the United States—
the basic geography" ("Greatest"). After acknowledging Imus's success in
doing so, Young comments on the choices Imus made:

> YOUNG: I'm looking at Chicago, and you've included—oh look,
> there's Wrigley Field. And a little icon where Northwestern
> University would be. And, oh, Grant Park. But I see, when
> I compare it, let's say, to the National Geographic map, you
> had to give up the town of South Haven. [Laughs] Which—
>
> IMUS: [laughs]
>
> YOUNG: —which would have been there. No offense to anyone in
> South Haven, but that's kinda cool, that there's Wrigley
> Field. So you made those choices it seems.
>
> IMUS: You know, I did, because, you know, Wrigley Field is a—
> an essential part of Chicago. It's part of what makes Chi-
> cago Chicago.
>
> ("Greatest")

While beleaguered Cubs fans certainly would agree with Imus's claim that
Wrigley is "an essential part of Chicago," residents of South Haven, Michigan, which is located just east of Chicago on the shore of Lake Michigan,

likely would take issue with Imus's decision. His motives, though, seem to rest on two related criteria: space and essence. The first is obvious. Even on a map as large as Imus's, there's only so much space to include details such as cities, towns, rivers, and parks. Essence certainly is a trickier concept, because, based on this example, it often comes down to someone's judgment as to what is or is not essential about a place. At some point, cartographers need to include some geographic features and leave others out.

Such choices, laden with motives, land us squarely in the rhetorical domain. As is well documented in rhetorical studies, maps make arguments because they aim to convince us as to what is important, as to what viewers should see (Anderson and Prelli; Harley; Monmonier; Reynolds; Wood). Maps thus function in ways that correspond to Kenneth Burke's concept of terministic screens: they direct attention by reflecting certain aspects of reality while deflecting others ("Terministic" 45). Including Wrigley Field as part of Chicago forwards the argument that Wrigley is, in Imus's terms, "an essential part of Chicago." In the process, South Haven is rendered as less significant, as nonessential. As Young put it in her interview with Imus, "[m]aps count" ("Greatest"). They do so because they function ideologically to forward a particular argument about what deserves space within a particular representation of a geography.

What does this discussion of mapping have to do with Christian rhetorics? Our purpose in this volume is to argue that Christian rhetorics not only belong on the map of rhetorical studies, but that they should be essential to the geography of rhetorical studies in the twenty-first century. While we certainly don't argue that locating Christian rhetorics on the map of rhetorical studies should oust other concerns—rhetorical studies as a field does not share the same spatial constraints that Imus faced—we are arguing that concerning ourselves with Christian rhetorics in particular and religious rhetorics in general tells us something *about* rhetoric itself—its boundaries, its characteristics, its functionings. We thus agree with Brian Jackson when he writes in this volume that defining religious rhetoric "might help us improve our rhetorical judgment" (this page 19).

In various ways, the contributors to this collection argue that Christian rhetorics specifically and religious rhetorics more broadly are *essential* to rhetorical studies. We fully recognize that essence is a thorny concept. But the question of what *belongs* on a map, of what features constitute the essence of a place, is an important one. It's a question that Nedra Reynolds discusses in terms of academic disciplines and cultural reproduction. She notes that scholars "use the language of mapping to show how the field is configured" and "where the borders lie" (80). Too often, the borders of rhetorical studies have been drawn in a way that excludes or marginalizes religious rhetorics. In a 2006 *Rhetorica* essay, for instance, Laurent Pernot begins his analysis "by locating rhetorical forms of religious expression in order to establish *a kind of map of religious discourse*" (237, emphasis added). Pernot's motives for doing so likely arise from awareness of his audience's proclivities, some of which may militate against taking religious rhetorics seriously. Pernot recognizes, for example, that "linking rhetoric and religion remains new and daring" and that "many academic circles remain reticent and unenthusiastic when it comes to rhetorical readings of ancient religious texts" (236).

The act of mapping, as Imus's interview suggests and as Pernot demonstrates, makes an argument about what is or should be significant—even essential—to a particular geography. *Mapping Christian Rhetorics* thus makes an argument about the space of religious rhetorics within rhetorical scholarship. We contend that religion *has been* to a lesser extent, *is becoming* to a greater extent, and *should continue to be* to an even greater extent, a central locus of inquiry in rhetorical studies. And while we focus in this volume on Christian rhetorics, we hope to encourage future work on other religious rhetorics as well.

The contributions that comprise this volume thus work toward helping rhetoricians rethink the "mental maps" they have of the relationship, or relationships, between rhetoric and religion. Reynolds relates mental mapping to "a person's cognitive capacity to understand where things are in relationship to one another" (82). Such mental maps are socially constructed and produce what she calls an "imagined geography" (Reynolds 84). In assembling original research on the intersections of rhetoric and Christianity from prominent and emerging scholars, *Mapping Christian Rhetorics* seeks to locate religion more centrally within the "imagined geography" of rhetorical studies in the twenty-first century. It does so by mapping the terrain of this scholarship in terms of four categories: *theory, rhetorical education, methodology*, and *civic engagement*. Readers familiar with scholarship dealing with the intersections of rhetoric and Christianity might protest that *history* is not one of the categories we name. That's because we see such scholarship as so central to each of the other threads that separating it would do it disservice. Indeed, many of the chapters in this volume draw on or speak to historical inquiry as it relates to Christian rhetorics. We also highlight the contributions of historical inquiry to theory, rhetorical education, methodology, and civic engagement in our chapter that closes this volume.

MAPPING: ACKNOWLEDGING, CONNECTING, CHARTING

We see the metaphor of mapping as useful for understanding and furthering research on Christian rhetorics. In this introduction and the volume as a whole, we use *mapping* in three overlapping ways:

1. Mapping allows scholars of rhetoric to *acknowledge* that which has been overlooked or ignored.

2. Mapping serves to *connect* territories or domains of knowledge that may remain disconnected or at least under connected.
3. Mapping helps scholars *chart* new avenues of rhetorical inquiry that might invigorate research, teaching, and civic engagement.

Mapping as Acknowledging the Overlooked

Mapping helps rhetoricians acknowledge and name territory that has been overlooked or passed by. This function of mapping is essential because religious rhetorics are often akin to landmarks that occupy an invisibly present space: they exist in abundance in the media, in academia, and in civic and public life—even in many of our own scholarly motives—and yet remain relatively ignored or underrepresented (see DePalma and Ringer, this volume).

By drawing attention to the variety of religious forms, Christian and otherwise, that existed in ancient Greece alongside the more familiar landmarks of classical rhetoric, Laurent Pernot's work exemplifies how mapping religious rhetorics can direct the attention to that which has always been there, even if we've passed over it (*Rhetoric*). Pernot argues that religious discourse in antiquity was ignored because conceptions of rhetoric encompassed primarily politics and civic action. As he shows, religious discourse in the form of prayers, hymns, oaths, panegyrics, apologies, and sermons *did* exist, and he contends that histories of ancient rhetorics need to account for them. Beth Daniell's contribution to this collection also seeks to chart that which has been ignored, though her concern is with contemporary religious rhetorics. She seeks to name a space that academics and media outlets often ignore, namely, the middle space between "Christians"—often portrayed as "narrow-minded, ignorant, oppressive, conservative, judgmental, faithful to dogma"—and "secular liberal academics"—commonly represented as "open-minded; enlightened; liberating; of course, liberal; accepting; and espousing critical thinking" (this page 243). Such a middle encompasses people who "hold liberal political views while practicing their faith," as well as people "who, while socially conservative, experience a Christian community focused on compassion and forgiveness" (this page 243). In her chapter, she goes on to name this middle space by articulating the attendant ideas and values related to biblical interpretation. What Daniell asks of readers, in other words, is that they reimagine rhetorical geography such that "Christian"—reconceived as moderate or even progressive—can find space within academia.

The problem to which Daniell responds—that of a "bifurcated map" that "excludes the possibility of a middle and ignores the complexities of human identity and thought" (this page 243)—speaks to Nedra Reynolds's "imagined geographies." Writing about composition studies in particular, Reynolds notes that the field has "created or invoked frontiers, cities, contact zones, safe houses, borderlands, community compacts, and various other territories that have influenced, at least metaphorically, concepts of literacy or learning" (27). She goes on to say that one consequence of such "territorial metaphors" is that they reify "notions of insider and outsider" (27). One way of understanding Daniell's purpose in her chapter is that she hopes to help readers rethink these boundaries between insider and outsider. The academy, for instance, has often constructed Christians as outsiders—and this because "Christian" so often leads metonymically to "fundamentalist" or, to use Sharon Crowley's term, "apocalypticist."

As a result, a wide range of religious rhetorics tend to remain invisible, buried within fuzzy categories that conjure radicalism and intolerance. Margaret D. Zulick speaks to this when she describes the rhetoric of religion as an "undiscovered country" that demands mapping (125). After mentioning Crowley's *Toward a Civil Discourse*, Zulick observes that "rhetorical criticism of religious discourse in the American situation has to date largely concentrated on prophetism and apocalyptic rhetoric" (132). She later notes that the terms *prophetic* and *apocalyptic* tend to be used interchangeably, despite the fact that not all prophetic rhetoric can be considered apocalyptic (133–34). What results from such conflation is a lack of nuance that can blind researchers to realizing fuller, more accurate understandings of the possibilities—and perils—surrounding the variety of Christian rhetorics (see Cope and Ringer, this volume).

Thus, the benefit of mapping Christian rhetorics—of acknowledging and naming them—is that scholars may come to see distinctions that have hitherto remained invisible. In his contribution to this volume, Brian Jackson gets at this notion when he defends his motivation to define religious rhetoric and explains why such a definition matters to rhetorical studies as a whole: "Pursuing a definition of religion, as fraught a quest as it is, might help us improve our rhetorical judgment by giving us the power to draw distinctions between rhetorical acts that, however similar they may be on the surface, are unique in some way" (this page 19). This resonates with Kenneth Burke's notion of motives. Indeed, elsewhere in his chapter, Jackson cites Burke's notion that "there is an *objective* difference in motivation between an act conceived in the name of God and an act conceived in the name of godless Nature" (*Rhetoric* 6). Jackson's "inclusive" and "supernatural" approaches to defining religious rhetorics certainly invite further dialogue, but he offers a compelling starting place, one that allows rhetoricians to name religious rhetorics *as* such and thus to acknowledge key distinctions between religious and nonreligious forms of rhetoric. In addition, Jackson makes the important claim that effective analysis entails recognizing distinctions that remain invisible.

Matthew T. Althouse, Lawrence J. Prelli, and Floyd D. Anderson's contribution to this collection also illustrates the importance of acknowledging Christian rhetorics that have been concealed. In "Mapping the Rhetoric of Intelligent Design: The Agentification of the Scene," Althouse, Prelli, and Anderson use pentadic cartography to examine the rhetorical dimensions of a leading example of intelligent design discourse: Lee Strobel's *The Case for a Creator*. By using Burke's dramatistic pentad to map Strobel's book, they uncover "the pivotal attitudes and motives of intelligent design" that other rhetorical critics have not acknowledged (this page 161). The act of acknowledging that Strobel's book restricts discourse about science and religion to idealistic or agent-centered terms enables Althouse, Prelli, and Anderson to invent "counterstatements" that bring its dominant and controlling terms into contact with the terms of otherwise excluded perspectives. In doing so, they hope to "open public discourse to as many perspectives as possible" (this page 175). They also provide a roadmap for future scholarship: "Perhaps there are other Christian perspectives that feature agent, purpose, or some other pentadic term that could also enter the dialectical conversation. Students of Christian rhetorics could use pentadic cartography to map out available perspectives as a prelude to encouraging their 'cooperative competition' by confronting them with counterstatements that expose their partiality" (this page 177). Mining Christian rhetorics through the methodology of pentadic cartography could thus serve to invigorate public discourse.

Lisa Shaver's work on Methodist women's rhetoric during the nineteenth century also illustrates the importance of acknowledging Christian rhetorics that have thus far been overlooked (*Beyond* 16–17). In her chapter, Shaver examines the legacy of the deaconess movement during the late nineteenth and early twentieth centuries. She discusses how Methodist deaconesses crafted a distinct group identity that functioned as symbolic action to induce acceptance of expanded women's roles in the church and society, and she traces how their rhetorical strategies served to transform the communities they served. Despite the far-reaching influences of the deaconess movement, it has received little attention in rhetorical studies. In unearthing this legacy of rhetorical and Christian influence, Shaver provides a historical model of rhetorical tactics that might be used to construct more socially just arrangements in twenty-first-century contexts.

Lisa Zimmerelli's chapter in this collection also acknowledges an important dimension of nineteenth century rhetorical history that has not received the attention it deserves: nineteenth-century defenses of women's preaching. In "'Heaven-Touched Lips and Pent-up Voices,' the Rhetoric of American Female Preaching Apologia, 1820–1930," Zimmerelli maps the debates surrounding nineteenth-century women preachers' activism, particularly in terms of the arguments women invented and employed in various genres. By acknowledging the integral role Christianity played in activist rhetorics, Zimmerelli argues that the texts produced by these women to defend their religious leadership serve as important examples of feminist rhetorical activism. Zimmerelli's chapter also provides a rich example of how religion and civic activism can inform one another.

The act of acknowledging previously ignored religious dimensions of rhetoric does more than simply add to scholars' understandings of rhetoric;

such acknowledgment stands to restructure how scholars think about such discourse and its possibilities. Take, for instance, Beth Daniell's contribution to a 1994 interchange in *College Composition and Communication*. In "Composing (as) Power," Daniell recollects how Ann Berthoff reminded a conference audience that Paulo Freire's pedagogical insights stemmed "as much from his Catholicism as from his Marxism" (238–39). Daniell goes on to note how this statement "fundamentally altered [her] view of reality," later explaining that "[e]conomic and political analyses had never seemed adequately to account for the success of Freire's method" (238–39). While Daniell does not discuss this moment in terms of geographic metaphors, she does highlight how recognizing Christian rhetorics as part of the imagined geography of rhetorical and pedagogical theory can significantly restructure one's view of once-familiar terrain. Berthoff didn't invent something new; Freire's Catholicism had always been there. But she named that which rhetoricians had ignored and, in so doing, prompted a restructuring of Daniell's perception of Freire.

Mapping as Connecting Domains

The second notion of mapping we employ is that of connecting: maps help readers perceive connections between domains of knowledge that remain under connected or even disconnected. In some ways, this function of mapping bears similarities to the previous—a map can help draw attention to that which has been ignored or overlooked. The difference rests in how the connecting metaphor serves to link two disciplines, scholarly discussions, or fields of knowledge. Zulick, for instance, notes key connections between rhetoric and religion but then laments that the two fields "rarely are correlated in the course of inquiry" (125). This leads her to observe that the rhetoric of religion demands charting and mapping—a kind of coming to grips with one's location within the terrain of a diverse, if not fractured, discussion (125). To do this connecting work, Zulick shows "where the interconnections lie between religious discourse, rhetorical theory, biblical exegesis, and public discourse" (126). Zulick further highlights the interdisciplinarity of her venture by observing that her chapter will "introduce some key literature in religion and biblical studies to rhetoricians and introduce some of the work in rhetoric to scholars of religion and biblical literature" (126). Her chapter thus connects domains of knowledge that previously were disconnected.

Similarly, Janice W. Fernheimer's introduction to the 2010 special issue of *College English*, titled *Composing Jewish Rhetorics*, emphasizes the notion of mapping as connecting. While her discussion is clearly directed at Jewish and not Christian rhetorics, the larger principles she names pertain. She begins on a personal note, reflecting on the "incongruities" she experienced as a graduate student travelling abroad to Israel in 2000: "These incongruities allowed me to begin contemplating how arguments over specific interpretations of Talmud, Midrash, and Tanakh might relate to conversations about post-structuralism, rhetorical theory, and pedagogy" (578). Drawing on Burke's "perspective by incongruity"—the connecting of "hitherto unlinked words" (Burke, *Permanence* 95)—Fernheimer muses on the possibilities such connections might afford:

> If Burke's notion of perspective by incongruity teaches us nothing else, it teaches us about the importance of *relationships and connections*, about the need to recognize that those connections (or perceived lack thereof) are always constructed symbolically, and thus can be reconstructed, differently connected, or perhaps even newly interconnected in ways not previously imaginable until experienced incongruously.
>
> (578)

Fernheimer's goal, then, is to chart new connections among rhetoric, writing studies, Jewish ethnicity, and Judaism. In doing so, she aims to address the gap that exists because "academic custom has not put the terms *Jewish studies* and *rhetoric* together" ("Talmidae" 578). Indeed, one of the principles Fernheimer identifies as part of the fabric of Jewish rhetoric is that of "to-ness," which is represented by the Hebrew letter *lamed* and emphasizes "relationship" (578).

Richard Benjamin Crosby does such connecting work in his contribution to this volume. In "The Agentive Play of Bishop Henry Yates Satterlee," Crosby charts connections between "theories of agency and basic assumptions about sacred rhetoric" (this page 50). Specifically, Crosby connects "recent discussions of rhetorical agency" to "revelatory, or prophetic, discourse" (this page 48). In so doing, he argues that "conceptions of the so called 'decentered' agent are not terribly far afield from ancient notions of the prophetic agent, and that a better understanding of the latter will lead to a better grasp of the former's rhetorical latitude" (this page 48). He does so by theorizing rhetorical agency as both kinetic and kairic. Ultimately, he concludes that "agency is not a possession or even a stable source of power, but it is an ephemeral space into and out of which the revelator moves in an effort to generate the maximum level of influence" (this page 49). Theorizing this "space" of rhetorical agency thus allows rhetoricians not only to connect the sacred and the rhetorical, but also to come to a more nuanced understanding of rhetorical agency.

Two other chapters in our collection foreground mapping as connecting. Brenda Glascott's examination of a nineteenth-century American Tract Society novella, *The Pilgrim Boy*, forges important connections between three spheres: rhetoric, masculinity studies, and evangelical Christianity. By investigating the rhetorical action made available to non-elite white males through evangelical Christian faith, Glascott prompts readers to "interrogate [. . .] methodological assumptions undergirding nineteenth century historiography" (this page 141) and thus foreground connections between "groups and individuals excluded from traditional rhetorical histories" (this page 141). Meanwhile, William Duffy's chapter connects Christian rhetorics to civic purposes by examining the sophistic rhetoric of Walter Rauschenbusch. In "Transforming Decorum: The Sophistic Appeal of Walter Rauschenbusch and the Social Gospel," Duffy reads the twentieth-century theologian's well-known *Christianity and the Social Crisis* in order to theorize what he calls the *transformation of decorum*, "a concept that highlights occasions when rhetors use specialized discourse like religious speech to expand how an audience is prepared to interpret that discourse" (this page 223). Beyond considering historical connections between Christianity and civic rhetoric, Duffy provides rhetoricians with suggestions regarding how to "ready religious discourse for civic purposes" (this page 235). By connecting Rauschenbusch's progressive Christian rhetoric to sophistic notions of decorum, Duffy offers rhetoricians ways of thinking about how religious discourse can help address contemporary social problems.

Mapping as Charting New Avenues

Finally, mapping helps chart new avenues of inquiry by helping rhetoricians identify and name new territories for scholarly investigation, civic engagement, and rhetorical education. One example of such work is Elizabeth Vander Lei's chapter. In " 'Where the Wild Things Are': Christian Students in the Figured Worlds of Composition Research," Vander Lei maps the current discussion about Christian students in rhetoric and composition. Drawing on Gee's analytical tool of *figured worlds* to examine discourse about religious students, Vander Lei showcases how such discourse has been influenced by a trope in composition studies: composition as a city. Her chapter prompts scholars in rhetoric and composition to consider how disciplinary metaphors influence our perceptions of religious student writers and the nature of academic writing. In doing so, Vander Lei charts new avenues for rethinking the relationship between Christian identity and rhetorical education. Thomas Deans's contribution to this collection also charts new directions in rhetorical education, though his concern is less with how we talk *about* students than with which texts—and through which theories—we engage with them. Drawing on his own experiences teaching courses in rhetorical and literary theory, Deans invites rhetorical educators to introduce sacred texts into courses where students might not expect them. He argues that "inserting one, maybe two, carefully chosen primary sacred texts into the reading list of a composition, rhetoric, literature, or communication course can trigger comparative analysis with secular modes of reading and awaken in students a fresh meta-awareness of their tacit interpretive habits" (this page 86–87).

Two chapters that chart new territory in terms of methodology are Heather Thomson-Bunn's "Empirical Hybridity: A Multimethodological Approach for Studying Religious Rhetorics" and Emily Murphy Cope and Jeffrey M. Ringer's "Coming to (Troubled) Terms: Methodology, Positionality, and the Problem of Defining 'Evangelical Christian.'" Thomson-Bunn argues that accounting for religious rhetorics demand new and expanded methodologies. In her chapter, she outlines how "empirical hybridity"—a methodological approach that blends empirical research design and analysis with analysis of composition scholarship involving religious literacy, discourse, and pedagogy—can invigorate scholarly discussions of Christian rhetorics. Cope and Ringer chart similar methodological terrain by exploring the complex role definitions play in research dealing with the writing that evangelical Christian students produce in university contexts. Specifically, they reflect on their separate experiences designing qualitative research studies that center on a contested term, *evangelical Christian*, and the increasingly diverse population it names.

Another domain of religious rhetorics that remains largely unexplored—and that demands methodological innovation—is that of prayer. William FitzGerald's contribution to this volume helps address this gap. Defining prayer as a discourse that remains elusive, FitzGerald terms it "thoroughly rhetorical" (this page 33). Despite the significance of prayer, FitzGerald notes an absence of scholarly attention to it in rhetorical studies and argues—with echoes of Pernot and Zulick—that prayer demands "charting" (this page 38). What results from his mapping of the rhetorical landscapes of prayer is an assertion with far-reaching implications: "*rhetoric is prayer*" (38). FitzGerald's chapter contributes not only to our theoretical understanding of the nature of rhetoric itself but also to our methodological repertoire for researching a rhetorical practice central to Christianity, as well as other religions.

Specifically, FitzGerald's use of Burke to analyze prayer promises rich possibilities for the study of religious rhetorics, territory that we have already begun to chart with Jim Webber in our 2008 analysis of then Senator Barack Obama's Pentecost 2006 address and Sharon Crowley's *Toward a Civil Discourse* (see DePalma, Ringer, and Webber). FitzGerald calls for "thick description of prayer in situ, as in ethnographic accounts of prayer" among various faith traditions (this page 43). FitzGerald's discussion of prayer charts new territory for rhetorical scholarship *and* establishes connections with terrain far more familiar to rhetoricians. In calling attention to the ways prayer itself challenges notions of a secular public square, Fitz-Gerald draws a connection between the rhetoric of prayer and publics theory. He also draws connections between prayer and epideictic rhetoric, the rhetoric of preaching, and material rhetorics, among others. By charting new territory, FitzGerald concomitantly identifies future lines of inquiry for rhetorical scholarship—work that is also accomplished by a range of contributors in this collection.

OVERVIEW

We divide the book into five sections. The contributions to the first section, "Christianity and Rhetorical Theory," argue that Christian rhetorics— which differ from rhetoric *about* Christianity or religion—offer much to discussions about rhetorical theory. Brian Jackson, Richard Benjamin Crosby, and William Fitzgerald contribute to this section. Next, "Christianity and Rhetorical Education," which includes contributions by Elizabeth Vander Lei and Thomas Deans, explores how acknowledging the intersections of rhetoric and religion might enrich pedagogical practices. The third section, "Christianity and Rhetorical Methodology," considers how accounting for religious rhetorics demands revised, expanded, and even new methodologies. Contributors include Emily Murphy Cope and Jeffrey M. Ringer, Heather Thomson-Bunn, and Brenda Glascott. Chapters that examine the relationship between Christian rhetorics and public discourse comprise our fourth section, "Christianity and Civic Engagement," which includes chapters by Matthew T. Althouse, Lawrence J. Prelli, and Floyd D. Anderson; Lisa J. Shaver; Lisa Zimmerelli; and William Duffy. Finally, our fifth section includes two chapters that map existing (and new) territory in relation to religious rhetorics. Beth Daniell's chapter opens this section, and Michael-John DePalma and Jeffrey M. Ringer's chapter closes it.

We see forging connections among these domains of scholarship as particularly important because the rapid expansion of scholarship on Christian rhetorics can lead to an unintended consequence: the formation of enclaves wherein theorists only talk to theorists, historians only talk to historians, and so on. And while such specialization can lead to greater nuance, it can also produce a kind of tunnel vision that can hinder advances in what scholars of rhetoric know—and *need* to know—about the intersections of Christianity and rhetoric. Our book aims to curb this trend by acknowledging the contributions of scholars working in these regions, forging connections among these domains of scholarship, and charting new avenues of rhetorical inquiry. In carrying out this work, we hope to highlight the value of research on Christian rhetorics in particular and religious rhetorics in general. We also aim to reorient scholars' mental maps of rhetorical studies and invigorate research, teaching, and civic engagement in and through rhetorical studies.

In short, our hope is that this collection prompts scholars to envision Christian rhetorics as essential to the "imagined geography" of rhetorical studies—as more Wrigley Field than South Haven. While we can't presume that every reader would experience the kind of shift in perspective Daniell underwent when she encountered Freire's Catholicism—or the kind of shift we experienced when encountering many of the scholars of religious rhetorics we discuss in our final chapter (see DePalma and Ringer, this volume)— we do hope at our most optimistic moments that readers' mental maps would be "fundamentally altered" with regard to the place of Christian rhetorics in rhetorical studies. We certainly recognize ways in which this volume has prompted *us* to think even more deeply about what it means to locate Christian rhetorics at the center of rhetorical studies.

Beyond demonstrating how Christian rhetorics are essential to rhetorical studies, our hope is that *Mapping Christian Rhetorics* will serve to provide a helpful point of departure into the realm of Christian rhetorics in particular and religious rhetorics in general for interested readers and researchers. We also hope that these essays will inspire future inquiry into key areas that the present collection, due to issues of scope, can only hint at. To do so productively, we must devote more scholarly energy to the study of Christian and other religious rhetorics, particularly in terms of the question we raise in our final chapter and that we echo here: What difference does it make when rhetorical action is motivated by religious motives, beliefs, identities, and assumptions, and how do we as rhetorical scholars account for those differences? (see DePalma and Ringer, this volume). We hope *Mapping Christian Rhetorics* prompts scholars in rhetorical studies to foreground such concerns with greater frequency, nuance, and depth.

REFERENCES

Anderson, Floyd D., and Lawrence J. Prelli. "Pentadic Cartography: Mapping the Universe of Discourse." *Quarterly Journal of Speech* 87.1 (2001): 73–95.

Burke, Kenneth. *Permanence and Change: An Anatomy of Purpose.* 3rd ed. Los Angeles: U of California P, 1984.

———. *A Rhetoric of Motives.* Los Angeles: U of California P, 1969.

———. "Terministic Screens." *Language as Symbolic Action: Essays on Life, Literature, and Method.* Los Angeles: U of California P, 1966. 44–62.

Crowley, Sharon. *Toward a Civil Discourse: Rhetoric and Fundamentalism.* Pittsburgh: U of Pittsburgh P, 2006.

Daniell, Beth. " 'Composing (as) Power.' Interchanges: Spiritual Sites of Composing." *College Composition and Communication* 45.2 (1994): 238–46.

DePalma, Michael-John, Jeffrey M. Ringer, and James D. Webber. "(Re)Charting the (Dis)Courses of Faith and Politics, or Rhetoric and Democracy in the Burkean Barnyard." *Rhetoric Society Quarterly* 38.3 (2008): 311–34.

Fernheimer, Janice W. "Talmidae Rhetoricae: Drashing Up Models and Methods for Jewish Rhetorical Studies." *Composing Jewish Rhetorics.* Ed. Janice W. Fernheimer. Spec. issue of *College English* 72.6 (2010): 577–89.

"The Greatest Paper Map of the United States You'll Ever See." *Here & Now.* Narr. Robin Young. National Public Radio. WBUR, Boston, 26 Jan. 2012. Web. 16 May 2014.

Harley, J.B. "Deconstructing the Map." *Cartographica* 26.2 (1989): 1.

Monmonier, Mark S. *How to Lie with Maps.* Chicago: U of Chicago P, 1996. *Harvard Library Bibliographic Dataset.* Web. 8 June 2013.

Pernot, Laurent. *Rhetoric in Antiquity.* Washington, D.C.: The Catholic University of America P, 2005.

———. "The Rhetoric of Religion." *Rhetorica* 24.3 (2006): 235–54.

Reynolds, Nedra. *Geographies of Writing: Inhabiting Places and Encountering Difference.* Carbondale: Southern Illinois UP, 2007.

Shaver, Lisa J. *Beyond the Pulpit: Women's Rhetorical Roles in the Antebellum Religious Press*. Pittsburgh: U of Pittsburgh P, 2012.

Zulick, Margaret D. "Rhetoric of Religion: A Map of the Territory." *The SAGE Handbook of Rhetorical Studies*. Eds. Andrea A. Lunsford, Kirt H. Wilson, and Rosa A. Eberly. Los Angeles: Sage, 2009. 125–38. *MLA International Bibliography*. Web. 8 June 2013.

Section I

Christianity and Rhetorical Theory

1 Defining Religious Rhetoric
Scope and Consequence

Brian Jackson

> Religion assumes the world to be directed by conscious agents who may be turned from their purpose by persuasion.
>
> —James Fraser, *The Golden Bough*

In December 2007, presidential candidate Mitt Romney told a friendly audience at the George H. W. Bush Presidential Library in College Station, Texas, that some of his fellow citizens were "intent on establishing a new religion in America—the religion of secularism" (Romney). Four years later, running against the incumbent Barack Obama, a practicing Christian of the United Church of Christ, Romney said something similar at a political rally in Milwaukee, Wisconsin. "I think there is in this country a war on religion," he said in reply to a question about birth control. "I think there is a desire to establish a religion in America known as secularism"—and the Obama administration, according to Romney, was leading such efforts with its health care policies (Volsky).

Because Romney did not elaborate on this point beyond saying that these secularizers were "wrong," we have to guess what he meant when he said that secularism is a religion. And my guess is that he assumes that *any* passionate ideology to which passionate people adhere can be considered a religion. Or perhaps he means that those who want to push religion out of the public sphere want to establish a different kind of compelling belief—one with its own rituals, communal observances, and exclusions. Or perhaps, if we want to be less generous, by using the word *secularism* he is simply blowing a dog whistle that will bring his believing audience to full alert. At any rate, it seems that Romney worries that the Judeo-Christian civil religion of America is being replaced, or significantly sidelined, by the religion of non-religion.

Does this line of reasoning make sense? Is calling *secularism* a religion like calling courage cowardice? Or misery happiness? Is establishing "a religion [. . .] known as secularism" like launching an energy drink called *Torpor*? The one term implies the total absence of the other. The word *secular* comes from the Christian Latin word *saeculum*, meaning "the world," a space—metaphorical or otherwise—to be distinguished from the sacred, the religious. Mircea Eliade, one of the most prominent students of religion in the twentieth century, writes that the central attribute of religion is "spatial nonhomogeneity," or the very real, lived sense that our reality is composed of two fields: one given special significance by something "wholly other" than ourselves—spirits, the gods, supernatural powers—and one *profane*, or natural or common or of-this-world (20). For Émile Durkheim, this division is *absolute*: the two worlds "have nothing in common" (38). Ironically, by declaring secularism *religious*, Romney unintentionally desacralized the cosmos, eliminating the distinction between the sacred and the profane and stripping religion of its "unique ontological status" (Eliade 23). If secularism is religion, then what *isn't* religion?

Because it implicitly, but confoundingly, draws our attention to the difference between a secular American and a Christian America, the Romney anecdote is a fitting place to begin a conversation about what constitutes Christian rhetorics and how such rhetorics might differ—in purpose, emotional salience, assumption, strategy, shape—from other kinds of rhetoric. To set up this distinction, though, I am going to take a perilous leap backward from Christian rhetoric to a higher level of generality: religious rhetoric. If we can tease out a working definition of religious rhetoric itself, we will better understand the unique *species* of religious rhetoric called, in this book, Christian rhetorics. As Romney's statement about secularism makes clear, when it comes to defining religious rhetoric, we have options, and each option has rhetorical consequences.

Specifically I explore two approaches: one I call *inclusive* and the other, *supernatural*. The inclusive approach is expansive—its adherents want to forestall a specific definition of religion so that all kinds of human symbolic behavior can be considered religious, even rhetoric that rejects what is commonly understood as religious belief or behavior (such as belief in God). At its most expansive, the inclusive approach becomes *hermeneutic* when we say that anything called religious rhetoric should be considered religious rhetoric and should be analyzed accordingly. The supernatural approach, on the other hand, would define religious rhetoric as symbolic action in a specific context of belief, behavior, and belonging: specifically, assuming supernaturalism or beings and forces "beyond human flourishing" (Taylor 20). While I lean more toward the transcendent approach, for reasons I give in the following, I see how both enrich our attempts to map religious and, in the case of this collection, Christian rhetorics in our never-ending quest to understand human communication.

THE INCLUSIVE APPROACH

As challenging as it might be, we should attempt to define the scope of the word *religion* if we're going to map its rhetorics. What is at stake, then, in the way we define religion? And what does it matter, in the end, if we let religion slip the leash and claim territory in places that don't fit someone's OCD (or OED?) understanding of where religion ought to go? In some ways, defining religious rhetoric is like trying to explain why a particular episode of *The Simpsons* is funny; all the magic is vacuumed out the second you open your mouth.

One could argue, however, that without somewhat of a distinction between what is religious and what is not, we are limited in our ability to study religious texts rhetorically. Rhetoricians study situational action in order to discover meaning, motive, and effect. Genre, for example, helps us understand rhetoric as symbolic action fitted to a particular situation and purpose, following a pattern to which audiences assent. It might not be too dramatic to say that *rhetorical judgment*—by which I mean the various acts of rhetorical criticism such as defining, interpreting, analyzing, or evaluating—hinges on our ability to make meaningful distinctions between this and that type of communication. Rhetorical judgment is situational; situations bear the stamp of peculiarity; analysis attends to peculiarity. Of course, our judgment changes as language use inevitably does, but rhetorical criticism, if I might steal liberally from the New Testament, is "living and active" when it divides "soul and spirit, joints and marrow" to judge "the thoughts and attitudes" embedded in rhetorical situations (*NIV Study Bible*, Heb. 4:12). Pursuing a definition of religion, as fraught a quest as it is, might help us improve our rhetorical judgment by giving us the power to draw distinctions between rhetorical acts that, however similar they may be on the surface, are unique in some way.

What, then, is religion? (I'm tempted here to write, *God knows.*) In some ways, defining religion is a fool's errand. Crack open the various encyclopedias of religion if you want vertigo; the various definitions (and evasions of definitions) leave you giddy, and often the attempts to define religion end up looking, in po-mo hindsight, like cultural imperialism. Over the years I've collected dozens of definitions of religion from figures such as E.B. Tylor ("belief in spiritual beings" [1: 424]) to Clifford Geertz ("a system of symbols which acts to establish powerful, pervasive, and long-lasting moods and motivations in men by formulating conceptions of a general order of existence and clothing these conceptions with such an aura of factuality that the moods and motivations seem uniquely realistic" [90]). In his definition of the Holy, Rudolf Otto throws down an incredibly high hurdle for the rhetorical critic by describing religion as an "aweful mystery," which is inexpressible, ineffable, unnamed, and unspeakable (25). Weber thought of religion as charisma; Marx, as opium; Freud, as illusion; and Christopher Hitchens, as poison.

Combined, all the definitions that take religion seriously may lead to a family resemblance of what religion is, but it's a pretty big, unruly family. (Think "family" in the capacious biological sense: *hominidae*, for example.) Should we accept Durkheim's social definition—"a unified system of beliefs and practices relative to sacred things [. . .] that unite its adherents in a single moral community" (46)—or William James's experiential one—"the feelings, acts, and experiences of individual men in their solitude, so far as they apprehend themselves to stand in relation to whatever they may consider the divine" (31–32)? Karen Armstrong sees religion as an ultimate "reality that transcended language" (15), and the 1980s band Edie Brickell & New Bohemians sang out, simply, enigmatically that "religion is the smile on a dog."

Surfing the Web reveals instance after instance of expansive usage: "Marxism as religion," "baseball as religion," "yogurt as religion." Once in a moment of parental overreach, I called potty training a religion because of its rituals, sacred spaces, taboos, rewards, rites, lavatory purgatories. I have friends who watch certain TV shows *religiously*. In *The Joy of Sports* Michael Novak tries to argue that sport is religion because of its "high ceremonies, rituals, and symbols," its "impulse of freedom," its "asceticism and dedication," its "sense of respect for the mysteries of one's own body and soul," its "sense of awe" and "fate" and "destiny," its "vestments," its "symbols of cosmic struggle" (19, 21). I can empathize with this semantic gesture. As a preteen fan of the Utah Jazz basketball team, I once threw myself on the stairs and sobbed after watching a painful loss to the Golden State Warriors in the playoffs.

There is indeed something mystical about sports—or politics or love or video games or gardening—that invites us to anoint these activities with holy oil, as Jacob did the stone he slept on, and call them religious. In many important ways they exemplify the vital guts of what we've come to think of as the essence of religious observance, from the sacred spaces (the line of scrimmage, the voting booth, the place where we first kissed) to the holy figures (LeBron James, John F. Kennedy, that one girl I met at that barn dance in junior high and never saw again). "There's something about you, Ethel," croons the prepubescent boy in the cartoon, "that gives me a sort of religious feeling" (qtd. in Geertz 98). Take sports again. Catherine Albanese points out that athletes "often wear special symbolic clothing to distinguish them from nonparticipants," just as priests or rabbis distinguish themselves from other worshippers with holy vestments (in Hoffman 7). Likewise, the *intensity* of feeling that accompanies something like the Olympic Games surely seems to invoke a Paul Tillich–like theology of ultimate concerns ("The thrill of victory! The agony of defeat! The human drama!"). I admit that watching the American swimmer Michael Phelps end his career at the London Olympics with twenty-two medals made me suspect something superhuman was taking place. And I'm not alone. Right before the 2014 Super Bowl, the Public Religion Research Institute published a poll showing that around fifty percent of sports fans see the hand of God in the success or failure of their favorite teams ("Half").

If we pursue an inclusive approach, we accept that what we call *religion* eludes tidy definition but still can be articulated through cultural attributes clustered in Venn-like overlap. Sometimes, as with Albanese's discussion of sports, religion becomes something vaguely "set apart" from other human behavior. Play, in fact, is central to religious studies because it acts out alternative realities in which daily life's struggles are suspended (see Bellah 74–97). Religion, to some, connotes intense adherence, the kind that draws people into systems of thinking and behavior that break common patterns of existence. To others, religion is stillness, an earnest search for meaning or inner strength and peace—again, through behavior set apart from the rat race. The popularity of the term *spirituality* set against the word *religion* might suggest that the core of what we're talking about is a nondenominational longing, searching, or questing in a kind of sweet homesickness for whatever is left unfulfilled in daily life.

In an attempt to bring these perspectives into some order while still remaining inclusive, Ninian Smart gives us six attributes of worldviews we should consider religious. Religions (1) have doctrines or declarative statements about the way things are; (2) tell stories about origins, in myths and narratives; (3) adopt ethical or legal systems to govern behavior; (4) have ritual practices; (5) evoke powerful emotions through experience; and (6) "create particular institutions" in social contexts (Smart 10). Smart does not claim that every religion has all six attributes; nor does he argue that these attributes explain all of religion. Furthermore, as Smart argues in *Worldviews*, one can find these attributes in Marxism or secular humanism, thereby expanding the map of religious rhetoric to include significant world ideologies.

If we adopt the inclusive approach, we can expand the map of religious rhetorics to include various forms of atheism as well. In the aptly named *Faith of the Faithless*, philosopher Simon Critchley defines "an atheistic conception of faith" (18) as "that force which can bind human beings together in association—without God" (20). Political discourse is religious rhetoric, for Critchley, when it seeks, through artful speech, to constitute the "supreme fictions" that bind people together in an *immanent* (i.e., worldly, secular, natural) political body. Coming from the perspective of scientific philosophy, Ronald Dworkin, in his equally aptly named *Religion Without God*, writes of the virtues of religious atheism, which is the reasonable and emotionally salient conviction of the "full, independent reality of value," particularly the value of human life and nature (10). Any rhetorical performance that attempts either to affirm some kind of ultimate power to unite people in political bodies or to argue for the self-sufficient value of human life or the natural world should be traced on the map of religious rhetorics.

If we follow the inclusive approach to the edge of its possibilities, we might stop trying to define religious rhetoric altogether and ask ourselves the more hermeneutical question: Why and how do people interpret rhetoric as religious? Naming something religious rhetoric may tell us more about the namer than about the name. In *Confessional Crises and Cultural Politics in Twentieth-Century America*, Dave Tell analyzes how calling a text a confession reveals political and cultural exigencies rather than "textual characteristics" (184). Tell is not interested in the "formal characteristics" of a genre called *confession*; he's more after the interpretive practices of the people who call texts confessions (8). As a result, the "cultural power" of religious rhetoric, if we follow Tell's logic, could not be attributed to a recurring dimension of the rhetorical situation but to the critical naming power of those who see religious rhetoric and call it religious rhetoric (18). What he sees as "confessional anxiety," then, can also be seen in the hundreds of mad attempts we've made to define religion to make it a useful interpretive concept. Maybe it would be better if we shifted from generic or definitional approaches to more receptional or hermeneutical ones, letting rhetorical actors themselves reveal their motives in the act of calling rhetorical performances religious.

I have tried to describe what an inclusive approach to religious rhetoric might look like. You cannot, in fact, describe this approach without leaving something out. Ultimately with this approach, there may not be a wall big enough on which to hang the map of religious rhetorics. Even attempting to map Christian rhetorics in an inclusive way would be daunting. We risk a blooming, buzzing confusion of potential texts and situations that deserve our attention as rhetorical critics of religion. One imagines a book such as the one you're holding but that is three feet thick, with articles on Martin Luther and Buddhist meditation and secular humanism and NCAA basketball and break dancing and tole painting the Grand Canyon and My Little Pony admiration and debates about mortgage-backed securities and Burning Man and (your turn)—all held together by the tenuous glue of the mere fact that we've called each text religious rhetoric. (Actually, that book sounds pretty awesome.) The inclusive approach is generous; by taking it, we seek to avoid looking exclusive or prejudicial. But like Pan, it also dances on the edge of incoherence: exuberantly, freely, playfully.

THE SUPERNATURAL APPROACH

There is a more contracted way to define religious rhetoric that I think performs important analytical work for those interested in mapping religious rhetorics such as Christian rhetorics. This approach draws back from what starts looking like a chaos of potential rhetorical performances to get at a more focused perspective. As anthropologist Clifford Geertz noted, when we expand the definition of religion to include any collective experience that provokes intense adherence, we lose the "empirical differentia" of religious experience as it has been understood through observation and reflection (98). While the supernatural approach is, as I've argued, not the only approach to understanding religious rhetorics, it is an approach that has a parsimonious advantage over the inclusive one. I believe it is also more harmonious with how we've come to understand religion's emergence in the cultural evolution of humanity. It is particularly suitable for understanding Christian rhetorics, because Christianity rests primarily on a supernatural condescension: God coming to earth in the form of Jesus Christ.

The *supernatural* approach superimposes over rhetorical situations the existences and activities of forces beyond the natural world. There is nature, there are humans, there is this world and the known universe . . . and then there is *something more*, some*where* more, some*one* more. Religion, at its core, evokes emotional salience concerning a world or sphere or being(s) "beyond human flourishing," as Charles Taylor writes (20). In his masterful work *A Secular Age*, winner of the 2007 Templeton Prize for religious scholarship, Taylor argues that the modern world is marked by a social transformation that occurred when belief in "some agency or power transcending the immanent order" became just one possible belief among many (20). This shift took centuries, starting in the sixteenth, as religion became separated from social life and science provided an alternative narrative to theology, which in time led to an "anthropocentric" and impersonal and natural world order (Taylor 221). What began as "an exclusive humanist alternative to Christian faith" among elites spread out, like a nova blast, into "whole societies," so that now it is quite common for people to live moral, purposeful lives believing that nature and humanity are self-sufficient (299). Secularism, then, contra Mitt Romney, is a turning away from belief and action oriented to transcendental powers or beings and a turning to an "immanent frame," one that exists "without reference to interventions from outside" (543).

By chronicling this transformation, Taylor helps us understand not only the modern world's self-sufficient secularity but also religion's essence as being concerned with (for lack of a better phrase) that-which-is-beyond-human-and-nature. The sociologist Rodney Stark provides us with a good starting point. "Supernatural," he writes, "refers to forces or entities beyond or outside nature that can suspend, alter, or ignore physical forces" (269). Stark points out that this definition is often ignored by anthropologists who won't accept that the people they study actually believe in supernatural forces or entities; it all seems so gauche, to the modern mind. The word itself—*supernatural*—smacks of ghost stories, fairy tales, or Marvel comics. Yet from this perspective, supernatural beings or forces have been at the center of religion from the beginning of culture. Scott Atran writes that "supernatural agency is the most culturally recurrent, cognitively relevant, and evolutionarily compelling concept of religion" (57). With his collaborator William Sims Bainbridge, Stark writes, "The ultimate source of religion is the fact that humans greatly desire rewards which are not to be found in this material world of scarcity, frustration, and death. Neither politics nor science [nor sports!] gives any convincing promise of freeing our species from its dire limitations" (312). God, gods, ancestors, spiritual beings—religion is what we believe about them and how one lives because of those beliefs.

I pause here to suggest that adopting the supernatural approach is a rhetorical, not an ontological, decision. In other words, it doesn't matter whether supernaturalist religion evolved from a neurobiological need to stipulate supernatural agents for group survival (Wade 15), represents the way language itself constructs and maintains "a sacred cosmos" that is "other than man and yet related to him" (Berger 25), or began with an actual break in the fabric of existence in which supernatural agents revealed themselves. By adopting the supernatural approach, we do not need to make an argument about what is *actually the case* when it comes to religion. "Whether there are gods or not," writes Kenneth Burke, "there is an *objective* difference in motivation between an act conceived in the name of God and an act conceived in the name of godless Nature" (Burke, *Rhetoric of Motives* 6). This point will become clearer later when I refer to Burke's *Rhetoric of Religion*. The supernatural approach posits that the cultural symbol system we call religion invites distinct rhetorical interactions—ones based on supernatural agents.

And actually the concept of supernatural agents coevolves with rhetoric in ways that I find compelling. We learn from evolutionary anthropology that religious ideas come from cognitive systems "devoted to making inferences about the beliefs, desires and intentions of other minds," like the minds of gods, spirits, or ancestors (Atran and Henrich 3). Belief in supernatural agents is counterintuitive; as both Stark and Pascal Boyer have written, supernatural agents both violate and preserve our expectations for the way the world works (Boyer 62). But because of the very concept of rhetorical agency, early societies assumed that these agents could be persuaded. Supernatural beings are *rhetorical beings*. Writing as a scientific journalist, Nicholas Wade defines religion this way:

> Religion is a system of emotionally binding beliefs and practices in which a society implicitly negotiates through prayer and sacrifice with supernatural agents, securing from them commands that compel members, through fear of divine punishment, to subordinate their interests to the common good.
>
> (15)

So the rhetorical situation is set: supernatural agents and believers are locked in a rhetorical counterpoise of commands and supplications. As "purveyors of goals and emotions," supernatural agents help to establish systems of believing, behaving, and belonging that mortals negotiate in communities of practice (Atran 66). The moral psychologist Jonathan Haidt explains that through engagement with supernatural agents, religious communities create "moral exoskeletons": "[i]f you live in a religious community, you are enmeshed in a set of norms, relationships, and institutions" that combine to endow such communities with power (269). And that power comes from the varieties of ways in which humans use rhetorical performances to gain access to supernatural power.

When we talk about *religious rhetoric* from the supernatural stand-point, we are talking about rhetorical situations in which speaker, audience, purpose, and strategy are tied up in assumptions related to sentient forces beyond humanity. But I suggest this approach goes even further than that, since there are many rhetorical performances *about* supernatural agency that do not assume such agency. For example, if religious rhetoric is simply any symbolic practice related to the topic of religion, then the contemptuous atheist Bill Maher uses religious rhetoric just as much as any Southern Baptist preacher. The supernatural approach distinguishes rhetoric *about* religion from religious rhetoric proper.

In the supernatural approach, religious rhetoric may be defined as persuasive symbolic action to, from, or about supernatural forces or beings *that assumes the existence of supernatural forces or beings.*

This definition may require some unpacking. By *symbolic action* I mean to imply any type of gesture, utterance, or symbol making meant to convince, persuade, or induce cooperation. (I'm influenced by Gerard Hauser's definition of rhetoric here.) I say *to, from, or about* to evoke a rhetorical triangle of sacred rhetoric that includes communication *to* spiritual beings (sacrificial offerings or oblations, prayers, incense burning, etc.), *from* spiritual beings (scripture, possession, aural revelations, totemic phenomena, shamanic pronouncements, or other persuasive signs assumed to have non-human origins), and *about* spiritual beings (sermons, conversations, rituals, worship houses, origin narratives, etc.). I've taken this triad from Laurent Pernot, whose incredibly useful article titled "The Rhetoric of Religion" makes this division in an attempt to account for the religious rhetorical practices of the classical world. "The very basis of religion," he writes, "is the supernatural" and therefore the essence of religious rhetoric lies "beyond the human realm" (Pernot 236, 238).

The last part of the definition requires some attention. I'm suggesting that from a supernatural standpoint, the participants of religious rhetoric to one degree or another *assume the existence of supernatural forces or beings.* I'm suggesting that a casual mention of God, gods, ancestors, spiritual beings, or any other supernatural force that is meant merely to describe belief in them or practice related to them is not, by my definition, religious rhetoric. When French anthropologist Pascal Boyer writes of the religious practices of the Fang people of Cameroon in *Religion Explained,* he is not writing religious rhetoric: he is writing rhetoric about religion, and his argument does not assume—or at least it need not assume—anything about whether God, gods, ancestors, spiritual beings, or supernatural cosmic forces exist and require our attention. (Boyer, in fact, argues that we have religious beliefs and practices because that's how we have evolved to think about the world.) But when the Fang themselves pray to their ancestors, they are using religious rhetoric. And when God commands Moses to ascend the mountain, that's religious rhetoric. And when the president of the U.S. says "God bless America," he is using religious rhetoric, because he assumes—or at least we assume he assumes—that there is a God and that this being is capable of casting benedictions at will on countries.

How do we actually know the president assumes there is a God when he says, "God bless America"? We don't. We *can't*. There is no sure way to tell whether someone, say, praying over the food at a family gathering believes she's persuading a mighty invisible being to accept gratitude for the food on the table; she might just be humoring a saintly mother to hide her agnosticism. I know a man from Botswana who, because of family pressure, poured homemade beer on his sidewalk for the spirits of his ancestors to drink, even though he did not believe his ancestors drank the beer—or even existed. Who knows what equivocations lurk in the hearts of men and women amid religious symbolic action? Yet this problem is not unique to religious rhetoric but to *any* kind of rhetoric. As rhetorical critics, we impute motives, analyze assumptions, and reconstruct arguments based on the performance of a text. The very act of analyzing or imputing the motives of a communicator is an act of faith—it is an imaginative act very much like empathy, since we cannot fully understand why people say what they do in the manner they say it. So when the president tosses out a "God bless America" every twenty minutes, we assume he doesn't mean, *merely*, "Gee, I hope America does well in the world!" We take him to mean "I hope God—an all-powerful nonhuman Something—will rain down beneficence on this specific country!" The phrase is meaningless otherwise. (Nonbelievers might argue that the phrase is meaningless *always*.)

At any rate, in the same way Eliade divides reality in sacred and profane categories, the supernatural approach divides religious from nonreligious rhetoric not to cast judgment on nonreligious language but to create a linguistic nonhomogeneity that assists in rhetorical work. I believe Kenneth Burke's ingenious essay *The Rhetoric of Religion* makes this point nicely by distinguishing between sacred language and its "usable secular analogues" (2). He calls his study of *logology*—or "words about words"—a "purely secular subject" because it does not require any assumptions about whether communication is to, from, or about the supernatural (5). Rather, he studies how nonreligious communication takes on the imprimatur of religious communication when it bears "a notable likeness" to its *dynamis*—like when, for example, we invent "god-term[s]" that connote an ultimate order not unlike the naming of God (14, 25). Burke's point, similar to the point I tried to make about baseball, is that nonreligious language can have attributes *similar* to religious language without *being* religious language itself. He implicitly recognizes the linguistic nonhomogeneity that functions as an analog to Eliade's spatial nonhomogeneity. Religious rhetoric belongs to a "wholly different order" of communication, since its concerns transcend human flourishing (Eliade 11).

Religious rhetoric constructs a "sacred canopy," in Peter Berger's words, and thereby constitutes an emotionally salient social order concerned with deeply important matters that involve life, death, and life after life. Through religious rhetoric, pitiful humans supplicate the Powers that Be for assistance in leading our lives—for forgiveness, inspiration, protection, vengeance. Through religious rhetoric, the Powers that Be speak back—in holy books, through prophetic intermediaries, in trances and dreams, in glossolalic ecstasy, in thunder and lightning, and in strange whisperings to the mind. Through religious rhetoric, we speak about these Powers—in what manner they exist or behave, what they expect of us, how we must live to garner their favor. Clearly religious rhetoric is a vital practice. It is also controversial, confusing, and mysterious.

So mysterious, in fact, that Karen Armstrong, in *The Case for God*, argues that the religious impulse actually springs from the *impossibility* of using language to describe or perpetuate it. We rhetoricians operate in the tradition of *logos*—the "pragmatic mode" that enables "people to function effectively in the world" (Armstrong xi). Religion, on the other hand, has its origins in *mythos*, in a "very different mode of consciousness" (10) oriented to transcendental mysteries that "lead to an appreciation of the limits of language and understanding" (26). An implicit advocate of negative (or apophatic) theology, Armstrong argues that revelation, paradoxically, tells "us that we [know] nothing about God," and "human language is not adequate to express the reality that we call 'God' " (110). The correct response, then, to the experience of the "primordial nothingness" is silence, not speech. In Plato's dialogue, Timaeus tells Socrates that even if we could understand the divine perfectly, we could never express that understanding because of the great gulf between the creator and the created, the eternal and the mortal. Likewise Augustine, in *On Christian Doctrine*, writes that "nothing worthy may be spoken" of God, and yet the deity accepts "the tribute of the human voice" in all its deficiencies (11). In an 1832 letter to a friend and fellow believer, the Mormon prophet Joseph Smith broke out in a plaintive prayer: "Oh Lord God deliver us in thy due time from the little narrow prison almost as it were total darkness of paper pen and ink and a crooked broken scattered and imperfect language" (Jessee 287). In the end, our symbolic storehouse is all we have. For many people religious rhetoric, broken and scattered and imperfect as it is, provides the only "cosmic guarantee" that a certain way of life is in harmony with the universe (Geertz 104).

From the supernatural perspective, calling activities such as baseball *religion* or calling various ideologies such as Secular Humanism *religious*—as Supreme Court chief justice Hugo Black did in the 1961 ruling *Torcaso v. Watkins*, giving Mitt Romney legal precedent for calling secularism a religion—does not enlighten us about the nature of religious rhetorical performances. In order to map religious rhetorics, it must be understood that religious rhetoric is a unique human activity with assumptions, goals, audiences, and purposes very different from other activities. Specifically, religious rhetoric is persuasive symbolic action to, from, or about supernatural forces or beings that assumes the existence of supernatural forces or beings.

What kind of work does this definition open up for us? I see several possibilities. First, it helps us *classify* and *define* rhetorical artifacts with more clarity. Though we can't really call religious rhetoric a *genre*, we can maybe call it a *supergenre* in that its various manifestations have at least this in common: they will assume the existence of supernatural forces or beings, and the rhetoric will be fashioned accordingly in recurring responses to recurring exigencies. From the perspective of this approach, there are some exigencies or predicaments that drive rhetorical actors to appeal to agencies beyond human flourishing. In his delightful book *Spiritual Modalities*, William FitzGerald suggests that the act of prayer serves as a "meta-rhetoric," a representative speech act embodying "the perfection of the possibility of connection and the promise of response" (131). In the supergenre of religious rhetoric, speakers are often at their most vulnerable, full of rhetorical hope and dread, depending on agents and authorities that have commanding cosmic presence.

Second, the definition I've proposed helps us see religious rhetoric operating in distinct rhetorical situations that likely will involve what in stasis theory is categorized as substance or conjecture arguments. In other words, religious rhetoric, by this definition, presupposes claims based on ultimate realities that often defy modernity's ways of knowing. This insight becomes particularly useful when we talk about religious rhetoric in public, because religious language, by its very nature, includes truth claims that will be inaccessible to others. Apologists for religious rhetoric in the public square have pointed out that though there is no constitutional requirement for religious folks to make their arguments secular, there are obvious *strategic* reasons for bracketing religious rhetoric in deliberations to access *koine* or the common experience of a public (see Audi and Wolterstorff; Stout). Jürgen Habermas, for example, late in his career said that religious rhetoric is welcomed in the public sphere, as long as religious *rhetors* translate their "religious utterances [. . .] into a generally accessible language," especially if they intend to get their issues on legislative agendas (Habermas 25). This caveat goes too far for some scholars, not far enough for others.

Finally, defining religious rhetoric in this way grants an analytical integrity to a certain way and how and why of communicating. It takes up the symbolic action of religious *rhetors* on their own terms and with their own assumptions, without having to judge in any way whether those terms or assumptions actually correspond to what's real. Another way to put that is that the supernatural approach holds religious *rhetors* accountable for the full measure of what they bring to a rhetorical moment. In these instances, the rhetorical triangle becomes the rhetorical pyramid: speaker, audience, and topic become connected to agents beyond the immanence of the situation. Such moments have an integrity that invites a rhetorical orientation more specific than what the inclusive approach, at its most expansive, provides.

Whether we adopt the inclusive or supernatural approach, religious rhetoric should also be celebrated in its own right as a practice meant to refine humanity—even though it often fails miserably to do so. To borrow Karen Armstrong's eloquence, religious rhetoric's task, "closely allied to that of art, [is] to help us to live creatively, peacefully, and even joyously with realities for which there were no easy explanations and problems that we could not solve: mortality, pain, grief, despair, and outrage at the injustice and cruelty of life" (318). When religious rhetoric *causes* pain, grief, despair, outrage, or injustice, a rhetorical critic should be on hand to analyze and evaluate its consequences. Like religion itself, religious rhetoric invites from critics a "dedicated intellectual endeavor" (Armstrong 319). I believe this collection is a salutary addition to that kind of endeavor.

REFERENCES

Armstrong, Karen. *The Case for God*. New York: Knopf, 2009.
Atran, Scott. *In Gods We Trust*. Oxford UP, 2002.
Atran, Scott, and Joseph Henrich. "The Evolution of Religion: How Cognitive By-Products, Adaptive Learning Heuristics, Ritual Displays, and Group Competition Generate Deep Commitments to Prosocial Religions." *Biological Theory* 5.1 (2010): 1–13.
Audi, Robert, and Nicholas Wolterstorff. *Religion in the Public Square*. Lanham: Rowman and Littlefield, 1997.
Augustine. *On Christian Doctrine*. Trans. D. W. Robertson. Upper Saddle River: Prentice Hall, 1997.
Bellah, Robert N. *Religion and Human Evolution*. Cambridge: Harvard UP, 2011.
Berger, Peter L. *The Sacred Canopy: Elements of a Sociological Theory of Religion*. New York: Anchor, 1969.
Boyer, Pascal. *Religion Explained: The Evolutionary Origins of Religious Thought*. New York: Basic, 2001.
Burke, Kenneth. *A Rhetoric of Motives*. Berkeley: U of California P, 1969.
———. *The Rhetoric of Religion*. Berkeley: U of California P, 1961.
Critchley, Simon. *The Faith of the Faithless*. London: Verso, 2012.
Durkheim, Émile. *The Elementary Forms of Religious Life*. Trans. Carol Cosman. Oxford: Oxford UP, 2001.
Dworkin, Ronald. *Religion without God*. Cambridge: Harvard UP, 2013.
Edie Brickell & New Bohemians. "What I Am." By Edie Brickell and Kenny Withrow. *Shooting Rubberbands at the Stars*. Geffen, 1988. CD.
Eliade, Mircea. *The Sacred and the Profane*. Trans. Willard R. Trask. San Diego: Harvest, 1957.
FitzGerald, William. *Spiritual Modalities: Prayer as Rhetoric and Performance*. University Park: Penn State UP, 2012.
Fraser, James G. *The Golden Bough*. Avenel: Gramercy, 1993.
Geertz, Clifford. *The Interpretation of Cultures*. New York: Basic, 1973.
Hauser, Gerard A. *Vernacular Voices: The Rhetoric of Publics and Public Spheres*. Columbia: U of South Carolina P, 1999.
Habermas, Jürgen. "The Political." *The Power of Religion in the Public Sphere*. Ed. Eduardo Mendieta and Jonathan VanAntwerpen. New York: Columbia UP, 2011. 15–33.

Haidt, Jonathan. *The Righteous Mind: Why Good People Are Divided by Politics and Religion*. New York: Pantheon, 2012.

"Half of American Fans See Supernatural Forces at Play in Sports." *Public Religion Research Institute*. 16 January 2014. Web. 16 January 2014.

Hoffman, Shirl J., ed. *Sport and Religion*. Champaign: Human Kinetics, 1992.

James, William. *Varieties of Religious Experience*. New York: Modern Library, n.d.

Jessee, Dean, ed. *Personal Writings of Joseph Smith*. Rev. ed. Salt Lake City: Deseret Book, 2002.

The NIV Study Bible. New International Vers. Grand Rapids: Zondervan, 1985.

Novak, Michael. *The Joy of Sports*. Rev. ed. Lanham: Madison, 1994.

Otto, Rudolf. *The Idea of the Holy*. Trans. John W. Harvey. London: Oxford UP, 1958.

Pernot, Laurent. "The Rhetoric of Religion." *Rhetorica* 24.3 (2006): 235–54.

Plato. *Timaeus and Critias*. Trans. Robin Waterfield. Oxford: Oxford UP, 2008.

Romney, Mitt. "Faith in America." Transcript. *NPR.org*. 6 December 2007. Web. 26 June 2012.

Smart, Ninian. *Worldviews*. 3rd ed. Saddle River: Prentice Hall, 2000.

Smith, Huston. *The World's Religions*. San Francisco: Harper San Francisco, 1991.

Stark, Rodney. "Micro Foundations of Religion: A Revised Theory." *Sociological Theory* 17 (1999): 264–89.

Stark, Rodney, and William Sims Bainbridge. *A Theory of Religion*. New Brunswick: Rutgers UP, 1996.

Stout, Jeffrey. *Democracy and Tradition*. Princeton: Princeton UP, 2004.

Taylor, Charles. *A Secular Age*. Cambridge: Belknap Harvard, 2007.

Tell, Dave. *Confessional Crises and Cultural Politics in Twentieth-Century America*. University Park: Penn State UP, 2012.

Tylor, E.B. *Primitive Culture: Researches into the Development of Mythology, Philosophy, Religion, Language, Art, and Custom*. 2 vols. 4th ed. London: John Murray, 1903.

Volsky, Igor. "Romney: Obama Hopes to Establish 'Secularism' as an Official Religion." *Think Progress.org*. 3 April 2012. Web. 26 June 2012.

Wade, Nicholas. *The Faith Instinct: How Religion Evolved and Why it Endures*. New York: Penguin, 2009.

2 Seeking, Speaking Terra Incognita
Charting the Rhetorics of Prayer

William T. FitzGerald

A prayer is a strategy for taking up the slack between what is wanted and what is got.

—Kenneth Burke, *Philosophy of Literary Form*

Prayer enables speech; it extends us beyond our known self into the unknown self. It sends our words toward this other whom we seek. We discover this way that what we thought was the seeking of our prayer is in fact a responding to the other's having sought us.

—Ann and Barry Ulanov, *Primary Speech:
A Psychology of Prayer*

Prayer is arguably simple. Mere children learn to do it. Indeed, a certain childlike confidence seems a basic requirement for prayer, a "second naiveté" that allows one to cultivate a religious imagination after traversing "a desert of criticism" (Ricoeur 349). At its simplest, prayer is *talking to God* (Spear), a likening of communication with divine beings to discourse among human beings. However, complexity abounds as soon as one admits the diversity of practices, motives, and assumptions that inform "talking to God." Consider the highly scripted prayer of Catholic and Anglican devotion, the contemplation of Christian mystics, or the studied informality of evangelical prayer. These and other forms of prayer depart, sometimes radically, from ordinary conversation to reveal "talk" as but one model of prayer, a model aimed, in part, at lowering barriers to an activity rightly recognized as difficult. Indeed, I am reassured by biblical scholar Walter Brueggemann's frank admission that "prayer is characteristically a dangerous act, and dangerous rhetoric is required to match the intent of the act" (xvi). To call on the heavens, to implicate the divine in human affairs, *is* "dangerous rhetoric." Absent a compelling need, who would dare pray? Implicit in Brueggemann's claim is an insight that prayer has become domesticated. Taking Brueggemann as a guide, how might we recognize prayer as "dangerous rhetoric"?

At the heart of prayer is an apprehension of privation, an awareness that danger looms. In etymological terms, prayer is not talking, but begging: "Out of the depths I cry to you, O LORD. LORD, hear my voice! Let your ears be attentive to the voice of my supplications!" (*HarperCollins Study Bible*, Psalm 130:1). Our default concept of prayer is appeal for aid beyond what may be obtained by our own power. As Kenneth Burke says with characteristic irreverence, "Prayer is a strategy for taking up the slack between what is wanted and what is got" (*Philosophy* 54). This insight suggests that everyday notions of prayer have things backward, that beyond earnest entreaty, prayer is cagily prospective. Daring and pragmatic, by turns, prayer sets sights on what may be "got" by conforming our words to reality. Prayer asks for daily bread, but not for manna from on high.

Prayer is also a response to need in a different sense, that of obligation. According to Ann and Barry Ulanov, "We discover [. . .] that what we thought was the seeking of our prayer is in fact a responding to the other's having sought us [. . .]. Prayer is as far as one can get from the self-indulgence of narcissism" (9). Burke's crafty realism and the transcendent idealism of the Ulanovs are prayer's systole and diastole. The duality of prayer is eloquently taken up in Jesuit Karl Rahner's collection of post–World War II sermons, *The Need and Blessing of Prayer*. An antidote to despair, Rahner's "prayer in the everyday" (38) weaves the warp of desire with the weft of demand. Rahner's text may stand here for myriad works presenting prayer as a response to urgencies rising from within or obligations pressing from without. However, if we consider how much has now been written about prayer, do we *need* another account? Yes, because despite much instruction and exhortation, prayer remains an elusive mode of discourse. We recognize prayer as a kind of religious activity performed *in the direction* of some divine being or higher power (see Jackson, this volume). Yet so diverse are prayer's forms and audiences, so multiple its contexts, it seems a thing too vast and protean to speak about as a totality. What can be said of prayer that has yet to be said?

In a familiar African-American spiritual, one is moved to exclaim, "I am standing in the need of prayer" (Schomburg). This hymn, itself a prayer, recognizes prayer as both necessary and possible. Indeed, prayer's unstated premise is that there is an audience for which prayer, of some sort, is the required response. In this chapter, I take as a starting point this dialectic of *necessity* and *possibility*. In agreement with Rahner, I understand prayer as premised on experiences of urgent need and "blessed" opportunity. Such experiences are typically manifested in prayer's complementary modes of petition and praise. We find a similar dialectic at work in the preconditions of rhetoric, expressed in terms of *exigence* and *kairos*—likewise, urgent need and blessed opportunity. For rhetoric is grounded in the possibility of effective response to exigent circumstances, a response conceived as sizing up situations and seizing moments of opportunity. The "dangerous rhetoric" of prayer concerns itself with apprehending situations requiring an appropriate response.

So rather than pit *authentic* prayer against *duplicitous* rhetoric, I approach prayer as thoroughly rhetorical speech. Can we not just claim prayer as a *species* of rhetoric, then, and proceed to read its situations—its exigencies, audiences, and performative constraints—using the tools provided by rhetorical analysis in its classical or modern formulation? We could, though we risk missing what is special about this species of rhetoric unless we also consider why prayer seems to be rhetoric with a difference. Prayer, conceived of as address (in the broadest terms) to divine audiences (in the broadest terms) is rhetoric *at the limits*. Prayer tests rhetoric's reach; it thus serves as a proving ground for human speech in general. Prayer, we might say, is a profound expression of our nature as *languaged* beings addressing *other/ Other* languaged beings. Attributing receptivity to nonhuman audiences to *our* speech, we are arguably never *more* human than when we communicate with the divine.

A bold preface here contrasts sharply with this observation: prayer is largely absent from consideration of the modes and aims of discourse in rhetorical studies. With one notable exception in Kenneth Burke, for whom prayer is a "key term" (FitzGerald, "Burkean") across all major works, rhetoric has said surprisingly little about prayer. Yet surely we cannot understand rhetoric without attending to its application in prayer. To date, the most substantive account of prayer in relation to rhetoric is my own *Spiritual Modalities: Prayer as Rhetoric and Performance*, the first systematic effort to bring prayer and rhetoric into dialogue. Employing Burkean dramatism as a methodological framework, *Spiritual Modalities* examines three essential motives of prayer: its *scene* of address, *act* of invocation, and *attitude* of reverence. These dramatistic overlays bring into relief various aspects of prayer's rhetorical character without presuming to offer an exhaustive account of prayer's rhetorical operations. The signature merit of this approach is that it recognizes prayer as forming a continuum with other modes of discourse even as it seeks to identify aspects of prayer that contribute to its distinctive character.

The present essay is more limited in scope, yet more global in approach. Here, I argue for prayer as a kind of *meta-rhetoric*. That is to say, prayer is discourse primarily concerned with the very possibility and necessity of discourse. In assuming a divine audience, prayer likewise addresses what we hope to gain when putting our needs and desires into words. The chapter proceeds in three parts. I begin by surveying efforts to identify prayer as an object of study in rhetoric and other disciplines. Next, using prayer as a compass, I venture deep into the forest of rhetoric to articulate how rhetoric as a whole may be understood as a kind of prayer. I conclude by exploring prayer as a phenomenon of agency and embodiment, suggesting how the study of prayer can contribute to advances in rhetorical studies.

PERSUADING UPWARD: PRAYER AS RHETORIC

The discipline of rhetoric has developed a robust set of tools for analyzing a wide range of discourse. In principle, prayer is no exception to the claim, by rhetoricians, that *all* communication is rhetorical. Indeed, a persuasive intent to gain the goodwill and cooperation of divine beings is evident in much prayer, Christian prayer included. Believers look to move God or to move themselves closer to God. Yet, viewed as a whole, appeals to socially significant, otherworldly addressees are distinct from *ordinary* rhetoric (see Jackson, this volume). Prayer manifests aims beyond mere persuasion. Indeed, it is not clear that divine audiences (e.g., God, saints) *are* persuaded by appeals addressed to them. How prayer "works," including whom prayer influences, is not easily accounted for, but it remains productively ambiguous. In reaching beyond the human plane, prayer is rhetoric that takes on added dimensions, both *vertical* (human-to-divine) and *horizontal* (human-to-human) movement.

A useful starting point is to consider prayer's *civic* dimensions. An art of shaping language to persuasive ends, rhetoric, concerned with the often fractious divides within human communities, has been conceived in largely *secular* terms. By contrast, relations between human and divine beings are the stuff of poetry. Yet a political role for poetry or prayer is undeniable. As a manifestation of human–divine relations, religion exercises a powerful role in the *polis*. Despite our efforts in the modern era to enforce separation, church and state inevitably overlap. In the civic arena, prayer performs vital *epideictic* functions as a celebration of institutions and ideals: the incorporation of prayer in twentieth-century presidential inaugurations (Medhurst) confers a double legitimacy on both civic institutions and Christian heritage. Even so, a fusion of prayer and politics in events such as prayer breakfasts is controversial in a culture of religious pluralism. A (re)turn to prayer as a mode of civic discourse challenges long-standing notions of a *secular* public sphere, described by Habermas as a site of "rational critical debate in which matters of the public good are considered" (132). Depending on how deeply prayer permeates an occasion, its performance can be understood as primarily religious, or as "civil religion" with ceremonial functions that sanctify social institutions (Bellah).

Despite the importance of religion in civic affairs, rhetoric has been slow to consider prayer, even as civic discourse. When rhetoric *does* so, it discovers speech of a particular kind—an address to a deity. However, in such complex scenes of address, one must consider prayer's speakers and its imagined audience. While the default setting of prayer is often one person addressing a divine being, this is not prayer's only setting. Many people can appeal *as one*, as with petitions in secular contexts in which multiple voices are assembled into collective action (Zaeske).[1] Scenes of *public* prayer are instructive for underscoring prayer as speaking *on behalf of* as well as *to* an assembly. Those gathered in public prayer function as both speaker *and* audience, even when particular persons perform distinct communicative tasks. When a Christian minister such as Rick Warren delivers an inaugural prayer, he speaks not only for himself, but for all those assembled. Hence, problems will arise through any effort to speak such a prayer in Jesus's name.

In negotiating pluralism and particularity, public prayer risks excluding someone from that assembly, praying *at* rather than *with* others. The more heteroglossic its cast of speakers, the less particular prayer can be. The more particular, the less a community's distinct voice can be resolved. These constraints explain how ostensibly non-sectarian prayer, addressing a generic God, quickly reaches its rhetorical limits. The very nature of public prayer, wherein collective address predominates, limits the possibilities for prophetic speech and reduces prayer to purely ceremonial ends. Rhetoric's secular frame helps explain a lack of attention to prayer insofar as religion is bracketed off from disciplinary concerns. Prayer's rhetorical operations have been left to theology or to secular forms of religious studies. Yet one finds a similar paucity of interest in prayer even here. Indeed, prayer seems to fall between the cracks of a divide between secular and religious modes of inquiry now that rhetoric has become largely secularized.

A notable exception to secular rhetoric is the tradition of *ars praedicandi*, or art of preaching. In the Latin West, this "sacred rhetoric" long paralleled civic oratory after Augustine adapted Ciceronian rhetoric to Christian culture in *On Christian Doctrine*. In the medieval era, preaching was a major rhetorical art, together with letter writing (*ars dictaminis*) and poetry (*ars poetriae*; Murphy, *Three*). Less prominent within rhetorical tradition are the *artes orandi*, or arts of prayer (Jaye).[2] Here, prayer is a form of "*rhetorica divina*" (Murphy, *Rhetoric* 331) in which human speech is directed to God. In secular accounts of rhetoric, such orientation is soon marginalized. Consider the *SAGE Handbook of Rhetorical Studies* (Lunsford, Wilson, and Eberly), a collection of essays surveying contemporary developments in rhetoric, including Margaret Zulick's "The Rhetoric of Religion: A Map of the Territory." Zulick's account of rhetoric's rapprochement with religion is grounded in notions of transcendence and address, yet nowhere is prayer considered along with theology, biblical criticism, and American religious rhetoric. But Zulick can hardly be faulted. Prayer has simply not been of vital interest in modern rhetorical studies. In another essay, "Religious Voices in American Public Discourse" (Darsey and Ritter), prayer is similarly mentioned only in passing. Indeed, that a turn to religion is not also a turn to prayer is a phenomenon worthy of speculation.

We can contrast this lack of attention to Laurent Pernot's call to reengage prayer in a keynote address at the 2005 conference of the International Society for the History of Rhetoric, later published in *Rhetorica*. Ken Dowden's "Rhetoric and Religion" seemingly responds to Pernot's invitation by analyzing prayer as persuasive discourse to the gods delivered in a highly ritualized style. Dowden further identifies material acts of sacrifice as analogous to prayer and examines prayer's vocative strategies. In light of such sporadic efforts, one detects a reticence to engage prayer as rhetorical performance in its own right. Only a handful of articles (e.g., Charney; Howard) and a single monograph (FitzGerald, *Spiritual*) consider prayer from a specifically rhetorical perspective. What might be said by way of review?

We might look to approaches to prayer in other disciplines and discover a field not so fallow, after all. For example, studies of prayer as *living* discourse have recently come from the social sciences, including history (Orsi), anthropology (Luhrmann), and sociology (Wuthnow). In a more historical vein, socio-rhetorical readings of prayer in the New Testament (e.g., Neyrey) follow groundbreaking work in Old Testament (Greenberg) and classical Greek (Pulleyn) prayer. Several monographs read prayer through a literary (Schoenfeldt; Targoff) or cultural lens (Kimelman). These studies suggest the rich possibilities for engaging prayer as performative and textual practice and for approaching prayer as argument, style, or contextualized discourse.

While we think of prayer as quintessentially religious language, prayer arguably straddles secular and sacred domains. In other words, prayer forms not only a continuum of practices from verbal appeal to divine beings, certainly but also a "downward" continuum of various kinds of address: from no one in particular to persons held in power or in high esteem, even to abstract entities signifying transcendent values. Beyond formal address, prayer can also be understood as various habits of mindfulness in performing daily routines (e.g., cleaning, baking, walking) and certain modes of concerted action toward some vision of the good; these practices have much in common with notions of prayer in strictly religious contexts. Indeed, a supple understanding of prayer beyond a particular set of agents helps to recognize prayer's architectonic role in shaping, not merely reflecting, religious sensibilities.

Given this protean character, prayer can seem impossibly ragged as an object of study—hence, a tendency to catalog its varieties and to construct hierarchies of prayer (e.g., mystical versus prophetic, individual versus corporate). The modus operandi for studying prayer is the panoptic survey, ranging from phenomenological accounts from a Christian perspective (e.g., Heiler; Ellul) to recent taxonomies that take a more syncretic approach (Foster; Zaleski and Zaleski). Of course, moving from the particular to the general meets significant challenges of definition. How do we bracket prayer off from *its* other? Under what conditions, say, is a moment of silence a prayer? Or practices such as yoga or meditation? Given its diverse aims and methods, prayer is akin to Wittgenstein's notion of games in possessing a range of family resemblances (Ahmed). Efforts to articulate a rhetoric of prayer, then, must confront necessarily partial accounts that represent certain forms of prayer as normative and recognize such accounts as arguments about the nature of selves and communities.

Here, we may recall the landmark definition of religion William James offers: "*the feelings, acts and experiences of individual men in their solitude, so far as they apprehend themselves to stand in relation to whatever they may consider the divine"* (31, emphasis in original). James couples his definition of religion with an identification of prayer as "the very soul and essence of religion" (337). Locating prayer in starkly individualist terms says much about the place of religion in James's liberal Protestant culture. For James, religion and prayer as its "very soul and essence" are at the furthest remove from scenes of public oratory, the domain of civic life. Jamesian prayer contrasts sharply with rhetorical notions of discourse as *socialized* performance *with* and *before* others. Significantly, James does not consider prayer's aim to move a divine audience to particular ends. In his psychological account, prayer is "the very movement itself of the soul, putting itself in a relation of contact with the mysterious power of which it feels the presence" (337). In effect, prayer acts only on the self—a view at odds with classical and biblical conceptions of prayer as persuasive speech that moves human and divine audiences alike. James rescues prayer from a crude anthropomorphism while echoing a classic formulation of prayer, attributed to St. John Damascene, as the "raising of the mind and heart to God" (*Catechism* 2559). Yet James is intentionally vague about the "mysterious power" with which prayer puts us, individually, in contact.

As I have noted, a focus on prayer as individual experience offers a model at odds with rhetorical models of persuasion that underscore the transactional character of discourse. In classical and biblical contexts, prayer involves pleading, flattery, and even bargaining with divine beings, much as with human beings. Yet James realizes that prayer is more than verbal action extended in anthropomorphic fashion to otherworldly audiences—in prayer, "*something is transacting*" (338, emphasis in original). This somewhat strained expression—*transacting* over *transacted*—suggests that prayer itself possesses a power into which practitioners tap. In a key insight, James concludes that in prayer "things which cannot be realized in any other manner come about: energy which but for prayer would be bound is set free and operates in some part, be it objective or subjective, of the world of facts" (338). James does not make clear the source of this "energy," only that prayer is chiefly concerned with actualizing what cannot otherwise be actualized. For James, prayer is a more a matter of agency than agents.

A sense of the uncanny here places prayer in opposition to ordinary discourse. Indeed, James presents prayer as language that *goes beyond* and whose master trope is *hyperbole*. Prayer is conceived as a mode of symbolic action that expands horizons of possibility. Emmanuel Levinas goes further to claim that the task of prayer is nothing less than "repairing the ruins of creation" ("Prayer" 233). Burke likewise grounds prayer in ethical vision: "the man [sic] who does not pray cannot build his character" (*Attitudes* 322). These various characterizations link prayer with the very nature of language, its potential and attendant obligations. They also serve to illustrate the range of motives—scene, act, purpose—that inform prayer.

What stands out in these accounts is recognition of prayer as an *extraor-dinary* dimension of language, one that involves a dramatic turn toward an *other/Other* to effectively enlarge the sphere of discourse. In the communi-cative space opened by prayer, one is heard and *over*heard. Crucially, prayer involves a double reception. Such psychodynamics as occur in prayer are taken up in Bakhtin: "the author of the utterance, with a greater or lesser awareness, presupposes a higher superaddressee (third), whose absolutely just responsive understanding is presumed, either in some metaphysical dis-tance or in distant historical time" (126). For Bakhtin, this superaddressee can be "God, absolute truth, the court of dispassionate human conscience, the people, the court of history, [or] science" (126). Prayer imagines some higher authority exercising the crucial functions of an audience, one whose *over*hearing entails a release of latent energy in any situation. Indeed, James' characterization of prayer as energy echoes classical rhetorical notions of *kairos* insofar as situations are opportunities to bring new situations into being by a timely response (see Crosby, this volume).

Surprisingly, prayer is discourse that gives voice to our situations, spelling out the conditions that call for prayer. Prayers "size up [their] situations, name their structure and outstanding ingredients, and name them in a way that contains an attitude about them" (Burke, *Philosophy* 130). Here are Burke's motives of scene, act, and attitude, which, I suggest, provide a use-ful heuristic for charting diverse rhetorics of prayer, whether conceived as intimate conversation, address upward, or the energy latent in any situa-tion. Rather than single out any particular characterization of prayer as normative, as a religiously motivated rhetoric of prayer inevitably does, the secular rhetoric of prayer I seek to characterize here must draw the widest possible circle around such diverse phenomena as petition and praise, song and silence, lament and accusation offered in solitude and performed in solidarity with others. No single mode being definitive, prayer inventively dramatizes a range of communicative situations and embodied responses.

"REVERENT BESEECHMENT," ULTIMATELY: RHETORIC AS PRAYER

A present task for rhetoric, then, is to engage the demands that prayer, in its variety, places on rhetoric as an architectonic art. The task is not, ulti-mately, to account for *prayer as rhetoric*, but to understand how *rhetoric is prayer*. This task is the more demanding, and the present effort goes only some way toward charting aspects of rhetoric that are most fully realized in prayer. Even so, I suggest that we gain an invaluable purchase by approach-ing prayer as meta-discourse through which we sound out the need and possibility of rhetoric.

This reading of prayer counters James's identification of prayer as "the soul and essence of *religion*" (337, emphasis added). Rather, it regards prayer in structural terms as exposed bedrock and as principally concerned with the constitution of discourse. Such concerns are evident in *liturgy* (in Greek, the "work of the people"), the means by which a community dramatizes its identity. Liturgical rites of every stripe, secular or religious, are arguably *prayer in the original*, with individual prayer an authorized extension. Even in praying alone, we use forms and motifs sanctioned by our communities. Viewed this way, it comes as no surprise that Burke, in introducing terms for analysis of symbolic action, chooses *prayer* to signal the "public, or communicative, structure" of a poem along with "subdivisions" of *dream* ("unconscious or subconscious factors") and *chart* ("the realistic sizing of up situations"; *Philosophy* 5–6). By design, prayer wrestles with what it means to *be in communication with* another.

Prayer, then, *is* the act of constructing scenes of communication, the ground that unites speakers and audiences. In the exposed bedrock of prayer, human speakers act out these scenes before divine audiences, such as when a supplicant voices not only some need but also the grounds on which one turns to prayer addressing a particular audience in one's need. The Lord's Prayer, for example, begins by recognizing God's sovereignty as the grounds for petitions that seek to align heaven and earth.

Grounded in scenic relations, prayer is also an encounter with the ethical demands imposed by communication. An audience places demands on a speaker, and prayer serves as a term for a rhetor's apprehension of those demands. As Levinas puts it, "the Other faces me and puts me in question and obliges me" (*Totality* 207). To face an other/Other is to radically encounter our nature as rhetorical beings open to the necessity and possibility of appeal. Before prayer is a demand to be heard, it is first an encounter with the demanding "face" of the Other. Levinasian "responsibility" (Nealon 131) finds its counterpart in Bakhtin's "answerability" (131), a term signaling the dialogic dimension of discourse. If prayer is not to be reduced to addressing a projection of its performer, it must be open to moments of genuine encounter. Hence Brueggemann's "dangerous rhetoric" of prayer, because in any act of communication we are always on a knife's edge between fictive and real address. Behind every prayer is a prayer that *this* prayer be genuine.

The performance of prayer thus manifests openness to a real encounter. Whether conceived as physically or psychically distant, prayer's audience must first be called into presence. Alternatively, prayer's speakers must perform a kind of self-summons into the presence of the divine. (This is especially the case in Christian prayer conceived as the raising of one's heart and mind to God.) Consequently, the core speech act of prayer is not petition or praise, but invocation. Not simply a prologue to prayer, invocations also open and, through repeated acts of address, sustain a communicative space. As an act that makes a divine audience present, invocations name their object of address and in doing so seek to gain an advantage. But invocation is also prayer at its most dangerously rhetorical. Invocations put claims on addressee and speaker alike—reciprocal to invocation's *call* is vocation's *response*. Invocation entails commitment to the demands of relationship claimed through prayer, so one had best be serious.

Regardless of how this challenge is understood, invocation must be sufficiently demanding if prayer is to retain an aura of mystery. Such mystery is inherent in communication between beings of different kinds. At its most profound, this communication approaches "pure persuasion," a scene of discourse that "in all purity would transform courtship into prayer, not prayer for an end, but prayer for its own sake, prayer as Adoration, or as the Absolute Compliment" (Burke, *Rhetoric* 252). Such "reverent beseechment" may not be fully realizable in any real situation, but pure persuasion "can be present as a motivational ingredient in any rhetoric, no matter how intensely advantage-seeking such rhetoric may be" (Burke, *Rhetoric* 178, 270). Burke thus extracts from prayer a disinterested form of interest, representative of the highest motives implicit in a communicative act: to desire nothing but to be *in communion with* the other. Such "pure persuasion" cannot be fully equated with prayer, which has its utilitarian ends as well.

This bedrock of pure persuasion, "logically prior to any persuasive act" and "the essence of language" (Burke, *Rhetoric* 252), finds outcroppings in language that would transcend, if not fully negate, pragmatic motives. Prayer thus stages encounters that exceed a strictly transactional scene while seeking what leverage may yet be had. This last point is crucial given a tendency to valorize prayer as transcendence of interest at the expense of prayer as strategy. Like all discourse, prayer desires *something* from its encounters with an audience. However, a motive of transcendence helps us understand the self-conscious and hyperbolic character of prayer. Prayer must dare to overcome interest if it is to escape becoming a monologue.

By slow turns, then, we move from notions of prayer as *exceptional* to *essential* rhetoric. Rather than regard prayer as the transcendence of rhetoric, we can recognize prayer as an appropriate name for the communicative motive in all its complexity of self-interest and regard for the other. There is a risk, then, in reading prayer's scenes too *simply* to account for such complexity. This is the case when certain modes of prayer are singled out as higher or as somehow more authentic or when prayer itself is elevated above all other discourse. At the same time, in approaching rhetoric as prayer it becomes clear that certain paradigms function as arguments about the nature of communication and community. In the gospels, Jesus uses conventions of Greco-Roman oratory as a foil to advance a counter-rhetoric of prayer: "When you are praying, do not heap up empty phrases as the Gentiles do; for they think that they will be heard because of their many words. Do not be like them, for your Father knows what you need before you ask him" (Matt. 6:8–9). Jesus further characterizes showy speech performed in public as *play*acting in contrast with the sincere *pray*acting performed in private. This is a kind of purifying of motive. Of course, such admonitions have only partially shaped Christian prayer. Distinctions between sincerity and showmanship retain their pungency because prayer continues to manifest mixed motives.

In any culture, available forms constitute a performative grammar of prayer. In gospel accounts, as elsewhere, these rhetorical forms signal basic stances. In the Reformation, a long-standing binary of scripted versus spontaneous prayer grew ideological, pitting the use of received forms in Catholic/Anglican tradition against a Protestant insistence that scripted prayer posed a threat to authentic communication with God. More recently, praying in the *orans* position (arms extended, palms facing upward) has been embraced by some as a reclamation of early Christian practice and has been critiqued by others for assuming a posture reserved for clerical leaders.

Prayer manifests the principle of appeal that many, following Burke, associate with rhetoric: *"the use of language as a symbolic means of inducing cooperation in beings that by nature respond to symbols"* (*Rhetoric* 43, emphasis in original). This definition is useful if only to underscore the question of which beings do, finally, respond to symbols, and thus whose cooperation may be induced. Does rhetoric, as prayer, operate beyond its natural range? As earlier noted, if anything characterizes divine beings, it is their addressability. But do they "respond to symbols"? Is prayer properly regarded as inducing cooperation in *human* beings, the real audience of prayer addressed *by means of* divine address? As I have endeavored to show, such a reading is (literally) hopelessly reductive and does no justice to the motivational reach of rhetoric.

This present effort locates prayer in a more expansive frame than communication with divine beings by considering the range of operations in modes of address. As noted, prayer is usefully approached in terms that challenge a religious–secular binary, especially through Burke's oxymoron of "secular prayer," or "the *coaching of an attitude* by the use of mimetic and verbal language" (*Attitudes* 322, emphasis in original). In this crucial formulation, Burke locates prayer at the nexus of two dramatistic motives: *act* (coaching) and *attitude*, a form of "incipient action" (*Grammar* 446).[3] Equating prayer with attitude formation places it at the center of *all* symbolic action, not just within the domain of religion. As Burke observes,

> It is of great importance to study the various strategies of "prayer" by which men [sic] seek to resolve their conflicts, since such material should give us needed insight into the processes of prayer ("symbolic action," "linguistic action," "implicit commands to audience and self") in its many secular aspects, not generally considered "prayer" at all.
>
> (Philosophy 313)

For Burke, "secular prayer" is not address before a particular audience but the property of address itself—the bedrock of speech. Religious prayer is thus a "representative anecdote" (Burke, *Grammar* 5) of "secular prayer" in the broad sense, because address to divine audiences, by nature ideal communicants, epitomizes the functions of address.

A notion of secular prayer also establishes a link between "mimetic and verbal language" (Burke, *Attitudes* 322). An early instance of a bodily turn in rhetoric, this identification marks a shift toward recognizing the body as a site of performance equally with words. Burke recognizes prayer as a speech act performed in words, but not only words:

> Secular prayer would not, by our notion, be confined to words. Any mimetic act is prayer. Even "psychogenic illness" may be a prayer, since it is the "substantiation of an attitude" in a bodily act. All mimetic procedures, in the dance, the plastic or graphics arts, music and verbalization are aspects of "prayer" in our technical sense of the term. And they have a great deal to do with the building of character. In fact, the man who does not 'pray cannot build his character.
>
> (*Attitudes* 321–22)

Burke stretches "prayer" beyond its ordinary semantic range to express its essence as *mimesis*, thus likening spiritual training to physical exercise. In mimetic terms, attitudes are not only *coached* but also *danced*: "The symbolic act is the dancing of an attitude" (Burke, *Philosophy* 9).

Of course, prayer may literally be danced as an analog or accompaniment to verbal performance (Snowber). The "spiritual exercises" of Ignatius of Loyola suggest that Burke's characterization of prayer as mimesis is not far afield from a religious understanding (Loyola). Prayer has long been understood as a spiritual discipline, crucially involving the body as an instrument of performance as well as an instance of verbal communication. For phenomenologist Jean-Louis Chretien, prayer "concerns our body, our bearing, our posture, our gestures," all of which "can be gathered together in a summoned appearance that *incarnates* the act of presence" (150). Insisting on the embodied nature of rhetorical performance, Burke's "secular prayer" anticipates this phenomenological account, negotiating binaries of physical and verbal, material and symbolic, presence and absence. Indeed, secular prayer resembles the strategies of children who "name the essence of their play objects" and discover "unseen existences" to thereby transcend "material reality"; employing the same strategies, an adult " 'sees' the class struggle" in "the welter of the world" (Burke, *Attitudes* 322).

One final insight into rhetoric as prayer can be credited to Burke in his notion of "literature as equipment for living" (*Philosophy* 293). Like proverbs, whose didactic aims Burke discovers operating in all literature, prayer never strays far from pragmatic ends. This notion of texts and stories as "equipment for living" is usefully extended to prayer as a site of *rehearsal* for living; prayer functions not only as a scene of transcendence or transaction but also as a site wherein we cultivate essential attitudes. One turns to prayer as a rehearsal space for broader rhetorical operations—we learn to communicate through the conditioning of character afforded by prayer. In this sense, prayer, the term for being in communion with others, serves as the epitome of rhetorical action.

BEYOND DESCRIPTION: CHARTING A NEW
COURSE FOR A RHETORIC OF PRAYER

How does one come down from the proverbial mountaintop and begin to articulate the relationship between rhetoric and prayer in ways that move beyond the playful speculation of rhetorical theory? In broad strokes, a "working" rhetoric of prayer takes inventory of prayer's speciation to disclose underlying principles. Despite a vast devotional literature, our understanding of prayer as utterance, composition, and performance remains rudimentary in the modern era now that the language whereby we understand rhetoric is far removed from the devotional language of prayer. We need thick description of prayer in situ, as in ethnographic accounts of prayer in evangelical (Luhrmann) or Catholic (Orsi) contexts.[4] Both Luhrmann and Orsi emphasize prayer as social imagination in personal relations with God (Luhrmann) or with the saints (Orsi). As a discipline, rhetoric has yet to contribute its due measure to accounts of prayer from humanistic or social scientific perspectives. In this increasingly vital inquiry, rhetoric risks marginalization.

Beyond these etic accounts of prayer are multiple emic perspectives, including spiritual classics (*Way of the Pilgrim*; Weil) and confessional works (Balthasar; Teresa of Avila) that explore internal topographies of prayer to illuminate Christian belief and practice. Such texts invite our close reading to better understand the rhetoric of prayer as lived experience. Beyond experiential accounts, one discovers a raft of primers that collectively comprise entire alternative traditions of rhetoric. Despite being among the most abundant and influential of applied rhetorics, such practical rhetorics of prayer (Bounds; Pennington) have largely escaped notice in our accounts of rhetorical theory or history. Again, we would do well to reclaim these spiritual rhetorics as a contribution to a full understanding of rhetorical thought and practice.

Finally, several promising lines of inquiry in contemporary rhetoric have long been central to prayer, none more so, perhaps, than emergent concerns with the material basis of rhetoric. As I have briefly touched upon, prayer is an encounter with communicative *agency* as much as agents. In particular, prayer is an encounter with the agency of language, verbal or otherwise. Spiritual communication depends on a formal vehicle to deliver eloquence. The remarkable fluidity of form that prayer enjoys stems in large measure from the performative resources available through our embodiment. Religious traditions each respond to the challenge of embodiment in different ways, embracing the body and its mediated extensions for the "dancing of an attitude" (Burke, *Philosophy* 9) or transcending bodily limitations through the spiritual resources of speech, including bringing the body and the spirit to order. Such ends are achieved in Christian contexts through embodied acts of prayer such as silence, stillness, or recurring gestures (e.g., bowed head, folded hands). In some contexts, prayer becomes synonymous with the psychosomatic discipline required to be free from distraction, to act with abandon, or to attain mystical states of consciousness. Embodied prayer likewise encompasses the use of media such as rosary beads as a devotional aid.

This line of inquiry into prayer as agency complements approaches to prayer as scene, act, or attitude. Indeed, prayer is productively understood as a *techné* for crafting selves in relationship to reality. A key contribution of rhetoric to a study of prayer (and vice versa) comes in recognition of the *tool value* of spiritual discourse without negating characterizations of prayer as persuasion of or communion with divine agents. Prayer is precisely a strategy for transforming situations through mimesis—a self-dramatizing, multimodal agency. Viewed in this light, prayer represents a compelling instance of Foucault's "technologies of the self" that "permit individuals to effect by their own means or with the help of others a certain number of operations on their own bodies and souls, thoughts, conduct, and way of being, so as to transform themselves in order to attain a certain state of happiness, purity, wisdom, perfection, or immortality" (18). An emphasis here on techniques of regulation and construction underscores the degree to which prayer is at once a form of *address* and a mode of *attention* that acts reflexively on the self, in individual or collective terms. Focusing on prayer as attention recognizes prayer as a mode of embodied subjectivity realized in modes of discursive production and reception.

Classical rhetoric categorized the mediated character of performance under *delivery*, the reciprocal relations between rhetorical acts and their uptake by audiences. Given the distance between prayer's human speakers and divine audiences, the delivery of prayer involves things *said* and *sent*, hence a focus on prayer as sending words and receiving answers or insight. Again, much prayer depends on instrumentalizing delivery through strategies of amplification and transmission, whether through material objects (e.g., candles) or intermediaries (e.g., saints). Similarly, performing prayer at particular sites or placing prayers in specific locations (e.g., the Western Wall in Jerusalem) lends a spatial dimension to delivery, conceived not just as a metaphorical sending of our thoughts but, often, as a physical, mimetic act that makes the notions of reaching a distant audience more palpable as well. As rhetoric seeks to understand the multimodal rhetorics of embodied performance, it has only to look to prayer as a rich set of practices ready for analysis.

Most recently, digital modes of composition and circulation of texts further enact the performative logic of delivery, particularly in the proliferation of virtual spaces in which prayer appears (Howard). Through practices that remediate (Bolter and Grusin) prayer's pre-digital forms, one can now post prayers to websites or use digital apps such as e-rosaries. Indeed, the rise of mobile technology highlights prayer's simultaneously social and instrumental dimensions. (In the age of the internet, it is harder than ever to follow Jesus's admonition to pray in secret.) The remediation of speech into text(ing) reveals that prayer unfolds within social networks, digital or otherwise, that authorize and even solicit its performance. It remains to be seen what effects new media will have on prayer when notions of a spiritual "toolbox" as nearby as one's mobile phone join traditional concepts of prayer as practice, discipline, and mode of being. Already, notions of prayer as virtual communication have been augmented by the affordances of new media. The rise of spiritual "apps" thus provides a valuable opportunity to gauge emergent "spiritual" literacies, their entrepreneurial development, and vernacular adoption (Howard).

Notwithstanding the power of technology to transform long-standing habits of devotion, it seems prudent to predict that prayer's future will accord with prayer's past. To claim that prayer in a fundamental sense *is* rhetoric is to identify in the fluidity of its motivational concerns the full range of rhetoric. Before prayer was religious, it was a language of appeal, a vital expression of our linguistic endowment. Burke's identification of rhetoric as "a function that is wholly realistic and continually born anew" (*Rhetoric* 43) suggests that prayer, synonymous with the communicative act, and prayer, the epitome of that act in dramatic relations with a divine audience, is no mere phase in our development but is an endemic feature of social cognition. Prayer is the very principle of symbolic action, the spirit of possibility measured against all recognizable limitations, and thus the beating heart of rhetoric.

NOTES

1 I am grateful to Susan Zaeske for her insight that political petitions function as a secular analogue to prayer. For the rhetoric of petitions, see Zaeske.
2 For a detailed account of a medieval *ars orandi* in practice, see Spence.
3 Burke would later add a sixth motive of attitude to his dramatistic pentad of act, scene, agent, agency, and purpose.
4 When God Talks Back (Luhrmann) richly portrays prayer life in the Vineyard, a fast growing Evangelical faith community. Orsi further portrays prayer as a social tapestry of human and divine beings in *Between Heaven and Earth: The Religious Worlds People Make and the Scholars Who Study Them. Thank You, St. Jude* (Orsi), is an equally insightful account of twentieth-century devotion, especially by women, to St. Jude, the patron of "lost" causes. Luhrmann, in particular, underscores prayer's dialogic dimensions.

REFERENCES

Ahmed, Arif. *Wittgenstein's "Philosophical Investigations": A Reader's Guide*. New York: Continuum, 2010.
Augustine. *On Christian Doctrine*. Mineola: Dover, 2009.

Bakhtin, Mikhail. *Speech Genres and Other Later Essays.* Trans. V. W. McGee. Eds. Caryl Emerson and Michael Holquist. Austin: U of Texas P, 1986.

Balthasar, Hans Urs Von. *Prayer.* San Francisco: Ignatius P, 1986.

Bellah, Robert. "Civil Religion in America." *Journal of the American Academy of Arts and Sciences* 96.1 (1967): 1–21.

Bolter, J. David, and Richard Grusin. *Remediation: Understanding New Media.* Cambridge: MIT P, 2000.

Bounds, E. M. *Complete Works of E. M. Bounds on Prayer.* Grand Rapids: Baker, 2004.

Brueggemann, Walter. *Awed to Heaven, Rooted in Earth: Prayers of Walter Brueggemann.* Minneapolis: Fortress P, 2002.

Burke, Kenneth. *Attitudes toward History.* 3rd ed. Berkeley: U of California P, 1984.

———. *The Grammar of Motives.* Berkeley: U of California P, 1969.

———. *The Philosophy of Literary Form.* Berkeley: U of California P, 1973.

———. *The Rhetoric of Motives.* Berkeley: U of California P, 1969.

Catechism of the Catholic Church. New York: Doubleday, 1995.

Charney, Davida. "Performativity and Persuasion in the Hebrew Book of Psalms: A Rhetorical Analysis of Psalms 22 and 116." *Rhetoric Society Quarterly* 40.3 (2010): 247–68.

Chretien, Jean-Louis. "The Wounded Word: Phenomenology of Prayer." *Phenomenology and the "Theological Turn": The French Debate.* Eds. Dominique Janicaud et al. New York: Fordham UP, 2000.147–75.

Darsey, James, and Joshua Ritter. "Religious Voices in American Public Discourse." Lunsford, Wilson, and Eberly 553–80.

Dowden, Ken. "Rhetoric and Religion." *A Companion to Greek Rhetoric.* Ed. Ian Worthington. London: Blackwell, 2010. 320–35.

Ellul, Jacques. *Prayer and Modern Man.* New York: Seabury, 1970.

FitzGerald, William. "Burkean Perspectives on Prayer: Charting a Key Term through Burke's Corpus." *Kenneth Burke and His Circles.* Eds. Jack Selzer and Robert Wess. West Lafayette: Parlor P. 2009. 201–21.

———. *Spiritual Modalities: Prayer as Rhetoric and Performance.* University Park: Pennsylvania State UP, 2012.

Foster, Richard J. *Prayer: Finding the Heart's True Home.* New York: Harper, 1992.

Foucault, Michel. *Technologies of the Self: A Seminar with Michel Foucault.* Amherst: U of Massachusetts P, 1988.

Greenberg, Moshe. *Biblical Prose Prayer as a Window to the Popular Religion of Ancient Israel.* Berkeley: U of California P, 1983.

Habermas, Jürgen. "Notes on a Post-Secular Society." *New Perspectives Quarterly* 25:4 (2008): 17–29.

The HarperCollins Study Bible: New Revised Standard Version. San Francisco, CA: HarperSanFrancisco, 2006.

Heiler, Friedrich. *Prayer: A Study in the History and Psychology of Religion.* Oxford: Oxford UP, 1932.

Howard, Robert G. "A Theory of Vernacular Rhetoric: The Case of the 'Sinner's Prayer' Online." *Folklore* 116.2 (2005): 172–88.

James, William. *The Varieties of Religious Experience.* London: Longman, Green and Company, 1902.

Jaye, Barbara H. *Artes Orandi.* Turnhout: Brepols, 1992.

Kimelman, Reuven. *The Rhetoric of Jewish Prayer: A Literary and Historical Commentary on the Prayerbook.* Plymouth: Littman, 2014.

Levinas, Emmanuel. "Prayer Without Demand." *The Levinas Reader.* Ed. Sean Hand. Oxford: Basil Blackwell, 1989. 227–33.

———. *Totality and Infinity: An Essay on Exteriority.* Norwell: Kluwer, 1979.

Loyola, St. Ignatius. *The Spiritual Exercises and Selected Works.* Ed. G.E. Ganss. Mahwah: Paulist P, 1991.

Luhrmann, Tanya M. *When God Talks Back: Understanding the American Evangelical Relationship With God.* New York: Knopf, 2012.

Lunsford, Andrea, Kirt H. Wilson, and Rosa Eberly, eds. *The SAGE Handbook of Rhetorical Studies.* Thousand Oaks: Sage, 2009.

Medhurst, Martin. "American Cosmology and the Rhetoric of Inaugural Prayer." *Central States Speech Journal* 55 (1977): 272–82.

Murphy, James. *Rhetoric in the Middle Ages.* Berkeley: U of California P, 1974.

———. *Three Medieval Rhetorical Arts.* Berkeley: U of California P, 1985.

Nealon, Jeffrey. *Alterity Politics: Ethics and Performative Subjectivity.* Chapel Hill: Duke UP, 1997.

Neyrey, Jerome. *Give God the Glory: Ancient Prayer and Worship in Cultural Perspective.* Grand Rapids: Eerdmans, 2007.

Orsi, Robert. *Thank You, St. Jude: Women's Devotion to the Patron Saint of Hopeless Causes.* New Haven: Yale UP, 1996.

Pennington, M. Basil. *Centering Prayer: Renewing an Ancient Christian Prayer Form.* New York: Doubleday, 2001.

Pernot, Laurent. "Rhetoric and Religion." *Rhetorica* 24.3 (2006): 235–54.

Pulleyn, Simon. *Prayer in Greek Religion.* Oxford: Clarendon P, 1997.

Rahner, Karl. *The Need and Blessing of Prayer.* Collegeville: Liturgical P, 1977.

Ricoeur, Paul. *The Symbolism of Evil.* Boston: Beacon P, 1967.

Schoenfeldt, Michael C. *Prayer and Power: George Herbert and Renaissance Courtship.* Chicago: U of Chicago P, 1991.

Schomburg Center for Research in Black Culture. *Standing in the Need of Prayer: A Celebration of Black Prayer.* New York: Schomburg Center, 2003.

Snowber, Celeste. *Embodied Prayer: Toward Wholeness of Body, Mind, Soul.* Kelowna: Wood Lake, 2004.

Spear, Wayne. *Talking to God: The Theology of Prayer.* Pittsburgh: Crown and Covenant, 2002.

Spence, Timothy L. "The Prioress' *Oratio ad Mariam* and Medieval Prayer Composition." *Medieval Rhetoric: A Casebook.* Ed Scott Troyan. New York: Routledge, 2004. 63–90.

Targoff, Ramie. *Common Prayer: The Language of Public Devotion in Early Modern England.* Chicago: U of Chicago P, 2001.

Teresa of Avila. *The Interior Castle.* Trans. Keiran Cavenaugh and Otilio Rodriguez. Mahwah: Paulist P, 1979.

Ulanov, Ann, and Barry Ulanov. *Primary Speech: A Psychology of Prayer.* Louisville: Westminster John Knox P, 1983.

Way of the Pilgrim. Trans. H. Bacovcin. New York: Doubleday, 1985.

Weil, Simone. *Waiting For God.* Trans. Emma Craufurd. New York: HarperCollins, 2009.

Wuthnow, Robert K. *The God Problem: Expressing Faith and Being Reasonable.* Berkeley: U of California P, 2012.

Zaeske, Susan. *Signatures of Citizenship: Petitioning, Antislavery, and Women's Political Identity.* Chapel Hill, NC: U of North Carolina P, 2003.

Zaleski, Philip, and Carol Zaleski. *Prayer: A History.* New York: Houghton Mifflin, 2005.

Zulick, Margaret D. "The Rhetoric of Religion: A Map of the Territory." Lunsford, Wilson, and Eberly 125–39.

3 The Agentive Play of Bishop Henry Yates Satterlee

Richard Benjamin Crosby

> Afterwards all the Israelites came near, and he gave them in commandment all that the Lord had spoken with him on Mount Sinai. When Moses had finished speaking with them, he put a veil on his face.
>
> —Exodus 34:32–33

The epigraph comes from the section of the Pentateuch in which Moses descends Mount Sinai with the Ten Commandments and communicates the will of God to the children of Israel. God has been speaking with Moses for forty days and nights and has conferred on him the authority to serve as revelator and prophet of the children of Israel. In this passage, Moses has become the literal conveyance for God's word, a conduit for the divine Logos. Perhaps the detail that gets the least attention in this familiar story is Moses's veil. The image suggests a deliberate self-effacement. The veil, applied over the face when "giving" (not advocating, arguing, deliberating, evaluating, interpreting, or contriving) God's will, directs attention away from the speaker and toward the revelation itself. When finished delivering the commandments, Moses would "take the veil off" (*HarperCollins Study Bible*, Exodus 34:34). As with the veil of the temple mentioned in Exodus 26:33, the veil over Moses's face serves to differentiate that which is "most holy" from that which is not, and it powerfully reminds his audience that a greater will speaks through him.

Moses's veil is an appropriate symbol for this discussion, because it communicates, rather literally, a strategic rhetorical effacement. Moses conceals his face when he delivers the word of God. When he does not deliver the word of God, his face remains strategically unconcealed. This chapter of *Mapping Christian Rhetorics* seeks to complicate recent discussions of rhetorical agency by situating them within the context of revelatory, or prophetic, discourse. I argue that conceptions of the so-called decentered agent are not terribly far afield from ancient notions of the prophetic agent and that a better understanding of the latter will lead to a better grasp of the former's rhetorical latitude. I am particularly interested in what I call *agentive elision*, which I define as the strategic concealment or elision of agency in the interest of assigning a particular message to a higher order source, thus lending the message greater power. I am also interested in demonstrating how this elision of agency is negotiated by strategic, occasional reassertions of agency. As I argue, agency is not a possession or even a stable source of power, but it is an ephemeral space into and out of which the revelator moves in an effort to generate the maximum level of influence.

In what follows, I account for current discussions about rhetorical agency and their relationship to revelatory rhetoric. I then perform an analysis of a particular religious event, the 1898 "Peace Cross Ceremony" at the so-called National Cathedral in Washington D.C. I use the analysis to demonstrate how a religious rhetor, Henry Yates Satterlee, first bishop of the National Cathedral, strategically concealed his own agency in framing the seminal event while constructing an identity for what is now the world's sixth-largest cathedral and one of the nation's most unique and politically charged sacred structures. Finally, I discuss how revelatory rhetoric and its embrace of the strategically concealed agent might inform the possibilities for rhetorical agents as discussed in the current literature.

AGENCY AND THE PROPHETIC RHETOR

Theories of agency can be a little unwieldy, perhaps because the current literature views the agent as a contingent actor in a highly complex world. The contingent actor is, as Althusser puts it, "always-already interpellated" in the situations and ideologies that precede his or her actions (176). Of course, this notion that an agent is interpellated contradicts older, more romantic notions of agency as the possession of an autonomous actor. Agency was thought to be something one possessed and deployed in an effort to exert influence. The distinction between these two interpretations is clear. Agents are unconstrained, self-guided individuals, or are mere media through which power structures speak. But these two interpretations represent less a dichotomy than a spectrum. It is now widely accepted that the old modernist subject (the older view of the agent as autonomous) has been "decentered," but this description does not mean the agent is unable to exert influence.

Carolyn Miller argues that agency is the property of an interaction among a variety of actors. Miller writes that "[t]he energy of agency is rhetorically functional only through interaction" (149). Here Miller borrows from Michael Leff's view that agency has always been interactive in the sense that a rhetor's audience inherently constrains her ability to persuade, and that notions of cultural "tradition" mediate "between individual and collective identities" (Leff 135). Miller elaborates this principle of interaction by introducing the metaphor of kinetic energy (150). There is a mutual attribution of influence between the rhetor and the audience; this mutual attribution is kinetic in that it generates persuasive power through a rhetorical give-and-take between the actor and the audience (see also Cooper 13).

Miller's claim that agency becomes functional only in the moment of interaction points to the fundamental instability of the concept. It is not a possession, nor is it merely a product, but it is "the deed in the doing, action itself" (Miller 147; see also Cooper 16). Scott Graham reads this refiguration of agency as a move from stable *commodity* to volatile *process* (380). Ultimately, then, Miller believes that agency's interiority has been chased out by the postmodern condition—that agency is now diffused across a spectrum of exterior variables that interact in an unpredictable, always altering condition. Agency, in this sense, cannot be generated except through dynamic distribution between and among potential actors (see also Sánchez 235). This interactive movement generates opportunities for meaningful action and suggests a link to the concept of *kairos*, the ancient idea of an always-shifting moment of opportunity that grows out of the contingencies of lived experience. Elsewhere, I have pointed out that Greek mythology interprets Kairos (the proper noun) "as a fleeting, youthful male with a lock of hair hanging from his forehead. He has wings on his shoulders and heels, suggesting that his body is in constant motion" (Crosby, "Cathedral" 134). He is, in this way, the embodiment of opportunity, a potentiality of influence that passes swiftly away. So the link between agency and *kairos* has rich implications, and Carl Herndl and Adel Licona's work on this topic is worth some attention.

Herndl and Licona take important steps to demonstrate this link between a kinetic agency and the principle of *kairos*. They argue that agents are structurally constrained subjects who may *enter into* and *perform* agency but not transcend it. Like Miller's kinetic theory of agency, Herndl and Licona's theory rejects the romantic notion that agency is something individuals possess. Quoting Bordo, they argue that "people and groups are positioned differently within (agency)" (qtd. in Herndl and Licona 137). The authors elaborate on this claim by noting that agency as a "social location" implies opportunities into and out of which rhetors move. Thus, Herndl and Licona build on Miller by suggesting that rhetors may be situated within interactive spaces, where persuasive power is generated. The kinetic energy that Miller references becomes, in Herndl and Licona's view, an ephemeral location in time and space that generates opportunity for change, a kind of *kairos*. Thus, Herndl and Licona reject agentive autonomy, while allowing individuals to recognize "when and where action is possible" (138). The *space* of opportunity becomes the source of authority. It is an opening—a *capacity* in the truest sense—that one inhabits.

Here, then, is where I locate the link between current theories of agency and basic assumptions about sacred rhetoric. Although Herndl and Licona do not design their theory with reference to religious discourse, their view of *kairos* points implicitly in theological directions. For example, some theorists see *kairos* as an essential principle of Christian revelation. Scholars of rhetoric traditionally view *kairos* as a principle inherent in a rhetor's response to temporal constraints imposed by occasions, contexts, rules of decorum, and so on. It is, simply put, "rhetoric's time" (Hawhee 66). However, when considering *kairos* within the context of sacred rhetoric, one must look to another conceptual framework. Dale Sullivan takes up the idea of a situationally emergent *kairos*, but he adds that out of the rhetorical situation "arises something like a magical power, dunamis" (320). Christian theology in particular embraces a sense of kairos as an inspired opening in the linearity of time. It assumes that important historical moments are divinely ordained. The opportune moment, or *kairos*, is a kind of revelation that the trained, sacred rhetor must be able to discern (see Duffy, this volume).

Jesus makes this point clear in Luke, where he takes to task "hypocrites" who understand the signs of natural events, such as rain and wind, but who cannot "interpret the present time" (12:56). In this view, kairic moments are not temporal coincidences of material and semiotic conditions that generate opportunities for rhetorical action; they are divine irruptions in linear time (*kronos*) that reveal imperatives for historical change. To put it another way, they are markers of God's intervention in the world. It is not surprising that *kairos* has been called "God's time," because it represents an occasion that "carries strategic imperatives for faith and action" (Sipiora 119). The power of this religiously inflected *kairos* derives from its transcendent source. The revelator, or sacred rhetor, is merely a conduit for God's will, one who does not create ideas ex nihilo but who plays an essential role in the sharing of ideas and the challenging of an audience. The sacred rhetor inhabits an authoritative space, what Debra Hawhee calls the "aperture" of "kairotic inspiration" (71). My point here is to show that there is a critical link between Herndl and Licona's notion of agency as a space into and out of which agents move, and what the literature on sacred rhetoric characterizes as revelation, or revelatory discourse. Herndl and Licona's theory may not mean to consider the puzzles of revelatory rhetoric, but it bears resemblance to revelatory process. In both cases, the rhetor must find and inhabit the kairic space of agency, and in both cases, the relationship between the rhetor and the authoritative kairos he inhabits is, in my reading, prone to flip. To put the matter in pentadic terms, the rhetor becomes the agency and the power that inheres the kairic space (the divine Logos) becomes the agent. The revelator does not seize the *kairos*; he allows the *kairos* to seize him and impel him to action.

A sacred rhetor's role comes back to the question of positioning, or his spatial relationship with the Logos and the audience. His unique burden is to stand "in place" of the Lord, to be a tool in the service of the Logos rather than to use logos as a tool, and finally, to "bear" God rather than to argue for God's probability. James Darsey's well-known work in this area highlights the point I am trying to make. "The role of the prophet," he writes, "is not a role one seeks; it is a role with which one is burdened" (Darsey 28).

Consequently, the prophet cannot retain prophetic authority without exchanging the self for the certainty or revelation. He must dissolve himself into a kind of transparency through which the "extraordinary, invisible, and personal (are made to be) understandable, visible, and public." In this way, the prophet is able "to present the uncolored word of Yahweh" (Darsey 32). God becomes "the true agent of the prophetic word and the prophet is reduced to the status of agency" (Zulick, qtd. in Darsey 17). But this negation of self is paradoxically also an assertion of authority, which derives from the kairos. By submitting himself to, or dissolving himself within, the character and power of the authoritative opening, the prophet masks his own temporal identity. Importantly, though, once the authoritative message is revealed as a basis, or premise, for new action, he or she steps out of the capacity and begins the process of instruction and interpretation. Given the persuasive power of this effacement, or what I am calling agentive elision, I offer the following analysis of its use.

ANALYSIS: BISHOP SATTERLEE AND THE AMERICAN "WESTMINSTER ABBEY"

In the space of a short chapter, it is impossible to recount the rich history behind the National Cathedral. Suffice it to say, the cathedral is not an ordinary church. Its official name, The Cathedral Church of Saint Peter and Saint Paul, points to the building's Anglican roots. In fact, the cathedral remains the mother church of the Washington, D.C., diocese of the American Episcopal Church. The exigency behind its now quasi-official nickname is revealing. In the late 1800s, when the cathedral was still just an idea, the Anglican Communion was composed of "a loose confederation of dioceses" (Hewlett, *Foundation Stone* 39). Some saw the D.C. cathedral's construction as a means to unite the communion, while other leaders, Bishop Satterlee among them, were still more ambitious. Satterlee believed that after certain reforms were in place and a symbolic national headquarters could be established in the form of the new cathedral, America's Protestant faiths would unite "under the aegis of the Anglican Church" (Hewlett, *Foundation Stone* 40).

This desire for Protestant unity was partly a response to the growing influence of Catholicism in the nation and, more specifically, in Washington, D.C. Materials from the cathedral archives reveal a palpable anxiety among cathedral organizers, including and especially Satterlee, that Roman Catholicism was better organized and positioned in the nation's capital than was Protestantism, specifically the Episcopalians. The cathedral would be an unmistakable reassertion of Protestantism's centrality to American identity (see "Letter from Senator Edmunds"). Satterlee even admitted privately that he was attempting to build the American "Westminster Abbey" (Satterlee, Letter to Bodley, undated). Once installed as bishop of the yet-to-be-built sanctuary, Satterlee established its three chief identities. The cathedral would be "a house of prayer for all people," "the chief mission church of the diocese," and "a great church for national purposes" (Hewlett, *Washington Cathedral* 3). Interestingly, the last identity on the list is a direct lift from Pierre L'Enfent, the eighteenth-century designer of America's federal city (see "Cathedral Timeline"). L'Enfent's master plan for Washington D.C. included "a great church for national purposes." The idea was jettisoned, presumably as a violation of the American aversion to state churches. Nevertheless, if the state could not sponsor a church, Satterlee saw no reason why a church could not sponsor the state.

I want to pause here to reaffirm just how radical and ambitious Satterlee's goals were. In a nation that legislated against such things as Westminster Abbey, he wanted to blend American identity and the Protestant faith so fundamentally that, in the practice of worship inside the cathedral, one could hardly be dissociated from the other. Realizing this expanded vision for the cathedral would require an aggressive and ongoing public relations effort. Satterlee proved to be a deft user of symbols, events, and media— not to mention a "master at achieving his goals without alienating those who disagreed with him" (Hewlett, *Foundation Stone* 63). The Peace Cross Ceremony provides a useful illustration of his abilities in this regard. More important, it shows a revelator–rhetor in action, strategically moving into and out of agentive spaces in an effort to exert further influence over an ambitious and controversial project.

The Peace Cross

In 1898, shortly after Satterlee's installation as bishop, the Episcopal Church was scheduled to hold its general convention in Washington, D.C. It just so happened that the convention coincided roughly with the end of the Spanish–American War, and Satterlee saw this coincidence as providential. Given that the cathedral was still only in the planning stages, Satterlee's idea was to erect a large "peace cross" on the cathedral grounds. He believed that the ceremony, if designed strategically, would establish a pattern for the cathedral to sacralize events that were national in scope and significance, thus setting a precedent for the cathedral's use as a universally recognized home for sacred events of national significance. If he could not legally create an American Westminster Abbey by an act of government, he would rhetorically construct the cathedral in such a way that the public would be persuaded to receive it as the nation's de facto religious center.

Satterlee immediately ordered the limestone to be quarried. It would need to be shipped from Indiana, carved, inscribed, and set in place—all in the space of a few weeks. Considering the breadth and force of Satterlee's efforts, it would be easy to assume that he was something of an aggressive character. But Satterlee's biographer, Richard Hewlett, indicates that the bishop was adept at avoiding total implication in the design and planning of major events. According to Hewlett, Satterlee preferred to lead others to believe that the ideas he advocated were originally theirs or those of someone else. He wanted to appear "merely as the implementer of ideas proposed by others" (Hewlett, *Foundation Stone* 67).

Satterlee's own words as outlined in his "Private Record" provide clues to this process and point to a rhetorically constructed *kairos* that gave Satterlee more leverage than might have been available otherwise. Because there is no record of Satterlee's private conversations other than what he wrote in his own private record, I am obliged to consider his own reflections as evidence of his rhetorical maneuvering. This constraint, however, is revealing. If one is to elide one's own agency, it is not surprising that the only evidence available for some record of the relevant action is to be found in a private record. The private record is also helpful because it not only provides a record of his interactions with other actors, but it also allows a glimpse into how he conceives of his own role in major events. We can see how he justifies that role and his actions in pursuing strategic goals. Consider the following excerpt. Positioning himself as the receiver—not producer—of ideas, Satterlee writes of the first moments in which the peace cross idea came to him:

> Then all suddenly, on the Sunday [. . .] while I was in the little Church in Twilight Park, the remembrance came back to my mind of the Communion service on Easter Monday of Bishop's guild, in which we had prayed so earnestly for peace. On that day the war with Spain was practically begun. Now it was practically over. Then came the remembrance of another service at Northeast Harbor, [. . .] we held a short thanksgiving service for the restoration of peace. This suggested the erection of a Cross of Peace as the first monument on the new Cathedral grounds with the inscription: "That it may please Thee to give to all nations unity, peace and concord, we beseech Thee to hear us, Good Lord!"
>
> (Satterlee, "Private Record" 99–100)

Satterlee does not recommend proposals or generate ideas. He does not even "remember" events. Rather, events come "back to [his] mind," and these "remembrances" in turn lead to self-evident conclusions. Note how the agentive memory "suggests" the erection of a "Cross of Peace"—as if the memory and not the one remembering would thus entitle the sculpture. Satterlee's language even implies that the memory is responsible for the proposed—and lengthy—inscription, which promotes "unity, peace and concord" for "all nations." Satterlee, playing the role of revelator, situates himself within a series of sacred spaces that ultimately lead to the revelation of the peace cross idea. Note that he inhabits places of divine inspiration, kairic openings through which revelation flows. As he sits passively in these places and prays, ideas are revealed to him, and he behaves as merely a worthy recipient.

Note also Saterlee's subtle shifts in subjectivity as the idea of the ceremony develops. Concluding his reflection on the Peace Cross idea, he writes, "At once I told the thought to my wife and daughter, also to Dr. and Mrs. Rives; and Dr. Rives said at once he would give the Cross. We all agreed that no more beautiful beginning could be made of the National American Cathedral of the Prince of Peace" (*Private Record* 100). Satterlee only situates himself as the agent when he is sharing *the* "thought"—not *his* "thought"—with other agents who might corroborate the inspired memory that produced the idea in the first place. The idea thus is not a claim to be argued but a truth to be disclosed, or revealed, and becomes viable only within a dynamic of social interaction. No fewer than four other actors are consulted, and they in turn urge the idea forth, affirming its self-evidence and providing the material resources to see it realized.

As a tactic of agentive elision, this dispersal of agency across actors serves at least two functions. First, as the idea is corroborated across a spectrum of other actors, it accrues rhetorical viability. That is, it is legitimized as part of a kinetic network of interacting variables that, in Miller's terms, creates the opportunity for change. Second, the idea's original revealer is insulated against liability as a larger spectrum of actors assumes a custodial role. The idea becomes a cause within a community. In the case of religious communities, the motivating force behind such causes is not the revelator but Providence itself. The revelator simply becomes a conductor within the larger network to which the community belongs. He is a contact point through which ideas are shared, not originated. Even then, he does not proclaim the idea as if from a mountaintop. As a sensitive persuader living within a modern, democratic culture, Satterlee creates additional layers of kinetic action in order vitalize the idea of the cathedral. He selects a particular audience and allows the idea to become viable in conversation. Indeed, the name Satterlee assigns to the cathedral (the "American Cathedral of the Prince of Peace") has no apparent source. Such a name is not mentioned in any other archival materials. We are left to assume it comes from Satterlee himself, though he will not, even in his private record, let alone in conversation with others, assume ownership of it. We only have a record of the action Satterlee creates around the idea.

From this time forward, Satterlee's role begins to shift. Once the idea has been introduced and gained traction, and assuming Satterlee has not been implicated as having personal or agentive motives, he is free to assume the role of evangelizer. The reader will recall Herndl and Licona's notion of agency as a *social location* into and out of which rhetors move—and, furthermore, that this location is shifting. Satterlee moves to inhabit a new social location once the idea is viable. He moves from revelator to evangelizer. He becomes the active, anxious agent of God's will. "But no time was to be lost," he writes. "The next day I wrote to Mr. Gibson, the architect of the Hearst School" (*Private Record* 100). In this way, Satterlee represents himself not as one who develops positions and arguments out of a deliberative process of searching and testing. Rather, he sees himself as a portal for inspired ideas that he in turn shares and advocates. The reader will note his abrupt shift from passive, third-person constructions to assertive first-person constructions once the idea has found social traction. He has begun the shift from agentive elision to agentive assertion, highlighting the duality of agency that is characteristic of revelatory discourse.

The example noted earlier is not the only instance in which Satterlee uses this agentive duality to his advantage. Given the length constraints of this chapter, I do not elaborate on other examples, except to say that his "Private Record" repeatedly shows him moving into and out of agency, from elision to assertion as the kairos demands. When an idea emerges, Satterlee evacuates agency by placing the proverbial veil over his face, but when the idea is to be conveyed, he occupies agency by removing the veil. For instance, in his preparations leading up to the Peace Cross event, Satterlee invites President McKinely to the ceremony and urges him to speak. McKinley's refusal to speak only prompts further prodding by the bishop. Referring to the morning when he traveled to the White House to pick up the president, Satterlee recalls, "On the way out I said to him: 'I wish I could venture to ask the President to speak, notwithstanding his refusal.' He [President McKinley] responded: 'I should not venture, Bishop, for he might refuse again.'" Undeterred, Satterlee pressed: "'But,' said I: 'This Cathedral is to last through coming centuries. One word from the President, if it were only a 'God bless this undertaking,' would make the occasion historic.'" At last McKinley provided an opening: "After your own speech is over you may appeal to me if you wish, and I will then decide whether or not to speak" (102). So Satterlee again elides his own agency. He does not say to the president, "Despite your refusal, I still want and invite you to speak at this ceremony." Instead, he says, "I wish I could venture to ask the President to speak," as if to act as an agent is forbidden, in spite of his own desires to do so. This paraliptic move is characteristic of such discourse, because it allows the rhetor to speak from a remove. The rhetor, feigning to mute himself, expresses his desire in the very act of forbidding its expression.

Satterlee as Director

This notion of communicating from a remove is important in agentive elision. In reading and analyzing Satterlee's journal, I have found myself alternating between an inclination to see him as one of several actors or as the hidden director in the social interactions that kinetically and kairically confer the agency behind his ideas. In the preceding analysis, Satterlee appears to characterize himself as a fellow actor. He plays an important role—that of revelator—but once the ideas and imperatives are revealed, he becomes another participant in vitalizing the idea. But there is also evidence that Satterlee serves as a director. He frequently instigates action from a place just out view. Consider his own reflection in his journal following the ceremony. He describes the events as though he is setting the stage and blocking the characters:

> The scene was indescribably beautiful, with the whole city of Washington spread out beneath us in the golden sunshine of the October afternoon. Bishop Dudley took the first part of the Service. Dr. Dix read the lesson. Bishop McLaren took the Creed and prayers [. . .]. Then I spoke and made the appeal to the President. He rose and made a beautiful little address.
>
> (Private Record 102)

Though his address was short, McKinley includes a sentence that undoubtedly pleased Satterlee: "Every undertaking like this for the promotion of religion and morality and education is a positive gain to citizenship, to country and to civilization, and in this single word I wish for the sacred enterprise the highest influence and the widest usefulness" (*Eminent Opinion* 29). The most prominent national political figure blesses the project as an advancement for "citizenship," "country," and "civilization," and urges work forward in a superlative fashion, wishing for the "highest influence" and "widest usefulness." Satterlee, still acting at a remove, recaps in his journal what happened next:

> Then I gave the signal. The American flag that enveloped the Cross floated down, giving the effect of a white Iona cross shooting up out of its folds and then from red clouds of glory. The whole choir of 250 voices, with the band, burst out with the hymn, "In the Cross of Christ I glory, towering o'er the wrecks of time." As Dr. Battershall described it, "It was the sensational moment."
>
> (Private Record 102–03)

Here Satterlee plays the director quite explicitly. In effect yelling "action" from just off stage, he orchestrates a performance that includes actors, images, and sounds all interacting—a field of relations over which he has quiet, invisible control. He would not have us believe he creates the message—the one subject position he refuses to adopt is that of author—but he certainly shapes it, and he clearly assumes the role of revealing it. He gives the orders as Moses gave the orders, but the source of those orders is always implicitly some higher will.

CONCLUSION

I hope this chapter of *Mapping Christian Rhetorics* has provided readers a sense of the complex and sophisticated negotiation of agency that inheres persuasive religious discourse. As rhetorical critics continue to try to come to terms with the nature of religious and Christian rhetorics, it seems increasingly likely that a unifying, rationalized theory of the way religion persuades will never be widely agreed on. We can, however, identify certain discursive features and exigencies that apply across a spectrum of religious texts. At the very least, there are theoretical concepts that play a significant, if contested, role in discussions of religious rhetoric. Agency is one such concept. There is a duality to agency in Christian discourse, and it can be identified according to specific needs and goals. On one side of the duality is the principle of agentive elision. The agent must subsume himself within a kairic capacity that confers authority by virtue of its transcendent origins. In this case, the agent must assume a passive position as a chosen vessel of an external, all-authoritative Logos. On the other side of the duality is the principle of agentive assertion. The agent may assume an active role only after the idea has been publicly, interactively affirmed, but once the affirmation takes place, the agent is called to act with faith and even urgency. The example of Bishop Satterlee illustrates how the movement from elision to assertion might take place within an explicitly religious context of goals, audiences, exigencies, and so on.

But while my central claims concern religious rhetoric, I believe there is potential to pursue this theory of agentive duality in other contexts as well. Given the remarkable success of Satterlee's seminal vision for the cathedral, I would propose at least two important considerations for discussions of rhetorical agency more broadly. First, elided agency is not necessarily a condition of disempowerment; it may actually be a condition of extraordinary empowerment. As Satterlee shows, some message sources are greater than others are, and in certain circumstances, people are not likely to be persuaded by someone who openly presents him- or herself as the source of an argument. It would be fruitful for rhetoricians to consider how this strategic effacement might be enacted in political and professional discourse. Undoubtedly, there will be examples of high-ranking actors making arguments that conceal their own interests while drawing on the demands of some higher hegemony. A politician may assign responsibility for an unpopular policy to the consensus of "science." An employer may assign responsibility for layoffs to "the market." How do well-positioned actors elide their own agency in the construction of persuasive arguments? And to what extent is this elision effective?

Second, Satterlee demonstrates that actors do not need to wait passively for that higher hegemony to speak its will. Rather, there are ways that actors can ascribe ideas and arguments to more universally persuasive structures. Satterlee shows that actors can occupy certain subject positions in strategic, kairic ways. Furthermore, he is not shy about instigating the kinetic energy necessary to vitalize the kairic revelation he receives, but he does so from a remove, the way a director works offset to constrain and enable important ideas, images, and actions. Once the idea is presented, he or she shapes it, shares it, seeks feedback, and even prods and pesters his or her targets, all the while concealing any sense of his or her own creative role in the matter. He sets the stage and directs the movement while veiling him- or herself as the origin of ideas. In much the same way, a CEO might read quarterly reports and market predictions and assume particular conclusions. The CEO may call meetings and set agendas, all designed to frame a matter as having an inevitable conclusion resulting from some higher force. But as this chapter is devoted essentially to religious discourse, I should like to return to the story with which I started things.

American Moses

Considering the example of Moses, a number of curious—if coincidental—parallels become evident. Well known is that when Moses descended Mount Sinai, he brought with him the famous Ten Commandments, but it is important to remember that he was sequestered with the Lord on Mount Sinai for forty days and forty nights, as the story goes, and he received a great deal more information than what is popularly known. Indeed, he returned from Sinai not only with a handful of commandments but also with a set of remarkably detailed construction plans for the temple and a laundry list of supplies that the people would need to provide:

> The hangings of the court, his pillars, and their sockets, and the hanging for the door of the court, The pins of the tabernacle, and the pins of the court, and their cords, The cloths of service, to do service in the holy place, the holy garments for Aaron the priest, and the garments of his sons, to minister in the priest's office.
>
> (Exodus 35: 17–19)

Satterlee, for his part, also revealed particularly detailed expectations for the cathedral. It was Satterlee's intention from the beginning that the cathedral's iconography should depict scenes and words from U.S. history—a history that he viewed as essential to American Protestants. In one letter to the cathedral's early principal architect, Satterleee wrote that the American historical scenes should be "intensely interesting," and "dear to the hearts of Puritans, Presbyterians and Methodists" (Letter to Bodley, 11 January 1907). Satterlee expands on these sentiments in other letters. Writing again to the same architect, he effectively whispers,

> [I]t is a National Cathedral, and sooner or later it will be in touch with the nation's life [. . .] Certainly in some part of the Cathedral there should be statues and perhaps bas reliefs presenting different events of American history. You yourself have suggested Washington and Pen (sic). I could add a great many other subjects. Some of them connected

with our own Church, like the baptism of Pocahontas, Washington reading the burial service over Gen. Braddock, etc.

(Letter to Bodley, undated)

Satterlee implies that the cathedral will inevitably become, in effect, the nation's church. And while clearly this becoming is rooted in Satterlee's own vision, the bishop characterizes it as self-evident, a vision from a divine source, which builders and designers might realize through, for example, "statues and perhaps bas reliefs presenting different events in American history." Satterlee is not just building a temple, however. The cathedral for him is itself a journey to a promised land. In unifying Protestant tradition and American identity, he is arguing for a particular interpretation of a chosen people residing in a chosen land.

Like Moses, Bishop Satterlee was not allowed to see the fulfillment of his massive religious and cultural project. He died in 1908 of apparent pneumonia, attributed to his incessant work for the cathedral, but his vision has indeed been realized. The cathedral now enjoys regular use as a venue for political solemnities, such as the funerals (or portions of the funerals) of Woodrow Wilson, Dwight Eisenhower, Harry Truman, Ronald Reagan, and Gerald Ford, and national prayer services, such as those that took place following the inaugurations of Franklin Roosevelt, Ronald Reagan, both Bushes, and Barack Obama. It has also become a place for national mourning, as evidenced by its prominent use after the September 11 attacks, and it is the last resting place of such prominent Americans as Woodrow Wilson, Helen Keller, Admiral George Dewey, U.S. senator Stuart Symington, and World War I hero Norman Prince.[1] Bishop Satterlee is also interred in the cathedral. The building's ubiquitous use as a political venue has become entirely uncritical. It is now assumed that, although the building is chartered as a church, and although it is sponsored by a specific religious denomination, and although it is overtly Christian, it is allowed to serve explicitly political purposes—namely, to sacralize the history and destiny of a nation that Satterlee, among others, regarded as chosen.

NOTE

1 This information is available on the cathedral's website: www.nationalcathe dral.org.

REFERENCES

Althusser, Louis. "Ideology and Ideological State Apparatuses." *Lenin and Philosophy, and Other Essays*. Trans. Ben Brewster. London: New Left, 1971. 127–88.
"Cathedral Timeline." *Washington National Cathedral*. n.d. Web. 30 January 2012.

Cooper, Marilyn. "Rhetorical Agency as Emergent and Enacted." Watson Lecture, February 26, 2010.

Crosby, Richard Benjamin. "Cathedral of Kairos: Rhetoric and Revelation in the 'National House of Prayer.'" *Philosophy and Rhetoric* 46.2 (2013): 132–55.

Darsey, James. *The Prophetic Tradition and Radical Rhetoric in America.* New York: New York UP, 1997.

Eminent Opinion: Regarding the Cathedral at Washington: Representative Americans State their Views. 1929. Washington Cathedral Executive Committee, Cathedral Archives, 132–5–20. Washington, D.C.

Graham, S. Scott. "Agency and the Rhetoric of Medicine: Biomedical Brain Scans and the Ontology of Fibromyalgia." *Technical Communication Quarterly* 18.4 (2009): 376–404.

The HarperCollins Study Bible: New Revised Standard Version. San Francisco: HarperSanFrancisco, 2006.

Hawhee, Deborah. *Bodily Arts: Rhetoric and Athletics in Ancient Greece.* Austin: U of Texas P, 2004.

Herndl, Carl, and Adela Licona. "Shifting Agency: Agency, Kairos, and the Possibilities of Social Action ." *Communicative Practices in Workplaces and the Professions.* Eds. Mark Zachry and Charlotte Thralls. New York: Baywood, 2007. 133–53.

Hewlett, Richard G. *The Foundation Stone: Henry Yates Satterlee and the Creation of Washington National Cathedral.* Washington: Washington National Cathedral, 2007.

———. *Washington Cathedral and its National Purpose: The Emergence of an ideal, 1867–1990.* Collection: 163–4–5. National Cathedral Archives, Washington D.C., 1992.

Leff, Michael. "Tradition and Agency in Humanistic Rhetoric." *Philosophy and Rhetoric* 36.2 (2003): 135–47.

"Letter from Senator Edmunds to the Bishop of Washington." 25 January 1898. *Published in Cathedral of SS. Peter and Paul: Washington.* Collection: 2–15–2. National Cathedral Archives, Washington D.C.

Miller, Carolyn. "What Can Automation Tell Us about Agency?" *Rhetoric Society Quarterly* 37 (2007): 137–57.

Sánchez, Raúl. "Outside the Text: Retheorizing Empiricism and Identity." *College English* 74.3 (2012): 234–46.

Satterlee, Henry Yates. Letter to Bodley. 11 January 1907. Collection 162–7–2. National Cathedral Archives, Washington, D.C.

———. Letter to Bodley. Undated. Collection: 162–7–2. National Cathedral Archives, Washington D.C.

———. "Private Record." *The Foundation Stone: Henry Yates Satterlee and the Creation of Washington National Cathedral.* Ed. Richard G. Hewlett. Washington, D.C.: Washington National Cathedral, 2007.

Sipiora, Philip. Introduction to *Rhetoric and Kairos: Essays in History, Theory, and Praxis.* Eds. Phillip Sipiora and James S. Baumlin. Albany: SUNY P, 2002. 1–22.

Sullivan, Dale. "*Kairos* and the Rhetoric of Belief." *The Quarterly Journal of Speech* 78.3 (1992): 317–32.

Zulick, Margaret D. "The Agon of Jeremiah: On the Dialogic Invention of Prophetic Ethos." *Quarterly Journal of Speech* 78.2 (1992): 125–48.

Section II

Christianity and Rhetorical Education

4 "Where the Wild Things Are"

Christian Students in the Figured Worlds of Composition Research

Elizabeth Vander Lei

Sustaining a self and sustaining a culture are ceaseless activities. Both projects are always under construction and under repair, although this endless work may escape our notice until a moment of crisis makes the grind of the machinery audible to us.

—Richard Miller, "The Nervous System"

The fog of the monster's breath marks the line of division between the realm of the verbal and the realm of infantile formlessness (where all things are patchy combinations wholly alien to the realm of Order as we know it).

—Kenneth Burke, *The Rhetoric of Religion*

Kathleen Blake Yancey opens "Made Not Only in Words: Composition in a New Key" by reminding us that important moments, like those Miller describes in the epigraph, are what we make of them: "Sometimes, you know, you have a moment. [. . .] These moments: they aren't all alike, nor are they equal. And how we value them is in part a function of how we understand them, how we connect them to other moments, how we anticipate the moments to come" (297). I see the publication of *Mapping Christian Rhetorics* as a significant moment for rhetoric and composition, an opportunity for us to examine our rhetorical negotiations about religious faith and religious students, particularly Christian students (because they have received the most attention in our scholarship). Examining these negotiations is important because such an examination makes audible to us the grind of the cultural machinery in rhetoric and composition. It draws attention to unexamined attitudes about the place of composition in the world and the place of students, particularly religious students, in composition.

In this chapter, I use James Paul Gee's analytical tool of *figured worlds* to examine our discourse about religious students, showcasing how that discourse has been influenced by a figured world commonly used in composition studies: composition as a city. This figured world appears in two versions: composition as an urban center surrounded by uncivilized space, and composition and religious faith as remote civilizations separated by dangerous space. Both versions position Christian students in particular and religious students in general outside the borders of composition in the wild places populated by monsters, creatures that simultaneously fascinate and intimidate us. In a third version that both relies on and challenges these figured worlds, composition teachers and their students eschew the safety of the city to explore frontiers where the wild things are. Through this review, I hope to encourage rhetorical scholars and educators to acknowledge how much our disciplinary metaphors influence how we imagine religious student writers and, indeed, the nature of academic writing. Doing so may help us imagine rhetorical education, and the students we teach, in new ways.

FIGURED WORLDS

Cognitive linguist James Paul Gee uses the term "figured worlds" to name the "models or pictures that people hold about how things work in the world when they are 'typical' or 'normal.' We all use them so that we do not have consciously to think about everything before we talk and act" (*How* 173). Gee's concept of figured worlds derives from the linguistic axiom that "human physical, cognitive, and social embodiment ground our conceptual and linguistic systems" (Rohrer 27). In our linguistic systems, cognitive linguists argue, we pay attention to a "trajector," the entity that interests us, and the "landmark," the background against which we locate the trajector and track its motion (Zlatev 327). For example, when people engage in regular activities, such as researching at a library, they rely on a generalized model of the activity—a figured world—that includes characters (e.g., students, professors, researchers, librarians) and actions (e.g., using a database to find a source, using a library catalog to locate that source on the shelves, checking out a book) that are considered normative or appropriate for that activity (see Oakley 216).

Through rhetorical acts of metonymy and metaphor, we emphasize and de-emphasize features of real-life characters to fit them neatly into existing schema. In the library example, we are likely to include details such as students' backpacks, textbooks, and computers and exclude details such as students' car keys, hairstyles, or body shapes. Cognitive linguists propose that people do not develop these figured worlds idiosyncratically. Rather, they do so in community, and people hold many figured worlds in common with others (Stockwell 16). One important communal function of figured worlds is projecting as normative and appropriate a communal understanding of complex identity issues such as race, gender, sexuality, and social class. Because of their metonymic nature, a community's figured worlds identify who is part of the community (and what role they play) and who is not: "Figured worlds involve us in exclusions that are not at first obvious and which we are often unaware of making" (Gee, *Introduction* 77). Unsurprisingly, these exclusions advantage some people and disadvantage others as they seek "'social goods' [. . .] like power, status, or valued knowledge, positions, or possessions" (Gee, *Introduction* 91–92).

And figured worlds shape a community's discourse. Summarizing the work of Charles Fillmore, cognitive linguist Alan Cienki notes that people rely on schemas (or frames) to assert a particular relationship between reader and writer:

> We not only employ cognitive frames to produce and understand language, but also to conceptualize what is going on between the speaker and the addressee, or writer and reader. This introduces the idea of framing on another level, in terms of "interactional frames." Such interactional frames provide a tool for talking about the background knowledge and expectations one brings to bear for the production, and interpretation, of oral or written discourse, particularly in relation to accepted genre types.
>
> (173)

Gee proposes that

> for any communication, we want to ask what typical stories or figured worlds the words and phrases of the communication are assuming and inviting listeners [or readers] to assume. What participants, activities, ways of interacting, forms of language, people, objects, environments, and institutions, as well as values, are in these figured worlds?
>
> (Introduction 72)

Applying this question to the composition scholarship about religious students offers sobering—and hopeful—answers.

At this point, many readers will have noticed that cognitive linguists themselves rely on geographical metaphors, such as Gee's "figured worlds" (see Oakley 217). Such images are echoed in the title of this collection and in the figured worlds of composition studies itself. For example, in his 2013 College Composition and Communication (CCCC) Chair's address, "Climate Change," Chris Anson considers social changes happening "all around universities" (325).[1] Anson thus enacts what Nedra Reynolds argues we all do in rhetoric and composition: place composition at the center of "an imagined geography big enough to hold [its] ambitions" (32). Geographical metaphors, such as the university campus that Anson's Professor Nathan Shield views, serve as valuable reminders of the materiality of the classroom and, beyond that, "of the material situatedness of all textual practices" (Ede 16). Moreover, they lend "specificity and concreteness to [our] observations and invite readers to relate these observations to their own experiences" (16).

Through the figured worlds constructed through such geographical metaphors, we define ourselves as a community concerned about the immediate needs of students and the rhetorical consequences—material and ideological—of the scholarly texts that constitute a significant portion of our discourse.

Reynolds notes that the geographical figured worlds in composition scholarship emphasize boundaries: "Generally, as composition has encountered postmodernism, metaphors of inside and outside, margin and center, boundaries and zones have become increasingly familiar, appealing, and even comfortable" (28). Lakoff and Johnson highlight the essential nature of this particular figured world—that of container—by pointing to the way we imagine ourselves as self-contained entities and "experience the rest of the world as outside us" (29). Due to such self-understandings, Lakoff and Johnson argue that "even where there is no natural physical boundary that can be viewed as defining a container, we impose boundaries—marking off territory so that it has an inside and a bounding surface—whether a wall, a fence, or an abstract line or plane. There are few human instincts more basic than territoriality" (29). This essential metaphor shapes our communal figured world of composition as an urbane environment, populated by citizens who write and behave in appropriate ways (see Donehower, Hogg, and Schell 13). Invoking the metaphor of an enclosed city, Reynolds suggests that "the ways in which we imagine space and place have a direct impact on how we imagine writing and acts of writing as well as the inhabitants of composition studies—and its outsiders, real or imagined" (27). Richard Miller borrows the container metaphor of a stage from James Scott to contrast students' academic writing—their "public transcript"—with their often-unvoiced, nonacademic allegiances—their "hidden transcript"—that are part of "the religiopolitical equipment of historically disadvantaged groups" (qtd. in Miller, "Arts" 15). Miller describes public transcripts as inauthentic except for the bits of hidden transcripts that enter from the outside:

> [S]lipping in enough of the hidden transcript to preserve their sense of self-respect, [students] write papers that lifelessly respond to the assignment; they contradict themselves, saying what they want to say and what they think the teacher wants them to say at the same time; they publicly announce their interest in the work at hand while manifesting no visible sign that their interest requires anything from them. They hunker down and try to get by.
>
> ("Arts" 18)

Indeed, Miller emphasizes the rhetorical space of the composition classroom: students "never forget where they are, no matter how carefully we arrange the desks in the classroom, how casually we dress, how open we are to disagreement, how politely we respond to their journal entries, their papers, their portfolios. They don't forget; we do" ("Arts" 18).

MONSTER THEORY

Reynold's comment about outsiders and Miller's description of hidden transcripts might make us think about the characters that populate the uncontained spaces beyond the boundaries of the composition class. These spaces provide a habitat for creatures—what I call "monsters"—that trouble the very figured world that produced them. In Baumgarter and Davis's terms, "this distancing from the monster creates the very space for monsters to exist and to flourish" (1). Of the community but not in the community, monsters and their ambiguous citizenship challenge the boundaries the community erects as a safeguard against difference: "From this space, the monster irrupts into the stability of the normal order. The monstrous other destabilizes the comfortable binaries of inside/outside, internal/external" (Baumgartner and Davis 1). The very presence of these uncontainable creatures comprises one of Miller's moments of crisis and reminds the community that created them of the inherent instability of boundaries.

Scholars in cultural studies have demonstrated that monsters have always been with us: they appear in our most ancient myths (such as the Greeks' Sphinx, Cyclops, and Sirens) and star in recent movies (such as *Men in Black* and *Super 8*). Perhaps monsters are so prevalent in our cultural texts because they evoke complex human emotions, not only horror and disgust but also curiosity and even attraction (Baumgartner and Davis 1). While "monster" might first seem a necessarily negative term, any viewer of movies for children knows that we can find monsters loveable, too—and useful: Asa Simon Mittman argues that " [m]onsters do a great deal of cultural work, but they do not do it nicely. They not only challenge and question; they trouble, worry, and haunt. They break and rend cultures, all the while constructing them and propping them up" (1). Throughout time and across the globe, monsters have embodied the instability of culturally negotiated understandings of gender, race, heredity, hierarchy, emotion, science, and sexuality. In composition, religious students do some of this monstrous work.

In *Monster Theory*, Jeffrey Cohen proposes that it is possible to learn much about a community by examining its monsters because a monster is "an embodiment of a certain cultural moment—of a time, a feeling, and a place. [. . .] The monster's body is pure culture" (4). Within a community, Cohen claims, monsters disrupt the smooth operation of the cultural machine, throwing sand in the works through their "refusal to participate in the classificatory 'order of things' [. . . T]hey are disturbing hybrids

whose externally incoherent bodies resist attempts to include them in any
systematic structuration" (6). As "disturbing hybrids," monsters embody
questions and concerns that are "rhetorically [. . .] distant and distinct"
from the very communities from which they "originate" (Cohen 7). Stories
of these monstrous hybrids evoke fear, and fear encourages members of
the community to stay within the safety of the well-lit city: "the monster
of prohibition polices the borders of the possible, interdicting through its
grotesque body some behaviors and actions, envaluing others" (Cohen 12).
So while the figure of monster does important cultural work for a community by challenging boundaries, the fear of monsters conserves and even
reinforces those boundaries.

WRITING INSIDE THE CITY: STUDIES OF RELIGIOUS
STUDENTS IN COMPOSITION

Composition scholarship about religious faith includes stories of teachers
erecting walls to quarantine the composition classroom from the outside
influence of religion, as Priscilla Perkins describes her colleagues doing when
they "cordoned off all Bible talk" ("Radical" 587). Similarly, Shari Stenberg describes instructors dismissing "religious inquiry or even testimony as
inappropriate for intellectual work" (282). Some composition teachers even
use military imagery to describe their efforts to check incursions of religious
faith into the composition classroom, as Chris Anderson's teaching assistant
does when she wonders "whether she should mount some kind of frontal
attack or restrain herself" when responding to "Cathy's" description of a
conversion experience (12). Commonly, composition is considered a formal
academic setting that must be protected from religious zealotry or passion.
Such passion is imagined to be "proper [only] in certain situations," those
being outside the composition classroom (Anderson 13). Janice Neulieb uses
language similar to Richard Miller's when she describes how the Advanced
Placement (AP) scoring system reinforced—"naturalized," in Stenberg's
terms (279)—formal academic discourse by offering benchmark essays
that "were often distanced, cool discourse that would leave both reader
and writer untouched by the affective transaction of the text" (Neulieb 42).
These instances and others imagine composition as a walled city in which
most academics are content to stay. In academia, Reynolds notes, "most
people are reluctant to travel, or even leave their neighborhoods, without
having a very good reason," even though "firm stay-at-home attitudes,
keeping yourself to yourself, contradict many philosophies of learning that
value, for example, challenging texts" (45–46).

Students, too, rely on a figured world of composition as a city when
they imagine a figurative wall separating school from the rest of their lives.
Sociologist Tim Clydesdale notes that the first-year college students he studied viewed higher education instrumentally, as a means to secure a good job

and financial stability (3). Consequently, students did not bring to school what they deemed to be personal:

> [R]ather than see schooling as an opportunity to examine oneself and one's place in the larger world, most American teens keep core identities in an "identity lockbox" during their first year out [. . .]. That lockbox preserves teens' mainstream American identity from intellectual or moral tampering that would put them out-of-step with the communities that shaped them or hinder their efforts to pursue the individual achievement that they have always envisioned for themselves.
>
> (4)

I experienced this kind of walled thinking myself growing up among Christian fundamentalists who sent their children to state universities rather than to Calvin College because they believed that the religious faith of their children would be out of bounds at the university, whereas that faith would be tested and refined through use ("liberalized" was their true fear) at a religious school such as Calvin, as Perkins's research suggests it would ("Radical" 594–95). For my neighbors, the purpose of school was to develop knowledge and skills, narrowly defined as those that prepare students for work; if students were to develop emotionally, spiritually, or socially, they would do so outside the university.

In composition scholarship about Christian students, Stenberg relies on a similar metaphor when describing how students choose what they will, and will not, include in their academic discourse: "students whose values and knowledge are dismissed by critical approaches may do one of two things: reject them entirely and resist the pedagogy, or if they want to be accepted within a new discourse community, keep that identity closeted" (279). According to Stenberg, when composition students find themselves walled off from religious faith, they have two choices: fight or hide. Amy Goodburn records her student Luke's invocation of this wall in his complaint that Goodburn is "supposed to be this unbiased grader. You present your viewpoints and the grade, not grade for the content of ideas, but for grammar and punctuation and development of ideas. That kind of thing" (345). If he had it his way, Luke would limit Goodburn's influence to topics appropriate to the public space of composition as city, to "social graces" such as grammar and punctuation. Brad Peters records a third option students consider: fleeing from the container. He describes a problematic tutoring session wherein the tutor begins by suggesting that the student writer remove all references to the Bible from the rough draft of her paper, a draft that referenced, among other things, the Ten Commandments (Peters 122). Peters describes the outcome: "When the student left, I suspected we'd never see her again—and I was right" (123).

The figured world of composition as a city positions rural spaces outside its boundaries; as a result, some have argued that "rural experiences are erased, denied, or deemed unimportant, where those who are rural are seen as having less 'experience, skill, or wits' rather than those of a different kind" (Donehower, Hogg, and Schell 14). In composition scholarship about religious faith, according to Phillip Marzluf, Christian fundamentalists are associated with rural spaces, the American Midwest, "farming communities," and the "Bible belt" (275). Indeed, in her essay about Christian fundamentalist students, Perkins describes herself as a "non-evangelical transplant to the Bible Belt" ("Radical" 586); similarly, Shannon Carter emphasizes her geographical position by titling her essay "Living inside the Bible (Belt)." New to these rural communities, both Perkins and Carter use boundary language to describe the adjustments they make to their teaching of writing. Carter notes that teaching writing in the Bible Belt taught her "the limits of my tolerance for difference" (572). Perkins describes her research on fundamentalist Christianity as crossing a gulf between bounded worlds: "a sanity saver, a lifeline to the cultural and academic world I had just left" ("Radical" 587). But these studies do not necessarily denigrate what happens beyond the boundaries of composition. Rather, some scholars build on the figured world of composition as a city to emphasize the rich possibilities beyond the city gates. Consistent with Miller's model of "public" and "hidden" transcripts, Perkins describes her students like this:

> While we [Perkins and her fellow instructors] all struggled in the classroom, faculty stories of our students' extramural ingenuity were legion: the same students who supposedly could not write essay exams in history classes were printing poems, novellas, and razor-sharp movie and music reviews in our campus publications. When they were not in school, they ran small businesses, raised large families, put in overnight shifts at the local tire factory, drove tanks to the practice grounds of the army base that bordered town.
>
> ("Radical" 588)

Contrasting the sterility of students' academic discourse to the fecundity of students' discourses outside the university, Perkins emphasizes differences between the university and its surrounding blue-collar, deeply religious neighborhood. Carter uses the language of boundaries to contrast herself and evangelical Christian students when describing a visit to an evangelical church in her student Keneshia's neighborhood. Carter admits that her own "functional illiteracies in this community of practice were apparent from the minute [she] walked through the door" of the True Love Baptist Church (589).

Sometimes functional literacies such as those Carter describes come as a surprise. For example, in *Toward Civil Discourse*, Sharon Crowley describes making an off-hand comment to graduate students about an audio version of *Left Behind*, the wildly popular end-times book, that she had listened to during her commute to the university. According to Crowley, the graduate students "recognized the tale immediately," leaving her as "the only person in the room who had never heard of John of Patmos or read the biblical book of Revelation" (102). In her telling, Crowley emphasizes the difference between the university and the surrounding neighborhood by noting that she borrowed the audiobook from her local library, assuming it to be "similar to the other light fiction I often listen to while commuting" (102). Her students' familiarity with *Left Behind* emphasizes their connection to the world outside the university. Crowley's description of her own response to this event, on the other hand, emphasizes her citizenship in the university and its scholarly work: "Fascinated by the story, and a bit ashamed of my ignorance, I began to study Christian apocalyptism" (102).

I myself emphasize the boundary between Christian students and school when I describe my student "Marty" suddenly appearing at my office door clutching a book that, he claimed, contained all the physical evidence he needed to prove that the biblical flood occurred exactly as it is described in the Bible ("Ain't" 94). The book and the potential research topic of Noah's flood excited Marty, while the alternative "academic" topic that he and I ultimately agreed on I cannot remember. Was it mere coincidence that I describe my office door separating Marty and me? Or was I invoking the figured world of composition as city to position Marty outside and myself inside the " 'univocal' story of the academic research paper in which I was expert and Marty novice" ("Ain't" 98)? I believe it was the latter.

COMPOSITION AND RELIGION AS DISTANT CITIES

Sometimes, in the composition scholarship about religious students, composition and religion are each imagined as civilizations separated by some distance. Scholars such as Goodburn and Stenberg search for common ground among these far-flung communities, as Krista Ratcliffe suggests people are inclined to do (67). Indeed, Patricia Bizzell directly challenges this metaphor of distance between composition and religion. Bizzell demonstrates that, in the theological debate between the Jewish scholar known as Nahmanides and the Dominican friar Paul Christian, both interlocutors used "mixed discourses, borrowing from one another's discourse communities to effect persuasion. [. . .] Indeed, as is often the case when we analyze mixed discourses, we discover that the discourses being mixed were not so separated to begin with" ("Rationality" 14–15).

But other scholars emphasize a dangerous no-man's land between the communities that students and teachers must learn to traverse. Shannon Carter describes this space as "a gap that liberal academics and evangelical Christians may find impossible to traverse—intolerable, in fact" (573). Making use of Gee's concept of Discourse, Doug Downs, too, relies on this metaphor when he describes the gulf between two competing Discourses—True

Believers and Real Scholars—that are "constituted by mutually exclusive and negating epistemologies" (40). In fact, he describes his student Keith as impossibly "stretched between" these two Discourses (44). Other scholars invoke this figured world when they recommend pedagogical strategies. For example, Lynell Edwards proposes that when teachers model "moral self-fashioning," they "provide their students with discursive habits that will allow them successful and safe passage into new disciplinary homes" (23). Carter relies on this geographic metaphor to frame her goal of helping

> students speak to and across difference by employing [. . .] a pedagogy of rhetorical dexterity, an approach that trains writers to effectively read, understand, manipulate, and negotiate the cultural and linguistic codes of a new community of practice based on a relatively accurate assessment of another, more familiar one.
>
> (574)

With the help of composition teachers, it is imagined, students can learn to cross the barren spaces between communities, code-switching among appropriate discourses. Such imagining presumes that students enter college capable of managing such cognitive complexity and motivated to do the work that this code-switching would require of them.

Other scholars employing this figured world argue that the distant religious community and its discourse can serve as a resource for students. Studies of the literacy practices of particular religious and quasi-religious communities—Andrea Fishman's *Amish Literacies: What and How it Means*, Beverly Moss's *A Community Text Arises*, and Beth Daniell's *A Communion of Friendship: Literacy, Spiritual Practice, and Women in Recovery*—support such a view. While Crowley might view these distant religious communities instrumentally, as sites "available for plunder" (54), most scholars imagine students using this resource respectfully. For example, Stenberg suggests that "we might consider what possibilities are opened by beginning with students' religious literacies, by assuming that they are not only deserving of study and reflection, but may in fact also serve as a resource for critical projects" (282). Similarly, Michael-John DePalma suggests, "From the perspective of pragmatism, [. . .] it becomes possible to see how students' religious discourse might contribute to discourses in the academy" (224). Brad Peters enacts something similar when he draws on features of African American sermonic discourse to imagine a tutoring session that could provide an African American student of faith "with the means to develop her critical powers without attempting to erase or repress her faith" (131).

Emphasizing the differences among human communities, this version of the figured world of composition as city presents students, teachers, and even scholars as strangers in a strange land, struggling, as tourists might, to describe what they are experiencing "with anything like fairness and accuracy" (Crowley ix). For example, Goodburn describes how her student Luke's allegiance to biblical authority skews his perspective on the course she was teaching so that Luke sees class content as promoting moral relativism rather than critical thinking (346). Like tourists, scholars can struggle with unfamiliar terms, as Carter (and presumably the editorial staff at *College English*) does when she refers to evangelicals as "evangelists," a misnomer no evangelical would use (580). Some scholars use "fundamentalist" and "evangelical" as synonyms, though many, perhaps most, fundamentalists and evangelicals would not accept this conflation because it elides distinctions that, while they may appear inconsequential to the tourist's gaze, are considered important by many Christians (see Cope and Ringer, this volume).

Researchers may recognize the difficulty of understanding no better than a tourist, but that recognition alone is not always enough to maintain objectivity (Gee, *How* 29). For example, despite her declared "functional illiteracies," Carter beautifully describes the unfamiliar-to-her experience at the True Love Baptist Church (589). And yet, elsewhere in her essay, Carter struggles, as we all do, to describe familiar and unfamiliar cultural and discourse practices evenhandedly:

> The social and cultural theories with which I most identify celebrate difference both empathetically and explicitly, yet much of the traditional conservatism through which evangelical Christianity resonates seems to embrace familiarity above all else, representing difference not as a benefit to embrace but as a threat to overcome.
>
> (373)

Whereas Carter uses the inclusive image of "embrace" to characterize rhetorical education and its goals, she depicts evangelical Christianity's reaction to difference in negative terms, as a "threat to be overcome." Similarly, Sharon Crowley posits a conflict between the "two powerful discourses [of] liberalism and Christian fundamentalism," the first one familiar to Crowley and the second one unfamiliar (2). Crowley presents liberalism (associated with academia) as neutral and positioned at the center, having "little or nothing to say about beliefs and practices deemed to reside outside the so-called public sphere" (3). She describes "fundamentalist Christians" as aiming to capture the center and its attendant hegemonic advantages; their goal is "to 'restore' biblical values to the center of American life and politics. If they have their way, Americans will conduct themselves, publicly and privately, according to a set of beliefs derived from a fundamentalist reading of the Judeo-Christian religious tradition" (3).

Sometimes the figured world of composition and religion as distant cities conflicts with the figured world of composition as an urban center. This conflict can pose problems for students, as it does in the AP test prompt that Neulieb describes:

> The first chapter of *Ecclesiastes*, a book of the Bible, concludes with these words: "For in much wisdom is much grief, and increase of knowledge is the increase of sorrow." Write a carefully reasoned, persuasive essay that defends, challenges, or qualifies this assertion. Use evidence from your observation, experience, or reading to develop your position.
>
> (41)

While the author of this test question may have thought of the Bible as merely a source of interesting commonplaces, some students saw the biblical reference as an invitation to use the Bible and religious experience as resources for their writing. Neulieb describes the AP readers as "appalled" by students' use of religious faith as a resource, which they punished with an "instant low score" (42). While Neulieb deems this response to student writing unfair, the AP graders do not. In the end, Neulieb is forced to translate students' religious writing into a secular academic equivalent, the dialect of the urban center, so that the AP graders could grade more fairly. Why did Neulieb sense the problematic nature of the rhetorical situation when the AP graders did not? I believe it is because Neulieb invoked the figured world of distant cities and the AP graders invoked the figured world of composition as a city inhabited by speakers of the public transcripts that Miller describes.

MONSTERS OF PROHIBITION IN COMPOSITION SCHOLARSHIP ABOUT RELIGIOUS FAITH

In the figured world of composition as city, religious students exist positioned outside the container, in a shadowy outer world inhabited by monsters. And in scholarship about religious students, Christian students in particular sometimes do the cultural work of monsters, troubling the sterility of the civilized composition classroom. This work can be seen positively and negatively, and I propose that composition research has imagined its religious monsters in mainly negative terms. I began this project after reading Marzluf's study of a purported conflict narrative present in scholarship about Christian students, a narrative that relies on "stock figures" of "secular, liberal teachers and their narrative counterparts, fundamentalist, Christian students" as it "depicts instructors as antagonists who ridicule or reject religious expression as a way to talk about identity or to support claims" (267). While a figured world of conflict is used by some scholars, notably Anderson, Carter, Downs, Neulieb, and Perkins,[2] most describe Christian students in less agonistic terms, as a source of a "problem" like disruptive classroom behavior (see Goodburn; Perkins, "Radical" and " 'Attentive' ") or disturbing writing (see Anderson; Downs; Goodburn; Neulieb; Smart; Vander Lei, "Ain't"). Authors commonly showcase the nature of this problem by focusing on a single problematic student. Those familiar with composition scholarship about religious faith are likely to recognize the pseudonyms of these problem students: Anderson's "Cathy," Goodburn's "Luke," Edwards's "Nate," Down's "Keith," Williams's "Mohammed," Perkins's "Clifford" and "Tina" ("Radical" and "Attentive"), and my own "Mike" and "Marty" ("Coming" and "Ain't"). Reduced to a single, troublesome character, religious students are easily positioned in one of composition's figured worlds. But what role will this character play? The nature of the reduction itself points to an answer. Several scholars have noted that scholarship reductively constructs all religious students as "problematic" (Daniell, "Whetstones" 80–81; DePalma, Ringer, and Webber; Rand; Vander Lei "Ain't"; Cope and Ringer, this volume). By means of this reduction, intentional or otherwise, compositionists place all religious students outside the city gates where troublesome monsters lurk. As Juanita Smart puts it, "within the academic community [. . .] the student's profession of faith is perceived as a kind of ill-formed, if not illegitimate, monster—a rhetoric that offends and threatens rather than instructs or enlightens other members of the composing community" (14).

According to Jeffrey Cohen, monsters threaten a community in part by transgressing the community's values. The community responds by exaggerating this difference in values into a threat against itself (7–8). And a review of composition scholarship about religious students produces examples of scholars exaggerating the presence or effect of religious faith into something monstrous. For example, I compare religious faith to a gun that usually occupied the empty holster on my student Mike's belt ("Coming"). By aligning religious faith with a deadly weapon, I exaggerate faith into an inartistic proof of physical danger that overwhelms the artistic proofs of rhetoric to which I hold allegiance. Similarly, Doug Downs and others have noted our tendency to exaggerate the inadequacies of the writing of problem religious students, prompting, in turn, aggravated responses of "impatience, disagreement, and even dejection with those arguments" (39). Our unreasonable responses to bad reasoning associated with religious faith testifies not only to the extent that religious faith offends our community values but also, ironically, to our own monstrous capacities: we willingly violate our own community values in an attempt to banish (or even eradicate) the monsters that threaten us, just as medieval Christian Spaniards violated central Christian beliefs in their quest to eliminate Jews from their community (Bizzell, "Rationality"). And as the instructor does in the comment on a student's paper that led to the troubling tutoring session Peters describes: "Hopeless paper. Go to the Writing Center" (122).

Composition scholarship often caricatures Christian students as monsters of prohibition who "police [] the borders of the possible" (Cohen 13). Like images of sea serpents drawn on medieval maps "to discourage further exploration" (Cohen 13), such exaggerations of Christian students and their faith discourage teacher and student alike from exploring the rhetorical possibilities afforded by religious faith. Additionally, when we tolerate exaggerated responses from intolerant academics such as Anderson's teaching assistant (TA) and Neulieb's Advanced Placement (AP) graders, we position those academics to act as monsters of prohibition. They certainly serve this function for Peters's writing center tutor when she explains why she recommended eliminating religious elements from a paper: "Some T.A.s won't even accept a paper when students quote the Bible or mention God" (123). Similarly, Lauren Fitzgerald describes giving similar advice when she was a TA; reflecting on that moment, she and I propose the following: "Had the student written about any other aspect of her identity—her race, ethnicity, class, sexuality, and/or disability—Lauren would have applauded her for using her new-found freedom" (Vander Lei and Fitzgerald 186). As a testament to the monstrous power of intolerant readers, I must admit that while I was drafting this chapter, I met with a Calvin student who was preparing a Fulbright application. We discussed how evaluators might respond to her inclusion of the Bible as an influential text. Fearing a monstrous response and desiring the opportunities that the Fulbright would provide, we removed it from the list.

Sometimes scholars "monster" Christian students not by exaggerating the threat they pose but by drawing attention to their patched-together nature, a hybridity that results from their membership in both religious and academic communities. But in composition studies we have viewed these monsters positively, too, as Kristine Hansen's students at Brigham Young University likely viewed her after she disclosed her political leanings: "I seem so orthodox in the faith, it's hard for them to imagine how I could be—gasp!—so liberal, a word that most have heard used mainly as a term of derision" (26). Cohen notes that monsters are "disturbing hybrids whose externally incoherent bodies resist attempts to include them in any systematic structuration. And so the monster is dangerous, a form suspended between forms" (6). Stitched together from various fragments of their experience in religious and academic communities, religious student writers, Jeff Ringer argues, "construct hybrid subjectivities that value various aspects of their identities" (275). Ringer examines how "Austin," a first-year writing (FYW) student, uses a passage from the Bible to support an academic argument. Ringer argues that the process of grafting religious faith to academic discourse distorts—casuistically stretches—not only academic discourse, as many studies have demonstrated, but also religious faith itself. Ringer's description of casuistic stretching as "a process through which an individual not only engages with a perspective other than one's own, but also comes potentially to identify with it and then interiorize it," provides a helpful image of grafted fragments fusing into a functioning, if ill-formed, whole (276).

Sometimes this grafting leaves a scarred rhetorical surface, as is evident in the results of the National Study of Youth and Religion. Focusing on "the religious and spiritual lives of American 18- to 23-year-olds," this survey points to a "great sensitivity to the belief 'Everybody's different'" (Smith and Snell 3, 48). Smith's interviews capture emerging adults casuistically stretching religious belief to accommodate cultural values of tolerance, as in this example:

> In the middle of explaining that for religious reasons she does not believe in cohabitation before marriage, a young evangelical woman, who is devoted to gospel missionary work overseas, interrupted herself with this observation: "I don't know, I think everyone is different so. I know it wouldn't work for me, but it could work for someone else."
>
> (52)

Patched together from Christian morality and cultural mores, this woman's response bears linguistic and logical scars that testify to its grafted nature. It is possible that examining the grafted writing of Christian students may help us see the grafted nature of most academic writing, casuistically stretched to accommodate a variety of experiences and agendas. Bizzell argues that we should encourage such casuistic stretching by referencing the adage of the blind men examining an elephant: "If we want to see the whole beast, we should be welcoming, not resisting, the advent of diverse forms of academic discourse, and encouraging our students to bring all their discursive resources to bear on the intellectual challenges of the academic disciplines" ("Intellectual" 9). Ringer also believes this to be possible: "Perhaps when we help students understand the identity implications associated with writing academically for diverse audiences, we also help them achieve the agency to negotiate such challenges effectively and arrive at a place of commitment" (297). With Burke, Ringer and other compositionists might be inclined to imagine that we are, all of us, rhetorical monsters, fascinating, complicated, and powerful.

Notably, some composition scholarship, including scholarship in which a single student serves as a representative anecdote, showcases students whose writing demonstrates an ability to be simultaneously, seamlessly religious and academic—students such as Nowacek's "Alan," "Betty," and "Tigra"; Fitzgerald's "Daniel"; DePalma's "Thomas"; Ringer's "Austin"; and Geiger's Lauren Spink and Ryan Graham. And some scholars, such as Virginia Chappell, Beth Daniell, Anne Gere, and Kristine Hansen, also testify to the positive effect of religious faith in their own scholarship. Bronwyn Williams, for instance, finds that "the emphasis on individual enlightenment and negotiated social truths makes it relatively easy to be a Quaker and accept a postmodern worldview" (111).

COMPOSITION AS A FRONTIER

Finally, a third version of the figured world locates religious faith and rhetoric in the territory outside the traditional boundaries of composition. In this version, religion and rhetoric are a frontier for students and instructors to explore and map. Nedra Reynolds suggests that the metaphor of frontier may originate with Mina Shaughnessy and that it "appears again and again in the literature of composition studies" (30). Scholars who invoke this figured world encourage instructors and students to explore the topics and arguments that shape their daily existence. Instructors and students learn about rhetoric, social discourse, and themselves as they struggle with difficult, sometimes distasteful, sometimes perplexing words and ideas (see Miller and Santos). The goal of this exploratory pedagogy parallels Krista Ratcliffe's admonition to treat difficult concepts such as race and gender not "as problems to be eradicated," but rather as "differences" that can be "successfully defined, negotiated, and celebrated" (135).

Hansen sees value in engaging complex and sometimes troublesome topics like religious belief because, she argues,

> the changing landscape of American politics and the diversity of our society will require rhetorical sensitivity and dexterity if we are to engage religiously motivated argument while promoting understanding and sufficient national unity to prevent prejudice, divisiveness, rebellion, or opting out of the process altogether.
>
> (32; see also Vander Lei and Hettinga)

Bronwyn Williams makes a similar claim, though with a global perspective. Reflecting on teaching writing to international students at a British satellite campus of an American college, Williams concludes,

> There are no simple solutions to cross-cultural conflicts involving faith and rhetoric. Yet it is folly to imagine that they are not already in the classroom with us. We must bring religion into open discussion—including our own backgrounds and feelings—so that we can engage in thoughtful conversation about its influence on how we write and read.
>
> (117)

DePalma, Ringer, and Webber envision a similar approach in this counterstatement: "In an attempt to open discourse on religion and politics beyond procedural 'tolerance,' we recognize beliefs and attitudes that embrace non-negotiability and pretenses to certainty" (330). Rather than muffling the "ceaseless activities" of "sustaining a self and sustaining a culture" that Richard Miller describes in the epigraph, the rhetorical stance that DePalma, Ringer, and Webber propose generates "moments of crisis" that amplify the "grind of the machinery" so that students can hear and perhaps even begin to refurbish it. Relying on Burke's image of the human barnyard, DePalma, Ringer, and Webber suggest that when students and teachers explore what may seem transgressive or monstrous, they "generate incongruities and thus reveal the blindspots [. . .] in our current political climate" (328). With the goal of fostering democracy in the U.S., they promote "a Burkean anarchic democracy that would give voice to perspectives that counter liberal pragmatic discourse" (332).

Promoting a pedagogy that erases any division between "composition" and the "real world," TJ Geiger argues for a "free exercise of rhetoric" that understands religion as "rhetorical, discursive and political as well as personal: religious beliefs and arguments are produced and exist in contexts (not outside of them), and they have consequences involving other people-of-faith and secular folks—all of whom have complicated relationships with religious communities and traditions" (256). A writing pedagogy that does so "stir[s] the economy of affects that brings into focus for students and myself where we reach the limits of our ability to identify with others and ideas" (Geiger 256). Unsurprisingly, engaging in such pedagogy involves a degree of risk not unlike exploring a frontier: "Repositioning and disidentification require opportunities for misrecognition, misreading, and confusion. [. . .] Unpredictability is desirable" (Geiger 256). Such risky teaching requires courage, commitment, skill, a humble openness to students' religious and cultural experiences, and a patient understanding of potential student resistance. Because of the real-world nature of the free exercise of rhetoric, all this risk taking can produce disappointingly realistic results.

Reflecting on the annihilation of medieval Spanish Jews, Bizzell describes what little (though valuable) knowledge students and instructors might acquire as a result of engaging in such exploration: "how resourceful rhetoricians make use of the materials at hand, however flawed, to do something, however limited, on behalf of their causes" ("Rationality" 28). Perhaps, too, students and instructors might both learn something about the limits of their own fundamentals, like an allegiance to freedom of speech (Williams 116) or rational argumentation (Bizzell, "Rationality" 28). Bizzell's forthright description of what we might actually be able to teach students is a valuable counter to our sometimes idealistic claims for rhetoric, but it may cause instructors and administrators to wonder if the risky work of producing crisis is worth this outcome.

In *Rhetorical Listening*, Krista Ratcliffe suggests that

[w]e may not always choose or control the discourses that socialize us; neither may we choose or control our conscious responses to these discourses. But we can, to a limited degree, articulate our conscious identifications and choose to respond to them (or not); in this way we become responsible for our words, our attitudes, and our actions.

(30)

Having considered some of the figured worlds that shape composition scholarship about Christian students, we are left to consider our responsibilities: the harm and the opportunities for students that we are creating by means of our figured worlds. Jeffrey Cohen approaches the same point by directing our attention one last time to monsters:

> Monsters are our children. They can be pushed to the farthest margins of geography and discourse, hidden away at the edges of the world and in the forbidden recesses of our mind, but they always return. [. . .] These monsters ask us how we perceive the world, and how we have misrepresented what we have attempted to place. They ask us to reevaluate our cultural assumptions about race, gender, sexuality, our perception of difference, our tolerance toward its expression. They ask us why we have created them.

(20)

As rhetoricians and compositionists, we reinscribe the dominant figured worlds of our discipline when we create and then interact with monstrous religious students. While such a rhetorical act is unavoidable—who can communicate without shared figured worlds?—it is a rhetorical act so laden with social and rhetorical consequences that we should map with care.

NOTES

1 It's important to note the presence of another figured world that influences composition research about Christian students: human development as a path. Length constraints preclude me from analyzing that figured world in this essay.
2 If there is conflict, teachers and students experience it internally rather than externally: teachers struggle to respect students' right to free speech even as they honor the outcomes of the course, and students struggle to fix words to what they are thinking and believing.

REFERENCES

Anderson, Chris. "The Description of an Embarrassment: When Students Write about Religion." *ADE Bulletin* 94 (1989): 12–15.

Anson, Chris. "2013 CCCC Chair's Address." *College Composition and Communication* 65.2 (2013): 324–44.

Baumgartner, Holly Lynn, and Roger Davis. "Hosting the Monster: Introduction." *Hosting the Monster*. Ed. Holly Lynn Baumgartner and Roger Davis. New York: Rodopi, 2008.1–9.

Bizzell, Patricia. "The Intellectual Work of 'Mixed' Forms of Academic Discourses." *AltDis: Alternative Discourses and the Academy*. Eds. Christopher Schroeder, Helen Fox, and Patricia Bizzell. Portsmouth: Heinemann, 2002. 1–10.

————. "Rationality as Rhetorical Strategy at the Barcelona Disputation, 1263: A Cautionary Tale." *College Composition and Communication* 58.1 (2006): 12–29.

Burke, Kenneth. *The Rhetoric of Religion.* Berkeley: U of California P, 1961.

Carter, Shannon, "Living inside the Bible (Belt)." *College English* 69.6 (2007): 572–95.

Chappell, Virginia. "Teaching—and Living—in the Meantime." *The Academy and the Possibility of Belief: Essays on Intellectual and Spiritual Life.* Eds. Mary Louise Buley-Meissner, Mary McCaslin Thompson, and Elizabeth Bachrach Tan. Cresskill: Hampton P, 2000. 39–63.

Cienki, Alan. "Frames, Idealized Cognitive Models, and Domains." Geeraerts and Cuyckens 170–87.

Clydesdale, Tim. *The First Year Out: Understanding American Teens after High School.* Chicago: U of Chicago P, 2007.

Cohen, Jeffrey, ed. *Monster Theory: Reading Culture.* Minneapolis: U of Minnesota P, 2006.

Crowley, Sharon. *Toward a Civil Discourse: Rhetoric and Fundamentalism.* Pittsburgh: U of Pittsburgh P, 2006.

Daniell, Beth. *A Communion of Friendship: Literacy, Spiritual Practice, and Women in Recovery.* Carbondale: Southern Illinois UP, 2003.

————. "Whetstones Provided by the World: Trying to Deal with Difference in a Pluralistic Society." *College English* 70.1 (2007): 79–88.

DePalma, Michael-John. "Re-envisioning Religious Discourses as Rhetorical Resources in Composition Teaching: A Pragmatic Response to the Challenge of Belief." *College Composition and Communication* 63.2 (2011): 219–43.

DePalma, Michael-John, Jeffrey M. Ringer, and Jim Webber. "(Re)Charting the (Dis) Courses of Faith and Politics, or Rhetoric and Democracy in the Burkean Barnyard. *Rhetoric Society Quarterly* 38.3 (2008): 311–34.

Donehower, Kim, Charlotte Hogg, and Eileen E. Schell. "Constructing Rural Literacies: Moving Beyond the Rhetorics of Lack, Lag, and the Rosy Past." Donehower, Hogg, and Schell 1–36.

————, eds. *Rural Literacies.* Carbondale: Southern Illinois UP, 2007.

Downs, Douglas. "True Believers, Real Scholars, and Real True Believing Scholars: Discourses of Inquiry and Affirmation in the Composition Classroom." Vander Lei and kyburz 39–59.

Ede, Lisa. *Situating Composition: Composition Studies and the Politics of Location.* Carbondale: Southern Illinois UP, 2004.

Edwards, Lynell. "Writing, Religion, and the Complex Spiritual Site of Evolution." *Language and Learning across the Disciplines* 5.2 (2001): 4–25.

Fishman, Andrea. *Amish Literacy: What and How it Means.* Portsmouth: Heinemann, 1988.

Fitzgerald, Lauren. "Torah U' Madda: Institutional "Mission" and Composition Instruction." Vander Lei and kyburz 141–54.

Gee, James Paul. *How to Do Discourse Analysis: A Toolkit.* New York: Routledge, 2011.

————. *An Introduction to Discourse Analysis: Theory and Method.* 3rd ed. New York: Routledge, 2011.

Gere, Anne Ruggles. "Revealing Silence: Rethinking Personal Writing." *College Composition and Communication* 53:2 (2001): 203–23.

Geeraerts, Dirk and Hubert Cuyckens, eds. *The Oxford Handbook of Cognitive Linguistics.* New York: Oxford UP, 2007.

Geiger, TJ, II. "Unpredictable Encounters: Religious Discourse, Sexuality, and the Free Exercise of Rhetoric." *College English* 75.3 (2013): 250–71.

Goodburn, Amy. "It's a Question of Faith: Discourses of Fundamentalism and Critical Pedagogy in the Writing Classroom." *JAC: A Journal of Rhetoric, Culture, & Politics* 18.2 (1998): 333–53.

Hansen, Kristine. "Religious Freedom in the Public Square and the Composition Classroom." Vander Lei and kyburz 24–38.

Lakoff, George, and Mark Johnson. *Metaphors We Live By*. Chicago: U of Chicago P, 1980.

Marzluf, Phillip P. "Religion in U.S. Writing Classes: Challenging the Conflict Narrative." *Journal of Writing Research* 2.3 (2011): 265–97.

Miller, Keith, and Jennifer M. Santos. "Recomposing Religious Plotlines." Vander Lei and kyburz 63–83.

Miller, Richard. "The Arts of Complicity: Pragmatism and the Culture of Schooling." *College English* 61.1 (1998): 10–28.

———. "The Nervous System." *College English* 58.3 (1996): 265–86.

Mittman, Asa Simon. "Introduction: The Impact of Monsters and Monster Studies." *The Ashgate Research Companion to Monsters and the Monsterous*. Eds. Asa Simon Mittman and Peter J. Dendle. Surrey: Ashgate, 2012. 1–14.

Moss, Beverly. *A Community Text Arises: A Literate Text and a Literacy Tradition in African-American Churches*. Cresskill, NJ: Hampton P, 2003.

Neulieb, Janice. " 'Spilt Religion': Student Motivation and Values-Based Writing." *Writing on the Edge* 4.1 (1992): 41–50.

Nowacek, Rebecca Schoenike. "Negotiating Individual Religious Identity and institutional Religious Culture." Vander Lei and kyburz 155–66.

Oakley, Todd. "Image Schemas." Geeraerts and Cuyckens 214–35.

Perkins, Priscilla. " 'Attentive, Intelligent, Reasonable, and Responsible': Teaching Composition with Bernard Lonergan." Vander Lei et al. 73–88.

———. " 'A Radical Conversion of the Mind': Fundamentalism, Hermeneutics, and the Metanoic Classroom." *College English* 63.5 (2001): 585–611.

Peters, Brad. "African American Students of Faith in the Writing Center: Facilitating a Rhetoric of Conscience." Vander Lei and kyburz 121–34.

Rand, Lizabeth. "Enacting Faith: Evangelical Discourse and the Discipline of Composition Studies." *College Composition and Communication* 52 (2001): 349–67.

Ratcliffe, Krista. *Rhetorical Listening: Identification, Gender, Whiteness*. Carbondale: Southern Illinois UP, 2005.

Reynolds, Nedra. *Geographies of Writing: Inhabiting Places and Encountering Difference*. Carbondale: Southern Illinois UP, 2004.

Ringer, Jeffrey M. "The Consequences of Integrating Faith into Academic Writing: Casuistic Stretching and Biblical Citation." *College English* 75.3 (2013): 272–99.

Rohrer, Tim. "Embodiment and Experimentalism." Geeraerts and Cuyckens 25–47.

Smart, Juanita. " 'Frankenstein or Jesus Christ: When the Voice of Faith Creates a Monster for the Composition Teacher." Vander Lei and kyburz 11–23.

Smith, Christian, and Patricia Snell. *Souls in Transition: the Religious and Spiritual Lives of Emerging Adults*. New York: Oxford, 2009.

Stenberg, Shari J. "Liberation Theology and Liberatory Pedagogies: Renewing the Dialogue." *College English* 68.3 (2006): 271–90.

Stockwell, Peter. *Cognitive Poetics: An Introduction*. New York: Routledge, 2002.

Vander Lei, Elizabeth. "Ain't We Got Fun?: Teaching Writing in a Violent World." Vander Lei et al. 89–104.

———. "Coming to Terms with Religious Faith in the Composition Classroom: Introductory Comments." Vander Lei and kyburz 3–10.

———, et al., eds. *Renovating Rhetoric in Christian Tradition*. Pittsburgh: U of Pittsburg P, 2014.

———, and Lauren Fitzgerald. "What in God's Name? Administering the Con-flicts of Religious Belief in Writing Programs." *Writing Program Administration* 31.1–2 (2007): 185–95.

———, and Donald R. Hettinga. "A Comment on 'A Radical Conversion of the Mind': Fundamentalism, Hermeutic, and the Metanoic Classroom." *College English* 64.6 (2002): 720–23.

———, and bonnie lenore kyburz, eds. *Negotiating Religious Faith in the Composition Classroom.* Portsmouth, NH: Heinemann, 2005.

Williams, Bronwyn T. "The Book and the Truth: Faith, Rhetoric, and Cross-Cultural Communication." Vander Lei and kyburz 105–20.

Yancey, Kathleen Blake. "Made Not Only in Words: Composition in a New Key." *College Composition and Communication* 56.2 (2004): 297–328.

Zlatev, Jordan. "Spatial Semantics." Geeraerts and Cuyckens 318–50.

5 Sacred Texts, Secular Classrooms, and the Teaching of Theory

Thomas Deans

We are used to hearing sacred texts in sacred spaces. Still, we expect to see them in some quarters of the university, particularly religion and theology departments, as well as pockets of English departments—for example, *Bible as Literature* courses, or Native American literature surveys that feature creation stories. In the Great Books courses and curricula that remain, selections from the Old and New Testaments, the Upanishads, the Baghavad Gita, the Tao Te Ching, and the Koran are read alongside secular classics. Yet sacred texts have never played a significant role in the first-year writing curriculum, at least as measured by the frequency of reading selections in the most widely used anthologies. No primary sacred texts are reprinted frequently enough in composition readers to be included in Lynn Bloom's "Essay Cannon" for composition, and even essays on religious topics are becoming more and more rare in such anthologies.[1]

Given that context, when religious texts surface in courses where they don't seem to have a natural provenance, they can provoke anxiety—in part because they are perceived as transgressing the boundary between church and state but, more important, because they interrupt habitual academic reading and reception processes. In either case, because such texts feel unnatural, off the map, in courses that have no disciplinary or thematic truck with religion, they carry, I have found, a distinct pedagogical potential. Their intellectually and emotionally unsettling presence opens opportunities to theorize the very processes of reading, rhetoric, and reception. When those texts come from the Christian tradition, they raise additional generative complications—some potentially motivating, as when students within that tradition see texts integral to their own faith reflected in the curriculum, and some potentially alienating, as when other students either wish to keep their faith and student lives separate or to experience such texts as complicit in an assertive dominant culture (see Vander Lei, this volume).

Here I argue, drawing on my own teaching experiences, that inserting one, maybe two, carefully chosen primary sacred texts into the reading list of a composition, rhetoric, literature, or communication course can trigger comparative analysis with secular modes of reading and awaken in students a fresh meta-awareness of their tacit interpretive habits. To be clear, I am not campaigning for instructors of composition or communication to convert a substantial proportion their syllabi to sacred texts or religious questions. That may make perfect sense for classes that take up religious themes, but such courses are not what I am considering here. Instead, I am suggesting small, strategic uses for primary sacred texts in courses where reading, writing, and rhetoric are the chief topics of inquiry.

THE GENESIS OF REFLECTION

In the beginning are two teaching narratives, neither my own, that hinge on introducing passages from Genesis in public university classrooms. One features a devout student, one a devout teacher, and both speak to the productively disquieting role that scripture can play in drawing students into critical reflection on their own reading processes—not to mention fundamental issues in literary and rhetorical theory.

In "Everyday Literacy: Secular Institutions, Religious Students, and the Commute between Incommensurate Worlds," Richard Miller describes an introductory theory course for English majors that focuses on reading practices and is somewhat similar to the seminar I discuss later in this essay. Miller had assigned David Denby's *Great Books*, which recounts Denby's experiment of returning to college to experience Columbia's great books course. Miller neither venerates nor bashes the Great Books model but, rather, interrogates it. While discussing Denby's account, the class expressed an interest in reading something from great books curriculum, and they opted for the first book of Genesis. Miller then goes on to show "how disruptive this moment proved to be" for Rachael, an older student from a conservative Orthodox Jewish community in New Jersey (77).

To reveal the kind of intellectual work he encourages in the class, Miller publishes in full an essay of Rachael's. In it she writes that "[t]he Orthodox Jewish tradition that's formative for me is not an oral one, but a written tradition that is extraordinarily deeply rooted and much venerated in my community and family. Everything else that I read is seen through the screen of those beliefs. I consider them absolute truths through and against which I can measure good and bad, just and unjust, right and wrong in everything" (79). When Rachael encounters texts and ideas in her college courses that are at odds with her faith commitments, she either interprets them in ways that are consonant with her beliefs or screens them out. She even rejected the version of Genesis that Miller selected: "The footnotes were clearly antithetical to Orthodox Jewish beliefs about the divine authorship of the Bible, and I could not read them. The New Testament and much of the writings of the ancient philosophers are in this group as well" (80). Miller concedes that the pluralism of the public university and the religious homogeneity of Rachael's home community are "incommensurate worlds," yet he celebrates how she reflects critically and self-consciously on her own interpretive habits. Rachael is *doing* thoughtful literary and rhetorical theory, Miller argues, and although he does not say so, the kind of theory she seems to be doing has strong resonances with reader-response criticism and Burkean terministic screening. Her process of rejecting all that is inconsistent with her home interpretive community is more deliberate and intentional than the tacit process of reading through interpretive communities that critics such as Stanley Fish describe, but the larger point is that Rachael is foregrounding the role of the reader in making meaning. The sacred text was the pivot on which her insights about identity, community, and reading turned.

Likewise, Christopher Anderson, in *Teaching as Believing*, shares his experience of teaching Genesis in a public university classroom. When introducing Genesis in a survey course on masterworks of Western literature, Anderson, a deacon in the Catholic Church, makes a dramatic pedagogical move: he brings his clerical garments to class and slowly, deliberately, silently dons his vestments in front of the class (26–29). He knows that this will jar his students, even provoke some anger and resentment, especially because he is teaching in Oregon, which is perennially listed among the most "unchurched" states. Anderson is, through this performance, announcing his faith commitments and triggering a class discussion about the assumptions that readers bring to Bible—their various commitments to faith or secularism, their attitudes toward religion and religious institutions, and their preconceptions about the content of Genesis (often based, he finds, more on cultural defaults than on the text itself). Anderson writes that "[t]he most important expectations that students bring to Genesis are expectations about the nature of texts and of reading, expectations that come from ignorance and lack of experience" (36–37). He ultimately wants his students to approach the text anew, to do a close reading of Genesis grounded not in prior assumptions about the Bible but instead in what Genesis delivers: concrete images and complex narratives, not dogma or abstract propositions. He wants "to move students toward a literary appreciation of the work" (Anderson 54) and along a trajectory that begins with recognizing the Bible first as story. Ultimately Anderson, who later in the course introduces selected New Testament texts alongside literary classics, is interested in showing how literature both models and precedes a Christian worldview. Paraphrasing C.S. Lewis approvingly, Anderson writes that "Christianity has a literary structure and requires a literary way of knowing" (94). Anderson does not proselytize in his public university classroom, but he does aim to impart this "literary way of knowing." He aims "to establish the connection between Christianity and interpretive open-endedness," and that interpretive open-endedness, for Anderson, is not doctrine but instead is an attitude of "humility and precision," both of which, he claims, are espoused as core values by Christian tradition and the university (106, 133).

I find myself in league with both Anderson and Miller, though not fully with either. Miller's aim, like mine, is to offer all students, including devout ones like Rachael, a greater vocabulary for reflecting on how their own experiences relate to established theories of reading, rhetoric, and communication.[2] Like Anderson, I want to push students to question their default assumptions and read the full range of available texts, including scripture, with a greater humility and precision. Yet his conflation of literary and Christian interpretive habits, while intriguing, is not an angle I wish to pursue. I am also hesitant to adopt his degree of self-disclosure as a teaching strategy, not only because it cuts against my personal demeanor but also because I want the sacred text itself, not the teacher, to do the disrupting.

NATURALIZING THE SACRED TEXT THROUGH THE FORMALIST OR RHETORICAL ANALYSIS

As many English departments have done over the last decade, mine has revised its major requirements to include more deliberate entry and exit experiences. In my department this has meant instituting a new required introductory course at the front end of the major and a new capstone seminar at the back end. Introduction to Literary Studies serves as that front-end gateway to the major and focuses on close reading, research skills, and literary theory. In my section we devote most of the semester to doing a tour of various schools of theory—formalism/New Criticism, reader-response, psychological approaches, literary history, deconstruction, feminism, Marxism, cultural studies, rhetorical criticism—and I try to model the dominant interpretive moves for each so that students can build a repertoire of theories. The subject of the course, at its most basic, is *reading*.

Bringing a sacred text into such a literary theory course is not especially novel. Indeed, the textbook we use features the parable of the prodigal son (Luke 15:11–32) as one sample on which to practice New Critical methods (Lynn 58–60). The appearance of a Biblical passage surprises some students, but because it is positioned alongside poems by Ben Jonson, Gwendolyn Brooks, Lucille Clifton, and Stephen Shu-ning Liu (which Lynn clusters because they all take up the theme of fathers and children), the clear message is that the parable is a literary text like the others, all equally ripe for New Critical analysis. The context dictates that the Biblical excerpt, like the poems, should be treated as a text to be mastered: identify themes, unpack the oppositions, analyze the relationship of parts to whole and of form to meaning, recognize the narrative's complexity in unity, and appreciate the paradoxes and ironies. This formalist approach is familiar enough to most students. They may not have had a name for it, or not have performed it with college-level rigor before, but the kinds of New Critical close reading that we do in this unit refines their analytical skills rather than troubles their basic assumptions about how texts (and English classes) work.

The same basic approach is available for courses focused on rhetoric. Just as aptly chosen sacred texts present artful narratives that open themselves to formalist literary analysis, they also offer intriguing case studies of persuasion that invite a close reading of rhetorical moves. Peter Wayne Moe recognizes this and illustrates, by focusing on the parables, how Jesus can "be read as a rhetor, one making calculated moves within particular contexts with specific aims and audiences in mind. He is a rhetor who relies upon narrative and metaphor to hold together his rhetorical practice" (72). Moe suggests that such parables could fruitfully be introduced in a composition classroom—one not necessarily focused on religious texts or themes—to reveal Jesus's "rhetoric of evasion" through which "the speaker does not make a claim outright but lay an argument alongside a narrative" (73). Such analysis could be leveraged further by juxtaposing the Jesus's indirect and opaque rhetoric with the direct and thesis-driven rhetoric typical of academic argument (Moe 73). Consistent with my unit on formalism, this pedagogical approach naturalizes the sacred text within the ecology of the curriculum, turning it into yet one more useful text for imparting fairly standard methods of academic analysis.

This kind of pedagogy demands that students maintain a critical distance and bracket off personal experience as they practice sanctioned modes of reading that treat the text as object. Such a posture is consonant with the ethos of our large, public university in the Northeast, where students come from diverse faiths and where multiculturalism and inclusivity are core values, even while overt expressions of religious identity generally make people uncomfortable. In that context some students—Christian and not, religiously observant and not—no doubt feel uneasy treating scripture as just another source for academic analysis, some for political reasons such as the perception that it transgresses the line between church and state and some for personal reasons rooted in their own faith commitments. In my course, at least during the unit on formalism, I don't give students much opportunity to voice such feelings. Instead, we push on with New Critical methods, tamping down the disruptive potential of the sacred text. And yet, one of the most important junctures in the course comes soon after, when we shift from this formalist criticism to reader-response criticism, which invites them to revisit some of those earlier anxieties. The full value of introducing a sacred text, at least as I do it, is realized through a two-step process: first imposing this sort of distanced analysis, then reflecting on how readers make meaning.

THE SHIFT TO READER-RESPONSE

Following on the heels of the formalism/New Criticism unit, I introduce reader-response criticism through Steven Lynn's chapter in *Texts and Contexts* and Stanley Fish's essay "How to Recognize a Poem When You See

One." Then I follow it with units on psychoanalytic, gendered, deconstructive, and Marxist theories, teaching those various lenses for reading. Both Lynn and Fish explain how reader-response theories shift the locus meaning from the text to the experiences and expectations of the reader, especially as those are conditioned by the interpretive communities to which they belong. Fish's essay is especially fitting because it opens with an anecdote set in a classroom. After teaching a class on linguistics, he was poised to teach a different course in that same classroom, this second one on seventeenth century English religious poetry. Fish left on the blackboard the names of five linguists he had been discussing earlier, and when his poetry students arrived, he told them that what they saw on the blackboard was a religious poem of the kind they were studying and that they should interpret it, which they proceeded to do, teasing out several potential literary allusions in the names and several potential structural patterns in how the words related to one another (Fish 322–25). Fish uses this anecdote to argue that readers recognized the words as a poem not because of anything in the text but because of their own expectations: "As soon as my students were aware that it was poetry they were seeing, they began to look with poetry-seeing eyes, that is, with eyes that saw everything in relation to the properties they knew poems to possess" (326). He then goes on to argue that the students perform in relative unison because they are all part of an interpretive community that conditions their expectations and interpretations. Students saw a poem because they expected to see one and treated the text as a poem because their context, their socialized habits, their interpretive community encouraged that mode of reading. Fish argues that shifting the focus to how readers *make* the text may affirm the contingency of meaning (because there is no stable meaning *in* the text), but it does not doom us to utter subjectivity because we make meaning collectively, through interpretive communities, according to institutionally and socially conditioned norms.

When I ask students to consider the interpretive community as an analytical concept, as a distinct way of doing theory that turns our attention to readers and communities of readers, they usually nod in affirmation that they get it. But most don't *really* get it until we briefly revisit the sacred text we studied not along ago—that passage from Luke—and then devote a full class session to the story of the woman accused of adultery in the Gospel of John (8:1–10). I ask students to recall their experience with the Luke passage, to reflect on their own reception of it during the New Criticism unit. Most behaved in accord with how they have long been socialized in school: treat the Prodigal Son parable as a text awaiting objective analysis in a pluralistic university classroom, following the teacher's lead and the usual classroom protocols. Through such seemingly innocuous habits, they—we—made the scripture a literary text inclined to formalist interpretation, much as Fish's students made the list of linguists a poem.

At this point I ask them to do two things: consider how changing the context and interpretive community changes our reception of the text; and revisit their personal and emotional responses to first encountering the Prodigal Son parable in our class. These shift us from analysis of the drama among characters *within a text* to analysis of the drama among readers *within our classroom*. While we rely on the language of Lynn and Fish to do this, we could just have readily relied on the key terms of rhetoric rather than of literary theory. That is, instead of relying on the language of Fish to account for how interpretive communities make meaning, we could just as readily employ the language of Aristotle, Bitzer, or Burke to account for how audiences respond.[3] Regardless of the heuristic used, I have found that when engaging in inquiry that shifts our gaze to the role of the reader/audience in making meaning, sacred texts generate more visceral engagement—and more immediate intellectual breakthroughs—than secular texts do.

I invite students to consider how sacred texts from any religious tradition are typically received in sacred spaces. Students know in their bones, for example, that when they hear scripture read from the front of a church or synagogue or mosque, they are poised to receive an ethical prescription or lesson for living. The collective, often tacit, expectation that sacred texts received in church will be mined for ways to act in the world ethically or faithfully conditions how and what the story "means."[4] For example, when they see the Prodigal Son parable through churchgoing eyes, they are predisposed to find in it maxims that guide attitudes and behaviors: that it is never too late to seek God's redemption, that we should ever be open to forgiving others, and so on. Sure, they have also been conditioned to read literature for "the lesson," though as budding English majors they also understand that such didactic habits are typically perceived as naïve in college; they instead need to seek out complexity and appreciate ironic detachment (Fahnestock and Secor). In some ways, all this is commonsensical to students: different audiences will read a text differently. But in other ways a reader-response approach is jarring because it insists that meaning resides more in readers and communities of readers than in texts. Some confront a dissonance between how they experience the very same text in church as opposed to in a university classroom. Even those who tend to partition their faith lives from their student lives are invited to reflect on how they shuttle between those overlapping interpretive communities (see Vander Lei, this volume).

When I ask students to freewrite about their personal and emotional reactions to first encountering the Biblical story of the Prodigal Son in an English class at a public institution, they register a wide range of responses. Some Christian students are pleasantly surprised; some are uneasy—even angry—because they object to treating the passage from Luke as just another literary text rather than as divine revelation. Students from other religious traditions tend to split along similar lines: some are eager to learn more about other religions; others find the presence of such a text alienating. Some who profess a commitment to separation of church and state are miffed, or at least puzzled. Many are nonplussed and simply see it as an occasion for dialogue or perhaps more cynically as just another class assignment.[5] The permutations of response change with each class enrollment, as they would in a different institutional or regional context. And this is to the point: who they are as readers and how their reception habits are conditioned by the interpretive communities to which they belong shape their reception of the text. I don't force students to reveal their current state of belief or disbelief or questioning because I want to respect their rights to privacy and self-disclosure—though I do suggest that they work from *some* base of belief, religious or secular (Ringer) or some "final vocabulary" (a phrase Mark Edmundson, in one of our earlier class readings, adapts from Richard Rorty), even if they can't fully articulate it.

I revisit their initial reaction to the Luke passage because it feeds the larger intellectual project of paying attention to the process of reception and interpretation; doing so also primes discussion of the next text I introduce: John 7:53–8.11. In practice, the two days during the semester when we discuss sacred texts are consistently among the most lively and spirited of the semester—many students speak up because these texts stir strong emotional and personal responses. But what happens when we raise the stakes? With the Prodigal Son parable, Jesus may be the narrator, but he is not *in* the narrative; it is a story at one remove from the main narrative of Luke, making it somewhat safer to extract and approach from a secular perspective. The story of the woman accused of adultery recounted in John 7:53–8.11, in which Jesus is front and center, is another matter. This is the episode where the scribes and Pharisees approach Jesus and challenge him to condemn a woman. In response, Jesus writes on the ground and utters, "Let anyone among you who is without sin be the first to throw a stone at her" (*HarperCollins Study Bible*, John 8:7) and writes on the ground again, after which the crowd silently disperses. I select this passage for several reasons: some practical (it's short); some aesthetic (it holds up well as a complex but unified, even quite beautiful, literary narrative); some rhetorical (it features an adversarial scenario and acts of persuasion); some cultural (it is among the most famous episodes in the Bible, and even those not familiar with the Bible have encountered the commonplace of "not throwing the first stone"); some emotional and ethical (the text is controversial for its depiction of Jews as villains); some situational (in my class of thirty I can count on having students of various religious traditions, including but not only Christians and Jews, who bring various degrees of religious commitment, including a number with none at all); and some personal (although as I tell my students, the personal becomes the theoretical when trafficking in reader-response criticism).

The adulteress story could be domesticated by applying New Critical methods—unpacking the oppositions, revealing the structure, articulating the ironies—and in fact, we begin by doing that. Yet I quickly turn our attention to a meta-discussion about textual reception. I ask them to take one step back and speculate on how Christians and Jews are positioned to read this passage differently. Can those who do and don't assume the divinity of Jesus read the story the same way? Critics such as Fish would presume not. Each cohort can imaginatively and intellectually stretch to identify with the point of view of the other, yet that takes extraordinary effort, and some cannot or will not adopt a subject position that violates their core beliefs (see Bizzell). Perhaps more revealing are the quieter, tacit habits of interpretation that we can start to track. Jewish readers, for example, are attuned to the depiction of the Jewish religious authorities as villains and how that depiction participates in a long history of anti-Semitism. Where Christians may see mercy and nonviolence, Jews may see an oppressive, triumphalist ideology that positions the Hebrew tradition as "old" law, awaiting replacement by Jesus' "new" law. Most Christian students don't register that cultural violence until they hear classmates of different identities articulate it. In many ways this text is destined to alienate Jewish readers not only because of what is *in* it but also because of its complicity in a history of oppression. New Critics would have us dismiss such feelings of alienation as a distraction, as the "affective fallacy," as a critical dead end, but reader-response critics would have us pay attention to what is behind such readers' experiences—real, socially situated readers, not just idealized ones. So would those committed to rhetoric and rhetorical criticism, as this approach highlights the role of audience and pathos in the rhetorical situation.

Time does not allow us to work through how every constituency in the class responds, but the larger question of how the reader's identity—especially his or her complicity in interpretive communities—govern interpretation is, I hope, on the minds of all. (The conversation also reveals that *difference* is about more than personal and political preferences.) I assume that throughout this exercise some will be feeling alienated: those who are not Christian and are either unfamiliar with the gospel story or uneasy in feeling pressed to engage with sacred texts outside their own belief system (think of students such as Miller's Rachael); those, Christian or otherwise, who are uneasy in *any* discussion of religion; those offended that we are troubling the separation between church and state; and those who see assigning a second Christian text as doubling down, imposing the dominant culture at the expense of minority cultures. But alongside those feeling alienated or resistant are those especially motivated at seeing another Biblical text part of required reading. Some devout Christian students, for example, perk up not only because they know the text so well but also because it speaks directly to their faith commitments. As we explore the range of our emotional and intellectual responses, we find ourselves in the thick of reader-response theorizing. Even students who insist that Divine Word or Absolute Truth precedes the text—whether evangelical Christians, whose experiences Lizabeth Rand explores, or Orthodox Jews such as Rachael, whom Richard Miller describes—can find themselves using the language of reader-response theory to account for their positions and to affirm their allegiance to the religious/interpretive communities that they prize most.

I also have found that by orchestrating this extended exercise of comparing formalist to reader-response modes of criticism, students are better poised to experiment with other schools of theory that we will soon encounter—feminist, psychological, Marxist, and so on. In fact, I emphasize that each school of theory is itself an interpretive community that powerfully conditions how critics within it read. Feminist critics who read the John 7:53–8.11, for example, cannot help but critique the troubling gender politics in this story (see Green). This is when I typically tip my own hand as a reader responding. I share with students that while I first encountered this story in church as a child and looked to it (as cued by that community) for the moral cautions it delivered about not judging others, now my professional investments in writing and rhetoric predispose me to a very different kind of reading, one not only more historical, analytical, and academic but also that focuses specifically on the two moments when Jesus bends to write (Deans). Looking at the story through "rhetoric-and-composition-seeing eyes," I emphasize the pedagogical and adversarial rhetorics in the story, the particular capacity of writing to provoke reflection, and the rhetorical impact of public silent writing. It's not that scholars of the Bible have not commented on Jesus's writing—many have—only that their own interpretive communities averted them from registering this particular nexus of writing and reflection, one filtered through theories of literacy and rhetoric rather than of theology or history. My approach could be explained as individual creative thinking, as *my* reading, or perhaps cynically as biased and parochial. But using the lens of reader-response theory my reception of John can also be theorized as a social phenomenon—social in the broad sense that it is complicit in an academic research community (and its genres) that ever prioritize newness and innovation over established knowledge or moral precepts. And social in the more local sense that it is conditioned by the language, logic, concepts, habits, assumptions, and attitudes of the rhetoric and composition discourse community. Even concepts that were not originally of personal interest to me, such as the rhetoric of silence, shaped my reading because they were as much *in* the social and intellectual matrix of my discipline as they were evident *in* the text.

That I read the text as my home academic interpretive community has trained me to do is not the only or even the end point. I emphasize that we all abide in overlapping discourse communities, and occasionally those bump up against each other in revealing ways (indeed, that is what is happening as we read sacred texts in school settings). I often share the anecdote of being at a Catholic Mass a day after returning from an academic conference where I had delivered a paper analyzing the strands of writing, rhetoric, and literacy in John 7:53–8.11. By coincidence, that was also the gospel reading that Sunday. In his homily, the priest drew on the forgiveness theme to urge parishioners to go to confession as part of preparing for Easter. That particular community gathered in that particular sacred space may not have expected that particular message—over the years I've heard a range of quite different homilies—but they did expect the priest to participate in the pretty standard clerical rhetoric of drawing from scripture lessons for personal and collective behavior. But to most, drawing a line between the story of the woman accused of adultery and going to confession would seem idiosyncratic or even illogical, a reading simply not viable outside the Catholic interpretive community—not in the protestant church next door, and certainly not in the Louisville hotel where I had been presenting an academic paper on that very same text about twenty-four hours earlier. Yet to that gathering on that Sunday morning the priest's homily seemed natural, consonant with the text because of an unspoken familiarity with Catholic doctrine about confession—and, ironically, an unspoken skepticism about confession, common among contemporary Catholic churchgoers, which created the exigency for the priest to urge them to go in the first place. That weekend delivered a pocket case study in reader-response criticism.[6]

CONCLUSION: SMALL AND STRATEGIC

Some rhetoric and communication courses investigate religion or belief in a sustained way. Some literature surveys explore how Christianity is woven into the Western literary tradition. As is no doubt clear by now, my Introduction to Literary Studies course harbors no such aspirations. Yet sacred texts have still proven particularly valuable—as small, strategic disruptions—for introducing and enacting modes of theory that focus on reception processes. That small but strategic sense of proportion mirrors Peter Wayne Moe's proposal (some snippets of which I shared earlier) for introducing sacred texts in composition courses that emphasize rhetorical criticism: "I do not want to be misread as suggesting Christ's parables, or any religious discourse, become a, or the, cornerstone of a composition classroom," he writes. "Rather, I am imagining a classroom that has found a way to access (if only for a lesson plan or two) the rich cross-cultural, cross temporal resources of religious texts" (74). I see additional parallel possibilities in the increasingly popular "writing about writing" approach to composition (Downs and Wardle), although to my knowledge no one has yet discussed how sacred texts might enrich that pedagogy.

Ideally, such curricular experiments should be matched with empirical studies of students and student learning. My instructional narrative, a composite of several iterations of teaching this same seminar, testifies to a pattern of student breakthroughs. But as ethnographies in writing studies have consistently affirmed, teacher narratives tell only part of the story; there are in play motives, identities, ideologies, resistances, and outcomes that become visible only when students are interviewed in depth and over time. Fortunately in composition studies we are seeing more and more such textured case studies of student writers that focus specifically on how they negotiate their faith in the writing classroom. Still, most such naturalistic studies are compelled to take as given that the syllabi of nearly all of composition, literature, rhetoric and communication courses will be populated with exclusively secular texts. We still have much learn about what happens when students happen on sacred texts where they do not expect to find them.

NOTES

1   In a personal e-mail, Bloom explained in more detail: "There is no primary sacred text that was reprinted enough times (20 or more in my 20% sample of Readers, including all of the most widely reprinted) 1946–1996 to be included in the Essay Canon. The most 'classical' of the Readers I examined were the early editions of the Norton Reader, especially the first edition, 1965. That edition included 'Thou Art the Man' Book of Samuel 2pp (Ethics section) and Matthew Parables of the Kingdom 3 pp (Religion)." Myra Salcedo's more recent examination of sixteen best-selling university composition textbooks published between 1990 and 2012 reveals that eight of those anthologies included a full chapter on religion in at least one edition during that period, yet she found that by 2012 four of those eight had cut chapters on religion.

2   Rachel's insistence on incommensurability, however, strikes me as something of an exceptional case. In my experience, even devout students are willing to engage with sacred texts within and outside their own religious faiths, even if at the cost of some personal conflict. That is, I don't think we need to choose between reflection on one's own terministic screens and direct engagement with the text—we can have both. I find, like Marzluf, that the "conflict narrative" emphasized in much scholarship on faith in composition does not align with my own teaching experiences.

3   It is not coincidental that the heyday of reader-response criticism a period of sustained engagement across literary theory and rhetorical theory—a window of exchange that we haven't seen since. Critics such as Fish celebrated rhetoric, and compositionists brought the interpretive community/discourse community into the mainstream of its scholarship.

4   I also introduce two more terms from literary theory to help frame the discussion: *hermeneutics* and *poetics*. Each is keyed to a different purpose, though hermeneutics has an association with religion, as Jonathan Culler explains: "Here there is a basic distinction, too often neglected in literary studies, between two kinds of projects: one, modeled on linguistics, take meanings as what has to be accounted for and tries to work out how they are possible. The other, by contrast, starts with forms and seeks to interpret them, to tell us what they really mean. In literary studies this is a contrast between poetics and hermeneutics. Poetics starts with attested meanings or effects and asks how they are achieved. (What makes the passage in a novel seem ironic? What makes us sympathize with this particular character? Why is the ending of this poem ambiguous?) Hermeneutics, on the other hand, starts with texts and asks what they mean, seeking to discover new and better interpretations. Hermeneutic models come from the fields of law and religion, where people seek to interpret an authoritative legal or sacred text in order to decide how to act" (62).

5   Doing inquiry in the interpretive processes of primary sacred texts is, I think, less polarizing than is reading essays that stake a claim in political debates

(abortion, same-sex marriage, etc.) where one side or the other is closely associated with institutional religious authority or advocacy.

6   At home after Mass that day, bemused by the contrast between the academic conference reading and the one in church, I decided to experiment further. I read the passage to my children, then ages seven and ten (they hadn't been paying much attention to it in church), and asked them what they thought it meant. They responded, "When you do something wrong, you should say you're sorry." Of course. We condition children to look Bible stories for a lesson. My kids delivered the interpretation that their socialization (and their developmental stage) made available to them. While too young to grasp the complexities of adultery or Mosaic Law, they recognized the woman in the story as a vulnerable target about to be punished, the forgiving reprieve offered to her by an authoritative protector, and the final command to sin no more. They saw themes—transgression, punishment, mercy, forgiveness—from their familiar, overlapping secular and religious communities and picked the ones that made the most sense to them. Their interpretation was based on the text but it wasn't *in* the text. It was in their social worlds and in their expectation that Bible stories deliver lessons in moral comportment. And yet, interpretive communities need not overdetermine a reading. My ten-year-old son, ever logical, paused after delivering his first answer and added, "But it also means that Jesus sinned." I was taken aback and asked him to explain. He said, "Well, he never threw a stone, so he must have sinned too." My own interpretive communities hadn't prepared me for that novel reading, nor had I encountered it anywhere in my review of scholarly commentary on this passage. Interpretive communities may be powerful, but they do not foreclose the possibilities for resistance, creativity, and novelty.

REFERENCES

Anderson, Chris. *Teaching as Believing: Faith in the University*. Waco: Baylor UP, 2004.

Bizzell, Patricia. "Faith-Based World Views as a Challenge to the Believing Game." *The Journal of the Assembly for Expanded Perspectives on Learning* 14 (2008–2009): 29–35.

Bloom, Lynn. "The Essay Canon." *College English*. 61.4 (1999): 401–30.

———. Personal email correspondence. 12 March 2013.

Burke, Kenneth. "Terministic Screens." *Language as Symbolic Action: Essays on Life, Literature, and Method*. Los Angeles: U of California P, 1966. 44–62.

Culler, Jonathan. *Literary Theory: A Very Short Introduction*. New York: Oxford UP, 2000.

Deans, Thomas. "The Rhetoric of Jesus Writing in the Story of the Adulteress (John 7.53–8.11)." *College Composition and Communication* 65.3 (2014): 406–29.

Downs, Douglas, and Elizabeth Wardle. "Teaching about Writing, Righting Misconceptions: (Re)Envisioning 'Introduction to Composition' as 'Introduction to Writing Studies." *College Composition and Communication* 58.4 (2007): 552–84.

Edmundson, Mark. *Why Read?* New York: Bloomsbury, 2005.

Fahnestock, Jeanne, and Marie Secor. "The Rhetoric of Literary Criticism." *Textual Dynamics of the Professions: Historical and Contemporary Studies of Writing in Professional Communities*. Eds. Charles Bazerman and James Paradis. Madison: U of Wisconsin Press, 1991. 77–96. Web. *WAC Clearinghouse*. 10 May 2014.

Fish, Stanley. "How to Recognize a Poem When You See One." *Is There a Text in This Class? The Authority of Interpretive Communities.* Cambridge: Harvard UP, 1980. 322–37.

Green, Elizabeth E. "Making Her Case and Reading it too: Feminist Readings of the Story of the Woman Taken in Adultery." *Ciphers in the Sand: Interpretations of the Woman Taken into Adultery (John 7.53–8.11).* Ed. Larry J. Kreitzer and Deborah W. Rooke. Sheffield: Sheffield Academic P, 2000. 240–67.

The HarperCollins Study Bible: New Revised Standard Version. San Francisco: HarperSanFrancisco, 2006.

Lynn, Steven J. *Texts and Contexts: Writing About Literature with Critical Theory.* 6th ed. New York: Pearson, 2011.

Marzluf, Phillip P. "Religion in U.S. Writing Classes: Challenging the Conflict Narrative." *Journal of Writing Research* 2.3 (2011): 265–97. Web. 24 April 2014.

Miller, Richard E. "Everyday Literacy: Secular Institutions, Religious Students, and the Commute between Incommensurate Worlds." *Teaching/Writing in the Late Age of Print.* Eds. Jeffry Galin, Carol Peterson Haviland, and J. Paul Johnson. Cresskill: Hampton, 2003. 75–82.

Moe, Peter Wayne. "Some Thoughts on Rhetoric, Method, and Belief." *Rhetoric Review* 33.1 (2014): 72–74. Web. 18 March 2014.

Rand, Lizabeth. "Enacting Faith: Evangelical Discourse and the Discipline of Composition Studies." *College Composition and Communication* 52.3 (2001): 349–67.

Ringer, Jeffrey M. "The Dogma of Inquiry: Composition and the Primacy of Faith." *Rhetoric Review* (2013): 349–65.

Salcedo, Myra. "Negotiating the 'Sacred' in Secular Writing Spaces: The Rhetoric of Religion in University Composition Textbooks." Conference on College Composition and Communication Convention. Las Vegas. 14 March 2013. Presentation.

Section III

Christianity and Rhetorical Methodology

6 Coming to (Troubled) Terms
Methodology, Positionality, and the Problem of Defining "Evangelical Christian"

Emily Murphy Cope and
Jeffrey M. Ringer

In this chapter, we explore the complex role definitions play in research dealing with a subset of Christian rhetoric, namely, the writing that evangelical Christian students produce in postsecondary educational contexts. Specifically, we reflect on our own experiences designing qualitative research studies that center on a contested term, namely, *evangelical Christian*.[1] Despite conducting our studies in different regions, we experienced similar challenges defining, sampling, and recruiting our participants. These aspects of research design were especially challenging because of the troubled history of *evangelical*, a term rife with political baggage that is often defined reductively. Moreover, *evangelical* identifies a rapidly shifting population, rendering it simultaneously frustrating and invigorating to study.

Because we both claim evangelical Christianity as part of our heritage, we had to consider our own positionality in relation to *evangelical* and the participants we hoped to recruit. On one hand, our experiences within evangelicalism opened up methodological possibilities. Because we are insiders, our awareness of the inadequacy of various scholarly constructions of evangelicals prompted us to research this population empirically. Our insider status also helped us identify (with) other evangelicals, largely because we are able to "speak the same language" and foster trust with potential participants, which aids significantly in participant recruitment. On the other hand, our ability to identify as insiders complicated our studies. Because of our proximity to evangelicalism, we were wary of projecting our experiences onto others or misinterpreting what our participants wrote or said.

Furthering complicating our positionality is the fact that each of us has a conflicted relationship to evangelicalism. While we both retain strong ties to evangelical subculture, particularly in terms of our faith and relationships with family and friends, we maintain significant reservations. We lament the Religious Right's co-opting of American evangelicalism and the narrow political agenda that ensued (see Balmer, *Making*). As Will Duffy and Lisa Shaver separately argue elsewhere in this volume, American evangelicalism once played a significant role in furthering efforts that aimed to address social ills such as gender inequality and economic injustice. We lament that evangelicalism lost this prophetic focus in the late twentieth century. But we agree with

Beth Daniell, who argues—also in this volume—that American Christianity, evangelicalism included, is more complex than popular representations suggest. Our experiences within evangelicalism sensitize us to its complexities; as insiders, we know firsthand that evangelicalism comprises an expansive discourse that allows for a range of manifestations and internal critique.

Researchers have long discussed problems surrounding definition and positionality in research design (Denzin and Lincoln; Powell and Takayoshi). Our focus on a particularly contested term brings into relief key challenges that researchers face when studying Christian rhetorics in the twenty-first century. Those challenges center on the problem of labels and the populations they purport to name. Illustrating this problem is the rise of religiously unaffiliated Americans. While "the nones" reject labels associated with faith traditions, they often espouse many of the same religious beliefs as previous generations and thus cannot be dismissed en masse as nonreligious (" 'Nones' "). This trend certainly exists among evangelicals in particular, who often have highly conflicted relationships with and thus distance themselves from *evangelical*, even if they meet received definitions (Kinnaman; Putnam and Campbell). Given these trends, how should researchers go about researching vernacular religious forms, particularly in terms of identifying and recruiting participants? Should researchers only use emic terms—terms individuals would use themselves—or might researcher-based etic terms prove beneficial in certain instances? These are the challenges we take up in this chapter.

In doing so, we hope to encourage rhetoricians to revise existing and develop new methodologies for mapping the terrain of one of the most dynamic variants of Protestant Christianity in the twenty-first century (Noll, "Future"). Given that terms such as *evangelical* function symbolically to shape attitudes and create or reify social realities, it behooves rhetoricians to investigate labels empirically and revisit definitions frequently. Doing so can lead to more ethical and nuanced understandings of the diverse attitudes and expressions of frequently maligned populations such as evangelicals. More complex understandings of labels can have far-reaching implications for how we go about researching varieties of Christian rhetorics. Equally important, such empirical research might trouble our assumptions about which discourses are welcome in academic and civic contexts. A more robust understanding of evangelicals might allow for the inclusion of "vital and nonfundamentalist" religious voices that can lead to a more democratic discourse (Habermas 25) both in the public sphere and in the "protopublic classrooms of rhetorical education" (Gilyard 61).

EXIGENCIES: PERSONAL, SCHOLARLY

Given our proximity to evangelicalism, we begin with brief narratives about our backgrounds and research interests. Emily was raised in conservative, nondenominational evangelical churches in the Midwest and western New York and attended a Bible college in the Midwest. Through undergraduate courses in religion and theology, Emily came to understand her own American evangelicalism as historically and culturally bound. In particular, Emily questioned the subculture's narrow epistemology, authoritative claims regarding gender roles, and use of legal and political power to impose values on others. Like many millennials, Emily doesn't feel any strong institutional ties but is currently part of a faith community with a mainline denomination—Presbyterian Church (U.S.A.). Emily's begin to develop her research interests as a graduate teaching assistant at the University of Tennessee, Knoxville (UTK). Workshops designed to initiate new writing teachers the first-year writing (FYW) featured discussion of particular groups of students—athletes, ethnic minorities, and lesbian, gay, bisexual, and transgender (LGBT), among others. No one discussed evangelical Christian students even though they likely constitute the single-largest subculture at UTK. Since then, Emily has frequently heard colleagues expressing frustration when students invoke faith in their writing. Given that graduate students and instructors in English are unlikely to espouse evangelical beliefs (Anderson; Brown and Olson; Tobin and Weinberg), Emily wondered why new composition teachers received no guidance about how to interact with evangelical Christian students. This exigency led to questions she continues to explore in her dissertation, a qualitative study of evangelical undergraduates' writing at public universities.

Jeff's exigency resonates with Emily's. He grew up in the Pentecostal tradition in New England and attended Lee University, an evangelical institution in the Southeast. While there, he took a number of courses that, like Emily's experience, alerted him to the historical and cultural situatedness of his faith. He also encountered a broad range of perspectives among the diverse student population, prompting him to question many of his received beliefs. After graduating, he started teaching FYW at the University of Vermont (UVM) as part of his MA program. There, Jeff interacted with a largely white population of students that overwhelmingly identified with no faith whatsoever, save for the occasional Catholic or Jewish student. When he returned to Lee in 2003 as a visiting instructor, he was blindsided by the difference in student writing. While his UVM students premised their arguments on various political assumptions, Lee students often made arguments that assumed the Christian God to be the source of Truth—for *everyone*. The irony was thick: a Lee alum, Jeff was unprepared to work with evangelical Christian students because his pedagogical training hadn't prepared him to do so. When a colleague informed him that the scholarly discussion about this population was growing within rhetoric and composition, he decided to explore the interrelationships between evangelicalism and academic discourse in his doctoral work at the University of New Hampshire (UNH).

By the time we separately began pursuing these interests as graduate students in the mid-to late 2000s, the field's attention to religiously motivated student writing was increasing. When we delved into the scholarship about evangelical students, we could hardly recognize many of our students or friends—not to mention ourselves—in the narrow characterizations of evangelical faith and identity we encountered. We already had questioned and revised many of the theological and political beliefs we had received within the subculture, and we knew many other evangelicals who were doing the same. The degree to which scholars in our field underestimated the diversity of American evangelicalism surprised us, and we independently sought to design qualitative studies that uncovered the nuances of contemporary evangelical Christian identity.

We quickly came to realize that researching this population is fraught with methodological difficulties. What exactly *is* an evangelical Christian? And who would describe themselves as such, especially given the label's negative connotations? These issues arose because we aimed to enact a more representative sampling method than what we saw in existing scholarship. Most articles featured teachers describing their experiences with evangelical students who breached the expectations of academic discourse (Anderson; Browning; Dively; Goodburn; Perkins; Smart; see also Vander Lei, this volume). Based on this teacher-research method of selection, rhetoric and composition perpetuated a narrow view of evangelicals as "problem students" who refused to think critically, parroted narrow-minded bigotry, and maintained fierce allegiances to hyper-conservative political and theological views (Gilyard 58; Goodburn; Montesano and Roen). Because we hoped to offer a more complex view of evangelical student writing, we knew we needed to avoid methods of recruitment that led to narrow portrayals. But if we were not identifying students who explicitly enact evangelical discourse in academic writing, how would we identify them, especially given that not all students who fit definitions of *evangelical* identify as such? The short answer is that we each chose a different sampling method: while Jeff relied on affiliation, Emily adopted self-identification. We discuss both designs in the following.

HOW WE DEFINE *EVANGELICAL*

What *is* an evangelical Christian? And why do individuals who fit definitions of *evangelical* reject that label? There is no easy answer to the first question—researchers have wrangled over defining evangelicalism for decades (Balmer, *Mine*; Bebbington; Hunter; Marsden; Noll, "Future"; Smith; Steensland et. al; Woodberry and Smith; Wuthnow). Timothy Beal, for instance, laments that "as soon as evangelicalism becomes a subject, it splinters and splits," while Nathan Hatch claims that "there is no such thing as evangelicalism" because it has ceased to name anything in particular (97–98). Despite the challenges of working with the term, we believe *evangelical* is useful because it names phenomena for which no better terminology exists.

Evangelical is an umbrella term, a category that contains a number of Christian traditions. Historians use *evangelical* to name a subset of Protestant Christianity, specifically movements, denominations, and institutions that arose from eighteenth and nineteenth-century revivals in the U.K. and U.S. (Noll, "Future" 421). These popular revivals engendered a transdenominational religious culture that refocused Protestant theology around the death of Christ and the authority of scripture, prioritized personal conversion and piety, and mobilized adherents to social action and proselytizing (Bebbington). Taking this genealogical view, many movements (e.g., charismatic revivals, fundamentalism), denominations (e.g., Southern Baptist Convention, Assemblies of God), organizations (e.g., Young Life, *Christianity Today*), and institutions (e.g., Wheaton College) meet historical definitions of evangelicalism because their values derive from the transatlantic revivals.

Evangelical also denotes "a consistent pattern of convictions and attitudes" (Noll, "Future" 422). Pollsters such as the Barna Group often use behavioral or theological criteria to define evangelicalism, but such criteria tend to be so culturally and historically bound that they elide changes to and diversity within religious life.[2] Many scholars instead rely on historian David Bebbington's "quadrilateral" definition of evangelicalism, which outlines four evangelical priorities that arose during the transatlantic revivals and have persisted on both sides of the Atlantic for more than three centuries (2). According to Bebbington, evangelicalism prioritizes

1. *conversionism*, the understanding of conversion as a personal experience that that significantly transforms each Christian's life;
2. *biblicism*, the premise that the Bible is the ultimate authority for Christian living;
3. *activism*, the impulse to spread and enact faith through relief/social work; and
4. *crucicentrism*, a focus on the substitutionary death of Christ. (3)

This attitudinal definition has been widely circulated by historians and resonates with other definitions (Balmer, *Mine*; Noll, "Future"). Some scholars, however, emphasize the first three priorities, since crucicentrism tends to align with a particular version of Protestant theology that excludes Catholic evangelicals (Lindsay 3–4).

In addition to these historical and attitudinal definitions, scholars understand evangelicalism as a subculture or web of related subcultures. Christian Smith's sociological research corroborates Bebbington's attitudinal quadrilateral and finds that contemporary evangelicals share "a set of minimal, baseline, supradenominational theological beliefs," as well as a "sensibility about strategy for the Christian mission in the world" (87). This "shared sensibility" underscores evangelicalism as a subculture, which Smith defines as a "distinct, publicly recognizable collective identity" (15; see also Balmer,

Mine; Gallagher; Webber; Wilcox). As a subculture, evangelicalism partic-ipates in and provides an alternative to American culture. Randall Balmer, for instance, demonstrates how evangelicalism has adapted to larger cul-tural shifts within American politics and society since the eighteenth century (*Making*).

Bebbington's "quadrilateral" remains valuable because of how well it integrates the historical, attitudinal, and subcultural senses of evangelical-ism. The four priorities it names comprise what James Gee might call the "identity kit" of evangelical discourse. Gee defines capital-D "Discourses" as entailing "ways of speaking/listening and often, too, writing/reading *cou-pled* with distinctive ways of acting, interacting, valuing, feeling, dressing, thinking, believing with other people [. . .], so as to enact specific socially recognizable identities engaged in specific socially recognizable activities" (155). Discourses help members of a subculture identify (with) each other via enacting shared values. The Institute for the Study of American Evan-gelicals (ISAE) notes that *evangelical* "denotes a style as much as a set of beliefs, and an attitude which insiders 'know' and 'feel' when they encoun-ter it," suggesting that evangelicalism operates as a Discourse (Eskridge, "Defining"). Thus, while Bebbington's hallmarks highlight core tenets of evangelical theology, they also name some of the "distinctive ways" that evangelicals speak, write, value, feel, and believe with each other.

A TROUBLED TERM

With this layered definition of *evangelical* in mind, we return to our second question: Why do individuals who fit scholarly definitions of *evangelical* tend to reject that label? One answer involves the term's negative conno-tations. Although scholars often use *evangelical* as an umbrella term that encompasses a range of political, theological, and social persuasions, the term is often mistakenly treated as synonymous with *fundamentalist* or *socially conservative Republican*. When conflated with fundamentalism, *evangelical* conjures notions of literalist interpretations of the Bible and patriarchal and homophobic attitudes. When conflated with socially con-servative Republican, *evangelical* implies hyper-individualist Americanism, acritical acceptance of capitalism, and fearmongering. Often, these confla-tions coincide. For instance, while Keith Gilyard initially works to distin-guish between "fundamentalist or evangelical," he ultimately reduces both to "fundamentalist," which he links to "conservative Christianity" and its affiliations with "conservative political actions" (58).[3]

Numerous scholars have pointed out, though, that *evangelical* and *fun-damentalist* are far from equivalent (Balmer, *Mine*; Hunter; Marsden; Noll, "Future"; Smith; Stephens and Giberson; Woodberry and Smith). In fact, the historical definition helps clarify the relationship between evangelicals and fundamentalists. In the early twentieth century, fundamentalism emerged as a splinter movement within evangelicalism, reacting against perceived "liberalization at work in some American denominations" (Noll, "Future" 422). While fundamentalists are part of the evangelical family, not all evangelicals are fundamentalists. *Fundamentalist* "denote[s] literalistic, moralistic, pietistic, and even militant impulses *within the larger tradition*" (Balmer *Mine* xv, emphasis added). Marsden cheekily describes a fundamentalist as "an evangelical who is angry about something" (1). When scholars conflate *evangelical* and *fundamentalist*, they elide lived distinctions that exist within and between religious traditions (see Daniell, this volume).

Fundamentalists are separatists who resist change; evangelicals strive to be culturally relevant (Balmer, *Making*; Smith; Webber). Balmer illustrates this fluidity when he describes four key "turning points" in the history of American evangelicalism: (1) from Calvinism to Arminianism during the First Great Awakening, (2) from postmillennialism to premillennialism in the late nineteenth century, (3) from engagement with society to separation from it following the Scopes trial, and (4) from seclusion to political engagement in the late twentieth century (*Making*). Each turning point coincides with cultural exigencies. When evangelical views of salvation shifted from the Calvinism of Jonathan Edwards to Arminianism of Charles Finney, they did so partially in response to populism and the burgeoning belief in the American Experiment. As Balmer explains, Finney's theology, which rejected Calvinist determinism and banked on one's personal decision to accept Christ, resonated with "the temper of the times" (*Making* 21). "Among a people who had only recently taken their *political* destiny into their own hands," Balmer writes, "Finney assured them that they controlled their *religious* destiny as well" (*Making* 21).

While evangelicals also came to be identified with social and political conservatism of late-twentieth-century movements such as the Moral Majority and Religious Right, those affiliations are splintering as the social and political context changes and as millennial evangelicals distance themselves from traditional social concerns of the Republican Party (Balmer, *Making* 80; Pally; Webber). Thus, while Sharon Crowley and others have shown that evangelicalism remains inflected with premillennialism and apocalypticism, evidence indicates their grip on the subculture is loosening. For instance, on the day we drafted this paragraph (December 16, 2013), the website of the National Association of Evangelicals (NAE) listed the following topics as trending: "Contraception mandate," "Immigration," "Environment," "Human Trafficking," "Marriage," and "Syria." While the contraception mandate and marriage reflect traditional concerns of American evangelicals, the rest indicate how much evangelicalism has changed since the 1980s. In fact, the NAE has supported comprehensive immigration reform since 2009, well before Republicans called party leaders to rethink their opposition after the 2012 elections. And while not every evangelical considers herself an environmentalist, interest in "creation care" has surged of late, largely because evangelicals en masse are returning to New Testament concerns about the poor (Prelli and Winters). In saying this, we do not mean to imply that socially and politically liberal evangelicals are good and thoughtful while conservative evangelicals are less so. We are arguing, however, that evangelical values support a broad range of political and social positions, including nonfundamentalist varieties of conservatism that engage deliberatively with other perspectives.

Despite contemporary evangelicalism's diversity, negative stereotypes persist, leading many individuals who fit definitions such as Bebbington's to reject the label or distance themselves from it. Many of our research participants demonstrated this ambivalence. One of Jeff's participants, Austin, a male evangelical student enrolled at a public university in the northeastern U.S., noted in an interview that he wanted to "break down the stereotype of [. . .] what people perceive to be Christianity." When Jeff asked him to talk further about this stereotype, Austin said,

> Um, kind of the crazy evangelical Christian, holier than thou, like, saying—you know, just going up to someone and saying, "You're a sinner, you need to have Jesus." Like, that's not gonna get people—like, that just puts people on a guilt trip. You know? [. . .] There's so many stereotypes built up about Christians. Like, um, the guy who stands on the corner on a soap box saying, "The world's gonna end in so many years! You need to have Jesus!" Like, that's not gonna get people to be Christians.

Note how Austin enacts Bebbington's hallmarks: he implies a desire to share his faith (activism) in order to attract people to Christianity (conversionism). And while he doesn't speak to his views of the Bible or of Christ's substitutionary death in this passage, he does so elsewhere (see Ringer). Austin distances himself from *stereotypes* of evangelicals, not from evangelical *practices*.

Indeed, Austin's comment suggests he is as concerned with legitimacy as he is conversion. D. Michael Lindsay notes that while populist evangelicals identify wholeheartedly with evangelical subcultures, cosmopolitan evangelicals tend to be more conflicted because they seek legitimacy in the wider culture (218–23). Cosmopolitan evangelicals reason that if evangelicalism comes to be seen as legitimate, "it will gain both prestige and prominence and will be embraced by more people" (Lindsay 221). This desire for legitimacy, though, implies awareness that evangelicalism isn't legitimate yet: in Austin's words, the "stereotypes built up about Christians" work against widespread acceptance of evangelical Christianity. Many of our participants are ambivalent about identifying as evangelical because they know its negative stereotypes make spreading their faith more difficult. The distance Austin sought to establish from the connotations of *evangelical* is not an isolated phenomenon—we saw it over and over in the interviews we conducted with students from various parts of the U.S.

In addition to distancing themselves from the negative connotations of *evangelical*, younger evangelicals may reject the term simply because it is a label. One of Emily's participants exemplifies this resistance. For Ember, all labels are inauthentic, but she uses them to communicate with others. Ember explained her flexibility with and resistance to labels in her interview:

> I've had so many terms that I've used over the years [. . .]. I call myself a "Free Believer" to people who know what it is, just because they can say, "Oh! I know who you are." [. . .] I don't think I really fit any exact category because I think when it comes to relationships with God, no one fits an exact category [. . .]. I think that it's almost an unhealthy obsession that we've developed as a society with these terms, so I would personally—I'll tell someone, "Sure, I'm an evangelical Christian if that helps you understand me," but I just view myself as a person who is fortunate enough to have a relationship with some amazing being.

Like Austin, Ember distances herself from *evangelical*, but does so because of a millennial sense of entitlement to a label-free identity (see Twenge and Campbell).

Ember isn't unique in this regard. She fits within the category of "nones" who retain religious belief and practice; recent polls show that 68 percent of the "nones" believe in God, 37 percent consider themselves "spiritual," and 21 percent pray daily ("'Nones'"). Ember's resistance toward labels also resonates with that of the Emerging Church Movement (ECM) popular among millennials. Marti and Ganiel describe the ECM as a movement that seeks "social legitimacy and spiritual vitality by actively disassociating" itself from evangelicalism (ix). They go so far as to characterize the ECM's resistance to labels as "passionate and obsessive" (Marti and Ganiel 5). Millennials such as Ember, and movements, such as the ECM, even if their beliefs and practices correspond to Bebbington's hallmarks of evangelicalism, challenge how researchers use and define existing labels. Traditional measures of religiosity that rely on affiliation may become increasingly unhelpful in describing the lived religious experiences of many young Americans.

PARTICIPANT RECRUITMENT: AFFILIATION AND SELF-IDENTIFICATION

Negative connotations of *evangelical*, preferences for label-free identities, the rise of the "nones," the growth of the ECM—these trends posed methodological challenges for our studies. How do we identify a population of students who fit definitions of *evangelical* but distance themselves from it or reject labels altogether? Should we use emic terms for recruitment? Most evangelicals describe themselves as "Christians" or "believers," not as "evangelicals." *Evangelical* thus functions as an etic term, an analytic category more salient to researchers than participants. Should we ask participants to self-identify with the etic term *evangelical*? If we use *evangelical* in our recruitment materials, might we run the risk of scaring off viable participants who seek to distance themselves from the label? But if we avoid the term, how do we ensure they *do* fit the definition?

We adopted two different strategies to negotiate this conundrum: Jeff identified participants through affiliation with evangelical ministries, while Emily relied on self-identification. Here, we discuss our reasoning behind each method and reflect on the benefits and shortcomings of each. In doing so, we invariably broach the topic of researcher positionality. But while methodological discussions of positionality tend to center on issues of data collection, analysis, and representation (Powell and Takayoshi), concerns about positionality in terms of participant recruitment are often overlooked. Given the troubled nature of *evangelical*, we had to think carefully about how we positioned ourselves in relation to that label in our recruitment processes to avoid alienating potential participants.

Identification via Affiliation

Jeff's research involved case studies with six evangelical Christians: three FYW students and three doctoral students in rhetoric and composition. In this discussion, he'll focus on the undergraduate portion of his study. Jeff's main research question involved how students negotiated their evangelical identities in relation to the academic discourse they were learning in the context of a public university. Because "negotiation" is an ongoing process that requires reflection over time to acknowledge, Jeff based his case studies on a series of five interviews spread out over roughly two to three months for each student. At the outset of his study, Jeff chose to avoid *evangelical* when recruiting participants. Given the context for his study—a midsized state university in the Northeast, where few students identified religiously at all, much less as evangelicals—he knew the term could alienate potential participants.

To identify participants, Jeff partnered with the leaders of evangelical campus ministries. The assumption behind this method is that students who affiliate with an evangelical subculture through involvement with a campus ministry are likely to identify with the values and beliefs promoted within that subculture. Of course, this assumption isn't always true; in parts of the U.S. such as the South, where forms of evangelicalism are so pervasive that a kind of cultural Christianity exists, individuals who affiliate with a particular evangelical community may not fit the definition of evangelical (Eskridge, "How Many"). Researcher identification based on affiliation with an evangelical community likely would not have worked for Emily's study in the Bible Belt. In the largely post-Christian Northeast, however, one can more safely assume that a state university college student who affiliates with an evangelical campus ministry will align him- or herself with the tenets of evangelicalism.

Still, affiliation is a complicated indicator, as is evidenced by the increase of religiously unaffiliated Americans who pray regularly and define themselves as "spiritual" ("Nones"). Nevertheless, research suggests that individuals who *do* still affiliate hold their beliefs with a higher degree of intensity and commitment: while affiliation to evangelicalism is decreasing among millennials, the Barna Group recently found that millennial evangelicals practice evangelism more frequently than previous generations of evangelicals ("Is Evangelism"). So, while affiliation might capture a smaller group of individuals than in previous decades, those it includes tend to fall square in the middle of what Smith and Snell call "The Devoted," the 5 percent of millennials who evidence high rates of religious attitudes and behaviors and see faith as central to their identities (259).

Partly because of the drawbacks of affiliation, Jeff partnered with campus ministry leaders who would know students well *as* Christians. This allowed Jeff to explain his study to leaders who could help identify students that met the profile he sought. Because he was asking these ministers to volunteer names and contact information for individuals for whom they felt responsible, Jeff had to gain leaders' trust. In the initial e-mails he sent to campus ministry leaders, he described his research as involving "the experiences of evangelical Christians in the secular university" and then established his evangelical ethos by noting he grew up in an evangelical family, attended a Christian college, participated in Graduate InterVarsity, and attended several area evangelical churches. Thus, in his communication with evangelical youth leaders, he positioned himself as someone with strong evangelical affiliations who understands the population as an insider.

These initial e-mails led to conversations with a number of campus ministry leaders, conversations wherein Jeff positioned himself as both researcher and evangelical insider. Jeff did not ask the campus ministry leaders to avoid using *evangelical* when talking with students about the study, so it is possible that they used the term, which may have influenced some students' level of interest. However, Jeff's partnership with campus ministries served as a first layer of screening. If, as Eskridge ("Defining") and Christian Smith suggest, evangelicalism functions as a kind of habitus, then the fact that evangelical campus ministry leaders "recognized" particular students as evangelical is a strong indicator of their evangelical identity. In fact, when campus ministry leaders e-mailed Jeff to tell him about a potential participant, they would often comment on the student's high level of devotion.

Jeff then sent brief e-mails inviting potential participants to join the study. This e-mail looked quite different from the one he sent to the campus ministry leaders. It opens with a brief introduction followed by recognition that their campus ministry leader was the source of the recipient's name and email address. Then Jeff explains the research project: "I've been a Christian my whole life, and my research has to do with the experiences of other Christians attending schools like NESU. I'm particularly interested in the experiences of Christians who are taking a first year writing course like English 101." Despite the absence of *evangelical*, the first sentence likely would alert evangelical students to the fact that this study is aimed at them.

Within American evangelicalism, stories abound about how the state university and those "liberal" professors have the singular goal of deconverting committed Christians from their faith (see Budziszewski). Thus the line "my research has to do with the experiences of other Christians attending schools like NESU" suggests that certain *kinds* of Christians have "experiences" at public universities worth studying. It should come as little surprise that the three FYW students who participated felt at least somewhat "embattled" as evangelicals attending a public university in the Northeast (see Christian Smith). Such subtexts bear significant persuasive appeal.

Jeff met informally with each potential participant to get a better sense of the student's faith and to foster trust. Initially, Jeff designed a questionnaire to ensure that participants met Bebbington's definition of *evangelical*. He abandoned this method, however, because it would have locked participants into a set of responses and essentialize a definition of *evangelical* that may not align with vernacular forms of faith (Howard; Primiano). Instead, Jeff held unrecorded conversations that dealt with each participant's faith background, family life, and educational background. He was not looking for lockstep agreement with the tenets of evangelicalism but, rather, for resonance with it. Did participants share a set of beliefs and attitudes that aligned with Bebbington's quadrilateral, even if their "lived" forms of faith pushed against the boundaries of abstract definitions? None of these discussions led Jeff to reject any potential FYW participants. Affiliation provided students from a range of backgrounds and with a range of evangelical practices who all attended the same local evangelical church and participated actively in the same the same campus ministry. Specifically, he identified a white male who spent his formative years in the South prior to moving to the Northeast; a female of partial Iranian descent who grew up Baha'i and converted to evangelical Christianity during high school; and a Jamaican-American female whose life was marked by conscious choices to participate actively in church-related activities.

Emily: Self-Identification

Emily limited her participants to a purposive sample of *self-identified* evangelical undergraduates at public universities (Berg 110). Self-identification was paramount for Emily because she wanted to understand how "ordinary," nonelite evangelicals write for college. Most studies of evangelical student writers rely on teachers' anecdotes about working with outspoken students and thus overestimate how frequently such students produce "problematic" texts (see Vander Lei, this volume). Emily avoided identifying participants via teacher-research methods. Instead of drawing on anecdotal classroom evidence, she analyzed the characteristics of academic writing by self-identified evangelical undergraduates and used semistructured interviews to understand how they experience academic writing situations.

Emily also settled on self-identification because of her context, a large public research university in the Bible Belt, where evangelicalism infuses the "ambient" religious culture (Engelke). Of Emily's ten participants, fully half would not have been visible: one participant had no institutional affiliation and four others attended mainline campus ministries or churches. The ambient evangelical culture also presented the challenge of *cultural evangelicals*—individuals who do not engage in characteristically evangelical practices such as church attendance, witnessing, or prayer but who remain embedded in evangelical culture and discourse (Eskridge, "How Many"). Cultural evangelical undergraduates may not attend church frequently but still sound like evangelicals to their instructors. Because evangelical Christianity is normative in the southeastern U.S., where the Southern Baptist Convention exerts outsized cultural influence, traditional measures of piety aren't useful for identifying individuals who enact evangelical discourse. Emily's pilot study confirmed the value of self-identification; she found that the existing literature ignored evangelical students who have largely assimilated the norms of the university but who believe their faith is relevant to academic writing.

Her pilot study also demonstrated the challenge of recruiting self-identified evangelical undergraduates. Emily experimented with three methods: approaching participants directly at evangelical campus ministries, visiting a classroom, and recruiting participants through mutual friends. She recruited only three participants[4] and realized that using *evangelical* likely alienated potential participants, especially those who didn't come to her through a trusted contact. Emily also realized that potential participants might trust her more if she disclosed her own evangelical identity. She had scrupulously avoided doing so because of her conflicted relationship with evangelicalism and her fear of being negatively perceived within the academy. However, Emily came to see her research as an opportunity for even ambivalent evangelicals to contribute to scholarly constructions of evangelical identity and discourse. To do so, she knew they would need to trust her.

For her institutional review board–approved study, Emily revised identifying as an evangelical. Because she wanted to capture a wide range of experiences and writing, she relied on a combination of snowball sampling, wherein participants help recruit other participants, and direct e-mail appeals to classes whose teachers allowed her to contact their students. Both methods foster identification and Emily made sure to enact evangelical discourse in the first-contact e-mail she wrote. Emily avoided *evangelical* in the beginning of the e-mail, using instead the emic term *faith* in the subject line ("Faith and Writing") and first paragraph: "Do you ever think about how your faith relates to what you learn in college? What about how your faith relates to your academic writing? Do you like to write about your beliefs or do you prefer to keep your faith and education separate?" *Faith* is not exclusive to evangelical Christianity, but Emily's use of it ("*your* faith") appeals to American evangelical individualism. Emily strengthened her insider status by explicitly identifying as a "Christian" scholar. Doing so allowed her to then use *evangelical*:

> If you'd be interested in talking about these issues, I'd love to discuss them with you as part of a study I'm conducting about the academic writing of evangelical undergrads at public universities. I'm working on a PhD in English and as a Christian scholar I've thought about these questions a lot. [. . .] If you're a Christian undergrad and this sounds interesting, please send me an email so we can set up a time to talk [. . .].

Within two weeks, six participants had confirmed. Four more joined via mutual contacts and snowballing.

Emily set up unrecorded meetings with each potential participant to discuss the study, consent form, and *evangelical*. Emily foregrounded *evangelical* on the informed consent and explained she was using the term because while evangelicals had become the focus of significant discussion among writing teachers, that discussion didn't reflect all evangelicals. This became a selling point for participants who were keenly aware of negative perceptions of evangelicals. Emily also asked each participant if he or she felt comfortable identifying as evangelical and found that nine of her ten participants quickly agreed. Emily's method thus proved successful—every interested person who contacted her chose to participate. While Emily's interview data reveal that her participants do not use the label as the primary way of describing themselves or their faith, they all agree they are evangelicals.

All except Ember, that is, who laughed when Emily asked if she identified as an evangelical. Ember grew up in a church that, she said, "meets all the requirements of being a cult." She thus distances herself from *evangelical* because of wounds by other evangelicals. Nevertheless, Ember now reports having an "intimate" relationship with God. She no longer attends a church but meets Bebbington's definition of *evangelical* and agrees to identify as such. In her official interview with Emily, however, Ember admitted to discomfort even with *Christian*. After empathizing with Ember's ambivalence about identifying as an evangelical, Emily explained that she was using *evangelical* in a particular, scholarly sense and briefly outlined Bebbington's quadrilateral, pointing out that she wasn't using the definition as "a litmus test" but as a means of helping Ember determine whether she felt comfortable identifying as evangelical. Ember responded, "I think it would be hilarious if you classify me as an evangelical [laughs], because of the con—I called myself that for so many years." Ember was about to say "because of the *connotations*," which suggests that such concerns were paramount for her and that her self-identification was thus ironic. Still, Ember assented—in her own words—to each of Bebbington's hallmarks.

While Ember's description of her beliefs and attitudes falls within the framework of evangelicalism, other evangelicals might not recognize her. At one point, Ember said the following:

> I do believe that Jesus is special. I think that people can get to God through Jesus without knowing it, because the bible verse said, "No man can come to the Father, but through the Son." I think people will come to the Father. If they get to Him, they've gotten through the Son whether they know it or not. In that way, Jesus is very special. I would hope that everyone could have the opportunity to know Him, but in their own way, not in the way that someone prescribes to them.

Ember articulates a pluralistic evangelicalism here—people don't need to realize that Jesus makes their relationship with God possible. But her statement resonates with Bebbington's quadrilateral: a relationship with God (conversionism) is possible only through Jesus' sacrificial death (crucicentrism). And though she interprets it differently than many evangelicals would, Ember authorizes her pluralistic evangelicalism by paraphrasing John 14:6 (biblicism). Finally, when expressing her desire for others to "know Him" (activism), Ember critiques traditional evangelical models of conversion that specify one narrow route to God.

Emily's interactions with Ember reveal the challenges of self-identification to recruit evangelicals and the rewards of recruiting participants who resist *evangelical*. Regarding challenges, Emily was concerned with the ethics of asking Ember to identify as an evangelical when she so obviously rejected labels and affiliations. Although confident in Ember's evangelicalism, Emily valued the agency that self-identification allows. Ultimately, Ember identified as an evangelical because she shared Emily's desire to revise scholarly constructions of evangelicals; she was willing to participate as an insider because she wanted her voice to be heard. Recruiting ambivalent evangelicals takes time, sensitivity, and the willingness to let participants go rather than pressuring them to self-identify. However, because Ember pushes the limits of received definitions of *evangelical*, the rewards of recruiting participants like her are rich. When participants willingly negotiate the labels they resist, they contribute to our understanding of the diversity within identity categories. Participants such as Ember prompt scholars to enact robust dialectical research processes valued by qualitative researchers (Guba and Lincoln 193).

IMPLICATIONS

In closing, we discuss implications surrounding the ethics of using contested labels, researcher positionality in recruitment, and refining terminology through empirical research. In doing so, we focus on the importance of definitions for scholars designing qualitative studies of Christian rhetorics.

We also seek to help rhetoricians better understand Christian rhetorics and methodologies for researching them.

Ethics

We see two main ethical concerns arising from our discussion. The first is that researchers should use terms with sound definitions, especially when dealing with labels that categorize people. If researchers want to use labels ethically for sampling purposes, they need to use terms *descriptively* and *explicitly* and at the level of denotation. Labels that stereotype fail to meet these criteria. Within Christian rhetorics, many available labels can function as stereotypes or as descriptors. Through her analysis of scholarship on Protestants, for instance, Leslie Smith found that *evangelical* and *fundamentalist* rarely operate descriptively; unfortunately, scholars often use both to portray the people they name in terms of "anti-intellectualism, anti-modernism, and militancy" (208). The same is true of *conservative*, a label often used to pigeonhole evangelicals as narrow-minded. Using labels in this way pathologizes the populations they purport to name (see Leslie Smith). Our studies highlight the diversity of evangelical attitudes, and we found many of our participants to be thoughtful, "cosmopolitan" evangelicals who hold conservative political beliefs (see Lindsay).

When studying evangelicals, researchers need to consider their motives from an emic perspective and be open to the deliberative possibilities within political stances that might not match up with our own. In her study of Appalachian women's literacy, Katherine Sohn describes her desire to counteract labels such as "redneck" or "hillbilly" that stereotype Appalachian women as ignorant. She thus employs purposive sampling to recruit women who fit the definition of *Appalachian* (2). Sohn uses *Appalachian*, then, to *describe* a population from a particular region, and she is *explicit* early on in her study about why she uses that term. Her study serves as an example of how rhetoricians might consciously use labels explicitly as descriptors.

Even when researchers employ explicit and descriptive definitions, sampling via self-identification introduces ethical concerns. One limit of self-identification is that potential participants may still rely on popular definitions based on stereotypes, leading to research that further confirms those stereotypes. For example, one of the weaknesses of Emily's use of self-identification is that her sample is overwhelmingly white (nine of ten participants). Because *evangelical* connotes whiteness in popular usage, nonwhite Christians who meet definitions of *evangelical* may not have seen themselves as part of Emily's sample population. One unfortunate consequence of Emily's sampling, then, is that her research may render nonwhite evangelicals less visible.

Our studies raise a second ethical concern about definitions: whether researchers should apply a label to individuals who meet scholarly and descriptive definitions but resist or reject them. As we have shown, this problem will persist for researchers of Christian rhetorics because millennials largely reject labels. One question researchers must ask, then, is whether using a label that meets with resistance benefits the field's understanding of a particular phenomenon or population. Both Sohn and Robert Glenn Howard, for instance, use labels that their populations might reject, yet their studies make significant contributions. Jeff sees his study as following suit: the participants he worked with fit the definition of *evangelical* while also pushing against stereotypes. His hope, then, is that his study leads to more nuanced understandings of evangelical identity, discourse, and rhetoric. That said, if Jeff were to redo his study, he would consider following Emily's lead by having explicit discussions about *evangelical* with his participants in order to mitigate ethical concerns surrounding researcher identification. While both our studies did engage participants in conversations about *evangelical* and related stereotypes, Emily invited her participants to become cocreators of evangelical identity by explicitly discussing and negotiating definitions of the term. Such conversations can help redefine contested terms in both academic and public contexts.

Positionality

The second implication involves researcher positionality. In each of our cases, our ability to recruit participants and conduct successful interviews resulted from our ability to position ourselves as insiders to evangelical discourse. This does *not* mean that only evangelical insiders can research this population. We recognize the significant contributions that non-evangelical and non-Christian researchers have made to scholarly discussions about such rhetorics. We do contend, though, that there may be questions within the scholarly terrain best answered by those who can enact an insider status because participants may be more prone to trust someone they perceive as speaking their own language and sharing their values. Thus, we call for a dialectic of research into evangelical Christian rhetorics from insiders and outsiders. Having both can lead to deeper understandings of a changing population.

Neither of us enacted evangelical discourse as a façade—we both grew up in evangelical families, attended evangelical colleges, and maintain close ties to evangelicalism. But we did have to think consciously about our performance of self throughout our studies (Newkirk). Researcher positionality in recruitment isn't limited to the use or avoidance of a descriptor such as *evangelical*. We *both* identified as evangelicals from the start, albeit in implicit ways. Our experience suggests that qualitative researchers interacting with populations such as evangelicals need to consider when and how to enact their own relationship to the identities or discourses in question, as well as how gender, personality, mutual contacts, and regional and institutional contexts might influence identification.

Our experiences demonstrate how important *resonance* is for researchers and potential participants. One way to conceive of this is in terms of

Burkean identification—the motives locked within particular phrases in our recruitment materials evidenced an underlying evangelical substance (Burke 23). The persuasive force of such subtext, in relation to Christian rhetorics in particular and religious identification in general, comprises unmapped territory that could be fascinating to study from a rhetorical perspective. What terms function as "code words" to announce a marginalized identity to others who share it? In what contexts do such terms function? What cultural, historical, or social exigencies give rise to or prompt revisions of such terms?

Terminology

The final implication involves terminology itself. Our experiences researching *evangelical* lead us to argue that while researchers should use scholarly definitions, they should also view them as fluid. We used Bebbington's attitudinal definition of evangelicalism because it operates explicitly and descriptively *and* because so many scholars echo it. But we also interpreted it capaciously, which allowed us to identify participants who fit the definition of *evangelical* while pushing against its boundaries. Because of this dynamism, we contend that terms themselves should be the subject of empirical research. Such research, especially when conducted in relation to populations such as millennial evangelicals, can help scholars rethink existing labels and create new ones. James Bielo's anthropological study of "emerging evangelicals" led him to abandon historical, attitudinal, and subcultural definitions and instead explore the "contentious and collaborative" dialogues that "unfold among the individuals and institutions that claim a Christian identity" (201). Such a dialogic approach might help researchers arrive at terms that ethically and accurately name shifting and emerging populations.

This is especially true when it comes to labels that name a diverse, global, and dynamic demographic. While formal definitions of *evangelical* often come from institutional sources—various denominations, for instance, or organizations such as the NAE—scholarship that interrogates the vernacular forms of such faith can prompt rhetoricians to rethink categories. Howard's *Digital Jesus* exemplifies such work because it details how fundamentalist participants in online communities develop their beliefs apart from institutional authority. The implication of Howard's research is that vernacular Christian faith often departs significantly from institutional or doctrinal statements of faith. In the case of millennial fundamentalists, for instance, Howard observed increased tolerance toward diverse perspectives, a clear contrast from popular conceptions of fundamentalism (167). Terms that function to categorize people, especially those with loaded meanings such as *evangelical* and *fundamentalist*, must be the subject of continuous research, especially qualitative studies that examine vernacular forms. Qualitative research with "ordinary" people might complement and challenge terms that have become fossilized within public and academic spheres.

Stasis theory suggests that definitions constrain our perceptions of whatever is at issue, including its causes and consequences and our responses to it. We thus call for rhetoricians to interrogate, unsettle, and revise definitions of key terms that can serve to delimit the contours of Christian rhetorics in overly narrow ways. Doing so, we hope, will enable future researchers to chart the complexities and nuances of lived religious rhetorics—in ways, we hope, that lead to a more inclusive and more robust democratic discourse.

NOTES

1 We use italics to designate instances when we refer to terms as terms. Thus, *evangelical* means "the term evangelical."
2 See, for example, the Barna Group's "9-point" definition of *evangelical* ("Survey").
3 We reject generalizations that essentialize *conservative* as negative and *liberal* as positive. There are thoughtful, socially conscious evangelicals who ascribe to conservative politics; there are progressive evangelicals who maintain absolutist perspectives that shut down deliberative possibilities.
4 There are a number of reasons why three participants sufficed for Jeff's study but not Emily's. The main one is that while Jeff wanted to get at negotiation and development, which demands multiple interviews over time and thus limits the number of students one can work with, Emily aimed to show the diversity among evangelical Christian students, which demands more participants.

REFERENCES

Anderson, Chris. "The Description of an Embarrassment: When Students Write about Religion." *ADE Bulletin* 94 (1989): 12–15.

Austin. Personal interview. 7 October 2008.

Balmer, Randall. *The Making of Evangelicalism: From Revivalism to Politics and Beyond.* Waco: Baylor UP, 2010.

———. *Mine Eyes Have Seen the Glory: A Journey Into the Evangelical Subculture in America.* Oxford: Oxford UP, 1989.

Beal, Timothy. "Among the Evangelicals: Inside a Fractured Movement." *The Chronicle of Higher Education* (12 Dec. 2010): B6–B9.

Bebbington, David W. *Evangelicalism in Modern Britain: A History from the 1730s to the 1980s.* Oxford: Oxford UP, 2004.

Berg, Bruce. *Qualitative Research Methods for the Social Sciences.* Needham Heights: Simon & Schuster, 1989.

Bielo, James S. *Emerging Evangelicals: Faith, Modernity, and the Desire for Authenticity.* New York: New York UP, 2011.

Brown, Robert L., and Michael Jon Olson. "Storm in the Academy: Community Conflict and Spirituality in the Research University." *The Academy and the*

Possibility of Belief. Ed. Mary-Louise Buley-Meissner, Mary McCaslin Thompson, and Elizabeth Bachrach Tan. Cresskill: Hampton P, 2000. 153–69.

Browning, Mark. "Your Logos Against Mine." *Dialogue: A Journal for Writing Specialists* 6 (1999): 8–13.

Budziszewski, J. *How to Stay Christian in College*. Colorado Springs: Navpress, 2004.

Burke, Kenneth. *A Grammar of Motives*. Berkeley: U of California P, 1969.

Crowley, Sharon. *Toward a Civil Discourse: Rhetoric and Fundamentalism*. Pittsburgh: U of Pittsburgh P, 2006.

Denzin, Norman K., and Yvonna S. Lincoln, eds. *The SAGE Handbook of Qualitative Research*. 3rd ed. Thousand Oaks: Sage, 2005.

Dively, Ronda Leathers. "Religious Discourse in the Academy: Creating a Space by Means of Poststructuralist Theories of Subjectivity." *Composition Studies* 21.2 (1993): 91–101.

Ember. Personal Interview. 12 April 2012.

Engelke, Matthew. "Angels in Swindon: Public Religion and Ambient Faith in England." *American Ethnologist* 39.1 (2012): 155–70. *Wiley Online Library*. Web. 17 April 2014.

Eskridge, Larry. "Defining the Term in Contemporary Times." *Institute for the Study of American Evangelicals*. 1996. Rev. 2012. Web. 17 April 2014.

———. "How Many Evangelicals Are There?" *Institute for the Study of American Evangelicals*. 1996. Rev. 2012. Web. 17 April 2014.

Gallagher, Sally K. *Evangelical Identity and Gendered Family Life*. New Brunswick: Rutgers UP, 2003.

Gee, James Paul. *Social Linguistics and Literacies: Ideology in Discourses*. 3rd ed. New York: Routledge, 2008.

Gilyard, Keith. *Composition and Cornel West: Notes toward a Deep Democracy*. Carbondale: Southern Illinois UP, 2008.

Goodburn, Amy. "It's a Question of Faith: Discourses of Fundamentalism and Critical Pedagogy in the Writing Classroom." *JAC: A Journal of Rhetoric, Culture, & Politics* 18.2 (1998): 333–53.

Guba, Egon G., and Yvonna S. Lincoln. "Paradigmatic Controversies, Contradictions, and Emerging Confluences." Denzin and Lincoln 191–215.

Habermas, Jürgen. " 'The Political': The Rational Meaning of a Questionable Inheritance of Political Theology." Mendieta and VanAntwerpen 15–33.

Hatch, Nathan O. "Response to Carl F.H. Henry." *Evangelical Affirmations*. Eds. Kenneth S. Kantzer and Carl F.H. Henry. Grand Rapids: Zondervan, 1990. 96–102.

Howard, Robert Glenn. *Digital Jesus: The Making of a New Christian Fundamentalist Community on the Internet*. New York: New York UP, 2011.

Hunter, James Davis. *To Change the World: The Irony, Tragedy and Possibility of Christianity in the Late Modern World*. Oxford: Oxford UP, 2010.

"Is Evangelism Going Out of Style?" *Barna Group*. 18 December 2013. Web. 17 April 2014.

Kinnaman, David. *You Lost Me: Why Young Christians Are Leaving Church and Rethinking Faith*. Grand Rapids: Baker, 2011.

Lindsay, D. Michael. *Faith in the Halls of Power: How Evangelicals Joined the American Elite*. New York: Oxford UP, 2007.

Marsden, George. *Understanding Fundamentalism and Evangelicalism*. Grand Rapids: Eerdmans, 1991.

Marti, Gerardo, and Gladys Ganiel. *The Deconstructed Church: Understanding Emerging Christianity*. Oxford: Oxford UP, 2014.

Mendieta, Eduardo, and Jonathan VanAntwerpen, eds. *The Power of Religion in the Public Sphere*. New York: Columbia UP, 2011.

Montesano, Mark, and Duane Roen. "Religious Faith, Learning, and Writing: Challenges in the Classroom." Vander Lei and kyburz 84–98.

National Association of Evangelicals. *National Association of Evangelicals*. Web. 16 Dec. 2013.

Newkirk, Thomas R. *The Performance of Self in Student Writing*. Portsmouth: Boynton/Cook, 1997.

Noll, Mark A. "The Future of Protestantism: Evangelicalism." *The Blackwell Companion to Protestantism*. Eds. Alister E. McGrath and Darren C. Marks. Malden: Blackwell, 2004. 421–38.

" 'Nones' on the Rise." The Pew Forum on Religion and Public Life. *Pew Research Center*. 2012. Web. 17 April 2014.

Pally, Marcia. "The New Evangelicals." *New York Times*. 9 December 2011. Web. 27 May 2014.

Perkins, Priscilla. " 'A Radical Conversion of the Mind': Fundamentalism, Hermeneutics, and the Metanoic Classroom." *College English* 63.5 (2001): 585–611.

Powell, Katrina M., and Pamela Takayoshi, eds. *Practicing Research in Writing Studies: Reflexive and Ethically Responsible Research*. New York: Hampton P, 2012.

Primiano, Leonard Norman. "Vernacular Religion and the Search for Method in Religious Folklife." *Western Folklore* 54 (1995): 37–56.

Prelli, Lawrence J., and Terri S. Winters. "Rhetorical Features of Green Evangelicalism." *Environmental Communication* 3.2 (2009): 224–43. *Communication & Mass Media Complete*. Web. 26 March 2014.

Putnam, Robert D, and David E. Campbell. *American Grace: How Religion Divides and Unites Us*. New York: Simon & Schuster, 2010.

Ringer, Jeffrey M. "The Consequences of Integrating Faith into Academic Writing: Casuistic Stretching and Biblical Citation." *College English* 75.3 (2013): 272–99.

Smart, Juanita. " 'Frankenstein or Jesus Christ?' When the Voice of Faith Creates a Monster for the Composition Teacher." Vander Lei and kyburz 11–23.

Smith, Christian. *American Evangelicalism: Embattled and Thriving*. Chicago: U of Chicago P, 1998.

———, and Patricia Snell. *Souls in Transition: The Religious and Spiritual Lives of Emerging Adults*. New York: Oxford UP, 2009.

Smith, Leslie. "What's in a Name? Scholarship and the Pathology of Conservative Protestantism." *Method and Theory in the Study of Religion* 20.3 (2008): 191–211.

Sohn, Katherine Kelleher. *Whistlin' and Crowin' Women of Appalachia: Literary Practices Since College*. Carbondale: Southern Illinois UP, 2006.

Steensland, Brian, et al. "The Measure of American Religion: Toward Improving the State of the Art." *Social Forces* 79 (2000): 291–318.

Stephens, Randall J., and Karl W. Giberson. *The Anointed: Evangelical Truth in a Secular Age*. Cambridge, MA: Harvard UP, 2012.

"Survey Explores Who Qualifies as an Evangelical." *Barna Group*. 18 January 2007. Web. 17 April 2014.

Tobin, Gary A., and Aryeh K. Weinberg. *Religious Beliefs & Behavior of College Faculty*. Vol. 2. San Francisco: Institute for Jewish & Community Research, 2007.

Twenge, Jean M., and W. Keith Campbell. *The Narcissism Epidemic: Living in the Age of Entitlement*. New York: Atria, 2010.

Vander Lei, Elizabeth, and bonnie Lenore kyburz, eds. *Negotiating Religious Faith in the Composition Classroom*. Portsmouth, NH: Boynton/Cook, 2005.

Webber, Robert. *The Younger Evangelicals: Facing the Challenges of the New World*. Grand Rapids: Baker, 2002.

Wilcox, W. Bradford. *Soft Patriarchs, New Men: How Christianity Shapes Fathers and Husbands*. Chicago: U Chicago P, 2004.

Woodberry, Robert D., and Christian S. Smith. "Fundamentalism et al: Conservative Protestants in America." *Annual Review of Sociology* 24.1 (August 1998): 25–56. *EBSCO Academic Search Premier*. Web. 17 April 2014.

Wuthnow, Robert K. *The God Problem: Expressing Faith and Being Reasonable*. Berkeley: U of California P, 2012.

7 Empirical Hybridity
A Multimethodological Approach for Studying Religious Rhetorics

Heather Thomson-Bunn

Since the early 2000s, the need for sustained scholarly attention to religious rhetorics in general and Christian rhetorics in particular has come into sharper focus. For example, in *Negotiating Religious Faith in the Composition Classroom*, writing faculty from various institutions articulated some of the tensions surrounding the presence of religious rhetorics in the classroom—the frustration of receiving student work that seems dogmatic or dualistic (Downs; Smart), or the difficulty of asking students to critique deeply held beliefs (Montesano and Roen)—and illuminated the need for additional work in this area. Over the last few years, scholars such as Michael-John DePalma, TJ Geiger, and Jeffrey Ringer have explored the challenges and possibilities that arise when Christian rhetorics and academic writing come together.[1] And in 2014, Elizabeth Vander Lei et al. published *Renovating Rhetoric in Christian Tradition*, a collection of essays that "focuses attention on rhetors who press into service an array of rhetorical strategies—some drawn from Christian tradition and some contributing to Christian tradition—to achieve their rhetorical ends" (ix).

What has *not* yet received much attention within rhetoric and composition (henceforth, rhet/comp)[2] is the question of how the research methodologies we use to explore religious rhetorics inform our engagement with them. In fact, explicit discussion of methodology has largely been left out of the conversation, leaving us with an unnecessarily limited view of what it means to study religious rhetorics. In *Negotiating Religious Faith in the Composition Classroom*, for instance, seven of the ten essays draw from experiences instructors had with one or two religious students (another uses three) to frame at least part of the discussion and develop an argument about the role of religious rhetorics in the writing classroom. This reliance on one or two students seems to be more the rule than the exception (see Anderson; Carter; DePalma; Downs; Geiger; Goodburn; Perkins; Smart). Authors who compose this type of scholarship offer deeply reflexive work that has helped to develop and invigorate discussion of religious rhetorics, and I am in no way suggesting that scholars abandon this approach. Rather, I suggest that we can usefully supplement, complement, and extend this research by incorporating and combining other approaches. I agree with Ellen Barton that "the central problem of our field—how and why written language is produced, understood, learned, and taught in a variety of contexts—demands investigations from a variety of methodological approaches" (407).

If we want to understand religious rhetorics more fully—as sources of conflict, elements of diversity, shapers of culture, dimensions of writing and critical thought, and influences on social/political movements—we should interrogate and expand our methodological repertoire for approaching them. Recently, scholars such as Emily Cope and Ringer have conducted qualitative studies to explore Christian rhetorics, which is a valuable addition to the growing body of research in this area and a welcome expansion of the methods used to study it (see Cope and Ringer, this volume). As Catherine Marshall and Gretchen Rossman note in *Designing Qualitative Research*, "the qualitative approach to research is uniquely suited to uncovering the unexpected and exploring new avenues" (38). Religious rhetorics are a relatively "new avenue" in the scholarship of rhetoric and composition, and in this chapter I argue for an approach to investigating religious rhetorics that incorporates empirical qualitative methods as traditionally employed in the social sciences with modes of inquiry more common in rhet/comp. I call this approach empirical hybridity. While many of the scholars who reflect on their experience with a Christian student to analyze religious rhetorics do adopt certain qualitative *methods*, what I advocate is a robust, qualitative *methodology* that should be intentionally designed before research begins.

I employed empirical hybridity for a study I conducted that examined Christian rhetorics as they operate within college writing classrooms at a large, public, Midwestern university (henceforth, PMU). I used surveys and interviews of writing instructors and undergraduate Christian students to provide new insight into the relationship between Christianity and composition courses—in particular, how students' religious rhetorics affect instructors' pedagogies, the student–instructor relationship, and student engagement. The study combined empirical research design and analysis informed by social sciences with analysis of composition scholarship. What this meant for data analysis was that while hypotheses and claims were formed based on evidence from collected data, I sought out connections (and contradictions) between these hypotheses and claims and the arguments forwarded by other, published scholars. The integration of data and scholarship allows researchers to add multifaceted empirical data to an area of study traditionally grounded in teacher-based research. This is particularly valuable for exploring and engaging the many competing perspectives that come into play when we study religious rhetorics.

DEFINING EMPIRICAL HYBRIDITY

Empirical hybridity is a multimethodological approach to research that joins social sciences criteria for ethical research design, data collection, and validity with rhet/comp's emphasis on interdisciplinarity, intertextuality, and rhetorical argument. In some ways, empirical hybridity is similar to what Lee Nickoson proposes in "Revisiting Teacher Research." Nickoson suggests expanding "the models of teacher-research to include historical studies, interview and survey research, and discourse analysis, among others" (105). For Nickoson, this expansion entails bringing together a team of researchers working from various perspectives, such as faculty from multiple disciplines, to create "multimethodological, robustly collaborative inquiry" (108). While empirical hybridity is not strictly related to teacher research and does not necessitate multiple researchers, it does call for the inclusion of multiple *types* of data collection and analysis. A researcher using empirical hybridity might usefully combine methods such as surveys, interviews, focus groups, and observations, which can open new possibilities for scholarship.

Bob Broad's articulation of the differences between textual-qualitative research and empirical-qualitative research is also useful in defining empirical hybridity. Textual-qualitative researchers, Broad says, "take published written texts as their main pool of data," whereas empirical-qualitative researchers are most interested in "things people do, say, or write in day-to-day life," rather than published texts (199). Though he complicates this binary by noting that scholarship often presents both kinds of data, he distinguishes the two types based on the kind of data that rests "at the heart" of the research (199). Empirical hybridity requires that both empirical *and* textual data lie at the heart of the research; it not only incorporates data from lived experience but also treats published scholarship as data, which often represent the lived experiences of the writer. In other words, scholarship is not only functioning to provide a theoretical framework, a historical context, or a literature review; it is itself analyzed alongside—and assists in the analysis of—data collected from respondents as well.[3]

Empirical researchers use scholarship to frame and contextualize their work. While that is one way of using empirical and textual approaches together, empirical hybridity asks published texts to play a much more central role. In addition to providing context and background, ideas found in the published texts are put in direct conversation with the researcher's qualitative data. Empirical hybridity thus blurs the distinction between empirical and textual evidence. Both types of evidence were vital to my own study, with qualitative data analyzed alongside "textual" data. For example, one of the instructors interviewed for my study, Paige, wrestled with her reactions to Christian rhetorics in the classroom. Paige reflects on the difficulty of encountering a belief that strikes her as ignorant or discriminatory, particularly when it is "a belief [she] won't be able to move." Not only did I look at Paige's thoughts in conjunction with the data I collected from other instructors, but I also put them alongside the published voices of Douglas Downs and Juanita Smart, both of whom recount their own struggles with Christian student perspectives that they found troubling. Doing so places Paige in the context of an ongoing thread of inquiry for writing instructors and scholars and lends weight to what might otherwise be dismissed as the opinion of a single instructor at a single institutional site. Paige's reflections are compelling, but they become more significant when viewed in light of others' perspectives on this issue.

At the same time, Downs's and Smart's articles, each of which discusses the work of only one student, become part of a larger discussion as well, their experiences linked to those of the interviewed instructors. In other words, it's not data (e.g., student perspectives) versus the experts (e.g., published scholarship); it's one kind of data alongside another, both with the authority to shape and challenge the other. Such positioning elevates the status of student, graduate instructor, and contingent faculty voices without diminishing the status of published voices. Given how often the issue of power—historical, cultural, rhetorical, institutional—arises in discussions of religious rhetorics, this balance or an attempt at balance is one more reason that empirical hybridity is a helpful approach in this area of study. New voices can contest scholars' claims, but they can also help to confirm or extend published ideas, particularly those developed in response to a single subject.

THE BENEFITS OF A HYBRID METHODOLOGY

Putting claims and hypotheses developed from the qualitative data in conversation with scholarship[4] is a rhetorical move that would be out of place in purely social scientific research, where data results tend to be isolated and presented in an independent section (often labeled "findings" or "results"). A researcher adopting empirical hybridity still employs methods of rigorous interpretation according to accepted social sciences criteria but also examines the findings in light of and in response to themes and issues emerging from scholarship in rhet/comp and possibly other areas.

For example, a quarter of the Christian students surveyed for my study noted that writing was a form of self-expression, and religious discourses were therefore a natural and necessary element of religious students' work. A few went so far as to say that excluding such discourses went against the university's promotion of diversity, and lamented what they perceived as a limited view of diversity at the school. If I had been conducting a traditional social scientific study, the expectation would have been for these student responses to be presented as stand-alone data. An empirically hybrid approach allowed me to hear echoed in these responses the concern of Jewish Studies scholar Susan Handelman, who notes that "while we encourage a very free discourse about political and sexual identity, we are silent about our spiritual sides" (204). It also allowed me to grapple with Handelman's claim alongside the students' perspectives. This mutually informative relationship between student data and scholarship highlights one of the greatest advantages of empirical hybridity as an approach for studying religious rhetorics: it can be used to invite into research voices that are not always present.

Inviting these voices allows for a richer understanding of how religious rhetorics are shaping the experiences of various groups across institutional contexts. The writing instructors I surveyed and interviewed were graduate students and lecturers, most of whom were not reading or producing scholarship in rhet/comp. Their perspectives are important because these are the people teaching many of the writing courses across the nation (especially at large research universities). Surveys and interviews allowed them to speak for themselves and to describe lived experiences. Using empirical hybridity to investigate a potentially touchy issue such as religious rhetorics creates space for participants who are sometimes stereotyped—student, instructor, or otherwise—to make their own perspectives heard. Researchers using empirical hybridity to examine religious rhetorics can gain a more complex view of misunderstood or underrepresented groups and a fuller sense of those participants' perspectives.

In my own study, putting the seldom-heard voices of Christian students, graduate student instructors, and lecturers in conversation with existing scholarship allowed me to determine the extent to which their perspectives align with those of scholars writing about religious rhetorics. In doing so, I was also able to identify certain ideas and beliefs that aren't represented in the scholarship. For example, when asked whether it was appropriate for students to incorporate Christian discourse into academic writing, a number of instructors responded that they would be acceptable in personal but not academic writing—and left it at that. The distinction between the personal and the academic is one that scholars in rhet/comp have long since abandoned. As such, little if any discussion in recent scholarship concerning religiously committed students addresses this distinction in light of instructor perceptions regarding Christian discourse. Thus, there remains a need to further examine the ways students and instructors perceive the inclusion of religious rhetorics in personal versus academic writing—and how those perceptions may align with or depart from those of rhet/comp scholars who may not see such distinctions as salient. As this example suggests, one advantage of using empirical hybridity is identifying new avenues for future research as well as possible scholarly conversations that aren't yet taking place. Considering that scholarly attention to the role of religious rhetorics in relation to rhet/comp is a relatively new phenomenon, gaps in our professional discourse that help identify new avenues for future research are important.

Empirical hybridity also allows for replication because it can be analyzed and evaluated according to formal standards—for participant recruitment and consent, for data analysis, for establishing validity, for transparency regarding one's role and biases as researcher, and so forth. Rebecca Rickly argues that replication is key to maintaining and developing rigor as we explore new research methods. "By replicating existing research," she writes, "we know that the design is workable, and we are looking to see how the application in different contexts might influence the outcome" (266). Religious rhetorics are inevitably shaped by geography, institutional type, and student population, among other factors, and using an empirically hybrid research design means that researchers can replicate the study in additional contexts or by using different demographics. Replicating the study I conducted at PMU at a small private university in the Northeast, for example, would likely lead to significant points of overlap and divergence. Any researcher could refer to the Methods section of my completed study, find my survey questions, and use that same survey in different contexts in order to generate additional data and uncover new patterns of response. As such patterns accumulate, findings are potentially generalizable in a way that those emerging from a single study are not.

DEVELOPING EMPIRICALLY HYBRID RESEARCH

There is no single correct way to develop research of this nature; much depends upon the research goals, target population, issue in question, and institutional context. In my own study, I investigated Christian discourses in order to explore their relationships to discourses of rhet/comp. I decided to work with both undergraduate Christian students and non-tenured instructors because these two populations are rarely afforded the chance to speak for themselves in scholarship and because I believed that the disciplinary conversation surrounding Christian rhetorics would benefit from their perspectives. PMU's status as a public university meant that my institutional context was not one that came with official ties to any particular religious tradition (as a religiously affiliated institution might). These factors shaped my research design.

Of course, all research starts with a question or a set of questions that determine the specific qualitative methods and analytical tools used to answer it. There are, however, methods for conducting research and for analyzing data that will likely be especially useful for researchers planning to use empirical hybridity to explore religious rhetorics. In particular, surveys and interviews open a host of questions that are significant to a deeper understanding of the interplay between religious rhetorics and rhet/comp—questions, for example, about what a certain group of students believes about the relationship of academic work to spiritual development, about how faculty talk to their students about the role of religious rhetorics in the classroom, or about how students and teachers negotiate conflict concerning religious rhetorics.

Surveys

Religion can be both deeply personal and politically/socially loaded, so a form of data collection that allows for anonymity grants researchers a view of religious rhetorics—and of the people who use, reject, or are affected by them—that they may not otherwise see. Surveys allow participants to write honestly and openly about their experiences and ideas without having to worry about the potential impact on their reputation or their relationships with others. A student surveyed for my study wrote, "I have felt scared to share my views [at PMU]. Through observation, views of Christians or from a Christian view didn't receive weight, weren't considered intelligent or valid." Considering the role that fear played into this student's use (or avoidance) of religious rhetorics, an anonymous survey may have felt like a relatively safe place to articulate his or her experience.

In addition to the qualitative data provided by these responses, surveys also offer *quantitative* data that help shape interpretation of the responses. For example, as I analyzed my survey data, I compared the number of instructors who said that it was appropriate to draw on religious discourses in academic writing with the numbers of students who said that it was appropriate; the fact that these numbers differed dramatically helped me to pinpoint, and provide evidence for, a source of misunderstanding and a potential conflict between students and faculty. Working with quantitative data allowed me to form hypotheses about which problems and issues were most significant to the subjects. Quantitative data can also serve as a lens through which to examine and question the stereotypes and entrenched ideas surrounding religious rhetorics.

My project, though not especially large as qualitative studies go, brought together the voices of more than eighty individuals, which allowed for the identification of patterns of response and for descriptions not possible with a smaller sample. For example, the students who participated in my study challenged an all-too-common portrayal of Christian students in rhetoric and composition, namely, that they refuse to think critically about their beliefs, as is evidenced by examples such as Anderson's "Cathy," Downs's "Keith," Gooburn's "Luke," and Perkins's "Clifford." Some students in my study spoke thoughtfully about their desire to engage with people whose ideas differed from theirs and to be pushed intellectually by their instructors and peers. The instructor participants similarly troubled a broader cultural assumption about anti-Christian/antireligion faculty; they had a range of responses to Christian students and rhetorics, often demonstrating sincere consideration for their Christian students and arguing for greater inclusion of religious rhetorics in the writing classroom. Combating widely held assumptions and stereotypes is crucial for fostering productive conversations about religious rhetorics, and empirical hybridity is one useful tool in that struggle.

Interviews

Interviews allow the researcher to talk individually with a subset of participants, and they provide more in-depth discussion of the topic at hand. Interviews don't have to follow a script; as Mary Brenner notes, in open-ended interviews, "the intent is to understand informants on their own terms" and this type of interview "gives an informant the space to express meaning in his or her own words and to give direction to the interview process" (357). A "grand tour" question can be an effective way to begin the interviews that are part of empirically hybrid research. Brenner describes a grand tour question as one that asks the informant to speak broadly about the subject matter; this helps the researcher identify issues of importance to the informant and choose follow-up (or "minitour") questions that build on the foundation laid by the grand tour question (358).[5] Employing a conversational, semistructured interview style (after asking the initial grand tour question) allows participants to talk freely about whatever seems most significant to them and allows researchers to remain open to the unexpected—one need not anticipate every possible way that religious rhetorics influence writing, the classroom, student–teacher interactions, and so forth (likely an impossible task, anyway). Rather, the interviewee is free to help direct the conversation and reveal unforeseen features of religious rhetorics in the course of this semistructured interaction.

As I conducted an interview with a participant named Isabelle, for instance, I was struck by her thoughts on why some instructors have negative responses to Christian students (which she had mentioned previously). She hypothesizes that the negativity is based not so much on instructors' personal experiences with or feelings about Christianity but on the fact that instructors may see Christian students as too rigidly set in their worldview:

> [M]aybe another thing that professors may think is that once you have these beliefs that you really believe, you're already almost molded, whereas you're molded into-it almost makes you who you are [. . .]. Maybe, almost—you're stuck or you're not as—you can't think as creatively because you're already—you've got a lot of energy in one place.

Isabelle is, in fact, picking up on a concern voiced by some instructors about students with strong religious faith—that they are unable or unwilling to consider other perspectives or ideas. In Isabelle's words, students may appear to be "stuck" or unable to "think as creatively." The use (twice) of the word *molded* is worth noting, because it calls to mind the notion of education as a process by which passive students are shaped in particular ways by the instructor. The problem cited here, however, is that Christian students are "already almost molded," thereby proving resistant to the influences of the course or the instructor. In this case, the interview allowed a twenty-one-year-old neuroscience major to offer an insightful hypothesis about why some instructors may have reservations about working with Christian students—a hypothesis that was then put into conversation with published scholars discussing the same issue.

Also stemming directly from this semistructured interview were some useful, challenging questions that Isabelle's comments raised about Christian rhetorics in relation to pedagogy: What *are* we expecting from religiously committed students in our classrooms? In what ways do we seek to shape our students—and are we open to being shaped by them? Are we looking at Christian students and rhetorics from a "deficit" perspective? These questions developed organically from the interview. The discovery of unexpected lines of thought—one of the primary benefits of using qualitative methods more generally—is fostered by an empirically hybrid research design that incorporates semistructured interviews.

Discourse Analysis

Ellen Barton defines discourse analysis broadly as "the study of the ways that language is organized in texts and contexts"; more specifically, she writes, "discourse analysis can investigate features of language as small and specific as aspects of sentence structure, or it can investigate features of texts and contexts as large and diffuse as genres and sociocultural world views" (57). Discourse analysis allows us to look closely at discursive acts and form hypotheses about the realities that are reflected and constructed by them. Using discourse analysis, researchers examine subjects' responses (say, to survey and interview questions) with an eye for what these responses reveal about how participants are valuing certain practices over others, about how their beliefs shape their perspectives, about how they view others, and about how they respond to discourses that challenge their view of the world.

Take as an example the following brief excerpt from instructor Yvonne's interview transcript. I have marked with italics words and phrases that I paid particular attention to in analyzing this passage:

> PMU seems to me to go out of its way to really be, while separate, *very accommodating and tolerating of all religions*. So, so that feels *appropriate* to me. But at the same time, *I wasn't brought up in a very religious environment*, and *I don't know if I were someone who really did identify as an extremely devout person, I'm not sure. I don't know* how it would feel to me [. . .].

She begins with a strong evaluative statement about PMU's actions toward religion—it is "very accommodating and tolerating," and Yvonne deems this "appropriate." Immediately after sharing this perspective, however, Yvonne acknowledges that her own position as someone not brought up in a religious environment may influence her interpretation. As she considers how an "extremely devout" person might feel, her uncertainty about how that subject position might make her feel about PMU becomes clear in her use of "I'm not sure" and two uses of "I don't know." From these observations of Yvonne's language, I surmised that she recognizes the ways in which background and identity shape one's perspective and that she is unsure of how devout religious students experience PMU. I also noted, as I considered this excerpt in its larger context, that Yvonne's depiction of PMU as accommodating to religious belief seems to contradict an earlier statement she made during the interview that "outing" oneself as a Christian was a risky prospect for students.

Discourse analysis may also draw attention to voices or ways of knowing that have traditionally been marginalized or that have been discussed in a reductive way. This is a significant advantage when researching a topic such as Christian rhetorics, because believers are sometimes caricaturized and stereotyped based on preconceived notions about their beliefs and practices. By studying the discourses of members of particular groups, researchers can make these discourses more visible, and contribute to a fuller and more nuanced sense of how various groups—and individuals within those groups—make sense of the world (Cairney and Ashton; Godley). Such complexity works against oversimplified representations of particular communities and allows new voices to trouble stereotypes and challenge assumptions about how certain rhetorics operate. My study, for example, incorporates the written and spoken language of forty-five Christian students; though this is a relatively small number, there are a wide range of opinions and motivating factors even within this subset of Christian students. The data reveal both positive and negative student experiences in writing courses, a diverse array of ideas about writing and writing instructors, and patterns of uncertainty surrounding how religious discourses fit into a public university setting. Discourse analysis as part of an empirically hybrid design contributes to a multidimensional (though still partial) view of Christian rhetorics—an image that resists easy categorization and definition.

Putting the Qualitative Data in Conversation with Existing Scholarship

As previously noted, empirical hybridity combines research design and analysis informed by social sciences with analysis of scholarship; the researcher seeks out connections (and contradictions) between his or her initial hypotheses and claims (based on evidence from collected data) and the claims forwarded by other scholars. For example, when I discussed instructors' statements about Christian students' power or vulnerability, I put emergent patterns from the findings in dialogue with scholars who have also commented on issues of power in relation to Christian students. Doing so allowed me to situate my analysis of instructor data in the broader context of scholarship focusing on Christian students in the writing classroom and in higher education and to add a data set to this developing area of study. As findings form and develop, analyzing them in relation to other kinds of data (i.e., comparing the responses to surveys and interviews) and to scholarship helps researchers see whether or not a hypothesis that evolved from data analysis is supported (or contradicted) by other sources.[6]

Putting the results drawn from qualitative methods into conversation with scholarship constitutes a useful form of triangulation (see Yin 15), and engaging with other scholars in this way helps us to identify specific contributions that our own work makes, acknowledge and wrestle with points of discrepancy or doubt, and raise new questions. For example, the data I collected from Christian students at PMU complicated the image of the "problem student" often presented in scholarship about Christian rhetorics. Many student respondents demonstrated awareness and fear of the "judgmental" label and worried about not being liked by instructors or peers. Some expressed frustration with the conflation of Christian and conservative, noting the often-erroneous assumptions others made about their politics or stance on social issues. This is not to say that scholarship focusing on a difficult experience with a Christian student is somehow inaccurate or unimportant; it is to say, rather, that scholarship and the data collected in an empirically hybrid study can be used to complicate, challenge, confirm, and inform one another.

Validity, Empirical Hybridity, and Religious Rhetorics

The notion of validity or credibility[7] differs dramatically between the social sciences and rhet/comp. While rhet/comp scholarship can establish validity via demonstrated knowledge of the field, sound logic, sensitivity to diversity, and acknowledgment of counterarguments, social scientific research follows specific protocols for research design and gathering or interpreting data and grounds all claims in the data collected. Such protocols include obtaining institutional review board approval to work with human subjects, explaining the study goals and design to potential participants, protecting participants' anonymity, triangulating data during analysis, and soliciting participants' feedback on that analysis through member checking, among others.

It is especially important that researchers using empirical hybridity to explore religious rhetorics articulate the reasoning behind the research design to participants and obtain informed consent from those subjects, as a way to help establish trust. Religious rhetorics have the power to trigger strong emotional responses, and it is critical for researchers dealing with them to create an atmosphere in which subjects feel comfortable. For example, religious believers may be concerned that they will be mocked, cast as anti-intellectual, or assumed to be speaking for others. Establishing an atmosphere of trust is crucial not only in eliciting rich data, but also in making sure that participants—some of whom may be considered part of a vulnerable population—feel comfortable and encounter minimal psychological risk (see Cope and Ringer, this volume; see also Mortensen and Kirsch). Taking time at the outset to articulate the reasoning behind the research and the study design can go a long way in establishing that trust.

Another invaluable way to build trust is for the researcher to demonstrate the validity of his or her procedure for data analysis and then to share some of the specific findings. Participants want to know that they are not being judged and that their words will be represented accurately and fairly. Therefore, in empirical hybridity, subjects are invited into the analytical and interpretive process. Member checking, a facet of social sciences research in which the researcher solicits feedback from subjects on the analysis of survey or interview data, allows subjects to raise objections to the analysis of their ideas and ask questions, clarify points, and offer additional insights. Member checking enhances validity by increasing the certainty that the researcher is "accurately portraying the *meaning* attached by participants to what is being studied" (Johnson 285). While analyzing my own data, I sent an e-mail to each interview participant, asking him or her to read two brief excerpts from my work that incorporated and analyzed his or her language (and offering to share more with the participant if he or she chose). I invited participants to ask questions, to express points of confusion, to correct me if they thought I'd misinterpreted them, or to elaborate on a point they'd made in their interview. Doing so allowed me to assert claims more confidently, knowing that the participants themselves understood and supported them.

Not all participants responded, and most of those who did were supportive of my analysis. A couple of them expanded usefully on points they had raised, and one instructor troubled my reference to her as a "nonreligious instructor." She wrote,

> I'm having mixed reactions to the label "nonreligious instructor." On the one hand, as an instructor, I don't think of religion as influencing my pedagogy or practice and, in fact, feel compelled to let students know that arguments based on religion will not be effective with me if that is the only type of evidence they use. On the other hand, I don't think of myself, personally, as nonreligious (maybe this goes back to the public/private divide that came up in the interview). I'm unaffiliated and non-practicing, but think and talk about faith and God on a somewhat regular basis and can be fiercely protective over people's religious views/rights/beliefs in my personal life. But, I think, ultimately, that because you are using nonreligious with instructor and because you are focusing on what happens in the classroom, I'm fine with you choosing/using that label . . . for some reason, I felt compelled to complicate the issue a little.

I followed up with her, and we worked together until we found something she was comfortable with (in this case, we agreed that I would use the term *nonreligious instructor* but would include a footnote in which I complicated the label by quoting part of the preceding response). While collaborating in this way with respondents may be uncomfortable and complicate data analysis, it also allows the relationships between researcher and respondent and researcher and data to evolve and remain dynamic. Such openness and transparency also help protect vulnerable subjects (e.g., students, minors) by granting them power over their own and the researcher's words. While this would be an important consideration in research about any sensitive issue, it is uniquely significant in relation to religious rhetorics. Institutions of higher education—and the faculty who teach in them—are often characterized as hostile to religion, and to traditional religious belief in particular (Claerbaut; Edwards; Marsden; Nye; Turner). Whether or not this characterization is fair, it means that academic researchers must take extra steps to assure subjects that they are pursuing their research questions in good faith.

When it comes to analysis, researchers always risk seeing in data what they *want* to see, and it is important to push against the temptation to mold data to fit a particular hypothesis or support a claim, or to ignore data that disconfirms a favored theory. The design of empirical hybridity—with its parameters of validity and ethical research practice and its verification of research findings against existing scholarship (as well as against participants' own interpretations via member checking)—constrains and challenges the researcher's interpretive tendencies. Researchers using empirical hybridity must take reasonable steps to avoid unfounded generalizations, interrogate assumptions, represent others as accurately as possible, acknowledge any limitations of their findings, and reveal areas of uncertainty. This may be particularly significant as we research religious rhetorics, tangled up as they are with sociopolitical conflicts, diverse cultures, and deeply personal commitments.

For example, it would have been convenient for me to be able to refer to the student participants in my study as *evangelical* or *born again*, given the role that faith played in their personal and academic lives and their participation in specific Christian organizations. However, the fact that no student participants described themselves or their religious communities in this way made it seem unwarranted and perhaps unethical to apply these terms to them. The adjectives typically appearing in front of *Christian* in order to identify a group of believers often carry pejorative connotations. *Born again* and *fundamentalist* are two examples of descriptors sometimes used to depict specific Christians as radical, zealous, conservative, or intolerant. As Emily Cope and Jeff Ringer discuss elsewhere in this volume, even *evangelical* represents a "troubled term," as it is sometimes used as a more polite-sounding stand-in for *fundamentalist* or *conservative*. Avoiding labels that don't develop organically from the data means resisting impulses the researcher may have to project her own preconceptions onto the participants. Resisting such impulses may also help lay a foundation for "a willingness to acknowledge difference while remaining open to the necessity of respectful address to others and their positions" (Crowley 22).

CONCLUSION

There is a growing acknowledgment of the need for increased scholarly attention to religious rhetorics and of the importance of this scholarship to the work of rhet/comp (Daniell; Dively; Perkins; Vander Lei and kyburz; Wallace). Complicating any great push forward in this area, however, is the fact that religion tends to make many of us uncomfortable. Some scholars remain suspicious of religious rhetorics, especially as they relate to intellectual work. Sociologists Neil Gross and Solon Simmons, in their 2006 research, found that "while most professors believed in at least the possibility of God's existence, they were more than twice as likely to be skeptics or atheists as the general population" (Barlett). Of course, being a skeptic or an atheist does not prohibit a person from engaging sincerely and productively with religious rhetorics; in fact, it may allow the researcher to maintain a helpful cognitive and emotional distance from the data. However, if we inhabit an academic culture that tends to marginalize religious rhetorics, we have to be vigilant about finding effective and ethical ways of studying them—particularly when we are analyzing rhetorics that we may not like or fully understand.

I believe that empirical hybridity is a particularly useful way to study religious rhetorics because it forces the researcher to take a step back from initial reactions and responses in order to establish a valid and transparent means of conducting research—a form of research that can be replicated using different participant groups or in different contexts. Empirical hybridity can invite in the voices of individuals who enact or are affected by various religious rhetorics and put them in conversation with the published voices already found in scholarship. By doing so, empirically hybrid research extends anecdotal scholarship by weaving individual experiences into an ongoing, collaborative discussion. Such complex and multifaceted conversations are necessary in order for rhetorical scholars to engage with religious rhetorics more rigorously and understand how they are shaping and reshaping the topography of our field.

NOTES

1 DePalma uses a pragmatic lens to situate religious rhetorics as rhetorical resources, Geiger examines the interplay of discourses surrounding religion and sexuality, and Ringer analyzes the complicated relationship between writing and identity for evangelical students composing in and for a secular context.

2 Though I focus primarily on rhetoric and composition—the field I most identify with—I believe that this discussion is relevant to those working in communication and other fields related to rhetorical education, as well.

3 The use of scholarship as data is especially fitting in the realm of religious rhetorics, as more and more published scholarship is presenting qualitative data. Rather than acting as theoretical frames or pieces of lit reviews, these texts can function as data themselves, complementing and challenging a researcher's own qualitative data.

4 The scholarship need not be limited to the field of rhet/comp. Research in fields such as education, communication, philosophy, and religious studies may be useful as well.

5 My grand tour question, for both instructors and students, was, "Why were you interested in participating in this interview and talking about Christian discourses?"

6 See, for example, chapter 3 of *When God's Word Isn't Good Enough*, in which I discuss instructor data in relation to existing scholarship to form hypotheses about instructors' expectations for the use of religious rhetorics in an academic setting and their frustration with some students' use of these rhetorics.

7 Some scholars, such as Juliet Corbin, favor "credibility" over "validity." Corbin feels that "validity" carries too many quantitative implications that do not apply neatly to qualitative research (Corbin and Strauss 301).

REFERENCES

Anderson, Chris. "The Description of an Embarrassment: When Students Write about Religion." *ADE Bulletin* 94 (1989): 12–15.

Barlett, Thomas. "Some Evangelicals Find the Campus Climate Chilly—but Is That About Faith, or Politics?" *The Chronicle of Higher Education* 54.5 (September 28, 2007): B6.

Barton, Ellen. "Linguistic Discourse Analysis: How the Language in Texts Works." *What Writing Does and How It Does It*. Ed. Charles Bazerman and Paul Prior. Mahwah: Lawrence Erlbaum, 2004. 57–82.

Brenner, Mary E. "Interviewing in Educational Research." *Handbook of Complementary Methods in Education Research*. Ed. Judith L. Green et al. Mahwah: Lawrence Erlbaum, 2006. 357–70.

Broad, Bob. "Strategies and Passions in Empirical Qualitative Research." Nickoson and Sheridan 197–209.

Cairney, Trevor, and Jean Ashton. "Three Families, Multiple Discourses: Parental Roles, Constructions of Literacy and Diversity of Pedagogic Practice. *Linguistics and Education* 13:3 (2002): 303–45.

Carter, Shannon. "Living Inside the Bible (Belt)." *College English* 69.6 (2007): 572–95.

Claerbaut, David. *Faith and Learning on the Edge: A Bold New Look at Religion in Higher Education*. Grand Rapids: Zondervan, 2004.

Corbin, Juliet, and Anselm Strauss. *Basics of Qualitative Research*. 3rd ed. Thousand Oaks: Sage, 2008.

Crowley, Sharon. *Toward a Civil Discourse: Rhetoric and Fundamentalism*. Pittsburgh: U of Pittsburgh P, 2006.

Daniell, Beth. "Composing (as) Power." *College Composition and Communication* 45.2 (1994): 238–46.

DePalma, Michael-John. "Re-envisioning Religious Discourses as Rhetorical Resources in Composition Teaching: A Pragmatic Response to the Challenge of Belief." *College Composition and Communication* 63.2 (2011). 219–43.

Dively, Rhonda Leathers. "Religious Discourse in the Academy: Creating a Space by Means of Poststructuralist Theories of Subjectivity." *Composition Studies* 21.2 (1993): 91–101.

Downs, Douglas. "True Believers, Real Scholars, and Real True Believing Scholars: Discourses of Inquiry and Affirmation in the Composition Classroom." Vander Lei and kyburz 39–55.

Edwards, Mark U, Jr. *Religion on Our Campuses*. New York: Palgrave, 2006.

Geiger, II, TJ. "Unpredictable Encounters: Religious Discourse, Sexuality, and the Free Exercise of Rhetoric." *College English* 75.3 (2013): 248–69.

Godley, Amanda. "Literacy Learning as Gendered Identity Work." *Communication Education* 52.3–4 (2003): 273–85.

Goodburn, Amy. "It's a Question of Faith: Discourses of Fundamentalism and Critical Pedagogy in the Writing Classroom." *JAC: A Journal of Rhetoric, Culture, & Politics* 18.2 (1998): 333–53.

Handelman, Susan. "'Stopping the Heart': The Spiritual Search of Students and the Challenge to a Professor in an Undergraduate Literature Course." *Religion, Scholarship, & Higher Education.* Ed. Andrea Sterk. South Bend: U of Notre Dame P, 2002. 202–29.

Johnson, R. Burke. "Examining the Validity Structure of Qualitative Research." *Education* 118.2 (1997): 282–92.

Marsden, George. *The Soul of the American University: From Protestant Establishment to Established Nonbelief.* New York: Oxford UP, 1994.

Marshall, Catherine, and Gretchen B. Rossman. *Designing Qualitative Research.* 3rd ed. Thousand Oaks: Sage, 1999.

Montesano, Mark, and Duane Roen. "Religious Faith, Learning, and Writing: Challenges in the Classroom." Vander Lei and kyburz 84–98.

Mortensen, Peter, and Gesa E. Kirsch, eds. *Ethics and Representation in Qualitative Studies of Literacy.* Urbana: NCTE, 1996.

Nickoson, Lee. "Revisiting Teacher Research." Nickoson and Sheridan 101–12.

———, and Mary P. Sheridan, eds. *Writing Studies Research in Practice: Methods and Methodologies.* Carbondale: Southern Illinois UP, 2012.

Nye, Abby. *Fish Out of Water: Surviving and Thriving as a Christian on a Secular Campus.* Green Forest: New Leaf P, 2005.

Perkins, Priscilla. "'A Radical Conversion of the Mind': Fundamentalism, Hermeneutics, and the Metanoic Classroom." *College English* 63.5 (2001): 585–611.

Rickly, Rebecca. "After Words: Postmethodological Musings." Nickoson and Sheridan 261–68.

Ringer, Jeffrey M. "The Consequences of Integrating Faith into Academic Writing: Casuistic Stretching and Biblical Citation." *College English* 75.3 (2013): 270–96.

Smart, Juanita. "'Frankenstein or Jesus Christ?' When the Voice of Faith Creates a Monster for the Composition Teacher." Vander Lei and kyburz 11–23.

Thomson-Bunn, Heather. *When God's Word Isn't Good Enough: Exploring Christian Discourses in the College Composition Classroom.* Diss. U of Michigan, 2009.

Turner, James. "Does Religion Have Anything Worth Saying to Scholars?" *Religion, Scholarship, & Higher Education: Perspectives, Models, and Future Prospects.* Ed. Andrea Sterk. South Bend: U of Notre Dame P, 2002. 16–21.

Vander Lei, Elizabeth and bonnie lenore kyburz, eds. *Negotiating Religious Faith in the Composition Classroom.* Portsmouth, NH: Heinemann, 2005.

Vander Lei, Elizabeth, et al., eds. *Renovating Rhetoric in Christian Tradition.* Pittsburgh: U of Pittsburgh P, 2014.

Wallace, David L. "Transcending Normativity: Difference Issues in College English." *College English* 68.5 (2006): 502–30.

Yin, Robert K. "Case Study Methods." *Handbook of Complementary Methods in Education Research.* Ed. Judith L. Green et al. Mahwah: Lawrence Erlbaum, 2006. 111–22.

8 Evangelical Masculinity in *The Pilgrim Boy*

A Historical Analysis with Methodological Implications

Brenda Glascott

When constructing histories of nineteenth-century rhetoric and rhetorical education, rhetoricians have tended to look in the most likely places: universities and schools, textbooks, and rhetorical theory written by academics. Feminist scholars such as Jacqueline Jones Royster, Roxanne Mountford, Shirley Wilson Logan, Lisa Shaver, Nan Johnson, and Jessica Enoch, among others, have helped us see beyond the usual historical sites in order to locate women's rhetorical activity in clubs and domestic spaces and on lecture platforms and deathbed pulpits (Royster and Kirsch 32–34). *Mapping Christian Rhetorics* invites us to engage in further methodological expansion by exploring uncharted sites in our current histories and seeking artifacts that help us navigate and name previously unrecognized terrain. In this chapter, I invite rhetoricians to interrogate their methodological assumptions undergirding nineteenth-century historiography by investigating the rhetorical action made available to non-elite white males through evangelical Christianity as depicted in *The Pilgrim Boy, with Lessons from His History*, a nineteenth-century American Tract Society novella.[1] Because evangelical rhetorical action, including praying with family, testifying to neighbors, leading community prayer meetings, and teaching Sunday school, intertwines with the pilgrim boy's masculinity, *The Pilgrim Boy* (*TPB*) invites us to scrutinize how gender, rhetoric, and religion were interrelated for men. Such scrutiny reveals that some forms of nineteenth-century evangelical rhetorical action may not be as gender specific as historians of women's rhetorics have sometimes imagined. Nineteenth-century evangelical Christian rhetoric does not operate within an epistemology that strongly divides emotion from reason or domestic from public. This makes evangelical Christian rhetoric a fertile ground for developing a more nuanced analytical framework that identifies and describes the extent to which rhetorical action is gendered in the nineteenth century. It also invites rhetoricians to appreciate more fully the influence Christian rhetorics can have on gender constructions and to account for them when they are present.

My analysis of *TPB* builds on feminist rhetorical historiographical practices that allow scholars to identify groups and individuals excluded from traditional rhetorical histories. It does so by employing an interpretive lens that, though an outgrowth of feminist theory, has not yet been integrated fully into historiographical methodologies—namely, masculinity studies and gender history. Until we turn to a more comprehensive analysis of gender in rhetorical history—investigating, for instance, how nonelite evangelical men were invited to function as rhetorical beings—we cannot know how to assess the gender-specificity of women's rhetorical activities.[2] And until we account fully for the influence of religious faith on such rhetorical action, any claim we make about them may be incomplete.

THE PILGRIM BOY AND NINETEENTH-CENTURY EVANGELICAL MASCULINITY

Set in the early nineteenth century, *TPB* is an American frontier bildungs-roman that narrates the early schooling, lost adolescence, and eventual salvation of the pilgrim boy, who experiences economic hardship for his entire narrated life. The pilgrim boy is an orphan raised as a Christian. The early chapters of the novella focus on his early formal education and spiritual education. By the time he is ten, financial hardship forces the boy to work as a plowboy and give up school. His adolescence is marked by moral degradation as he progresses from telling his first lie to cursing, gambling, and eventually Universalism, which is seen as a permissive religion and thus antithetical to evangelical Christianity. The pilgrim boy marries at nineteen and struggles to support his family as a tenant farmer. Eventually, an illness leads him to convert to Christianity. The remainder of the novella follows his struggle to take up the public evangelical rhetorical action required of him to complete his conversion. This struggle is intense because the pilgrim boy lives in a "dissipated community" with a wife who dislikes Christianity (83). He ultimately converts his wife, teaches Sunday school, leads community prayer meetings, and helps establish and lead a church.

Like most tract literature, the novella is didactic, with a narrator whose interjections underscore a lesson for the reader.[3] The ultimate goal for the pilgrim boy is to work up the courage to undertake public evangelical rhetorical action. This struggle to assume this evangelical rhetorical work is intertwined with his performance of evangelical masculinity. Masculinity is still a rather new area of scholarly study (Gardiner, "Introduction"; Hobbs). As "a significant outgrowth of feminist studies" (Kimmel, "Foreword" ix), academic masculinity studies has relied on feminist methodologies for attending to gender. According to Judith Kegan Gardiner, masculinity studies has been "influenced by queer theory, 'race' studies, and various post-structuralisms as well as by the full range of feminisms" ("Introduction" 2). Masculinity studies thus investigates how masculinity functions "as ideology, as institutionally embedded with a field of power, as a set of practices engaged in by groups of men" (Kimmel, "Foreword" x). It prompts attention to masculinity as a gender construct in relation to other culturally specific identity markers, including religion.

Early attempts to theorize nineteenth-century American masculinity have emphasized the importance of autonomy and self-fashioning to its performance (see Leverenz). Such work describes the pressures on nineteenth-century American men to perform a masculine identity tied to diligent work and ever-rising fortunes, not unlike nineteenth-century bootstrapping stories and modern political rhetoric. Michael Kimmel links nineteenth-century masculinity to success in the "emerging capitalist market" that "freed individual men and destabilized them" (*Manhood*, 17). Released from antiquated expectations and roles, men had to perform the identity of the "Self-Made Man," which necessitated successful economic striving: "[s]uccess must be earned, manhood must be proved—and proved constantly" (Kimmel, *Manhood* 17). Models of nineteenth-century masculinity emphasize economic autonomy.

The performance of masculinity measured against economic daring and success has served as a counterpoint to scholars' discussions of nineteenth-century anxieties about the potentially feminizing effect of religion on masculinity. In her 1977 *Feminization of American Culture*, American literary and cultural studies scholar Ann Douglas famously bemoaned the emasculation of a robust Calvinist masculinity by the rise of a softer, liberal, non-evangelical Christianity in the nineteenth century. Douglas focuses on elite, New England non-evangelical clergymen whom she claims "courted, with whatever ambivalence, a feminized image" as a way of justifying their failure to live up to an aggressive masculine norm (91). These clergymen rejected the aggressive masculinity of the self-made man. Douglas likens these Christian men to domestic women, claiming that they often suffered from ill health and were "more drawn to their homebound, religious, and supposedly 'weaker' mothers than to their more secular-minded, active fathers [. . .]. In other words, a poor physical constitution could be linked to, even confused with interest in 'feminine,' domestic, and religious pursuits" (89). Even though her book is almost forty years old, Douglas has had a profound influence on how historians of rhetoric and literary critics conceptualize the relationship between religion and nineteenth-century masculinity (see Shaver, "Women's"). The "feminization" of religious expression in the nineteenth century would seem to be supported by other factors. Women outnumbered men in congregations and more women were gaining a foothold as preachers (Mountford 51; see also Shaver, Zimmerelli, this volume). Cultural anxiety about effeminacy and religion accounts for the "muscular Christianity" that emerged at mid-century to alleviate anxieties about the emasculation of churchmen (Mountford 56). Drawing on Richard Storr and Austin Phelps, Roxanne Mountford describes the "manly" characteristics of the muscular Christian as including courage, honesty, physical fitness and "great intellect" (54, 59).

TPB does not easily fit into this model, or any model that links the performance of masculinity with economic success or muscular Christianity. The pilgrim boy is not feminized in the story—he is a naughty boy, hunting when he should be at church; he is a dissipated young man who associates with a rough frontier crowd. The pilgrim boy's evangelical masculinity cannot be adequately understood through the trope of the self-made man. The evangelical masculinity depicted in *TPB* does not culminate with personal fortune or class climbing, but with the pilgrim boy becoming a public evangelical rhetor as a Sunday school teacher, a local preacher, and a prayer leader. Thus, the evangelical construction of masculinity depicted in the tract corresponds to historian Janet Moore Lindman's argument that evangelicalism "reshaped the performance of white masculinity" by the end of the eighteenth century, ushering in "[a] new manhood based on acts of piety, sobriety, and nonviolence" in place of "drinking, gambling, fighting, and fornicating" ("Acting" 416). Originally, evangelicalism "posed a profound challenge for white men: how to embrace the new religion, change their lives, and renounce aspects of traditional manliness without rendering themselves powerless by their new status or losing their sense of self as men" ("Acting" 396). Lindman suggests the evangelical men risked feeling emasculated by embracing a construction of masculinity that featured traits associated with femininity. Evangelical Christianity asked men to embrace "emotionalism, empathy, and corporeal spirituality," traits not normatively attached to masculinity ("Acting" 397). Eventually, in adopting the evangelical construction of masculinity, nonelite men were able to access leadership positions within evangelical communities. Because it was possible to be elected to a governing position within the church, embracing temperance, piety, and affective performance of spirituality "potentially open[ed] up new positions of power for white men, especially for those of middling or lower status" ("Acting" 414).

Though *TPB* does evidence connections between economic success and American masculinity, it reflects Lindman's description of evangelical masculinity. The pilgrim boy's failure to achieve economic success even after his conversion demonstrates how evangelicalism offered alternative expressions of masculinity. Despite his low status, the pilgrim boy accesses power through his evangelical rhetorical action by becoming a Sunday school teacher, a local preacher, and a prayer leader. These are public leadership positions the pilgrim boy assumes through his merit as a serious, humble, and emotionally demonstrative evangelical man.

In fact, the pilgrim boy's trajectory and the narrator's didactic interjections decouple masculinity and economic success from the "self-made man." In one of his interjections, the narrator assures his readers that while "Franklin was a poor boy" who "became the next man to Washington in his day," economic success is not the outcome of individual action: "[God] may withhold riches from you for your good; many boys could not bear riches, and you may be one of them; and to save your soul, he may deprive you of them in love and mercy" (*TPB* 9–10). In this version of masculinity, the boy who hopes for economic and public success has limited autonomy. He may "aim at great things" and "bend all [his] energies to that end" (9), but economic rewards are not guaranteed. God, who is benevolent and knows that riches might compromise the boy's soul, may withhold wealth. Poverty might be an expression of God's love and compassion. This message, embedded in a text produced by a middle class organization, should be understood as part of a broader context in which " 'middle-class' discourse and practice [. . .] sought to reform the culture and reading of the 'lower classes' " (Denning 46). Michael Denning's examination of the dime novel publishing industry reveals that literature produced for the laboring class emphasized honesty for men instead of self-making entrepreneurship (46). Tracts targeted the same readers as the dime novel industry.[4] Consequently, Denning provides a nuanced understanding of the masculine identities available to male tract readers.

Reformist writing aimed at "producing classes," which included "craftworkers, factory operatives, laborers, and servants," celebrated the honest character and not necessarily the success of the self-made man (Denning 45). Nonelite evangelical men were prompted to embrace virtues similar to those Denning identifies as promoted for the "producing classes." While we might see the nonelite evangelical men as benefiting more from adopting these virtues than do Denning's "producing classes" (because they use these virtues to claim leadership positions in their communities), we might also note the ways these leadership positions are circumscribed, at least in *TPB*. The pilgrim boy exercises significant influence as an evangelical rhetor, but his leadership is exercised in modest circumstances—his focus is local, and his concern is with the interior lives of his community.

Feminist revisions of nineteenth-century rhetorical history have centered on how women expanded their rhetorical space (see Shaver, this volume; Zimmerelli, this volume). Female rhetors had to negotiate ideology and the separate spheres of action and influence to which women and men were "assigned." This cultural ideal, promoted via conduct manuals and popular magazines, placed men in a public sphere where they were political and economic actors. White, middle-class women, limited to the domestic sphere, were expected to encourage their husband's (or sons') virtuous behavior in the public sphere. Women were to provide domestic refuge for public men and exemplify virtue for male relatives. Men moved between both spheres while women remained in the domestic. Although husbands occupied the hierarchical pinnacle in any family or household within this cultural ideal, wives, mothers, sisters, and daughters theoretically filled the domestic space with their virtuous influence.

Feminist historians have had to contend with the cultural ideal of separate spheres. One approach has been to recover female rhetors who participated in the public sphere; another involves examining the kinds of rhetorical action that were (im)possible in the domestic sphere. Nan Johnson, for example, argues that women "found themselves stranded in the parlor with little hope of securing a voice in public affairs" because "a conservative agenda based on gender is an obvious part of the successful promotion of rhetorical literacy throughout the nineteenth century" (14). The "stranded" women Johnson identifies are passive victims of a conservative rhetorical literacy agenda. For Johnson, women are excluded literally from particular spaces. Nina Baym has argued against literal separate spheres and cautions scholars against perpetuating its ideology. She contends that the "public sphere" must be understood as a metaphor and that "public and private were different ways of behaving in the same sphere" (Baym 11). Assuming otherwise distorts what historians will recognize as public and private modalities.

In her discussion of how separate spheres ideology overwrote women's public advocacy work as "an extension of women's domestic and maternal roles," Lisa Shaver does the kind of work Baym calls for. Shaver argues that Methodist women used rhetoric to blur boundaries between the domestic and public spheres, and that this blurring is obscured by an ideology that insists that women's rhetorical activities in the public sphere (sites such as newspapers and city streets) are domestic ("Stepping," 63). Shaver demonstrates how separate spheres ideology functioned in the nineteenth century to contain threats to it: women could not escape the parlor because whatever site they inhabited *became* the parlor.

Texts such as *TPB* also trouble how historians of rhetoric have gendered certain spaces and rhetorical activities—particularly the evangelical rhetorical activity located in domestic spaces—and prompt scholars to rethink methodological assumptions. Such historians need to carefully evaluate the usefulness of an analytical frame that distinguishes domestic from public. The pilgrim boy operates as an evangelical rhetor in domestic spaces; he uses his home for public prayer meetings and Sunday school; his outreach in the community involves going into other people's homes. These domestic spaces are the only venues available to the pilgrim boy because of the poverty in his community. Class, masculinity, and religion intersect in *TPB* to complicate associations between domestic spaces and feminine virtue in the cultural ideal of separate spheres. Like middle-class white women subject to separate spheres ideology, the pilgrim boy does not have the luxury of acting in broader political or economic spheres. Thus, his evangelical rhetoric blurs distinctions between public and domestic spheres. And like middle-class white women who undertake evangelical rhetorical action, the pilgrim boy earns his right to minister to family, friends, and neighbors by cultivating his evangelical character through the right kind of reading.

BAD BOOKS AND EVANGELICAL CHARACTER

Evangelical leadership was tied, as Lindman argues, to "merit" and depended on the community recognizing the virtuous character of the would-be leader. Good character, not economic achievement, is the goal of the masculine evangelical in *TPB*.[5] Reading is central to the development of a good evangelical character and so becomes a crucial factor in undertaking public rhetorical action. Evangelical readers, both male and female, had to practice the right ways of reading and read the right kind of materials. Bad reading risked the reader's soul.

The pilgrim boy becomes a public rhetor in the final third of the novella; the first two-thirds chart the development of his character. These developments parallel the pilgrim boy's reading habits. He learns recommended evangelical reading practices as a young child, accompanying his foster mother to frontier "preaching-place[s]" where he "sat by her side, with an old Bible, printed in 1718, in which he hunted out the proof-texts, and marked them by turning down a leaf" (23). Evangelical literacy, as described here, is interpretative, emphasizing understanding and use of textual evidence. The narrator explains:

> In those days the minister quoted his proof-texts, chapter and verse, giving the people time to find and mark them [. . .]. In those old-fashioned times, the first thing the minister did was to read and explain the portion of the Psalm to be sung, so that the people might sing with the understanding, which often took nearly an hour.
>
> (23–24)

By giving the people time to mark proof texts—Bible passages that illustrate a claim—the minister models using textual evidence as a literacy practice. Written texts, such as psalms, are understood as interpretable. According to Candy Gunther Brown, "Evangelicals understood everyday activities, such as writing, publishing, and reading, within the same framework as revival meetings or specifically religious rituals, interfacing doctrine and emotion, denominational and evangelical identity, social and religious experience" (18). For example, the Sabbath ends in *TPB* with children repeating the psalm and "giv[ing] all the divisions of the subject" because "[e]very pious household was then a Sunday-school" (25). These evangelical literacy practices—careful reading, recitation, and interpretation of psalms—are not gender specific.

The pilgrim boy's fall into sin and loss of character are accompanied by a misguided reading practice that was overly ambitious and motivated by fear and unhappiness. The narrator condemns the pilgrim boy's diligent pursuit of education (he reads on his own at night after working) because the motives driving this pursuit do not evidence trust in God. The pilgrim boy's persistence is remarkable: "before he was fifteen he has read through a good circulating library that was kept in the neighborhood, and had acquired more general information than most boys in the community where he lived" (50). Despite his diligence and prayer, "[h]e felt that God was angry with him; and in order to please him he read and prayed more. While other boys were at their play, he was at his books" (51). Because the pilgrim boy turned to books and prayer out of disappointment with his lot in life, "he was an enemy to God; he served him through fear, and not from love" (52). Outward appearance of good character—hard work, extra study, prayer—cannot attest to one's actual character or salvation.[6]

Because reading practices reflect and construct the reader's character, choosing reading material as an evangelical is highly fraught. The pilgrim boy's collapse into sin, which results in his cynicism toward God, is precipitated by reading a "bad book." His experience is echoed in other tract literature about "bad books" in which the threat posed by the books is gendered. For instance, while a female reader might be harmed by novel reading, male readers are harmed more seriously by books about religion. Wayward male readers in tract literature are much more likely than wayward female readers to become disbelievers, drunks, gamblers, and fornicators. The evangelical anxiety about bad books reflects a broader cultural anxiety about the reading of novels and sensationalist publications during the mid-nineteenth century.

As a countermeasure against "bad books," evangelical tract and Bible societies operated extensive literacy campaigns to provide and regulate the materials that readers might encounter. Tract literature that incorporates scenes of reading, writing, and schooling often allude to the benefits of reading texts provided by evangelical literacy campaigns and Sunday schools—reading the right kind of books builds character. Tract readers are encouraged to imagine that developing good character overrides any initial economic disadvantages:

> The merchant was moved with the boy's tale, and said, 'Can you not get some one who knows you to testify to your character?' The boy pulled out of his pocket a well-worn Testament; on the title page was written, 'Given as a reward of merit to a good boy, by his Sunday-school teacher.' He was employed at once, and is now a rich merchant.
>
> (*TPB* 65)

Books were frequently used as awards in Sunday schools, and this vignette instructs the tract reader about the utility of displaying good character and of the value of the Bible and other evangelical texts. This example also suggests tension between the dominant understanding of masculinity, which is tied to self-making and economic success, and evangelical masculinity, which is not. Even though the narrator had warned readers that God might benevolently withhold wealth, he still deploys the dominant cultural understanding of wealth as reward. But the story of the rich merchant does not emphasize his hard work; the most important element in the story is that a Sunday school book has given him tangible proof of good character. This is a subtle shift in the dominant narrative of achieving economic success: the goal here is to work on Christian character, not to concentrate on being a hard-working merchant's boy. *TPB* echoes other tracts and tract society reading suggestions by recommending the following to readers:

> Let the Bible be your daily companion, and make yourself familiar with such books as have been written by the best of men on doctrinal and practical piety, together with biographies of the best men that have lived in this or other ages [. . .]. While reading their lives, you are brought in contact with pure and holy men, and your tastes and character must be influenced by them.
>
> (79–80)

Through reading the right types of books, evangelical male readers are mentored by "the best men" and "pure and holy men." Books shape character.

Rhetoricians and literary scholars have documented how nineteenth-century anxiety about novel reading exposes itself in descriptions of reading in a range of secular and religious texts. Reading was widely characterized as a form of ingestion in a broad range of texts spanning the entire nineteenth century (Davidson; Mailloux, "Cultural," "Use"; Nord 113–30). Reading could be an act that nourishes or poisons the reader. According to Steven Mailloux, the nineteenth-century trope of reading as eating should be understood figuratively and literally, as "slightly different aspects of the same activity, the physical ingestion of nourishment (for mind and body)" ("Cultural" 22). This trope highlights the minefield evangelical readers faced in choosing reading material. A poor choice could radically change the reader; lingering effects pollute the blood and are difficult to flush from the system. The *TPB* narrator writes,

> The reading of bad books has done more during the last twenty years [. . .] to poison the minds of young men, lower the standard of high moral rectitude, and shut the heart against the word and Spirit of God, than almost any other evil in the land. Show me the youth that pores over tales of fiction, and drinks their intoxicating poison, and I will show you a fictitious character, vacillating and unreliable [. . .]. A family library is an index to family character; the bookcase reflects the moral features. Better not read at all, than read bad books.
>
> (77)

By consuming the text, readers risk ingesting negative character traits.[7] The character of the text becomes integrated into the reader's character. As the narrator cautions, "the time you spend in reading a bad book is so much time spent in company with a bad character, and you cannot come in contact with filth without some of it sticking to you" (76).

Corrupting texts also pose dangers by inducing a thoughtless reading practice that contrasts against the careful reading recommended by evangelical literacy. Nineteenth-century critics of the novel worried that "engrossed reading of the wrong text [was] a kind of seduction or even a state of possession" (Davidson 43). Male characters in tract literature do risk novel reading, but the pilgrim boy falls to the most "fatal" of "dangerous books": "those that oppose evangelical religion" (*TPB* 77). The pilgrim boy's corruption derives from his dalliance with Universalism. Lindman characterizes early American Universalism as an optimistic post-Revolution alternative to the dour message of Calvinism (" 'Bad' " 263). Unlike Calvinism, Universalist doctrine "preached the salvation of all people no matter what their past behavior" (Lindman, " 'Bad' " 266). Universalism combined the emotionalism of evangelicalism with the Enlightenment celebration of reason (Lindman 260). The pilgrim boy's flirtation with Universalism begins when he debates a former schoolmate who had married into a Universalist family and zealously "advanced his sentiments [about his new religion], the same that Satan preached in Eden" (*TPB* 73). The pilgrim boy longs to believe that Universalism, which is characterized as "flesh-pleasing" (76), might be true—it seemed to offer an easier path wherein one could sin and be forgiven. However, the pilgrim boy's early religious literacy training—the discussion and identification of proof texts—makes it difficult for him to accept Universalism until his friend lends him Hosea Ballou's *Treatise on the Atonement of Christ*. Ballou was the "best-known American Universalist theologian of the nineteenth century" (Holifield 228). Reading Ballou, who suggests that sin is temporary, erases the pilgrim boy's doubts: "Before he was half through the book, he began to lay plans for the gratification of all the evil desires of his heart" (73–74). The pilgrim boy then begins to doubt his Universalist faith after reading Ballou's "Notes on the Parables" and finding the "reasoning [. . .] foolish and absurd in the extreme" (74). Nonetheless, the pilgrim boy professes Universalism for four years before reconverting to evangelical Protestantism, "a flesh-crucifying system of religion" that promises salvation (76).

OVERCOMING FEAR: EVANGELICAL RHETORICAL ACTION

The pilgrim boy, he cannot consider himself fully saved until he undertakes the evangelical rhetorical action that signals his acceptance of the submission required of evangelical masculinity. The types of evangelical rhetorical action he is called to make include praying with his family, testifying to neighbors, leading community prayer meetings, and starting and teaching in a Sunday school. This undertaking is a struggle for him because he fears ridicule from his disbelieving neighbors and, most particularly, his wife. As a child, the pilgrim boy encounters persuasive evangelical speech as both scourge and salvation. For instance, in the chapter that recounts the pilgrim boy's "*first lie*," the pilgrim boy is punished with rod and rhetoric for his attempt to break the Sabbath by lying (*TPB* 31). The rhetorician in this case is his adopted mother who addresses him "with a sermon on the terrors of the law, two miles long, preached to him by the way; and a similar one on the way home" (33). The narrator assures his readers that "it was the best sermon [the pilgrim boy] had ever got; he not only felt it on his skin, but in his heart" (33). As an adult, the pilgrim boy later thanked the woman for "that very whipping" (34).

While the pilgrim boy finds eventual salvation in his early lessons, his years of dissolution are accompanied by forms of rhetoric, particularly profanity, which he mistakenly associates with masculinity: "The pilgrim boy foolishly thought that if he could swear and chew tobacco, he should be a full-grown man, and fit for all classes of society" (*TPB* 55).[8] Always a precocious student, the pilgrim boy quickly learns to "swear pretty scientifically" and to chew tobacco so that "he was fit for a ringleader; and he stepped out of his boy's clothes, booted and spurred, as a companion of young men and women" (56). The acts of swearing and chewing tobacco make the pilgrim boy feel like "a full-grown man" and reflect the normative masculinity Lindman suggests evangelical men had to reject. To complete his fall, the pilgrim boy marries an unbeliever and lives in an unbelieving community.

His reconversion is a process marked by struggle to undertake the public rhetorical action required of him as a believing Christian man. It is sparked by an illness from which he expected to die. While he lay on what he thought was his deathbed, the pilgrim boy recalls "The Bible, the sermons, and pastor's counsel, his old mother's warnings, and the religious books he had read, [which] were all arrayed against him as so many witnesses for God, testifying, I have called, but you have refused" (*TPB* 95). Evangelical rhetoric in the form of sermons, counsel, and warnings represent evidence of the pilgrim boy's willful decision to reject God. Even though illness scares the pilgrim boy into wanting to return to religion, he only begins in earnest after reading *The Afflicted Man's Companion* in which he found inspiration from the "dying sayings of Christians" (97). Saved by the witnessing of the Christians in this book, the pilgrim boy inherits the burden of spreading the word as an evangelical rhetor; his conversion remains incomplete if he fails to do so. However, he risks embarrassment as an evangelical rhetor in a hostile community.

Evangelical conversion required submission and self-abnegation of both men and women. Susan Juster has argued that evangelical conversion was not strongly gender differentiated but, instead, "involved" both "male and female converts" in "a breaking down of the unregenerate will and sense of self, and its reconstitution under the divine power of Spirit" (37). To be an evangelical meant submitting completely to a God who might withhold economic reward, regardless of one's human striving. In this way, submission, not autonomy, is the keystone to evangelical masculinity. Because of its emphasis on submission, nineteenth-century evangelical conversion necessitated alternatives to the self-made man as an expression of masculinity.

The major barrier to the pilgrim boy's conversion and his evangelical masculinity is his fear of ridicule. He felt that to be a Christian he must make "a public acknowledgement of Christ" but "shrunk from the duty" because he feared "derision" from his wife and neighbors (*TPB* 98). The pilgrim boy forces himself to "ask a blessing at his table," which "seemed to be a hard task before an irreligious wife" (99). He avoids eating at others' houses because he fears being asked to give a blessing. His courage likewise falters at home. Although he persists in asking for blessings before meals, he quails before the task of instituting family prayer: "For six months he set every Sunday night to begin. He spent hours in the woods praying to God for strength, but when night came, and the moment drew near, he would tremble like an aspen-leaf, and retire without prayer" (99). Ashamed of his cowardice, the pilgrim boy contemplates suicide, but "finally resolved to begin family worship, or die in the attempt" (100):

> [H]e arose, grasped the Bible with a trembling hand, and with a deter-mination to read a chapter and pray, or die in the attempt. He broke the silence by saying, 'My dear wife, God has said he will pour out his fury on the family that call not on his name, and I am constrained to begin to-night. Will you join me?' She was silent; he opened the Bible, the struggle was over [. . .] the duty was performed, and peace of mind followed. His wife looked alarmed, but remained silent; he told her of his long struggle; she seemed deeply impressed for a long time, but did not give evidence of a change of heart for many years after.
>
> (101)

Far from conforming to the stereotype of the nineteenth-century husband confident in his dominance over his household, the pilgrim boy is terrified to undertake evangelical rhetorical action even within his own home.

The narrator is particularly critical of men who do not initiate family prayer in their homes. In a chapter titled "Grieving God's Spirit," the narra-tor explains that family prayer is the duty of the "head of the family" (120). While many histories of female public rhetoric explore how women use evangelical belief to authorize their claims to public platforms (see Shaver, this volume; Zimmerelli, this volume), *TPB* asks us to imagine the obsta-cles to evangelical rhetorical action in the domestic space. Suggestively, the obstacle facing the pilgrim boy is fear of his wife's response, and the nar-rator assumes his male readers may identify with the pilgrim boy's "diffi-dence" in instituting family prayer. This dynamic complicates constructions of the domestic sphere as sites of virtuous female influence. The pilgrim boy's world is not neatly bifurcated into domestic and public spheres, possibly because his shaky economic footing doesn't allow for what is a middle-class privilege of marking the home off from the public. The narra-tor also presents an alternative to distinctions between domestic and public spheres: "The family altar is a quadrant, by which the piety of the church may be measured. The church is composed of families" (120). The domestic "quadrant" is indivisible from the public institution of the church.

Furthermore, far from being "the angel of the house," the pilgrim boy's wife opposes his increasing evangelical activity, calling it "wild enthusiasm" and "so much time lost" (*TPB* 137). Because the husband is faulted for emotionality and for not turning time into profitable activity, these responses resist assumptions we have of nineteenth-century gender and religion. When the pilgrim boy undertakes more public evangelical work through the influence of another man who had started a Sunday school nearby, his wife strenuously opposes his efforts. On visiting the school, the pilgrim boy sees "seventy boys and girls, mostly children of godless parents, learning to read the Bible, [and] he felt it was a good work" (129). He agrees to sponsor similar literate activity in his neighborhood, opening a Sunday school and starting a weekly prayer meeting during which "he usually read one of Burder's village sermons" (130). Both took place in his house. His efforts are rewarded with "a deep religious interest" that leads to his election as an elder of the church (130). Initially, the pilgrim boy faces resistance from his wife and declines to be an elder. However, he eventually accepts the position because he is "determined to forsake all and follow Christ" (131). The pilgrim boy's evangelical masculinity necessitates he recognize that the "Christian's life is a constant warfare," even in the home (134).

The pilgrim boy's wife remains unmoved even by the pilgrim boy's second near-death illness, which gives him the opportunity to minister and convert even more people through his deathbed pulpit. Shaver describes the deathbed pulpit as "a site of worship in which dying individuals along with the crowds surrounding their deathbeds are presented participating in prayers, devotions, hymn-singing, scripture-reading, and praise" in published memoirs ("Women's" 30). While Shaver acknowledges that male ministers are occasionally depicted as occupying deathbed pulpits, she argues that they are "sacred and feminized space[s]" ("Women's" 22). Moreover, the deathbed pulpit is a rhetorical space particularly associated with women, and women's deathbed pulpits are emotional and melodramatic as opposed to the intellectual pulpits of men (Shaver, "Women's" 30–31). *TPB* disrupts this gender distinction: the pilgrim boy uses his deathbed pulpit to offer counsel and even converts a "married woman" who "wept and trembled, and returned home a mourning penitent, and soon found peace in believing, lived some years a consistent Christian, and died rejoicing in hope of glory" (133). Depictions of his deathbed pulpit are also heavily melodramatic:

> At another time, when his family and many of his neighbors were gathered around his bed to see him die, God was pleased particularly to manifest himself [. . .]. At his bed stood a weeping wife, with three little children, poor and helpless; and by her stood some of his pupils, besides many others, in their sins. Before him heaven seemed to be open with all its glories to receive him; his physical frame nearly a skeleton [. . .]. The

tears of his wife and little children stirred all the feelings of his nature. The suspense of his mind was awful, the struggle severe. At last he cried, from the inner-most recesses of his heart, "O, Lord, if it is for thy glory, and the good of dying souls, let me live; if not, let me die."

(133)

The pilgrim boy achieves complete self-abnegation by surrendering himself to God's will, particularly because he asks to live to continue his conversion work. In its appeals to pathos and self-surrender, the pilgrim boy's deathbed pulpit resonates with those of the women Shaver explores. According to Lindman ("Acting") and Juster, however, submission and emotional display are also elements of evangelical masculinity. The pilgrim boy causes other men to occupy deathbed pulpits; he eventually converts a "gay and thought-less" young man who soon becomes ill and preaches on his own deathbed pulpit, converting his father and other family members (140). Deathbed witnessing comprises public rhetorical action: the domestic space becomes a public pulpit that attracts visitors, and stories about the dying circulate in religious publications.

CONCLUSION

The contours of the evangelical rhetorical landscape presented in *TPB* sug-gest new directions for historians of women's rhetorics, of religious rheto-rics, and of gender and rhetoric. More work needs to be done on how class intersects with gender and religion in determining under what conditions domestic spaces function as publics for emerging rhetors. Because of the opportunities for nonelite rhetorical action within evangelical Christian-ity, these Christian rhetorics are a particularly fertile ground for studying class. The features of the rhetorical activities available to the pilgrim boy as part of nonelite white evangelical masculinity are similar to those femi-nist historians of rhetoric have associated with middle-class white women rhetors. This similarity has methodological implications for historians of nineteenth-century rhetoric.

Recognizing the similarities between the rhetorical activity linked to evan-gelical masculinity in *TPB* and the activity identified with nineteenth-century women presses the need for historians of rhetoric to embrace a reorientation from women's history to *gender* history. Reconceived as such, a method-ology that focuses on gender studies more broadly conceived could help create topographical maps that chart the layered relationships between gen-der constructions and other ways identities are indexed. While gender is frequently invoked in histories of women and rhetoric, it often becomes a synonym for female.[9] When masculinity is explicitly investigated in terms of gender, as in Mountford's *The Gendered Pulpit*, elite or middle-class white masculinity is set up as a counterpoint to what Jacqueline Jones Royster and Gesa E. Kirsch call "the three Rs"—"rescuing, recovering, and re(inscribing) women into the history of rhetoric" (18).[10] Because the historical study of gender in rhetorical studies has focused almost exclusively on women, non-gender marked history continues to be associated with men, reaffirming the fundamental bias that that which is neutral is male. Feminist theologian Rita M. Gross explains that when gender studies focuses on women exclusively,

> [w]omen are put in the odd and uncomfortable position of carrying the whole burden of human genderness by ourselves, thus freeing men to go about the business as usual, unencumbered by gender issues and gender concerns, as unknowledgeable as ever about the content of women's studies.
>
> (19)

There are two obvious problems with attempting to redress gendered exclusions in the history of rhetoric by continuing to focus primarily on placing women back into the historical record. One, alluded to by Gross in the preceding quote, is that the male subjects in rhetorical history continue to enjoy a neutral, normative position even in our current histories. The second is that we introduce distortions into our understanding of women's history if we do not also account for the complexities of gender and rhetoric as it extends to various ways gender intersects with class, race, geography, sexuality, and religion. Those of us who identify as feminist historians in rhetoric and composition are still primarily focused on what is most accurately labeled women's history rather than gender history (see Bock; Scott, "Gender," "Unanswered"; Meyerowitz; Rose). We might worry that turning to gender history will deflect us from the crucial recovery work still needed or dilute the importance of working towards positive social change. However, I would argue that a broader gender history approach does the opposite. We might think of gender history as a tool for mapping the layered relationships between gender constructions and other categories of difference. Gender history necessitates that we attend to the ways genders always exist in multiplicities: nonelite evangelical masculinity differs from contemporaneous masculinities such as muscular Christianity and self-made entrepreneur masculinities. We can locate sources for the differences among these masculinities at the intersections of class, geography, religion, and race. Recognizing this heterogeneous terrain affords us a vantage from which we can revisit our current understandings of constructions of women's identities in rhetorical history. We can begin by reconsidering "the parlor," particularly in relation to religious rhetorics and gender history.

Finally, this analysis of the pilgrim boy and his evangelical submission and emotional display points to terrain still to be charted in our study of

Christian rhetorics. For instance, what further connections exist between Christian masculinities and emotional vulnerability? How might this emotional vulnerability function rhetorically? We might find, for example, that men are drawn to an emotionally vulnerable evangelical masculinity because it allows them an emotional life not available in other masculinities. Pursuing these questions will allow us to explore how the emotional demands of Christian masculinities might constitute ways of being that function rhetorically by allowing for a fuller range of appeals, pathos included. Such a construction of masculinity would challenge assumptions that male subjectivities and modes of communication are primarily rational—men deploy pathos only in crafted sermons and otherwise inhabit the roles of dominating husband or emotionally distant father. In other words, actively deconstructing our own cultural assumptions concerning the subjectivities Christian men occupy in rhetorical history might prompt us to rethink our mental maps of gender, class, and rhetorical history. Equally important, it would tell us more about Christian rhetorics themselves.

NOTES

1 While the tract does not include a publication date, its references to American history suggest the tract was published in the 1840s.

2 I say "invited to function" because the tract I am looking at is the production of a mainstream publishing effort that should be understood to represent dominant culture. The tracts distributed by the American Tract Society are often intended for the "struggling classes" but are not necessarily representations of their thoughts, hopes, or worldviews.

3 Tract literature was published widely by local, regional, and national tract and Bible societies; it was freely distributed by traveling missionaries and Sunday school teachers. See Nord.

4 The two publishing worlds even shared authors. James Alexander, a Presbyterian minister, whom Denning identifies as a writer of "books about and for workers," also published with tract societies (31). See also Brown.

5 Poor readers of the tract are encouraged to balance their poverty with good character: "If you are a *poor* boy, resolve to be honest and honorable; make up for your poverty by the dignity and purity of your character" (8). Wealthy readers are threatened with poverty as a result of poor character enabled by wealth and other vices (63–64).

6 The disjunction between appearance and character leads to anxiety about knowing whether one has been saved or not. One chapter describes the "stages of feeling through which the sinner may pass before he is converted," a process which is incomplete until the sinner can identify evidence of the change within himself: "the very thing he loved most before, he now hates, and the things he once hated, he now loves" (104–05).

7 In a rare moment of humor, the narrator reports that the pilgrim boy "ate one small copy of Latin grammar to get it out of the way" (13).

8 The dangers of swearing are described in detail by the narrator: "Did you ever think that every oath you utter is a prayer to God to damn you? Suppose he should take you at your word, and answer your prayer, how awful it would be in hell, to think for ever that you received just what you prayed for" (60).

9 While Mountford pays significant attention to how masculinity is constructed, the guiding questions in *The Gendered Pulpit* seem to equate gender with women (13).

10 This is not to diminish the significance of recovery work or to suggest historians should stop finding and "reinscribing" women back into rhetorical history. One need only look at the skeptical questions Royster faced in response to her recovery of African American women's literacy clubs to understand its importance (Royster and Kirsch 9). Royster's careful recovery work has made a significant contribution to our field's understanding of nineteenth-century rhetorical history.

REFERENCES

Baym, Nina. *American Women Writers and the Work of History, 1790–1860*. New Brunswick: Rutgers UP, 1995.

Bock, Gisela. "Women's History and Gender History: Aspects of an International Debate." *Gender & History* 1.1 (1989): 7–30.

Brown, Candy Gunther. *The Word in the World: Evangelical Writing, Publishing, and Reading in America, 1789–1880*. Chapel Hill: U of North Carolina P, 2004.

Davidson, Cathy N. *Revolution and the Word: The Rise of the Novel in America*. New York: Oxford UP, 1986.

Denning, Michael. *Mechanic Accents: Dime Novels and Working-Class Culture in America*. Rev. ed. New York: Verso, 1998.

Douglas, Ann. *The Feminization of American Culture*. New York: Knopf, 1977.

Enoch, Jessica. *Refiguring Rhetorical Education: Women Teaching African American, Native American, and Chicano/a Students*. Carbondale: Southern Illinois UP, 2008.

Gardiner, Judith Kegan, ed. "Introduction." Gardiner 1–30.

———. *Masculinity Studies and Feminist Theory: New Directions*. New York: Columbia UP, 2002.

Gross, Rita M. "Where Have We Been? Where Do We Need to Go? Women's Studies and Gender in Religion and Feminist Theology." King and Beattie 17–27.

Hobbs, Alex. "Masculinity Studies and Literature." *Literature Compass* 10.4 (2013): 383–95.

Holifield, E. Brooks. *Theology in America: Christian Thought from the Age of the Puritans to the Civil War*. New Haven: Yale UP, 2003.

Johnson, Nan. *Gender and Rhetorical Space in American Life, 1866–1910*. Carbondale: Southern Illinois UP, 2002.

Juster, Susan. " 'In a Different Voice': Male and Female Narratives of Religious Conversion in Post-Revolutionary America. *American Quarterly* 41.1 (1989): 34–62.

Kimmel, Michael. "Foreword." Gardiner ix–xi.

———. *Manhood in America: A Cultural History*. New York: Oxford UP, 2006.

King, Ursula, and Tina Beattie, eds. *Gender, Religion, and Diversity: Cross-Cultural Perspectives*. New York: Continuum, 2005.

Leverenz, David. *Manhood and the American Renaissance*. Ithaca: Cornell UP, 1989.

Lindman, Janet Moore. "Acting the Manly Christian: White Evangelical Masculinity in Revolutionary Virginia." *The William and Mary Quarterly* 57.2 (2000): 393–416.

———. " 'Bad Men and Angels from Hell': The Discourse of Universalism in Early National Philadelphia. *Journal of the Early Republic* 31.2 (2011): 259–82.

Logan, Shirley Wilson. *We Are Coming: The Persuasive Discourse of 19th Century Women*. Carbondale: Southern Illinois UP, 1999.

Mailloux, Steven. "Cultural Rhetoric Studies: Eating Books in Nineteenth-Century America." *Reconceptualizing American Literary/Cultural Studies: Rhetoric, History, and Politics in the Humanities*. Ed. William E. Cain. New York: Garland, 1996. 21–56.

———. "The Use and Abuse of Fiction: Readers Eating Books." *Reception Histories: Rhetoric, Pragmatism, and American Cultural Politics*. Ithaca: Cornell UP, 1998. 128–48.

Meyerowitz, Joanne. "A History of 'Gender.'" *The American Historical Review* 113.5 (2008): 1346–56.

Mountford, Roxanne. *The Gendered Pulpit: Preaching American Protestant Spaces*. Carbondale: Southern Illinois UP, 2003.

Nord, David Paul. *Faith in Reading: Religious Publishing and the Birth of Mass Media in America*. New York: Oxford UP, 2004.

The Pilgrim Boy, with Lessons from his History. A Narrative of Facts. New York: American Tract Society, n.d.

Rose, Sonya. "Introduction." *International Labor and Working-Class History* 63 (2003): 6–8.

Royster, Jacqueline Jones. *Traces of a Stream: Literacy and Social Change Among African American Women*. Pittsburg: Pittsburg UP, 2000.

———, and Gesa E. Kirsch. *Feminist Rhetorical Practices: New Horizons for Rhetoric, Composition, and Literacy Studies*. Carbondale: Southern Illinois UP, 2012.

Scott, Joan W. "Gender: A Useful Category of Historical Analysis." *The American Historical Review* 91.5 (1986): 1053–75.

———. "Unanswered Questions." *The American Historical Review* 113.5 (2008): 1422–29. Web. 14 July 2014.

Shaver, Lisa. "Stepping Outside the 'Ladies' Department': Women's Expanding Rhetorical Boundaries." *College English* 71.1 (2008): 48–69.

———. "Women's Deathbed Pulpits: From Quiet Congregants to Iconic Ministers." *Rhetoric Review* 27.1 (2008): 20–37.

Section IV

Christianity and Civic Engagement

9 Mapping the Rhetoric of Intelligent Design

The Agentification of the Scene

Matthew T. Althouse, Lawrence J. Prelli, and Floyd D. Anderson

Creationism and intelligent design are often seen as exemplary of the ideas, theories, and beliefs of evangelical Christianity in the early twenty-first century. That exemplary nature is exhibited clearly when evangelicals attack the perspectives they presumably would replace as science. As Michael Ruse observes, some evangelicals interconnect their critiques of Darwinism with their critiques of social issues such as abortion, theological issues such as premillennialism, and political issues such as American support for Israel (267–69). This situation points to an "all-encompassing" view of knowledge "from which moral prescriptions flow" (269). Discourses that relate creationism and intelligent design to science have been examined critically within a variety of contexts and from different perspectives. Studies have examined those discourses from the vantage of argumentation (Condit; Hayes; Prelli 234–35), narrative appeal (McClure, "Resurrecting"; Woodward 24), media coverage (Martin et al.; Taylor and Condit), tactics in public debates (Klope), and usefulness in teaching science (Lessl; Lyne). None of these studies has examined the underlying attitudes and motives of creationism or of intelligent design. In this chapter, we employ Kenneth Burke's dramatistic pentad in an analysis that reveals the pivotal attitudes and motives of intelligent design.

We examine a book about intelligent design using a critical approach called "pentadic cartography" (Anderson and Prelli). That approach uses Burke's pentad as a method for disclosing whether and to what extent a discourse is open or closed to a variety of distinct perspectives about problematic situations. Moreover, that approach looks to invent strategies that work to open discourses largely closed to perspectives other than the one that has become dominant and controlling. Pentadic cartography has been applied in critical studies of a philosophical work and a television commercial (Anderson and Prelli), birth trauma narratives (Beck), a presidential speech and a book on religion and civic discourse (DePalma, Ringer, and Webber), media coverage of a natural disaster (McClure, "Media Coverage"), and maternity leave discourse (Meisenbach et al.). We "map" a representative example of intelligent design discourse in this critical study.

We selected Lee Strobel's book *The Case for a Creator: A Journalist Investigates Scientific Evidence that Points toward God* as the focus of our analysis. Strobel's book has had wide influence and thus is worthy of sustained, critical analysis. When published in 2004, *The Case for a Creator* (hereafter, *TCC*) debuted on the *New York Times* best-seller list (McCoppin, para. 21). *Christianity Today* named it a 2005 "Best Book" ("*Christianity Today*"), and, for sales exceeding 720,000 copies, the Evangelical Christian Publisher Association gave it a 2008 "Gold Award" ("Gold"). Strobel is interviewed frequently by major media outlets on matters of Christianity as one of the evangelical community's most well-known apologists ("Lionsgate"). Strobel is a journalist and not a scientist, but the book contains interviews with some of intelligent design's foremost thinkers and, thereby, provides us with a discourse that captures the purported science's leading positions.

It might be anticipated that any work advancing intelligent design would feature perspectives exhibiting one or a combination of two attitudes. Because intelligent design is advanced as science, one anticipated attitude is that intelligent design is provable on naturalistic, empirical, or material evidential grounds secured by the use of scientific procedures and instrumentations. Because intelligent design is also associated with evangelical Christianity, the other anticipated attitude is that acceptance of intelligent design is warranted by faith in the deity's purposes. Surprisingly, neither of those expectations is fulfilled. Strobel's text induces readers into a perspective on intelligent design that makes its scientific status contingent on their identification with evangelical agents themselves and on acceptance of the opinions, dispositions, and qualities of mind of the "right" people. As we show, this orientation invites readers to view both science and Christianity from a severely narrow and restrictive perspective while obscuring alternative understandings.

In the sections that follow, we first elucidate the leading precepts of pentadic cartography. That section is followed by a detailed analysis that applies pentadic cartography to Strobel's discourse, yielding a map that discloses its symbolic features and forms that, together, close the universe of discourse about intelligent design and the matters of science and religion it addresses. The last section generates strategies for opening that closed universe and creating possibilities for elaboration of more matured perspectives, with particular attention to a more mystical Christian perspective that clashes with Strobel's orientation.

PENTADIC CARTOGRAPHY

Pentadic cartography uses Kenneth Burke's pentad to chart how terminological perspectives operate to open or close a body of discourse. As is well known, Burke correlated featured pentadic terms with associated philosophical vocabularies. Those vocabularies featuring "act" exhibit a philosophy of realism; "scene," materialism; "agent," idealism; "agency," pragmatism; and "purpose," mysticism (*Grammar* 128–29). Thought and discourse are constrained when terms are so featured that, as Burke put it, we "treat all five in terms of one, by 'reducing' them all to the one or [. . .] 'deducing' them all from the one as their common terminal ancestor" (127). These reductions or deductions reveal a "featured" term's dominance. For example, Anderson and Prelli argue that technical vocabularies feature agency and, thus, operate according to a "strict instrumentalism" that "not only transforms acts, agents, and scenes into terms of agency, but even purposes themselves become meaningful only when nearly synonymous with agency" (80). Close inspection of how "verbal terrain both restricts and opens the range of possibilities for contextual meaning" (80) involves disclosure of terminological starting points and their extensions within a discourse. Pentadic terms never stand alone but always in combination with other terms. Such combinations are called ratios (e.g., scene:act, agent:agency, act:purpose, etc.). "All statements that assign motives can be shown to arise out of ratios," Burke observes (*Grammar* xvi). Once identified, ratios disclose the featured attitude of a given discourse. Mapping featured terms and dominant ratios enables pentadic cartographers to precisely identify and assess the various vocabularies employed in human talk about problematic situations.

Pentadic cartography is premised on Burke's belief that no single terminological orientation is entirely right or wrong ("Terministic Screens" 45) but that each makes "discoveries" about situations that are enabled by and have "objective validity" within its own particular terms (*Permanence* 257). Pentadic maps enable critics to see how terminological orientations adduced to size up problematic situations conceal some meanings even as they reveal others. A central task of the pentadic cartographer is to restore greater proportion among perspectives by overstressing the understressed and understressing the overstressed in a body of discourse. Critics engage that task through invention of incongruous counter-statements that bring overstressed perspectives into dialectical contact with the terms of under-stressed perspectives (Prelli, Anderson, and Althouse 118–19).

The "verbal atom-cracking" (Burke, *Attitudes* 308) of juxtaposing incongruous perspectives generates "understandings of social reality that transcend those of a dominant orientation" and opens "possibilities for qualitative social change" (Anderson and Prelli 79). Rather than negating dominant perspectives, counterstatements challenge such perspectives' presumed dominance by disclosing their partiality and need for revision. This occurs via confrontation with terms that reveal competing meanings that also have "objective validity," and such terminological confrontation creates a democratic dialectic. This dialectic provides each protagonist with the "maximum opportunity to modify his thesis, and so mature it, in the light of the antagonist's rejoinders" (Burke, *Philosophy* 444). Each perspective evoked to come to terms with a situation "represents but one voice in the dialogue, and not the perspective-of-perspectives that arises from the cooperative competition of *all* the voices as they modify one another's assertions" (Burke, *Grammar* 89). Only when alternative and necessarily partial perspectives are brought into communicative contact can disputants develop an encompassing, "matured" orientation that "transcends the partiality of the parts" (Burke, *Grammar* 89; Prelli, Anderson, and Althouse 116–18).

DePalma, Ringer, and Webber illustrate pentadic mapping in their analysis of Sharon Crowley's *Toward a Civil Discourse*. Crowley was concerned with how citizens who value liberal democracy could resist the absolutism of Christian fundamentalism. DePalma, Ringer, and Webber chart a materialistic-pragmatic orientation in Crowley's work that, they contend, reflects a liberal perspective rooted in the scene that restricts "legitimate discourse" largely to perspectives structured according to scene:agency ratios (321). All other ratios are delegitimized, including especially the perspectives of Christian fundamentalists, whom Crowley perceives as the primary antagonists to liberal protagonists in a divisive universe of political discourse. DePalma, Ringer, and Webber conclude that Crowley's effort to "open discourse," somewhat surprisingly, "unwittingly promotes a single terminology as the perspective of perspectives and thus recloses the universe of discourse" (322). Accordingly, DePalma, Ringer, and Webber invent lines of thought with which to challenge Crowley's preferred "liberal-pragmatic" perspective. A Christian fundamentalist might counter that perspective with incongruous counterstatements such as "Faith always comes before reason" and "There is no compromising Truth" (329). Those who share Burke's "anarchic" tendencies might contribute counter-statements to the liberal-pragmatic perspective such as "Disrespect the 'respectable' and respect the 'disrespectable'" or "Civil deliberation deserves disruption" (329).[1]

STROBEL'S QUEST FOR TRUTH

Let us turn our attention to an analysis that discloses the leading motives and attitudes within the symbolic forms and structures of Strobel's text. Strobel structures *TCC* with the same formula he used in other books. That formula involves characterizing himself as the balanced, open-minded, skeptical journalist on an objective quest for the truth. Strobel sought the truth about such topics as "the evidence for Jesus" in *The Case for Christ*, "the toughest objections to Christianity" in *The Case for Faith*, and "attacks on the identity of Christ" in *The Case for the Real Jesus*. The pattern also is used in *TCC*, in which we find Strobel, again a skeptical journalist, disclosing "scientific evidence that points toward God" and that makes "the case for a creator." Moreover, he invites his readers to join him on his intellectual quest by adopting the same dispositions he himself exhibits. "Strip away your preconceptions as much as possible and keep an open mind as you eavesdrop on my conversation with these fascinating scientists and science-trained philosophers," he exhorts. "At the end you can decide for yourself whether their answers and explanations stand up to scrutiny" (*TCC* 28–29).

A major source of *TCC*'s appeal with readers sympathetic to intelligent design is the author's persona as atheist-turned-Christian apologist. Strobel emphasizes his skeptical cast of mind and appreciation of "hard facts" because of his training in journalism and the law (*TCC* 26–29). His journalistic training especially inclined him to seek out all perspectives to write stories professionally. His narrative begins in chapter 1 with an episode that exhibits the states of mind, attitudes, and personal traits that powered his inquiring activities. The scene is rural West Virginia in 1974. Working as a journalist, Strobel covered a religious protest against Darwinism in public schools (*TCC* 8–9). Local activists raged against evolutionary theory in science texts and denounced literary classics, such as *The Lord of The Flies*, *Moby Dick*, and Plato's *Republic*, in which they discerned the same situational ethics perceived in Darwinism (*TCC* 10–11). As an atheist, Strobel viewed the activists dismissively:

> Why couldn't these people get their heads out of the sand and admit the obvious: science had put their God out of a job! White-coated scientists of the modern world had trumped the black-robed priests of medieval times. Darwin's theory of evolution—no, the absolute *fact* of evolution—meant that there is no universal morality decreed by a deity, only culturally conditioned values that vary from place to place and situation to situation.
>
> (*TCC* 16)

After completing his assignment in West Virginia, Strobel thought, "I had been fair to both sides [. . .]. But, frankly, it had been difficult" (*TCC* 15). As his narrative unfolds, the same skeptical and objective inclinations that evidently culminated in his atheism would enable him to make the case for a creator—*after* he underwent conversion.

Chapter 2 sets the stage for Strobel's conversion. The chapter begins with Strobel's youthful views of science and Darwinism. As a teenager in America's post-Sputnik era, science impressed him: "It fit well with my logical way of looking at the world, an approach that was already tugging me toward the evidence-oriented fields of journalism and law" (*TCC* 17). Furthermore, he claims that it was "no accident that my admiration for scientific thinking was developing at the same time that my confidence in God was waning" (*TCC* 18). If one studies Darwinism, Strobel implies, holding religious convictions becomes difficult (*TCC* 19–26). He dramatizes this thinking by referring to cultural shifts in the 1960s, a time marked by "relativism" and "situational ethics." These shifts exacerbated his doubts about God and bolstered his estimation of science. Faith became "mere opinion, conjecture, superstition" (*TCC* 18).

Strobel's attitude about faith changed after his wife, Leslie, embraced Christianity. Predictably, Leslie's conversion angered the skeptical Strobel. He asked her in a "venomous and accusatory tone: '*What has gotten into you?*' I simply couldn't comprehend how such a rational person could buy into [. . .] wishful thinking, make-believe, mythology, and legend" (*TCC* 27). Yet, as Leslie "became a more loving and caring and authentic person, I began asking the same question, only this time in a softer and more sincere tone of genuine wonderment: '*What has gotten into you?*'" (*TCC* 27). As he made explicit later in the book, "the positive changes in my wife after she became a follower of Jesus" induced him to redirect his drive for "objectivity" in investigations of religious faith (*TCC* 275): "I began asking more questions [. . .] about faith, God, and the Bible," he writes. "I was determined to go wherever the answers would take me" (*TCC* 27). Thus began his quest for informed faith, which resulted in his writing books such as *The Case for a Creator*.

Strobel's conversion did not amount to trading empiricism for "mere faith." For Strobel, matters of faith do not involve belief in spiritual realities without evidence; rather, matters of faith seemingly are certifiable as true both empirically and logically. He claims to do precisely what Linus Pauling said scientists do: "search for the truth" (qtd. in Strobel 28). Strobel's goal in *TCC* is "to cross-examine authorities in various scientific disciplines." These interviewees were "doctorate-level professors who have unquestioned expertise, are able to communicate in accessible language, and who refuse to limit themselves only to the politically correct world of naturalism and materialism." Materialists and naturalists were excluded so that Strobel could work with "the freedom to pursue *all* possibilities" unimpeded by critics' "politically correct" and presumably closed-minded adherence to perspectives opposed to intelligent design. "After all, it wouldn't make sense to rule out any hypothesis at the outset," Strobel explains with unintended irony as he admits ruling out points of view other than those supportive of intelligent design (*TCC* 28). Of course, sympathetic readers would not very likely discern the irony but, rather, would probably become all the more intrigued by Strobel's quest given its daring unconventionality.

Strobel's persona as an open-minded fact-finder seeking the truth is enacted continuously throughout the book. Readers witness him engaging in question and answer interactions with his expert interlocutors. Chapters 3 through 10 consist largely of dramatic encounters between Strobel and leading exponents of intelligent design. Each expert exposes the pitfalls of Darwinism and the viability of intelligent design. These experts in cosmology, physics, astronomy, biochemistry, "biological information," and "consciousness" articulate the distinctive kinds of evidence that are combined in making the case for intelligent design summarized in the book's concluding chapter. Each encounter, then, induces readers' participation in what Burke called repetitive form, or "the consistent maintaining of a principle under new guises" (*Counter-Statement* 125). Each interview enacts through a different expert the principle that scientific findings and philosophical conclusions point toward a creator and creation and away from Darwinism and evolution. The chapters methodically build toward the concluding case for a creator in the "step-by-step" pattern of syllogistic form (*Counter-Statement* 124). Strobel's readers are left to conclude that the case thus made is unassailable by fact or logic.

Agent: Act Ratios

Of the five pentadic terms, Strobel's drama features the agent and stretches that term's associated idealistic vocabulary to shape attitudes about intelligent design. Burke elaborated how featured terms are developed and extended using—rather conveniently for our purposes—agent as his example:

> Dramatistically, the different philosophic schools are to be distinguished by the fact that each school features a different one of the five terms, in developing a vocabulary designed to allow this one term full expression (as regards its resources and its temptations) with the other terms being comparatively slighted or being placed in the perspective of the featured term. Think, for instance, of a philosophy that had been established "in the sign of the agent." It must develop coordinates particularly suited to treat of substance and motive in "subjective," or "psychological" terms (since such terms deal most directly with the attributes of agents).
>
> (*Grammar* 127–28)

We can map Strobel's previously described quest as a terminological terrain dominated by "the sign of the agent" with motives and attitudes frequently structured in accord with agent:act ratios. Strobel exhibits the mental habits and inclinations that drive his investigative actions. Strobel's wife undergoes a conversion experience that changes her conduct for the better. Strobel himself undergoes a conversion after witnessing his wife's post-conversion conduct that reorients his own actions on issues of science and faith. All three of these specific instances are manifestations of the agent:act ratio. More generally, we see agent:act ratios manifested in Strobel's drama in three ways: (1) evangelical sages of science and philosophy expounding on the proper attitudes toward Darwinism and intelligent design; (2) the truth-seeker Strobel assimilating what he learned from those sages as prelude to further inquiry into intelligent design and Darwinism; and (3) interviewees and other agents bearing witness to how they came inexorably to the truth of intelligent design (and the deity) and the falsity of evolutionism (and of atheism) through objective and open-minded reasoning that enabled them to overcome prejudices induced by education in the latter. We examine in detail one chapter that illustrates all three.

In chapter 5, Strobel investigates the cosmological question of the universe's origin. He recounted background research that revealed "staggering" evidence and "exotic theories," all of which required a "certain degree of speculation" (*TCC* 93–95). His fact-finding disposition led him to consider fruitful hypotheses that explain the religious implications of the "Big Bang." That sort of consideration required that he avoid the "unsupported conjecture or armchair musings" of "pipe-puffing theorists" (*TCC* 95) and turn to philosopher and Christian apologist William Lane Craig.

Craig presents his *"kalam"* cosmological argument to Strobel, telling him that the Arabic word *kalam* means "speech" or "doctrine." That doctrine "came to characterize the whole medieval movement of Islamic theology" (*TCC* 98). The *kalam* argument bolsters a creationist line of thinking that can be traced back to ancient refutations of Aristotle's cosmology and traced forward to arguments from such diverse thinkers as Bonaventure, Locke, and Kant (*TCC* 97–98). According to the *kalam* argument, "[w]hatever begins to exist has a cause. The universe began to exist. Therefore, the universe has a cause" (*TCC* 98). Craig elaborates this argument with evidence from mathematics and physics (*TCC* 100–07). He further argues that the cause of the universe is a "personal creator" by adducing the idea of personal explanations. "Scientific explanations explain a phenomenon in terms of initial conditions and natural laws," Craig says. "By contrast, personal explanations explain things by means of an agent and that agent's volition" (*TCC* 110).

Consistent with his skepticism and objectivity, Strobel does not accept such ideas uncritically. Throughout the interview, he poses objections, heralded by phrases such as "hold on" and *"Not so fast!"* (*TCC* 108, 112) and advances counterarguments attributed to Carl Sagan and Stephen Hawking (*TCC* 113, 118). Craig responds successfully to Strobel's inquiries. As the interview closes, Strobel writes, "my mind could conjure up no rational scenario that could derail the inexorable logic of the *kalam* argument" (*TCC* 121). At the chapter's end, he reflects on the next stage of his intellectual journey: "Now that Craig had made a powerful case for God as Creator of the universe, it was time to consider the laws and parameters of physics. Is there any credibility, I wondered, to the claim that they have been tuned to an incomprehensible precision in order to create a livable habitat for humankind?" (*TCC* 123). Thus, the reader is prompted to anticipate another evidential proof of a personal creator from yet another expert in the next chapter.

Strobel offers an anecdote from Craig near the end of chapter 5. Craig remembered attending an academic conference with his wife, Jan, in Germany. There, they met a prominent physicist who claimed that studying physics "destroyed her belief in God." Jan responded, "[R]ead Bill's [Craig's] doctoral dissertation. He uses physics to prove the existence of God" (*TCC* 121). After several days, having perused the dissertation, the physicist announced to the Craigs: "I now believe in the existence of God. Thank you so much for restoring my faith in him" (*TCC* 122). Craig makes the anecdote's point explicit: "You asked whether God can use cosmology to change the life of a scientist. Yes, I've seen it. I've seen it happen with all kinds of skeptics" (*TCC* 122).

Notice the three manifestations of the agent:act form from earlier: the knowledgeable Christian expert expounding on the truth of a personal creator of the universe, Strobel assimilating that truth and setting out to conduct additional investigations, and skeptics undergoing conversion when confronted by the evidence of science.[2] Overall, then, the book is prominently circumscribed by the featured term of agent with its most frequent and extensive applications manifesting agent:act ratios. But these manifestations are parts of an overall cosmic drama structured according to agent, the featured term.

The "Agentification of the Scene"

When elaborating the idea of a featured term, Burke mentioned a terminological phenomenon that is operative in the language of intelligent design, at least as it is portrayed in Strobel's book. This phenomenon involves setting up antithetical relationships between two vocabularies that feature different pentadic terms so that the protagonist's preferred vocabulary permeates the symbolic terrain typically occupied by the antagonist's preferred terms. In this case, the idealistic vocabulary of intelligent design, featuring agent, supplants the materialistic vocabulary of Darwinian evolution, featuring scene. Following Burke, we call this phenomenon the "agentification of the scene." Burke explains this phenomenon as follows:

> Think of that stage where the philosopher, proud in the full possession of his coordinates for featuring the realm of the *agent*, turned to consider the areas that fall most directly under the heading of *scene*. Instead of beginning over again, and seeking to analyze the realm of scene in terms that had no relation to the terms he had developed when considering the realm of agent, he might proceed to derive the nature of his terms for the discussion of scene from the nature of his terms for agent. This might well, in fact, be the procedure of a thinker who, instead of using a terminology that was merely slung together, felt the logical and aesthetic (and moral!) desire for an internal consistency among his terms. And it would amount to an "agentification" of scene even though the terms for scene were placed in dialectical opposition to the terms for agent. For a scene conceived antithetically to *agent* would differ from a scene conceived, let us say, antithetically to *act* or *purpose*, the genius of the ancestral term surviving even in its negation.
>
> (Grammar 128)

The very words "intelligent design" illustrate the agentification of the scene because it carries forward the implications of an idealistic vocabulary that features agent and supplants the antithetical Darwinian vocabulary that features the material scene. Design, after all, is manifested intelligence and intelligence manifested *is* the universal scene that transcends, permeates, and encompasses the universe itself. Stephen C. Meyer amplifies this position during one of two interviews included in Strobel's book. "The cause of the universe must transcend matter, space, and time, which were brought into existence with the Big Bang," Meyer maintained. "The Judeo-Christian God has precisely this attribute of transcendence" (*TCC* 81). Naturalism, in contrast, "denies the existence of any entity beyond the closed system of nature" (*TCC* 81). To put the point in Burke's terms, the "intelligence" of the creator God enacts the wider circumference of meaning (*Grammar* 77), transcending and permeating all of matter, space, and time.

While Meyer appeals to scientific knowledge, J.P. Moreland during his interview with Strobel advances the idea of an all-encompassing intelligence based on "nonscientific knowledge." That sort of knowledge is derived through philosophical introspection that discloses the irreducibility of soul, mind, and consciousness to material phenomena such as the brain's operations. "Most of the evidence for the reality of consciousness and the soul is from our own first-person awareness of ourselves," Moreland said, "and has nothing to do with the study of the brain" (*TCC* 270–71). When scientists "are willing to open themselves up to nonscientific knowledge," they will "come to believe in the reality of the soul and the immaterial nature of consciousness" (*TCC* 270–71), Moreland maintained. "And this could open them up personally to something even more important—to a much larger Mind and a much bigger Consciousness, who in the beginning was the Logos, and who made us in his image" (*TCC* 271). The intelligent design position is that reality is permeated with the immaterial "substance" of Mind, Consciousness, or Intelligence.

The idealistic terms of intelligent design position Darwinism as its materialistic antithesis. The comments of Jonathan Wells, interviewed in chapter 3, are typical of this sort of antithetical framing. "The case for Darwinian evolution is bankrupt," he writes, because the evidence for it "is not only grossly inadequate, it's systematically distorted" (*TCC* 65). He concluded that "Darwinism is merely materialistic philosophy masquerading as science, and people are recognizing it for what it is" (*TCC* 66). Indeed, Wells believes that this point is so obvious that he asserts, "sometime in the not-too-distant-future—I don't know, maybe twenty or thirty years from now—people will look back in amazement and say, 'How could anyone have believed this?'" (*TCC* 65–66). When Strobel probes Wells to elaborate further, the scientific triumph of intelligent design over Darwinian materialism becomes all the more clear:

> "Let me get this straight," I said. "You're not merely saying the evidence for evolution is weak and therefore there must be an intelligent designer. You're suggesting there is also affirmative evidence for a designer."

"I am," he replied. "However, the two are connected, because one of the main functions of Darwinian theory is to try to make design unnecessary. This is what you experienced as you became an atheist. This is what I experienced. So showing that the arguments for evolution are weak certainly opens the door to design."

(*TCC* 66)

From the idealistic vantage of intelligent design, evidence ordinarily characterized in scenic and thus material terms becomes resonant with associations of intelligence, consciousness, and spirit. As the materialism of Darwinism is vanquished from the scene, the idealism of intelligent design takes up the slack. Examples of agentification of the scene abound in the book and are especially telling in discussions of evidence. According to Meyer, for instance, "[o]nly theism can provide an intellectually satisfying causal explanation for all of this evidence" (*TCC* 74). He elaborates the evidence that is susceptible only to idealistic rather than materialistic explanation:

If it's true there's a beginning to the universe, as modern cosmologists now agree, then this implies a cause that transcends the universe. If the laws of physics are fine-tuned to permit life, as contemporary physicists are discovering, then perhaps there's a designer who fine-tuned them. If there's information in the cell, as molecular biology shows, then this suggests intelligent design. To get life going in the first place would have required biological information; the implications point beyond the material realm to a prior intelligent cause.

(*TCC* 74)

Wells similarly adopts the perspective that phenomena can only be accounted for, scientifically, in idealistic rather than materialistic terms:

To me, as a scientist, the development of an embryo cries out, 'Design!' The Cambrian explosion—the sudden appearance of complex life, with no evidence of ancestors—is more consistent with design than evolution. Homology, in my opinion, is more compatible with design. The origin of life cries out for a designer. None of these things make as much sense from a Darwinian perspective as they do from a design perspective.

(*TCC* 66)

Wells's comments reflect an attitude shared by Strobel's interlocutors generally. Intelligent design is not only better on balance when compared with Darwinian and other naturalistic accounts; it is conclusively and definitively superior because it is true. "When you analyze all of the most current affirmative evidence from cosmology, physics, astronomy, biology, and so forth," Wells asserts, "you'll discover that the positive case for an intelligent designer becomes absolutely compelling" (*TCC* 67). "Maybe the world *looks* designed," Meyer quips, "because it really *is* designed" (*TCC* 71).

COUNTERSTATEMENTS AND OPENING
THE UNIVERSE OF DISCOURSE

Strobel's book enacts a universe of discourse on both scientific and theological matters circumscribed by an idealistic vocabulary that features agent as the dominant term. Readers are thus equipped with strategies for coming to terms with situations beset by controversies about the relationship of science and religion. "Rightly" disposed agents are continuously exhibited as acting in ways that foster acceptance of a designer and its intelligent design as true both scientifically and theologically. And, of course, alternative views are muted, if acknowledged at all, as though they are the outlooks of persons "wrongly" disposed. Moreover, we have shown how the featured term, *agent*, shifts from agent:act ratios to agent:scene ratios, manifesting what we have called, following Burke, the agentification of the scene. That terminological transformation is enabled by metonymy; it communicates the "incorporeal or intangible [. . .] in terms of the corporeal or tangible" (*Grammar* 506). The deity is reduced to a mere "designer" and complex natural and supernatural phenomena become the "design." The implication of this drama is that Strobel's quest yields the case that conclusively establishes the truth of intelligent design both scientifically and theologically.

We generate counterstatements from perspectives that are incongruous with the idealistic terms of intelligent design. It is important to stress at the start that our efforts to generate counterstatements neither presume their "truth" nor impugn the validity of intelligent design *on its own terms*. Nor do we suggest that supporters of intelligent design will be unable to respond to the counterstatements, again, *on their own terms*. The point is to bring excluded perspectives into contact with intelligent design by featuring terms other than those of an agent-based idealism. That contact opens a space for dialectic about the opposed terms. Accordingly, we shall invent counterstatements using materialist, pragmatic, mystic, and realist vocabularies. Those counterstatements, by their very enactment, disclose important perspectives on complex scientific, philosophical, or theological matters that Strobel leaves out of his account.

Materialism is a ready source of counterstatements. Opponents of intelligent design could take the well-traveled route of reasserting that non-materialistic perspectives are not scientific perspectives. Based on that widely accepted understanding of science, they could assert such counterstatements as the following:

- "The origins of the universe and life can be, and have been, satisfactorily explained in materialistic terms" (or, applying Occam's razor,

"Neither a designer nor any other supernatural force is needed to supplement adequate naturalistic explanations");

- "Intelligent design treats anomalies in material evidence for contemporary evolutionary theory as though they constitute positive evidence for an immaterial designer";
- "Intelligent design is an effort to subvert and overthrow the materialist world view for political rather than scientific reasons"; and
- "Intelligent design does not have the ability to predict events in the material world as other sciences do."

Critics of intelligent design could also spin off other possible counterstatements based on Burke's observation that "materialism [. . .] may be quite collectivistic in the ethical or political realm" (*Grammar* 129). From this scenic vantage, both intelligent design and Christianity may be critiqued as social products. Such is the position of Robert Wright who, in *The Evolution of God*, wrote, "as natural selection ground along [. . .] it eventually created a form of life [humans] so intelligent as to give birth to a second creative process, cultural evolution" (450). Moral orders known as "religions" evolved through "human nature, political and economic factors, technological change, and so on" (4). Based on this line of thought, one could enact the counterstatement "Intelligent design is part of the ongoing material development of an ever-changing, culturally permeated Christianity." Our first group of materialist counterstatements could be said to rematerialize idealistic science, while the last rematerializes idealistic religion and culture.

Resistance to intelligent design may also be found in pragmatism whose key term is agency. Agency focuses on the *techné*, means, or instruments of action rather than on purposes or aims. As noted earlier, one agency of intelligent design involves what Moreland calls "first-person awareness of ourselves" and an immortal "Logos" (*TCC* 270–71). Given this agency, it is clear that part of the movement's stance involves nonscientific methods. Typical counterstatements to intelligent design might challenge its lack of suitable *techné*:

- "Unlike physics or chemistry, intelligent design does not follow scientific procedures," or
- "Intelligent design is 'science' without method."

Agency-based counterstatements could be said to reinstrumentalize intelligent design's *techné*-free science.

Counterstatements to intelligent design can also be generated from the vantage of mysticism. It might seem odd that intelligent design does not feature purpose because mysticism is closely associated with idealism, as both tend to "reinforce each other" (Burke, *Grammar* 299) and both offer people sources of meaning beyond motion-driven survival. Mysticism, for Burke, involves the "unity of the individual with some *cosmic or universal purpose*" (*Grammar* 288, emphasis in original). Unlike idealism, then, mysticism rejects flat antitheses. Distinctions between body and spirit, form and matter, the one and the many, and the creator and the creation obscure efforts to secure cooperation and synthesis in a higher, unified purpose. Thus, the "body" may be "treated as a way into 'spirit'" (Burke, *Rhetoric* 189) rather than its dialectical opposite, because the very distinction between the two dissolves from the vantage of unitary, mystical, holistic purpose. The same could be said for all other distinctions, including the separation of creator from creation. Consider counterstatements from the vantage of Christian mysticism:

- "God is a universal and eternal living presence that is irreducible to a cosmic designer,"
- "Intelligent design is Christianity without the ineffable," and
- "Intelligent design ignores the living presence in creation of the creator."

Such counterstatements reenvision Christianity as a living, holistic, faith.

Finally, realism is a source of counter-statements that feature action. Burke maintains that "human acts are not 'verifiable' in the way that purely scenic statements are. The 'proof' of a human act is in the *doing*" (*Grammar* 282). What, then, do proponents of intelligent design *do* in their dramatic conflicts with evolutionism? They exhort, they argue, they debate, they extrapolate conclusions from established work across the sciences. What they don't do is empirical research related to the issues they rhetorically engage, regardless of whether they are credentialed as scientists. Realist counterstatements thus might include the following:

- "No intelligent designers *actually do* empirical research on testable hypotheses about intelligent design";
- "The precepts of intelligent design are irrelevant to what scientists do in biology, geology, and paleontology"; or
- "What 'science' have intelligent designers done that supports their 'paradigm'?"

Such counterstatements might be said to identify science as *doing* science rather than *talking* science.

We emphasize that Burke's dramatistic realism would acknowledge the objective validity of the various terminological perspectives we have discussed, including the perspective of intelligent design. All are considered partial perspectives of varying usefulness in coming to terms with the scientific and theological realities with which they grapple. Intelligent designers go wrong by their insistence that theirs is the definitive and conclusive perspective on those realities. The various counterstatements generated in this section show only some of the ways in which that presumption is wrong. Intelligent design is valid on its own terms, but to become a fully matured perspective it must undergo the revisions made necessary by other objectively valid perspectives such as those revealed in our counterstatements.

CONCLUSION

Strobel enacts a drama in which "rightly" inclined agents engaged in right actions in opposition to "wrongly" inclined agents who engaged in wrong actions (agent:act ratios). That conflict ultimately was resolved in the conclusion with intelligent design's triumph over Darwinism in establishing the truth about the divinely created and thus "agentified" universal scene (agent:scene ratios). His book, therefore, contains a universe of discourse closed to perspectives other than those that correspond or are consistent with this idealistic vocabulary.

We have shown how critics can attempt to open this closed discourse through invention of counterstatements that contrast the dominant orientation with otherwise excluded points of view. Accordingly, we generated counterstatements that brought intelligent design's idealistic perspective into contact with the terms of materialist, pragmatic, mystical, and realistic perspectives. Scenic counterstatements rematerialize intelligent design's idealistic science, as well as rematerialize intelligent design's idealized religious underpinnings as cultural products. Agency-based counterstatements contrast intelligent design's scientific stance with its lack of instruments and procedures; they reinstrumentalize science. Counterstatements featuring purpose contrast intelligent design with encompassing, unifying, mystical understandings of Christian faith; they reenvision intelligent design's scientistic religion as a living holistic faith. Act-based counterstatements challenge proponents of intelligent design to relate their science and their own practices to how science actually is done. Scientists do science as well as talk science.

Readers sympathetic to Strobel's perspective might conclude when reading the counterstatements that our intent was to discredit intelligent design, embarrass its supporters, or both. Such a conclusion is incorrect. Our task as pentadic cartographers is to open public discourse to as many perspectives as possible. We presume that intelligent design yields meanings that have "objective validity" from the vantage of its own terms, but any perspective becomes hegemonic when it excludes alternative points of view and confuses its own partiality for a complete and all-encompassing understanding. Such is the case with Strobel's book. The idealistic terms of Strobel's perspective yield important understandings, but they also conceal other important meanings that would be disclosed by the terms of different, and even critically opposed, orientations. The critic's task is to expose that partiality by bringing the dominant perspective into critical contrast with incongruous, excluded, but nonetheless valid, points of view. Counterstatements are the instruments for doing that; they open a space for a dialectic between otherwise excluded or muted perspectives and the dominant point of view. The very contact of different perspectives discloses their partiality and implies that the "whole transcends the partiality of the parts" (Burke, *Grammar* 89).

Consider the implication of pentadic mapping and the use of counter-statements for understanding the diversity of Christian perspectives. Our counterstatements make clear that Strobel's discourse about intelligent design not only is closed to all but a single Christian perspective but that it also is susceptible to a dialectic among a diversity of points of view. Strobel's idealistic perspective on the deity as creator and the universe as created ignores other valid Christian points of view. We suggested that Christian mysticism, featuring unifying cosmic purpose, is one sort of contrary view. We shall consider that point in more detail here.

An example of an alternative to intelligent design's orientation is Terry LeBlanc's articulation in *Sojourners* of Native American Christian beliefs. LeBlanc, a founder of the North American Institute for Indigenous Theological Studies, argues that Native Americans "shifted away from the dualistic philosophical frames within which European and Euro-North American theology has been classically undertaken to a more holistic philosophical frame of reference" (para. 3). From LeBlanc's perspective, dualistic thinking limits Christianity. "To Indigenous people," he writes, "life is not easily captured in the simple binaries and either/or realities common within Western thought. Our philosophy is much more akin to the Hebraic 'both/and' " (para. 12). LeBlanc elaborates:

> Compounded dualisms in classical Christian theology have also, from an Indigenous vantage point, created senseless divisions of reality into the sacred and profane, sacred and secular, natural and supernatural. Not everyone assumes life happens on two separated planes of existence, isolated from the rest of a supernatural creation by human-dictated delimitations. For most of us in the Indigenous world, everything expresses the sacred, for it all proceeds from God—regardless of the means of its creation. Not only is it fully sacred, but clearly, despite scientific discovery, it is still a significant mystery.
>
> (para. 15)

From LeBlanc's vantage, the portrayal of the deity as a designer in intelligent design would seem narrowly reductive, and efforts to justify those depictions through appeals to science would make that reduction all the worse. For the Christian mystic, the universal living presence of the deity is only obscured by the reductionism and discriminations of science. We can put the difference another way. Strobel's idealistic perspective is prefigured by metonymy; its attention is directed to parts or elements of a whole with special emphasis on the designer and the design. LeBlanc's mystical perspective, in contrast, is prefigured by synecdoche; its focus is on the cosmic unity of the whole.

Our example is offered to point a way to a dialectic between both perspectives and does not presuppose any preferred outcome. Only through an unfolding dialectic and its process of revision can one or the other or some more encompassing view emerge as the more "matured," more "rounded" (Burke, *Grammar* xv), and thus more valid perspective. Perhaps there are other Christian perspectives that feature agent, purpose, or some other pentadic term that could also enter the dialectical conversation. Students of Christian rhetorics could use pentadic cartography to map out available perspectives as a prelude to encouraging their "cooperative competition" by confronting them with counterstatements that expose their partiality.

Our example is thus generalizable. Pentadic maps assist in clarifying the diversity of available perspectives on the intersection of science and religion. After all, Strobel is not alone in enacting a drama about the relationship between science and religion that closes the universe of discourse to all but a single controlling point of view. Virtually any perspective has the potential to similarly dominate a discourse, presenting its perspective as the absolute and final perspective-of-perspectives. Synoptic understanding of the range of available perspectives that pentadic maps provide greatly assists in identifying both featured and privileged perspectives as well as those muted, neglected, and ignored. Such awareness enables analysts and critics to intervene when they encounter discourses that are insular, unitary, and hegemonic by introducing incongruous counterstatements that have the potential to open the closed universe of discourse.

NOTES

1 DePalma, Ringer, and Webber observe that Burke's interest in creating a democratic dialectic through terminological confrontation exhibits his "distinctly anarchic tendency" (316).

2 Some of Strobel's interlocutors are characterized to fit within this general story. Their open-mindedness and consideration of evidence led them to accept intelligent design, reject skepticism toward theism, or resist bias in favor of evolutionary theory, the atheism it purportedly induced, or both. In chapter 4, for instance, Stephen C. Meyer recalls how he became skeptical "of all naturalistic theories of origins" and turned with "excitement" and awareness of "powerful scientific findings" to intelligent design (Strobel, *TCC* 71). In *TCC*, also see Jonathan Wells (chapter 3, 33–34), Meyer (chapter 4, 70–71), Craig (chapter 5, 96–97), and Michael J. Behe (chapter 8, 193–95, 215). Robin Collins's background story is an exception. He became a Christian as a teenager before embarking on his professional, intellectual life (chapter 6, 129). Guillermo Gonzalez and Jay Wesley Richards in chapter 7 and J.P. Moreland in Chapter 10 are not characterized either way. For other anecdotes of skeptics-turned-believers see 69–71,122–23 125–26, 220–21, 249–50, 287–91. Strobel enacts and maintains his own intellectual quest narrative across the book's chapters through previews, transitions, interjections, and summaries (see 32–33, 34–35, 36–37; 66–67; 82, 84, 89; 95–96, 98, 123; 128, 130, 138, 140, 144–45, 150–51; 154, 158, 175, 177–78, 190–91; 196, 199, 201, 211, 216–17; 222, 228, 238, 244–45; 252, 255, 257, 267, 271–72; 275–76, 277, 283, 285, 291–92).

REFERENCES

Anderson, Floyd D., and Lawrence J. Prelli. "Pentadic Cartography: Mapping the Universe of Discourse." *Quarterly Journal of Speech* 87.1 (2001): 73–95.

Beck, Cheryl. "Pentadic Cartography: Mapping Birth Trauma Narratives." *Qualitative Health Research* 16.4 (2006): 453–66.

Burke, Kenneth. *Attitudes Toward History.* 3rd ed. Berkeley: U of California P, 1984.

———. *Counter-Statement.* Berkeley: U of California P, 1968.

———. *A Grammar of Motives.* Berkeley: U of California P, 1969.

———. *Permanence and Change: An Anatomy of Purpose.* 3rd ed. Berkeley: U of California P, 1984.

———. *The Philosophy of Literary Form.* 3rd ed. Berkeley: U of California P, 1973.

———. *A Rhetoric of Motives.* Berkeley: U of California P, 1969.

———. "Terministic Screens." *Language as Symbolic Action.* Berkeley: U of California P, 1966: 44–62.

Campbell, John Angus, and Stephen C. Meyer, eds. *Darwinism, Design, & Public Education.* East Lansing: Michigan State UP, 2003.

"*Christianity Today* Book Awards 2005." *Christianity Today.* 20 May 2005. Web. 9 December 2009.

Condit, Celeste Michelle. "The Rhetoric of Intelligent Design: Alternatives for Science and Religion." Campbell and Meyer 421–40.

DePalma, Michael-John, Jeffrey M. Ringer, and Jim Webber. "(Re)Charting the (Dis)Courses of Faith and Politics, or Rhetoric and Democracy in the Burkean Barnyard." *Rhetoric Society Quarterly* 38.3 (2009): 311–34.

"Gold/Platinum/Diamond Book Awards: Past Award Recipients." Evangelical Christian Publishers Association. N.d. 8 September 2009.

Hayes, James T. " 'Creation Science' Is not 'Science': Argument Fields and Public Arguments." *Proceedings of the National Communication Association/American Forensic Association Alta Conference on Argumentation: Argument in Transition, 1983.* Washington, D.C.: National Communication Association, 1983. 416–22.

Klope, David C. "Creationism and the Tactic of Debate: A Performance Study of Guerrilla Rhetoric." *Journal of Communication and Religion* 17.1 (1994): 39–51.

LeBlanc, Terry. "Reclaiming the Word." *Sojourners.* March 2014. Web. 16 May 2014.

Lessl, Thomas M. "Scientific Rhetoric as Religious Advocacy: Origins in the Public Schools." *Journal of Communication and Religion* 26.1 (2003): 1–27.

"Lionsgate Names Thomas Nelson, Inc. Exclusive Distributor in Christian Market." *Lionsgate.* Lions Gate Entertainment. 12 April 2007. Web. 17 May 2014.

Lyne, John. "Thinking Pedagogically About Design." Campbell and Meyer 525–32.

Martin, Justin D. et al. "Journalism and the Debate over Origins: Newspaper Coverage of Intelligent Design." *Journal of Media and Religion* 5.1 (2006): 49–61.

McClure, Kevin. "Media Coverage of Natural Disasters: Pentadic Cartography and the Case of the 1993 Great Flood of the Mississippi." *Kenneth Burke Journal* 8.1 (2012). Web. 16 May 2014.

———. "Resurrecting the Narrative Paradigm: Identification and the Case of Young Earth Creationism." *Rhetoric Society Quarterly* 39.2 (2009): 189–211.

McCoppin, Robert. "Local Boy Makes God: Lee Strobel Went from Atheist Newsman to Best-Selling Christian Author; Now He's Testing His Faith on TV." *Daily Herald* (Arlington Heights, IL) 7 October 2004, Suburban Living: 1.

Meisenbach, Rebecca J. et al. " 'They Allowed': Pentadic Mapping of Women's Maternity Leave Discourse as Organizational Rhetoric." *Communication Monographs* 75.1 (2008): 1–24.

Prelli, Lawrence J. *A Rhetoric of Science: Inventing Scientific Discourse*. Columbia: U of South Carolina P, 1989.

Prelli, Lawrence J., Floyd D. Anderson, and Matthew T. Althouse. "Kenneth Burke on Recalcitrance." *Rhetoric Society Quarterly* 41.2 (2011): 97–124.

Ruse, Michael. *The Evolution-Creation Struggle*. Cambridge: Harvard UP, 2005.

Strobel, Lee. *The Case for Christ: The Evidence for Jesus*. Grand Rapids: Zondervan, 1998.

———. *The Case for a Creator: A Journalist Investigates Scientific Evidence that Points toward God*. Grand Rapids: Zondervan, 2004.

———. *The Case for Faith: The Toughest Objections to Christianity*. Grand Rapids: Zondervan, 2000.

———. *The Case for the Real Jesus: Attacks on the Identity of Christ*. Grand Rapids: Zondervan, 2007.

Taylor, Charles Alan, and Celeste Michelle Condit. "Objectivity in Mediation: Coverage of Creation/Science." *Critical Studies in Mass Communication* 5 (1988): 293–312.

Woodward, Thomas. *Doubts about Darwin: A History of Intelligent Design*. Grand Rapids: Baker, 2003.

Wright, Robert. *The Evolution of God*. New York: Little, Brown and Company, 2009.

10 "Heaven-Touched Lips and Pent-Up Voices"

The Rhetoric of American Female Preaching Apologia, 1820–1930

Lisa Zimmerelli

> Answer, ye thousands of heaven-touched lips, whose testimonies have so long been repressed in the assemblies of the pious! Yes, answer, ye thousands of female disciples of every Christian land, whose pent-up voices have so long, under the pressure of these man-made restraints, been uttered in groanings before God!
>
> —Phoebe Palmer, *The Promise of the Father* and *Tongue of Fire*

In nineteenth-century America, Protestant churches were the point of origin for much of women's rhetorical discourse: women began their activist work in prayer circles, in Sunday school classrooms, and in church-associated reform and benevolent societies (see Boylan; Dodson). A subset of these women also felt called to preach, and for them an imperative and central rhetorical act was the performance and service of their ministry (see Brekus; DeBerg; Hardesty, "Minister," *Women*; Hassey; Ruether and Keller; Schneider). Although the pulpit itself was usually prohibited to them, women preachers found other spaces for their ministry: meetinghouses, drawing rooms, tents, and platforms. Initially, fledgling sectarian and separatist Protestant churches welcomed women's religious leadership, especially for activities that had the potential to contribute to church growth (e.g., membership campaigns and fund-raising efforts). However, as these churches attempted to gain denominational status, male leadership forcefully revoked their support of women's public religious speech.[1] In addition to formal church restrictions, male leaders across Protestant denominations disseminated objections to women's preaching. These objections were met by female preaching apologia by men and women, prompting debates in the pages of denominational presses and in pulpits and platforms (see Chaves; Gifford; Zikmund).

This chapter investigates the rhetorical features of one slice of this debate by analyzing nineteenth-century Protestant women's responses to objections to women's ministry. After outlining the most common arguments in these objections, I provide a rhetorical study of women's preaching apologia, closely attending to their navigation of genre as they map out different lines of argument. In so doing, I demonstrate how Protestant women from various backgrounds charted the blurry line between religion and activism.

The religious rhetoric that arose out of the nineteenth-century debate over women's preaching deserves special consideration as a unique subset of women's activism, contributing to our understanding of the negotiation of religious identity, public spaces, and public voices in this era (see Buchanan; K. Campbell; Levander; Logan; Ryan; Shaver). Sharing space with defenses of women's public address under the general umbrella of defenses of women, women's preaching apologia represent perhaps one of the broadest spectrums of political and social sympathies, with some arguing conservatively that women's voices should be limited to religious discourse and others arguing radically that women's equal religious status was representative of her equal social status. For preaching women, religion was an identity category as integral as race, gender, and class, and they were emboldened to claim direct inspiration from God in their ministry and activism. The texts generated in defense of Christian female leadership thus serve as important and representative examples of nineteenth-century feminist activism and religious rhetorical discourse. Moreover, nineteenth-century female preaching apologia also fit into the tradition of reformation-inspired rhetoric, a tradition of resistance and reclamation of rhetorical power that arguably can be traced over centuries.

OBJECTIONS TO WOMEN'S PREACHING

The rumblings of discontent over Protestant female religious leadership came to a head in the 1830s, as church leaders condemned the ministry of women in sermons and in pastoral letters read publically before congregations. These oral objections distinguished between female private and public speaking and took a broad stroke in their condemnation of women's public address. In the mid-nineteenth century, the debate moved beyond the confines of church walls and into the pages of the religious press, including such journals as the *Western Recorder*, the *Church Advocate*, the *Gospel Advocate*, the *Christian Standard*, the *A.M.E. Church Review*, the *Methodist Recorder*, the *Presbyterian Review*, the *Cumberland Presbyterian*, and *Congregational Quarterly*. By the late-nineteenth century, women's preaching became the central issue at national conventions such as the Presbyterian General Assembly and the Methodist Protestant General Conference.

The objections to women's preaching ranged from strong, even hostile opposition to conciliatory concession. At the far end of this spectrum, male church leaders called women's ministry a "subversion of Christian faith" (Wilkin 245) and a sign of "failure and apostasy" (Whittle 315). Biblical opposition to female preaching was supported by literal interpretation of Old and New Testament scripture. From the Old Testament, Eve was often referenced as "the 'second and revised edition' of man" (Weishampel "Female Preaching" 184); the woman who "made a little speech [. . .] that was the world's undoing" (Knwolton 332); and the person who passed on a "moral disability" whose "humiliation will abide even upon the last woman to the end of the age" (Needham 11).

The Old Testament arguments against female preaching, and particularly those references to the devastation wrought by Eve's intellectual liberties, were supplemented with New Testament "evidence" against female religious speech. The words of the apostle Paul figured most prominently, and two passages came to be known as the Pauline injunction. The first is from I Corinthians:

> Let your women keep silence in the churches: for it is not permitted unto them to speak; but they are commanded to be under obedience as also saith the law. And if they will learn any thing, let them ask their husbands at home: for it is a shame for women to speak in the church.
>
> (*Holy Bible*, 14:34–35)

The second is I Timothy 2:11–12: "Let the woman learn in silence with all subjection. But I suffer not a woman to teach, nor to usurp authority over the man, but to be in silence."[2] Calling Paul's prohibition against female preaching a "positive, explicit, and universal" rule (A. Barnes 294), male clergy held fast to a literal reading of Paul, arguing that Paul spoke with "the authority of God" (Brookes 253). They also cited as evidence the lack of female biblical authors, disciples, bishops, elders, deacons, and baptizers. In the words of African Methodist Episcopal (AME) minister J. P. Campbell, "Women always have been and are now recognized as helpers, and always ought to be so recognized and received, for that is the will of the Lord" (290).

Although Christian leaders claimed to rely on biblical support, the majority of objections were in fact based on cultural fears and assumptions. For example, one Congregational pastoral letter read:

> But when she assumes the place of man as a public reformer, she yields the power which God has given her for her protection, and her character becomes unnatural. If the vine, whose strength and beauty is to lean on the trellis-work, and half conceal its clusters, thinks to assume the independence and the overshadowing nature of the elm, it will not only cease to bear fruit, but fall in shame and dishonor into the dust.
>
> (qtd. in Brekus 282)

This letter represents one of the primary nineteenth-century arguments against women's preaching: that female preachers would throw off the divinely established natural hierarchy of the world. As religion historian

Catherine Brekus explains, objectors to women's preaching called up "virtually every negative stereotype of female preachers and reformers: they were 'manly' ('independent' and 'overshadowing'), sexually sterile (unable to 'bear fruit'), and promiscuous ('fallen')" (282). The stereotype of manliness carried particular weight in objections to female ministry: women were denounced by both men and women for appearing too masculine in their preaching, thus breaching feminine decorum. Itinerate preacher Nancy Towle was mocked in an editorial for being a man "in the costume of a female" (227), J. F. Weishampel calls women preachers "repulsive" ("Female Presumption" 190), and George Wilkin claims that under the leadership of women, "the churches are at war with manhood" (346).

God's natural place for women, argued objectors, was not the pulpit but the home, where their piety and morality could provide the domestic antidote to an industrialized, harsh world (see Glascott, this volume). In the words of Presbyterian Theodore Cuyler, "[t]here is a ministry that is older and deeper and more potent than ours. It is the ministry that presides over the crib and impresses the first gospel influence on the enfant soul" (4). Similarly, an editorial in the *Gospel Advocate* claimed that the "most contented little queen of the earth is the mistress of a true husband, a cosy cottage, a hen-coop, a cooking stove, a gentle cow, a good sewing machine, and a baby" (J. Barnes 451).

Along those lines, many argued that female preaching would discourage marriage and threaten the family. Objectors cited the biological burdens of pregnancy and breastfeeding and claimed that women could not cope with the exhausting regimen of preaching along with biological and household duties. The AME refusal of an 1848 petition for women's preaching read as follows:

> Must the Church, that needs the most manly strength, the most gigantic minds to execute her labors, confide them to those whom nature has fitted for the easier toil of life? [. . .] When his mighty truths were to be promulgated to a listless world, who was sent forth by heaven's Son, the tender, gentle daughter of Israel, or her more hardy enduring brothers?
>
> (qtd. in Dodson 92)

Similarly, clergy denounced women's intelligence as unsuitable for theological studies. Women, they claimed, were intuitive, not logical and reasonable, and their style of preaching would not appeal to men.

Some objectors made concessions for women's testifying and exhorting in private meetings, such as small prayer groups, but drew the line at public preaching to "promiscuous" or mixed gender assemblies: "Yet in ordinary social religious meetings, the instructions of the Apostle do not forbid her to take part. But they teach her to perform such part, at such times, and in such circumstances as become the subjection and modesty of her sex"

(Duren 22). These arguments insisted upon a distinction between appropriate and inappropriate womanly speech; women who spoke in front of men—whether in church or from the platform—shared a sin that warranted the "deepest condemnation" (P. Cooke 9). For these ministers, the issue was that women claimed public space, not divine inspiration; they were not concerned with the theological debate over women's preaching but, rather, with the social debate over women's public speaking.

In sum, the objections to women's preaching relied on scripture to support societal constraints on female public speech. Thus Protestant women rhetors had to negotiate carefully these two sources of objection—the Bible and social customs and mores. In defending women's preaching, women defied religious and cultural norms, but not always simultaneously, and it is in the parley between the two that we see the power and subtlety of the Christian rhetoric of this period.

THE GENRES OF WOMEN'S DEFENSES OF WOMEN'S PREACHING

A heterogeneous group comprised of different denominations, races, classes, political leanings, and geographic affiliations, Protestant female activists were prolific, publishing dozens of women's preaching apologia. Moreover, they were resourceful, using all genres available in their attempts to defend female ministry: spiritual autobiography, treatise, pamphlet, editorial, letter, and speech.

Most women who published female preaching apologia in the early nineteenth century did so through the spiritual autobiography, a genre common to evangelical traditions. Following a well-established narrative structure (the women detail their conversion, sanctification, call to preach, and itinerancy), the spiritual autobiography by its very generic nature is a de facto defense of the preacher who wrote it, providing evidence of a successful preaching career. Some women contain their female preaching apologia in standalone chapters of their spiritual autobiographies; for example, alongside such chapters as "Parentage," "Marriage," and "Mission Work," Sarah Cooke includes a chapter titled "Shall Women Preach the Gospel," and Maggie Newton Van Cott closes her spiritual autobiography with the chapter, "Shall Woman Preach." Many other women, such as Zilpha Elaw, Jarena Lee, and Lydia Sexton, embed their defenses of female ministry within the chapter of their spiritual autobiography that narrates their calls to preach. Others, such as Fanny Newell and Amanda Berry Smith, intersperse common lines of argument defending preaching throughout their narratives.

One of the more common genres for female preaching apologia by women was the pamphlet or treatise, a popular genre for addressing a variety of civil topics from the Reformation through the mid-nineteenth century. This genre was a bolder option than the spiritual autobiography because it extended the argument over female religious leadership into the civil and political realm and explicitly invited debate on the topic. Mary Boardman, Catherine Booth,[3] Barbara Kellison, and Deborah Pierce, for example, made aggressive attacks on the opposition to women's preaching in pamphlets, reprinting and circulating them multiple times, and Phoebe Palmer, Frances Willard, Louisa Woosley, and Fannie McDowell Hunter published book-length defenses of women's preaching. Moreover, several women defend women's preaching within treatises on women's rights. Both Sarah Grimke's *Letters on the Equality of the Sexes* and Elizabeth Wilson's *A Scriptural View of Woman's Rights* contain chapters defending preaching among other chapters covering a range of issues, including women's intellect, dress, and legal rights. Similarly, Jennie Fowler Willing embeds a defense of women's preaching in the chapter, "Talking," in *The Potential Women*, and Sara Duncan includes a brief defense of women's integral role in missionary work in *Woman a Factor in the Development of Christian Missions*.

In the mid- to late nineteenth century, Protestant women entered the discursive space of religious journals, thus inviting the broader Christian community to engage in the debate over female preaching via church-sanctioned publications. As columnists, Olympia Brown ("Women") and Jennie Willing ("Woman") frequently advocated for women's preaching in the *New York Evangelist* and *Guide to Holiness*, respectively. Other women wrote open letters and letters to the editor of a religious press, often over a period of several weeks, months, or even years—Antoinette Brown in 1849 in the *Oberlin Quarterly Review*, Ellen Stewart from 1851 to 1855 in the *Church Advocate*, and Silena Holman from 1888 to 1913 in the *Gospel Advocate*.

From the mid-nineteenth century on, women preachers took advantage of the newly emerging rhetorical space of women's rights conventions by delivering female preaching apologia speeches from the platform. Early conventions in the late 1840s to 1870s, such as the Worcester and Syracuse Women's Rights Conventions and the First Women's Congress of the Association for the Advancement of Women, devoted considerable space to women's leadership within the church and attracted female religious reformers, including Antoinette Brown, Lucretia Mott, Sojourner Truth, Elizabeth Wilson, Augusta Chapin, and Phebe Hanaford (see Stanton, Anthony, and Gage). The debate over women's preaching still raged on twenty years later at the World's Congress of Representative Women and the Congress of Women, both part of the World's Columbian Exposition held in Chicago, a World Fair devoted to social reconstruction efforts, with women's preaching apologia speeches given by Caroline Bartlett, Ida Hultin, Florence Kollock, Mary Moreland, Amelia Quinton, Mary Safford, and Eugenia St. John (a pseudonym for Martha Eugenia Berry).

Women also delivered women's preaching apologia directly from the pulpit; however, remarkably few of those sermons were later circulated. Olympia Brown ("Band") and Augusta Chapin defended female preaching at an ordination service of a woman and later published the apologia. In the early twentieth century, Church of Nazarene ministers Mary Cagle and Annie May Fisher defended their right to preach directly from the pulpit and then reprinted the sermons. The occasion evidently was not unique: Cagle writes that "as usual, she had to preach on 'Women's Right to Preach' " (61).[4]

THE TOPOI OF WOMEN'S DEFENSES OF WOMEN'S PREACHING

Using this broad collection of genres, Protestant female preaching apologists articulated a desire to accept women as authorized and legitimate rhetorical agents in their faith communities. In female preaching apologia, genre serves as one litmus test for the development and evolution of the debate over women's preaching as it intensifies over the course of the nineteenth century. In my study of women's defenses of women's preaching, I identify three topoi across the genres Protestant women selected for their apologia: reference to the power of the call to preach, a strategic blend of biblical interpretation that performs and invites female leadership, and a reconciliation of the role of female preacher within society. These topoi are employed with varying degrees; the female preaching apologists seem to have considered and understood the implicit and explicit "argumentivity" of these genres (Amossy 1), negotiating the suitability and effectiveness of these lines of argument within their selected genres.

Authorization: The Power of the Call to Preach

In her widely disseminated *Faith and Its Effects*, Phoebe Palmer emphasizes the call to preach as the primary source of religious and rhetorical authorization:

> And now, my dear sister, do not be startled, when I tell you that you have been *ordained* for a great work. Not by the imposition of mortal hands, or a call from man. No, Christ, the great Head of the church, hath chosen you, "and ordained you, that ye should go and bring forth fruit." O my sister, yours is indeed a high and holy calling.
>
> (290)

Palmer's rhetorical choice in emphasizing *ordained* as the term signifying and encompassing the power of the call to preach represents a common argument in Protestant female preaching apologia that the call was a literal, distinct command from God that trumped societal restrictions. The call to preach provided women with the rhetorical power of invoking a divine ethos as it simultaneously indicated the mandatory requirement to fulfill the duties of the call.

The divine call is a particularly important warrant in female preaching apologia of the spiritual autobiography tradition, most notably in those published in the early nineteenth century. The spiritual autobiography was a popular genre for religious leaders and laypeople alike, and thus including their call to preach within this expected and acceptable discursive practice allowed women preachers to defend their right to the pulpit in a passive, nonthreatening way (see Shaver, this volume). Furthermore, for evangelical sectarian women whose only option was itinerancy, the spiritual autobiography—often self-published—was the primary mechanism for convincing a congregation to accept her as a legitimate agent of God. Each congregation had the freedom to evaluate the authenticity of a woman's calling and her hermeneutic skills. Therefore, the narration of her call had to be rhetorically powerful enough to prove that authenticity and thus garner an invitation into the pulpit. A pattern emerges within the narration of these calls to preach, with the female preachers providing specific details regarding the moment of the call, their initial resistance to the call, God's punishment for this resistance, and, finally, God's role—explicit and implicit—in helping them follow the call.

In their narration of God's call to preach, the female preachers first provide precise details of the call. For many, the call is a distinct, audible voice from God, and the preachers relate the exact words, within quotation marks, that God or an angel delivers. Several women also describe the physical nature of the event. Zilpha Elaw, for example, tells of "a sensation as if I had received a blow on the head, or had sustained an electric shock" (79), followed by "a hand, touch me, on the right shoulder" (82), and Mary Lee Cagle claims that "the Lord put forth His hand, and touched my mouth" (71). For others, the call comes in dreams. Maggie Newton Van Cott relates a dream where she is called to preach and immediately answers that call, preaching to none other than John Wesley in her dreams (153); Julia Foote dreams that Jesus literally places a golden scroll in her bosom, telling her, "I have sent you to proclaim salvation to all" (71).

Almost universally, female preachers outline their resistance to God's call, citing culturally based pressures. As religious historian Louis Billington notes, all late-eighteenth- to early-nineteenth-century New England female preaching apologia "emphasized both publicly and privately the overwhelming compulsion of their calling and yet the fear and dread which it produced in them" (qtd. in Chaves 176). Lydia Sexton, for example, narrates how she was "possessed of a man-fearing spirit, and continually resisted the monitions of the Spirit" (223). The articulation of their hesitance to answer God's call highlights the predicament these female preachers found themselves in: they understood the call to preach as an expected rhetorical convention of the spiritual autobiography genre and an important warrant for congregations considering their application to preach; simultaneously, they were well aware of the limitations on women's public speech and widespread suspicions of female religious leadership. They resolve this rhetorical dilemma by trumping male resistance to their preaching with divine punishment for refusal to answer God's call.

For example, in 1817, Deborah Pierce warns, "Rise up ye careless daughters, for many, many days shall ye be troubled, for ye have not harkened to the voice of God yourself" (qtd. in Ryan 72). The consequences of ignoring her counsel are sprinkled throughout the other defenses, as women detail the physical, mental, and spiritual dangers of not heeding God's call. Not only did their own good health depend on their compliance, but they also risked the health and even the lives of their family, as well, if they failed to answer God's call. For example, Louisa Woosley first resists the call to preach because of her maternal duties, and her child falls ill. She writes, "The hand of affliction was laid upon my firstborn [. . .]. I felt that God was opening the way and intended to remove the hinderances, though it be by death" (98). She promises to follow God's call, but after the health of her daughter returns, she resists again due to a lack of confidence in her education and a lack of support from her husband. This time, her own health fails: "I was reduced to a frame, and as helpless as an infant" (98). It is only after "giving all to God" and seeking out an opportunity to preach that her health improves (98).

Many female preachers invoke scripture to describe the spiritual torment of resisting God's call, particularly Jeremiah 20:9: "Then I said, I will not make mention of him, nor speak any more in his name. But his word was in mine heart as a burning fire shut up in my bones, and I was weary with forbearing, and I could not stay." Also frequently cited is I Corinthians 9:16: "Necessity is laid upon me, and woe is me if I preach not the Gospel." Thus, female preachers answer commonly articulated societal restrictions on female ministry with evidence of the biblical and divine pressure to heed God's commands.

When the female preachers finally answer the call, they are careful to protect this constructed ethos by claiming little agency in their rhetorical power. Using metaphor, they refer to themselves as instruments for use by God. Harriet Livermore calls herself a "sharp threshing instrument in God's hands" (*Narration* 159), Fanny Newell a "poor feeble instrument" (144), Jarena Lee a "poor coloured instrument" (37), and Zilpha Elaw a "simple and weak instrument" (70). The women then describe how God literally provides their sermons and exhortations. Harriet Livermore comments that her "mouth was filled with praise" (*Narration* 118); Jarena Lee hears God's voice, which says, "Preach the Gospel; I will put words in your mouth" (35); and Mary Still Adams writes, "As soon as the Lord was pleased to give me strength I arose in obedience to my divine Master's command, and delivered the message which his Spirit dictated to me" (56).

This rhetorical technique is modified slightly in the conversion narratives contained in spiritual autobiographies published in the late nineteenth century, wherein female rhetors avoid deflecting agency solely to

God and rather reference more confidently their personal rhetorical abilities and their biblical knowledge. Lydia Sexton looks to the Bible and her religious community for support, citing scriptural passages that support her call, along with "encouragements by my brethren and sisters" (213–21). Often referring to the common biblical metaphor of God putting his "seal" on their preaching,[5] they highlight the mediatory role of the female preacher: God provides the inspiration and the authorization; women provide the rhetorical talent to deliver the message. "How He put his seal on this first work," writes Amanda Berry Smith, "to encourage my heart and establish my faith, that he indeed had chosen, and ordained and sent me" (158–59).

Nineteenth-century women preachers clearly recognized that the call needed to be rhetorically verifiable and supportable. Thus, they provide sufficient physical, literal, and scriptural evidence by establishing in their spiritual autobiographies that they are called to preach by God himself, that they have resisted due to real and potential objections from their communities, and that they preach only after divine provocation and threat. However, as Catherine Brekus, points out, by the mid-nineteenth century the call to preach lost much of its rhetorical efficacy, primarily because "most clerical leaders no longer believed that being called was sufficient preparation for the ministry" (288). Expectedly, then, the call to preach as a line of argument occupies a less prominent role in defenses outside of the genre of spiritual autobiography. In their pamphlets and treatises, Phoebe Palmer, Jennie Willing, and Frances Willard do not share their own calls to preach; however, they all refer to the call to preach as an important justification for preaching. Willing writes, "But shall women preach? Certainly, if God calls them to preach. He cannot make a mistake. He is not the author of confusion" ("Talking" 121). Similarly, in her platform speech defending female ministry, Augusta Chapin says, "Her call and commission are not from earthly councils but from Heaven; and the Church of to-day dares not—I cannot think it wishes even—to enforce upon her either inactivity or silence" (100).

The call to preach offered rhetorical power and was rhetorically generative. It was a source of authority because nineteenth-century women were expected to remain silent in almost all public spaces, and the call provided them with the necessary ethos to claim their role in public ministry. As a mandate from God, the call also constituted an exigency that demanded women respond. Moreover, their recognition of the call to preach as a discursively "safe" topos to leverage against the gender-biased cultural arguments of the day demonstrates their astute analysis of the constraints and opportunities of their rhetorical situation. To borrow Perelman and Olbrechts-Tyteca's concept of the hierarchy of values, female preaching apologists understood that within their particular community of Christian believers, obedience to God's will and the divine call was a more important "value" than the restriction of women's speech (80–81).

Biblical Hermeneutics: Employing a Range of Interpretation

Biblical hermeneutics includes the entire spectrum of interpretation, from using biblical stories for contemporary application to more formalized scriptural exegesis. Every woman who defended women's ministry employed a hermeneutic and thus demonstrated her scriptural knowledge. The articulation of their calls to preach served as evidence of a divine right to the pulpit despite societal restrictions; the use of a hermeneutic served as evidence of scriptural literacy, which female preachers could not simply claim or say was gifted by God. Rather, they had to demonstrate such literacy as proof of their capacity to fulfill the duties of the call to preach.

Across all genres, women referred to biblical stories to narratize a history of women's religious leadership; in treatises, pamphlets, and editorials, they employed more formalized, interpretative exegesis. Exegetical expertise, and particularly exegesis as a means of refutation, was relatively new territory for women and considered an acceptable practice only for male preachers and church leaders. Consequently, when female apologists performed what would be considered a more sophisticated exegesis to refute objections to women's ministry, they located their rhetorical power in their individualized religious experiences and in their mastery of a recognized *clerical* rhetorical act.

The historiographical strategy of reciting a lineage of women religious leaders in the Bible as foremothers is a particularly common topos for early-nineteenth-century female defenders. Because referencing Deborah, Miriam, Huldah, Jael, Anna, Priscilla, and Phoebe did not require scriptural "interpretation" per se, but rather a simple re-narratization of biblical stories, it fit the argumentative limitations of the spiritual autobiography in particular. Harriet Livermore, for example, devotes the majority of her defense—five letters and fifty-four pages—to detailing the stories of dozens of biblical women, beginning with Sarah and concluding with Mary Magdalene (*Scriptural* 32–86).

Within the pamphlet, treatise, and speech genres, especially those published from mid-century on, the topos of naming a lineage of biblical female precedence was often bolstered by references to contemporary female leaders, religious and secular. Susanne Wesley, Mary Bosanquet, and Sojourner Truth are just a few of the examples frequently cited as foremothers of a female clerical tradition; female pioneers in other industries—medicine, trade, astronomy, and education—are also cited. Supplementing the biblical lineage of preaching women with modern-day preaching women and women in other spheres of public life widens the sphere of activity for *all* women and invokes a broader genealogy of religious leadership. In her treatise chapter titled "The Outlook—Women's Prospects Brightening," Louisa Woosley lists the modern-day accomplishments—secular and religious—of more than two dozen women, interspersed with lines of collective or generic female accomplishments (e.g. "There are one hundred and ninety-six women operators in [. . .] the Western Union Telegraph Company" [88], and "Women are State librarians" [90]). She follows, then, with the specific Christian traits that these women have received and now advance from their biblical foremothers: "the boldness of Deborah," "the intercession of Esther," "the piety of Ruth," "the zeal of Priscilla," and so on (92).

When attempting to substantiate women's divine call to the pulpit, female preaching apologists pointed to either Joel 2:28–29 or Acts 2:17–18, a variation of the Joel passage:

> And it shall come to pass in the last days, saith God, I will pour out of my Spirit upon all flesh; and your sons and your daughters shall prophesy, and your young men shall see visions, and your old men shall dream dreams: And on my servants and on my handmaidens I will pour out in those days of my spirit; and they shall prophesy.
>
> (Acts 2:17–18)

These Pentecostal passages are central to the logical support of holiness women in particular. Phoebe Palmer refers directly to the Pentecost in the title of her defense, *Promise of the Father*, and Jennie Fowler Willing writes, "The Pentecost gave woman her Magna Charta" ("Woman" 21). According to Wesleyan scholar Susan Stanley, for holiness women, the authority of the Holy Spirit superseded any clerical prohibition against women's preaching (104). Female preaching apologists often cite or reference Acts 5:29 in support: "We must obey God rather than men." Coupled with the Pentecostal passages, this mandate compelled women to challenge the authority of those who attempted to prevent female ministry. As Palmer writes, "[w]here church order is at variance with divine order, it were better to obey God than man" (*Promise of the Father* vi), and Lydia Sexton asks, "How could they obey God and not Prophesy?" (254).

As the nineteenth century progressed, Pentecostal arguments diminished in effectiveness, partly because of a newly emerging denominational hierarchy in which presbyters, deacons, and bishops claimed greater ecclesiastical authority and de-emphasized prophetic authority. The decline of the rhetorical power and religious weight of prophetic authority mid-century is reflected in female religious rhetors' increased attempts to respond exegetically to the Pauline injunction, I Corinthians 14:34–35 and I Timothy 2:11–12. As Methodist Elizabeth Wilson explains in her 1849 treatise, "[t]here are but *two* isolated portions of Scripture on which the whole idea of women's prohibition of speaking in the church is predicated without any corroborating evidence" (149–50). Through their exegesis of these two passages, along with their comparative exegesis of other scripture, female apologists generated arguments refuting the Pauline injunction on three basic grounds: women spoke under the authority of the Holy Spirit and not in authority over men, Paul's injunctions were temporary and idiosyncratic when taken in historical context, and both passages were inconsistent with other scripture.

First, women argued that women's preaching did not in fact *usurp* authority, because women preached only under the influence and direction of the Holy Spirit. Defenses often reinforced this argument with the Pentecostal passages; thus, although defenders engaged in direct confrontation of male clergy through their refutation, they still articulated a theology that maintained the passivity of the female preacher as a vessel and conduit for God's new age. Women preachers also argued that women's submission to men was limited to the home and did not extend to the church, where God exercised authority over men and women. As Louisa Woosley writes, "[i]t is evident that the Scripture referred to in verse 34, applies solely to married women, and it has no reference to religious worship of any kind" (12).

Second, female defenders argued that Paul's injunction was uniquely specific to the early church and that biblical scholars had to be sensitive to the cultural conditions that gave rise to Paul's prohibitions. According to female preachers, women obviously prayed and prophesied publicly in the early church; Paul's restrictions referred to the *manner* of their speaking, that is, with propriety. For example, Phoebe Palmer argues in *Tongue of Fire* that the passages were written in the context of disorderly debates and only referenced disruptive women in the church of Paul's time as specific examples; Elizabeth Wilson claims that "the apostle's prohibition was *special* and *particular*, and not universal and general" (159); and Jennie Willing writes, "[Paul] gave [women] an injunction applicable only to their land and time" ("Talking" 119).

Third, female defenders argued that a too literal reading of Paul is inconsistent with other parts of the Bible. Citing Genesis 1:27 ("So God created man in his own image, in the image of God created he him; male and female created he them") and Matthew 28:10 ("Then said Jesus unto them, Be not afraid: go tell my brethren that they go into Galilee, and there shall they see me"), the women offer a revisionist reading of key scriptural passages and argue that they contradict the Pauline injunction. This argument also applied to other Pauline passages. The women refer to 1 Corinthians 11:4–5, wherein Paul authorizes women to "pray and prophesy," and Philippians 4:2 and Romans 16:12, in which Paul lists women who helped him spread the gospel, including Euodia, Syntyche, Tryphena, and Tryphosa. Frances Willard captures similar inconsistencies visually in what she calls "tabulated form" (27).

In addition to demonstrating their own careful exegesis of the Pauline injunction, female preaching apologists critiqued male exegesis as inaccurate, dogmatic, and "the result of old-fogyism" (Woosley 87). They question formal biblical translations, particularly King James, criticize the shift in Paul's reference to Phoebe from deacon or minister to servant, conjugate and analyze the Greek word *lalein* ("to speak") used in the Pauline injunction, and challenge gender pronouns. Most women refer to multiple Bible editions in their texts, including Elizabeth Cady Stanton's controversial *The Woman's Bible*. Elizabeth Wilson and Sarah Grimke reach as far back as a 1574 Bible for support. On one hand, this criticism is performative; the women construct a preacherly ethos by demonstrating deep awareness of scripture and church publishing history. On the other hand, this criticism is rhetorically strategic; the women extend the boundaries of their textual support with this larger canon of biblical history, biblical criticism, and Bible editions.

Misinterpretation of scripture, according to female preaching apologists, was not innocent, and they further argue that male clerical leaders willfully misread scripture for their own dogmatic ends. This particular criticism stretches back as far as the earliest nineteenth-century defenses. As Jarena Lee, warns, "O how careful ought we to be lest through our by-laws of church government and discipline, we bring into disrepute even the word of life" (36). Elizabeth Wilson similarly complains, "Some of our brethren are very good at *making Scripture*, in order to support a *favourite theory*" (153, emphasis in original). This strategy sends a powerful message: Biblical interpretation by male preachers in the service of rejecting female leadership is dissociated from true exegesis and associated, instead, with "ecclesiastical tyranny" (Stewart 188), and "imposed or borrowed theories of masculine authority" (Hultin 789). In her well-circulated transatlantic tract defending female ministry, Catherine Booth aptly sums up the importance of women's exegetical contributions:

> If commentators had dealt with the Bible on other subjects as they have dealt with it on this, taking isolated passages, separated from their explanatory connections, and insisting on a literal interpretation of the words of our version, what errors and contradictions would have been forced upon the acceptance of the Church, and what terrible results would have accrued to the world.
>
> (23)

Women's religious participation in the nineteenth century was a constant negotiation, with the Bible providing the strongest evidence both against and for female preaching. In addition to answering objections exegetically, female preaching apologists addressed directly the cultural and social biases underlying those objections. Ranging from conciliatory to aggressive, these exegetical arguments provided a foundation for female apologists' use of religious rhetoric in the resolution of women's traditional roles with women's religious leadership.

Women's Role in Society: Reconciling the Role of Female Preacher

Nineteenth-century dominant discourse offered a limited number of acceptable roles for women: slave, wife, mother, and teacher. A necessary topos, then, for all female preaching apologia was a consideration and negotiation of women's role within society. Nineteenth-century scholars generally agree that there were two primary methods of argumentation concerning the "woman question," namely, "difference" and "equality" (see Cott; Welter). Those who used a rhetoric of difference argued that because women differed from men in natural endowment, environment, or training, it behooved the natural balance of society to permit women equal access to education, work, and citizenship. Those employing equality argued that women were intellectually and spiritually equal to men, and thus deserved the same opportunities. Within women's preaching apologia, rhetors also argued from a position of difference or equality; however, the arguments based on equality were further divided into arguments based on scriptural equality and natural equality.

The arguments based on difference did not demand a reconfiguration of traditional male and female roles. Using domestic metaphors and allusions that emphasized middle-class social responsibility and piety, these rhetors offered women a vision of an expanded spiritual sphere while maintaining the constraints of her temporal sphere. Jennie Willing and Josephine Butler, for example, attempt to demonstrate that women's preaching was well within a woman's prescribed sphere by pointing to Jesus' parable of the talents (Matt. 25:14–30); they claim that God included the pulpit as an appropriate place to exhibit and use their talents. Notably, these talents are scripted as uniquely female: women preaching apologists argue that God purposely endowed women with specifically feminine gifts for the ministry. According to Catherine Booth, "God has given to woman a graceful form and attitude, winning manners, persuasive speech, and, above all, a finely-toned emotional nature, all of which appear to us eminent *natural* qualifications for public speaking" (3); similarly, Mrs. G. E. Taylor claims that "[f]rom the beginning of time, woman has represented the good, the true and the beautiful. She has been the personification of the world's ideals" (20).

An extension of the argument based on difference was an argument for women's preaching based on her unique role as mother. Such arguments were often used in women's defenses as a position with scriptural support that unified women's other sites of identity. The preacher as mother is a popular trope in female preaching apologia across genres and throughout the nineteenth century, because it enabled women to position themselves across the political spectrum.[6] In female preaching apologia of the early nineteenth century, women maintained a safe, acceptable identity by identifying as mothers. Fanny Newell never uses the term *preaching* except when she refers to preaching to her children (168); when engaged in public ministry, she "exhorts," "testifies," or "speaks." Similarly, throughout her work, Nancy Towle simply refers to herself as a "Mother in Israel" and "Sister in Christ" but never as a preacher (229). By mid-century, women expanded the definition of mother by claiming that "[p]astoral work is adapted to women, for it is motherly work" (qtd. in Brekus 340).

Other preaching apologists, such as Virginia Broughton, Caroline Bartlett, Florence Kollock, Mary Chapin, and Frances Willard, represent the role of mother as congruent with the role of minister and align the biological function of motherhood with the scriptural function of ministering. For example, Broughton, invoking the aforementioned topos of naming biblical foremothers, states that all women were descended from Mary; she thus claims women as specially privileged by God for both her family's conversion and the regeneration of humanity (cited in Higginbotham 129). Caroline Bartlett similarly argues that the church's regeneration depended on women's motherly ministry:

> But today, while the present abnormal state of things exists in the church, I believe that the greatest need of the church is to be *mothered* [. . .] until the motherhood as well as the fatherhood of God is recognized by this world [. . .] bringing it up to the true knowledge and glad service of our Father and Mother God.
>
> (232–33)

Florence Kollock further adds a mother's intellectual contribution to women's biological and scriptural functions, claiming that "mother's love and woman's wit" are needed in ministry (222). Through this phrase she successfully absolves the binary of mother/woman/maternal affection and masculine wit, suggesting instead that women can be both. Kollock further argues that women physically birthed the world's "great prophets, priests, and teachers" (221) and "[sustained] them in their efforts" (222), presumably through education and support. Through their biological and intellectual contributions of motherhood, women offered a matrix of support for male religious leaders throughout history.

Several defenses of women's preaching, particularly those given as speeches at women's rights conventions, suggest that women are not only uniquely gifted by God, but also necessary for humanizing religion. Mary Safford argues that through female ministry "religion will become less masculine in the pulpit, less feminine in the pews, more nobly human in both" (238), and Ida Hultin agrees that both man and woman are needed "both together—man thinking and doing in man's way, woman thinking and doing in woman's way. He, true manly; she, true womanly; each intelligently, responsibly, personally religious" (789). Similarly, Eugenia St. John claims that "woman's native intuition is as necessary in the pulpit as man's logical, reasoning powers" (233). The implication behind this line of argument is that if humanity is comprised equally of men and women, then the important roles in society—namely, teacher and minister—must be equally distributed to men and women; it is precisely because women and men are different that they should be equally represented in church offices.

Female rhetors who argue for equality based on scriptural rights do so primarily by referencing Galatians 3:28: "There is neither Jew nor Greek, there is neither bond nor free, there is neither male nor female; for ye are all one in Christ Jesus." According to Catherine Booth, "[i]f this passage does not teach that in the privileges, duties, and responsibilities of Christ's kingdom, all differences of nation, caste, and sex are abolished, we should like to know what it does teach, and wherefore it was written" (19). The women who cite Galatians negotiate a delicate balance, arguing for equality with men while maintaining women's separate sphere. In claiming that men and women are equal *in the eyes of God*, these women avoid direct confrontation with men over the debate of women's sphere in everyday life and distance themselves from the larger and more strident battles of equality then being waged. They do this partly by arguing that men and women are inherently and naturally equal in their Edenic state. They consider the current subjugation of woman to be a result of the fall: "It must be conceded, that in a state of innocency, there was a perfect equality between the sexes" (Livermore, *Scriptural* 26). Moreover, in redefining the "natural order of God"—an argument so often used against women—they maintain that it was actually male custom and prejudice that threatened the original natural order of God: "They were both made in the image of God. Dominion was given to both over every other creature, but not over each other" (Price 20).

Female preaching apologists who argued for equality from a position of natural rights borrowed rhetoric from the woman's rights and other social justice movements (see Donawerth). They still relied on scriptural support; however, that support either was on equal footing with or became secondary to their arguments based on natural equality. Furthermore, it was relatively easy and rhetorically seamless to borrow from other social justice movements, because, as Carl and Dorothy Schneider point out, these movements "originated in part because of men's refusal to let women speak [. . . and] at least at first understood themselves as promoting religious values [. . . and] afforded women experiences helpful in the pulpit" (59). It is thus not surprising to see rhetoric in these defenses that encourages political action and engagement. Jennie Willing writes that "[i]f the existing social order is not in harmony with the Divine plan, it will have to be subverted" ("Talking" 122). Similarly, Mary Lee Cagle warns that "[t]his is pre-eminently a woman's age. They are slowly but surely pressing their way to the front" (160).

Within their defenses, women encourage other female ministers to attend to a variety of social issues, including women's political disenfranchisement, slavery and racism, alcoholism, poverty, prostitution, and education. These defenses merge scriptural arguments for women's preaching with the natural rights arguments used in a variety of social reform movements; they also conflate the importance of eschatological witness with political action. In so doing, they present a theology aimed not only at transforming the individual, but also society (see Duffy, this volume; Shaver, this volume).

Particularly representative of a blended rhetoric of religion and social reform are the female preaching apologia delivered as platform speeches; these speeches invoke women's rights rhetoric and mask exegesis with a rhetoric of secular reason and logic. Whereas defenses in the other genres tend to *supplement* their scriptural defenses with secular, natural rights arguments, the rhetors at women's rights conventions *replace* the scriptural arguments for women's preaching with arguments based on the prevailing natural rights arguments of the day. It is telling that the speeches presented at the 1893 World's Congress of Representative Women were delivered in the forum titled "Science and Religion." Mary Safford, for example, references evolution in her extended metaphor: "As that monarch of the forest, the oak, is the result of the evolution of physical life, so woman's place in the church as a minister of religion is the result of that evolution of spiritual life which will yet transform the world" (236); Eugenia St. John claims that "intuition and reason have come to woman in the new era" (234); Ida Hultin refers to religion as "the science of the highest human development" (788); and Caroline Bartlett opens her defense with three "propositions," which she then explicates to demonstrate that her third proposition is true, due partly to "the law which governs 'the survival of the fittest' " (229).

Because theirs is not an exegetical argument, Kollock, Safford, St. John, Hultin, and Bartlett cite few, if any, biblical passages. Rather, their references to God are often masked by metonymy. For example, Kollock refers to God as "Logic" and "the power that gave woman being" (221), thus establishing a binary between logic and theology, with logic being a God-given power and theology a human, and specifically masculine, power. Her opening enthymeme sets the tone for her entire argument: "Woman in the world is the product of the will of the First Great Cause. Woman in the pew is the natural sequence of woman in the world. 'Woman in the pulpit' is the inevitable consequence of woman in the pew" (221). By identifying God as the "First Great Cause" and using the terms "product" and "natural sequence," Kollock naturalizes God and further establishes him as the precedence of all other causes to follow. She implies that such causes as temperance, suffrage, abolitionism, and education are a natural extension or evolution of this First Great Cause.

Regardless of whether they argued from a position of difference or equality, female religious rhetors recognized the need to define, redefine, or expand women's sphere. As they did so, the stakes were made clear, and women's right to the pulpit became intertwined with other civil and political rights. Female preaching apologists fused social reform and natural rights rhetoric with religious rhetoric, thus synchronizing the debate over women's preaching with other social reform movements. In so doing, they establish rhetorically reciprocal religious and secular arguments for defending women's right to the pulpit.

CONCLUSION

This chapter's attention to the synergy between genre and argument helps us make some tentative generalizations. Primarily using the genre of spiritual autobiography, the earlier defenses rely much more heavily on personal narrative that witnessed to their successful preaching careers. Their hermeneutical strategy is more historical than exegetical, and their use of the inspired call is a rhetorical choice to locate power with God alone, deflecting attention from the rhetorical agency of the woman preacher. In the mid-nineteenth century, exegetical defenses dominate, as women engage directly with clerical opponents to their ministry. Even as they attest that their inspiration is divine, the source of their rhetorical power lies in biblical hermeneutics as practiced by their male clerical counterparts. By the end of the nineteenth century, reliance on scriptural support becomes secondary to natural rights rhetoric. This is particularly true because women address public audiences via the platform at secular women's rights conferences. For these women, preaching is but one vocation of many that should be accessible for women.

However, it is as rhetorically interesting to investigate the boundaries between the genre and content of these works as fluid and negotiable. Spiritual autobiographers rely quite heavily on the call to preach as a means of justification. They also, however, employ a biblical hermeneutic, especially towards the middle of the nineteenth century with their use of Pentecostal scriptures. Similarly, while many treatise and editorial writers rely primarily on exegesis, they still also include their call to preach or reference the call as a viable defense. All the women preachers, whether paraphrasing biblical passages in their personal narratives, refuting objections to their preaching, or using metaphor to align their defenses with the women's rights movement, demonstrate a deep knowledge of the Bible and a commitment to their preaching sisters.

Overall, this recovery project reads the rich rhetorical features of this Christian debate as integrally woven into the fabric of nineteenth-century rhetorical practice. I hope that such an analysis demonstrates the value of using religious identity as one terministic screen through which we can understand and complicate the rhetors and the texts we study. This chapter does not simply cast religion as one more interesting dimension of nineteenth-century women's lives; it rather situates their Protestant identities as central to their rhetorical lives, compelling them to enter discourse and sustaining them in that discourse. In short, the Christian faith of female preaching apologists constituted an invitation and obligation to engage in rhetorical practice. To be in service of that faith through rhetoric was their ultimate goal.

NOTES

1 Women's religious speech generally fell under four umbrellas: Preaching, interpreting and expounding on Scripture before a congregation; exhorting, speaking passionately about one's faith to encourage conversion; testifying, sharing one's conversion and sanctification experience; and prophesying, allowing God to speak through oneself.

2 All biblical references are from the King James translation, the translation most popular in the nineteenth century and most cited within the debate over women's preaching.

3 Although Catherine Booth, founder of the Salvation Army, was British, I include her because she frequently toured in the United States and was influential in American religious and reform discourse. Her works *Who Shall Prophesy?* and *Who Shall Publish the Glad Tidings?* are examples of this influence.

4 Cagle uses the third person throughout her spiritual autobiography.

5 This is probably a reference to 2 Corinthians 1:22 ("[God] who hath also sealed us, and given the earnest of the Spirit in our hearts").

6 For an interesting comparison of Palmer's emphasis on woman as "prophet" and Willard's on woman as "mother," see Hardesty, "Minister."

REFERENCES

Adams, Mary Still. *Autobiography of Mary Still Adams, or, "In God we trust."* Los Angeles: Self-published, 1893.

Amossy, Ruth. "The Argumentative Dimension of Discourse." *Argumentation in Practice.* Ed. Frans H. van Eemeren and Peter Houtlosser. Philadelphia: Benjamins, 2005. 87–98.

Andrews, William L., ed. *Sisters of the Spirits: Three Black Women's Autobiographies of the Nineteenth Century.* Bloomington: Indiana UP, 1986.

Barnes, Albert. *Notes Explanatory and Practical on the Epistles of Paul to the Corinthians.* New York: Harper & Brothers, 1859.

Barnes, Justus M. "Woman Her Mission, and Her Education." *Gospel Advocate* 28 (21 July 1886): 451.

Bartlett, Caroline J. "Woman's Call to the Ministry." *The World's Congress of Representative Women.* Vol. 1. Ed. May Wright Sewell. Chicago: Rand, McNally & Company, 1893. 229–33.

Boardman, Mrs. W.E. (Mary). *Who Shall Prophesy?* Boston, MA: Henry Hoyt, 1873.

———. *Who Shall Publish the Glad Tidings?* Boston, MA: Henry Hoyt, 1875.

Booth, Catherine Mumford. *Female Ministry; or, Woman's Right to Preach the Gospel.* London: Morgan & Chase, 1859. Rpt. New York: Salvation Army Supplies Printing and Purchasing Department, 1975; and *Holiness Tracts Defending the Ministry of Women.* Ed. Donald Wilbur Dayton. New York: Garland, 1985.

Boylan, Anne. *The Origins of Women's Activism: New York and Boston, 1797–1840.* Chapel Hill, NC: U of North Carolina P, 2002.

Brekus, Catherine. A. *Strangers and Pilgrims: Female Preaching in America, 1740–1845.* Chapel Hill, NC: U of North Carolina P, 1998.

Brookes, James H. "Woman in the Church," *Truth, or, Testimony for Christ* 14 (1887–1888): 252–53.

Brown, Antoinette L. "Exegesis of 1 Corinthians, xiv, 34, 35; and 1 Timothy, ii, 11, 12." *Oberlin Quarterly Review* 3 (July 1849): 358–73.

Brown, Olympia. "Band of Fellowship." *Services at the Ordination and Installation of Rev. Phebe A. Hanaford, as Pastor of the First Universalist Church, in Hingham, Mass., Feb. 19, 1868.* Boston: C.C. Roberts, 1870. 29–31.

———. "Women Preachers." *New York Evangelist* (24 July 1872): 234.

Buchanan, Lindal. *Regendering Delivery: The Fifth Canon and Antebellum Women Rhetors.* Carbondale: Southern Illinois UP, 2005.

Cagle, Mary Lee. *Life and Work of Mary Lee Cagle: An Autobiography.* Kansas City: Nazarene P, 1928. 160–76.

Campbell, J.P. "The Ordination of Women: What the Authority for It?" *A.M.E. Church Review* (Apr. 1886). *Social Protest Thought in the African Methodist Episcopal Church, 1862–1939.* Ed. Stephen Angell and Anthony Pinn. Knoxville: U of Tennessee P, 2000. 289–90.

Campbell, Karlyn Kohrs. *Man Cannot Speak For Her: A Critical Study of Early Feminist Rhetoric.* Vol. 1. Westport, CT: Praeger, 1989.

Chapin, Augusta A. "Woman's Work in the Pulpit and the Church." *Papers and Letters Presented at the First Woman's Congress of the Association for the Advancement of Woman.* New York: Mrs. WM Ballard, Book and Job, 1874. 99–102.

Chaves, Mark. *Ordaining Women: Culture and Conflict in Religious Organizations.* Boston: Harvard UP, 1997.

Cooke, Parsons. *Female Preaching, Unlawful and Inexpedient. A Sermon.* Lynn: James R. Newhall, 1837.

Cooke, Sarah A. *The Handmaiden of the Lord or "Wayside Sketches."* Chicago: Arnold, 1896. Women and the Church in America, 149. Microform.

Cott, Nancy F. *The Bonds of Womanhood: "Woman's Sphere" in New England, 1780–1835.* New Haven: Yale UP, 1977.

Cuyler, Theodore Ledyard. *Recollections of a Long Life: An Autobiography.* New York: American Tract Society, 1902.

DeBerg, Betty A. *Ungodly Women: Gender and the First Wave of American Fundamentalism.* Minneapolis: Fortress P, 1990.

Dodson, Jualynne. *Engendering Church: Women, Power, and the AME Church.* New York: Rowman & Littlefield, 2002.

Donawerth, Jane. *Conversational Rhetoric: The Rise and Fall of a Women's Tradition, 1600–1900.* Carbondale: Southern Illinois UP, 2011.

Duncan, Sara. *Progressive Missions in the South and Addresses with Illustrations and Sketches of Missionary Workers and Ministers and Bishops' Wives.* Atlanta: The Franklin Printing and Publishing Company, 1906. *Documenting the American South.* 4 November 2004. Web.

Duren, Charles. "Woman's Place in Religious Meetings." *Congregational Review* 8 (January 1868): 22–29.

Elaw, Zilpha. *Memoirs of the Life, Religious Experience, Ministerial Travels, and Labours of Mrs. Zilpha Elaw, an American Female of Colour.* London: Published by the author, 1846. Rpt. Andrews 49–160.

Fisher, Annie May. *Woman's Right to Preach: A Sermon Reported as Delivered at Chilton, Texas.* San Antonio: Published by the author, 1903.

Foote, Julia. *A Brand Plucked from the Fire: An Autobiographical Sketch.* New York: George Hughes, 1879.

Gifford, Carolyn DeSwarte, ed. *The Defense of Women's Rights to Ordination in the Methodist Episcopal Church.* New York: Garland, 1987.

Grimke, Sarah M. *Letters on the Equality of the Sexes and the Condition of Woman.* Boston: Isaac Knapp, 1838.

Hanaford, Phebe A. "Woman in the Church and Pulpit." *Papers and Letters Presented at the First Woman's Congress of the Association for the Advancement of Woman.* New York: Mrs. WM Ballard, Book and Job, 1874. 102–05.

Hardesty, Nancy A. "Minister as Prophet? Or as Mother?" *Women in New Worlds: Historical Perspectives on the Wesleyan Tradition.* Ed. Hilah F. Thomas and Rosemary Skinner Keller. Nashville: Abingdon P, 1982. 88–101.

———. *Women Called to Witness: Evangelical Feminism in the Nineteenth Century.* 2nd ed. Knoxville: U of Knoxville P, 1999.

Hassey, Janette. *No Time for Silence: Evangelical Women in Public Ministry around the Turn of the Century.* Grand Rapids: Academe, 1986.

Higginbotham, Evelyn Brooks. *Righteous Discontent: The Women's Movement in the Black Baptist Church, 1880–1920.* Cambridge: Harvard UP, 1993.

Holman, Silena. "Let Your Women Keep Silence." *Gospel Advocate* 30 (1 Aug. 1888): 8.

———. "The New Woman, No. 2." *Gospel Advocate* 38 (16 July 1896): 452–53.

———. "A Peculiar People." *Gospel Advocate* 30 (2 May 1888): 12.

———. "The Scriptural Status of Woman." *Gospel Advocate* 30 (10 Oct. 1888): 2–3.

———. "The Woman Question." *Gospel Advocate* 55 (27 Feb. 1913): 198–99.

———. "The Woman Question, no. 2" *Gospel Advocate* 55 (6 Mar. 1913): 218–30.

———. "Women's Scriptural Status Again." *Gospel Advocate* 30 (21 Nov. 1888): 8.

The Holy Bible. New York: American Bible Society: 1999. King James Vers.

Hultin, Ida C. "Woman and Religion." *The Congress of Women: Held in the Woman's Building, World's Columbian Exposition, Chicago, U.S.A., 1893*. Ed. Mary Kavanaugh Oldham. Chicago: Monarch, 1894. 788–89.

Hunter, Fannie McDowell. *Women Preachers*. Dallas: Berachah, 1905.

Kellison, Barbara. *The Rights of Women in the Church*. Dayton: published by the author, 1862.

Knowlton, Stephen "The Silence of Women in the Churches." *Congregational Quarterly* 9 (October 1867): n.p.

Kollock, Florence E. "Woman in the Pulpit." Sewell 221–28.

Lee, Jarena. *Religious Experience and Journal of Mrs. Jarena Lee, Giving Account of Her Call to Preach the Gospel: Revised and corrected from the Original Manuscript written by Herself*. Philadelphia: published by the author, 1849. Rpt. Andrews 25–48.

Levander, Caroline Field. *Voices of the Nation: Women and Public Speech in Nineteenth-Century American Literature and Culture*. New York: Cambridge UP, 1998.

Livermore, Harriet. *A Narration of Religious Experience in 12 Letters*. 2 vols. Concord: published by the author, 1826.

———. *Scriptural Evidence in Favor of Female Testimony in Meetings for the Worship of God*. Concord: published by the author, 1824.

Logan, Shirley Wilson. *"We Are Coming": The Persuasive Discourse of Nineteenth-Century Black Women*. Carbondale: Southern Illinois UP, 1999.

Moreland, Mary. "Discussion of the Same Subject." Sewell 234–35.

Needham, Elizabeth Annable. *Woman's Ministry and other expository addresses*. New York: Fleming H. Revell, 1880.

Newell, Fanny. *Memoirs of Fanny Newell*. 2nd ed. Springfield, MA: Merriam, Little, 1832.

Palmer, Phoebe. *Faith and Its Effects: or Fragments from My Portfolio*. New York: published by the author, 1850.

———. *Promise of the Father; or, a Neglected Specialty of the Last Days*. Boston: Henry V. Degen, 1859.

———. *Tongue of Fire on the Daughters of the Lord; or, Questions in Relation to the Duty of the Christian Church in regard to the Privileges of her Female Membership*. New York: W.C. Palmer, Jr. 1869; Rpt. *Phoebe Palmer: Selected Writings*. Ed. Thomas C. Oden. New York: Paulist P, 1988. 33–49.

Perelman, Chaim, and Lucie Olbrechts-Tyteca. *The New Rhetoric*. South Bend: U of Notre Dame P, 1969.

Pierce, Deborah. *A Scriptural Vindication of Female Preaching, Prophesying, or Exhortation*. Carmel, New York. 1820.

Price, Abby. "Woman in the Church." *Proceedings of the Woman's Rights Convention, Held at Worcester, October 23rd & 24th, 1850*. Boston: Prentiss & Sawyer, 1851. 20–36.

Quinton, Amelia S. "Discussion of Same Subject." Sewell 240–41.

Ruether, Rosemary Radford, and Rosemary Skinner Keller, eds. *Women & Religion in America, Volume 1: The Nineteenth Century, a Documentary History*. San Francisco: Harper & Row, 1981.

Ryan, Mary. *Women in Public: From Banners to Ballots*. Baltimore: Johns Hopkins UP, 1992.

Safford, Mary A. "Woman as a Minister of Religion." Sewell 236–40.

Schneider, Carl J., and Dorothy Schneider. *In Their Own Right: The History of American Clergywomen*. New York: Crossroad, 1997.

Sewell, May Wright, ed. *The World's Congress of Representative Women*. Vol. 1. Chicago: Rand McNally, 1893.

Sexton, Lydia. *Autobiography of Lydia Sexton*. Dayton: United Brethren, 1882.

Shaver, Lisa. *Beyond the Pulpit: Women's Rhetorical Roles in the Antebellum Religious Press*. Pittsburgh: U of Pittsburgh P, 2012.

Smith, Amanda Berry. *The Story of the Lord's Dealings with Mrs. Amanda Smith, the Colored Evangelist*. Chicago: Meyer and Brother, 1893.

St. John, Eugenia (aka Martha Eugenia Berry). "Discussion of the Same Subject." Sewell 233–34.

Stanley, Susan. "Empowered Foremothers: Wesleyan/Holiness Women Speak to Today's Christian Feminists." *Wesleyan Theological Journal* 24 (1989): 103–16.

Stanton, Elizabeth Cady. *The Woman's Bible*, parts 1 and 2. New York: European Publishing, 1895/98. Rpt. Mineola: Dover, 2002.

———, Susan B. Anthony, and Matilda Joslyn Gage, eds. *History of Woman Suffrage*, Vol 1. New York: Fowler & Wells, 1881. *Project Gutenberg*. Web. 5 September 2009.

Stewart, Ellen. *Life of Mrs. Ellen Stewart Together with biographical Sketches of Other Individuals also a Discussion with Two Clergyman and Arguments in favor of Women's Rights; together with Letters on Different Subjects Written by Herself*. Akron: Beebe & Elkins, 1858.

Taylor, Mrs. G. E. "Woman's Work and the Influence in Home and Church." *African Methodist Episcopal Church Review*. 23.1 (1906): 20–24. *The African-American Experience in Ohio*. Web. 3 June 2005.

Towle, Nancy. *Vicissitudes Illustrated in the Experience of Nancy Towle in Europe and American Written by Herself*. Charleston: James L. Burges, 1832.

Van Cott, Maggie Newton. *Life and Labors of Mrs. Maggie Newton Van Cott, the first Lady Licensed to Preach in the Methodist Episcopal Church in the United States*. Dictated to John O. Foster. Cincinnati: Hitchcock and Walden, 1872.

Weishampel, J. F. "Female Preaching." *Church Advocate* (1 February 1855). Rpt. Stewart 184.

———. "Female Presumption Again." *Church Advocate* (19 April 1855). Rpt. Stewart 189–90.

Welter, Barbara. "The Cult of True Womanhood, 1820–60." *American Quarterly* 18.2 (1966): 151–74.

Whittle, D. W. "Daily Scripture Readings: Tuesday, November 1." *Record of Christian Work* 11 (October 1892): 315. *Bible Believers*. Web. 5 October 2009.

Wilkin, George Francis. *The Prophesying of Women: A Popular and Practical Exposition of the Bible Doctrine*. Chicago: Fleming H. Revell, 1895.

Willard, Frances. *Woman in the Pulpit*. Boston: Lothrop, 1888.

Willing, Jennie Fowler. "Talking." *The Potential Woman*. Boston, MA: McDonald & Gill, 1886. 111–27.

———. "Woman and the Pentecost." *Guide to Holiness* 68 (January 1898): 21–23; (February 1898): 54–55.

Wilson, Elizabeth. *A Scriptural View of Woman's Rights and Duties, in All the Important Relations of Life*. Philadelphia: W. S. Young, 1849.

Woosley, Louisa M. *Shall Women Preach? Or the Question Answered*. Caneyville: Published by the author, 1891. Rpt. Memphis: Frontier P, 1989.

Zikmund, Barbara Brown. "The Struggle for the Right to Preach." Ruether and Keller 193–241.

11 The Deaconess Identity
An Argument for Professional Churchwomen and Social Christianity

Lisa J. Shaver

Jacob Riis, famous photojournalist and social reformer, captured the image of a Methodist deaconess conversing with a merchant amidst a street crowded with people, hawker stalls, and stacks of castoff rubbish in one of New York City's slums. Published in 1911[1] alongside the photograph on the front page of the *Deaconess Advocate* (*DA*), Riis's description read as follows: "I have seen a deaconess through quiet and loving ministry in the chaos of a ghetto transform a street which was a jungle of junk into a spot that breathed of heaven's first law. It is the gentle and noiseless influence that makes mightily for the coming of the Kingdom" (*DA* 9/1911:1).[2] Even though Riis described the deaconess's efforts as a "noiseless influence," his camera was drawn to her. Deaconesses stood out; they were distinct by design. Not only were deaconesses transforming urban ghettos; they were also transforming the Methodist Church's role in poor urban neighborhoods and women's roles in the early-twentieth-century Methodist Church.

The deaconess movement was established in 1888 by the Methodist Episcopal Church[3] amid the heyday of the women's mission movement that dramatically increased the number of women dispatched as foreign missionaries. Deaconesses were single women, at least twenty years old, who devoted themselves to the service of Christ. While some traveled abroad as foreign missionaries, the largest number worked in city slums, assisting poor residents and immigrants through home visits, health care, and vocational training; they also established kindergartens for working mothers. Others served as pastors' assistants, worked in hospitals as nurses and administrators, or ran orphanages or homes for the elderly. Deaconesses wore distinct dress, long black or dark blue dresses with white ties at the collar. They received room and board and a small monthly allowance, but no wages. Most lived in communal deaconess homes, which were often located in or close to the neighborhoods they served. Although they resembled Catholic nuns, deaconesses did not take vows and were free to leave the office at any time.

When the deaconess movement formed, about twenty percent of all women were employed, yet most working women were from lower-economic classes, forced by necessity to take jobs as domestic servants, farm laborers, dressmakers, laundry workers, teachers, factory workers, housekeepers, and clerks. Even if they had the requisite qualifications, middle-class women struggled to enter professions (*DA* 8/1908:7; McClelland 83). Because women comprised the majority of congregations, church work would seem a natural profession. However, it was rigidly gendered: ministers were men and women were volunteers. Consequently, assuming professional roles required women to position themselves strategically within the Methodist Church in a way that would both garner institutional authority and distinguish them from female lay volunteers. To negotiate this complex situation, the Methodist deaconess movement crafted a distinct deaconess identity that functioned symbolically to induce acceptance of expanded women's roles in church and society. The deaconess movement achieved this by carefully negotiating and leveraging cultural constraints posed by nineteenth-century views on gender roles. Functioning rhetorically as symbolic action, the deaconess identity allowed deaconesses to transform themselves and make progress toward transforming women's roles in society and the material and spiritual conditions of their world.

BACKGROUND: THE DEACONESS MOVEMENT AND CULTURAL CONSTRAINTS

The deaconess movement in the late-nineteenth-century Methodist Church emerged in response to numerous social problems and cultural constraints. It grew out of the Christian conviction that churches had an obligation to help the growing poor and immigrant populations in American cities. In other words, they were fulfilling a Christian duty akin to the social gospel that William Duffy explores elsewhere in this volume. The deaconess office also answered some women's desire to pursue higher education and careers directly linked to their religious beliefs. Throughout much of the nineteenth century, church work including church-sponsored benevolent societies, missionary societies, Sunday schools, and tract and Bible societies were the province of women. Even though some of these organizations were still managed by men and male boards, volunteer churchwomen overwhelmingly provided the labor and made the day-to-day decisions as they canvassed neighborhoods, assessed needs, taught classes, and raised funds. Consequently, church work and religious organizations enabled countless women to enact their Christian beliefs and expand their rhetorical boundaries through their efforts as church volunteers (Shaver, *Beyond* 70–104). However, toward the end of the nineteenth century, women's expectations for themselves and the church began to change.

Whereas previous evangelical social ministries had sought to offer salvation to individuals, social gospel efforts endeavored to save society (see also Duffy, this volume). Responding to the rapid urbanization and industrialization during the latter half of the nineteenth century, the social gospel movement offered "a theological and practical response to the stark realities of poverty and economic injustice," and "a ringing indictment of the complacency of Protestantism" (Edwards and Gifford 3). While past scholarship on the social gospel focused almost exclusively on preachers and theologians who delivered sermons and published theological treatises, more recent scholarship has recognized women as early participants in social Christianity (Blue; Dougherty, "Social"; Edwards and Gifford). In the latter half of the nineteenth century, groups including the Women's Christian Temperance Union (WCTU), the Young Women's Christian Association, and Methodist deaconesses were already enacting "a grassroots version" of the social gospel (Dougherty, "Social"; Scott 85). Identifying these efforts as early social gospel work, Mary Agnes Dougherty argues that "the social gospel demanded a radical change in the attitude and actions of Protestant men [. . .] born only when male ministers and professors and lay*men* began to think and behave in ways which nineteenth-century American culture considered characteristic of womanhood" ("Social" 201).

Lucy Rider Meyer, the deaconess movement's founder, believed that Christian women could transform American society. Instead of part-time volunteers working around their duties as wives, mothers, and caretakers, Rider Meyer invented a different model of women's religious work. Working within societal and institutional constraints that discouraged and precluded women from entering many professions including ordained ministry, Rider Meyer sought to advance the kingdom of God by envisioning an office sanctioned by the church that would be filled by women who were specially trained and consecrated to Christian service. The deaconess office was sanctioned amid a heated debate about appropriate roles for women in the church. The 1888 Methodist General Conference that created the office of deaconess was the same conference that had refused to admit five female lay delegates—including WCTU president Frances Willard—on the grounds that they were not "laymen" as specified in the Methodist *Book of Discipline*.[4] This came eight years after the 1880 General Conference barred women from the role of local minister. Consequently, some viewed the office of deaconess as a compromise. In one sense, the move could be "viewed as supportive of women's increased responsibility and leadership, but from another perspective the diaconessate looked like a means to deflect women from their goal of equal rights in the church" (Gifford). Instead of a diversion or a compromise, the office of deaconess represented an entirely different strategy for elevating women's role in the church. Because it emerged out of pressing social needs, the deaconess office constituted "intentional, artistic, human action" (Patton 49). Rather than fighting along gender lines that had rigidly defined church work, the deaconess office effectively leveraged key social and institutional constraints in order to propose a new, sanctioned position for women.

GROUP IDENTITY AND SYMBOLIC ACTION

Specified within the deaconess office were elements that fostered a distinct deaconess identity including the deaconess name, required training, consecration (being set apart), and conservative dress. Kenneth Burke's notions of identification and symbolic action help explain how this deaconess identity helped position women within the church and society. Burke defined rhetoric as entailing identification and division; the former occurs when individuals see themselves as *consubstantial* with each other—as sharing similar interests—whereas the latter names "ways in which individuals are at odds with one another" (*Rhetoric* 20–23). Through naming, training, consecration, and dress, the deaconess identity operated as a shrewd form of Burkean identification, aligning women with traditional conceptions of feminine Christian service all the while distinguishing and elevating deaconesses above volunteer laywomen. Symbolic action, Burke reminds us, directs the "attention into some channels rather than others" ("Terministic" 45). At the same time, the deaconess identity situated deaconesses as professional church workers alongside Methodist ministers without raising concerns about women's clerical ambitions. In short, the deaconess identity struck a balance between identification with and division from social and institutional constraints concerning gender expectations and women's roles in the church and society. Doing so helped women claim a middle ground within the church that would allow them to exercise more authority.

Because Burkean division connotes discord, I use the term *distinction* in this chapter to refer to the rhetorical strategy deaconesses used to distinguish themselves from male church leaders and from female church volunteers. Deaconesses worked closely with female church volunteers who played critical roles as advocates, contributors, fund-raisers, board members, and workers. In her study of the St. Mark's Community Center in New Orleans, Ellen Blue describes the strong working alliances and deep friendships forged between laywomen and deaconesses, and the *DA* is replete with recognition of deaconess auxiliaries and supporters. Creating a strong deaconess identity did not negate these partnerships or the female bonds that had always undergirded women's religious and charitable efforts. Indeed, even when women left the diaconate to marry, many of these former deaconesses continued to work as church volunteers, subscribed and sent letters to the *DA*, and attended training school reunions. *Distinction* effectively captures this nuance while avoiding any suggestion that deaconneses and other members of the church, male or female, were "at odds" (Burke, *Rhetoric* 22).

Contemporary scholarship on group identity from the fields of social psychology and business help explain how the deaconess movement established and reinforced their distinct identity. Stephen Konzieczka and Lawrence Frey explain that group identity exists "when a relatively small number of people view themselves collectively as comprising an entity that is distinct from other entities" ("Group"). Group identity differs from social identity, which refers primarily to identification with broad social categories such as race or ethnicity. Moreover, Konzieczka and Frey stress that group identity accounts for how nonmembers view a group and members view themselves, thus highlighting group identity's internal and external rhetorical functions. Rhetorically, the deaconess identity simultaneously influenced the perceptions and actions of deaconesses and members of the church and community. Specifically, it helped transform how the church viewed women, how the women perceived themselves, how the church perceived its role in urban areas, and how urban residents viewed the church.

A successful group identity requires members to identify themselves as part of the group (Henry, Arrow, and Carini 562–63). Michael Pratt writes, "At its core, identity involves *self-referential meaning*. The questions, 'Who am I?' and 'Who are we?' capture the essence of identity by highlighting that identity is about an entity's attempts to understand itself" (164). Women were drawn to the deaconess movement because of their desire to enact their Christian beliefs and because few professional avenues were then available for doing so. These desires for deeper meaning and self-actualization are what attract individuals to a particular group (Wade-Benzoni 260–61). Indeed, throughout the nineteenth century, women were drawn to religious, benevolent, and reform groups, in part because of this desire for deeper meaning.

Members cultivate group identities and convey them to nonmembers through traditional communication channels (i.e., face-to-face, print media) and symbolic devices (i.e., language, ceremonies, dress, behavioral routines) that function rhetorically (Pratt 174–77). The deaconess movement used its periodical, the *Deaconess Advocate*, to communicate and reinforce its collective identity. In January 1886, just three months after opening the Chicago Training School, Rider Meyer began publishing and distributing the *DA* to deaconesses, subscribers, and key stakeholders in the church. As the movement grew, the periodical expanded from a four-page quarterly publication to a sixteen-page monthly with a circulation that reached 32,000 (Dougherty, "Methodist" 12, 188). Throughout the nineteenth century, periodicals functioned as an important rhetorical practice for secular and sectarian women's groups (Cassidy 174; Sharer 15–34). These self-produced publications enabled women to control the content, including their own depictions. Thus, the *DA* contributed to deaconesses' self-referential meaning in addition to the collective identity they conveyed to key stakeholders in the church. Deaconess training schools also helped inculcate a strong deaconess identity. Processes of socialization "whereby a member of a collective 'learns the ropes' about their job, role and the values and beliefs of the collective" comprise another component of group identity construction (Pratt 175). A group identity requires shared meaning: individuals act in ways that affirm their identity, and this behavior must be accepted and confirmed by others. As a result, a strong group identity fosters cohesion and a sense of belonging (Riley and Burke 64; Webster and Wong 44, 48).

The deaconess identity was also forged through several symbolic devices including the deaconess name, their consecration ceremony, and their dress. The deaconess name functioned symbolically to identify deaconesses with scripture and associate them closely with ministers. As symbolic action, the deaconess consecration ceremony similarly distinguished deaconesses from the laity and identified them with ministers. The most visible symbol of the deaconess identity was their conservative dress. Nineteenth-century women recognized dress as an important rhetorical medium that they used to express themselves and project an image (Mattingly 8). Indeed, dress has long been used as a symbol for religious witness and group membership. Ultimately, all three of these symbolic devices—name, ceremony, dress—functioned to affirm deaconess's Christian commitment within this collective and to witness to individuals outside of the group.

The office of deaconess provided an empowering transitional site for many women, affording them an education, a supportive network, opportunities, and immense responsibilities. However, religious careers such as that of deaconess and educational sites such as deaconess training schools are often overlooked in women's histories (see also Glascott, this volume). These absences narrow our understanding of the strategies women used to enter professions and the Christian convictions that motivated women's actions (see also Zimmerelli, this volume). For deaconesses, Christianity and civic engagement were intricately linked (see also Duffy, this volume). By becoming deaconesses and by establishing hospitals, industrial schools, city missions, and orphanages—along with pursuing early methods of social work—they modeled evangelism through service and persuaded by their actions. In the same way that a deaconess drew photographer Jacob Riis's attention and admiration, deaconesses' actions, highlighted by their distinct identity, influenced how communities viewed the church and how parishioners perceived deaconesses' roles in communities. Leveraging the cultural and institutional constraints they faced, the deaconess movement crafted a strong group identity to persuade themselves that they *could* do this work, and to persuade others that they *should* do this work. In the remainder of this chapter, I describe how the deaconess movement in the Methodist Church began, how the deaconess identity operated rhetorically to establish a professional role for women in the church, and how deaconesses transformed women, churches, and society.

IDENTIFICATION AND DISTINCTION THROUGH NAMING

In 1885, Lucy Rider Meyer and her husband Josiah Meyer opened the Chicago Training School (CTS). The inspiration for the deaconess office soon followed. The CTS was designed for women interested in pursuing missionary work at home and abroad. Students studied the Bible and methods for teaching the Bible, as well as basic medicine and nursing. Two or three afternoons each week, students made door-to-door visits to evangelize and provide basic healthcare and other practical assistance. They also directed residents to community resources for aid, employment, and education. During the summer of 1887, the school became a temporary deaconess home; eight women devoted their summers to city missionary work. Rider Meyer explained the experiment as an opportunity to use their school for "the advance of the Kingdom," concluding with the prescient statement: "We believe this thought of a Headquarters for lady missionaries and an organization of their work may be a seed with a life-germ in it which shall grow" (*DA* 6/1887:8). When school reconvened in the fall, the school's executive committee took a leap of faith, renting a flat and establishing a deaconess home even though funding was not secured (*DA* 10/1887:8; Meyer 155–57).

Although she chose the name *deaconess*, Rider Meyer claimed that it was months later before she learned about the deaconesses in Europe. Fifty years before the Meyers opened the CTS, Lutheran pastor Theodore Fleidner and his wife Friedericke established a deaconess training institution in 1836 at Kaiserwerth in Germany to prepare women to serve the poor by training them in theology and nursing. Kaiserwerth's most famous student was Florence Nightingale, and the need for nurses prompted the opening of other deaconess institutions in Germany, Europe, and Great Britain. Many churches in America supported deaconesses in the nineteenth century, including the Lutheran, Episcopal, and Presbyterian churches, but with Rider Meyer's rendering of the office, the Methodist church became their strongest sponsor (Meyer 31–44; Prelinger and Keller). Stressing the exigencies they faced, Rider Meyer underscored their motives for choosing the title *deaconess*: "Our only thought was an effort to *make such work possible* in answer to the urgent cries that came to us from all parts of the great city lying at our door" (*DA* 5/1902:8, emphasis added). The titled itself functioned as symbolic action aimed at inducing acceptance of the deaconess office and the societal transformations they hoped to achieve.

Using a rhetorical move frequently employed by women, proponents for the office of deaconess also claimed scriptural authority through Phoebe, a member of the primitive church (see Zimmerelli, this volume). Romans 16:1–2 reads, "I commend to you our sister Phoebe, a deacon of the church at Cenchreae, so that you may welcome her in the Lord as is fitting for the saints, and help her in whatever she may require from you, for she has been a benefactor of many and of myself as well." Phoebe, whom Paul entrusted to carry his epistle from Corinth to Rome and who had cared for the sick and suffering in her community, became a powerful model for nineteenth-century deaconesses (Dougherty, *My Calling* 3–5). The words *deacon* and *deaconess* derive from the Greek *diakonos* ("servant") and *diakonia* ("service"). In the Methodist Church, *deacon* is reserved for ordained ministers. Thus, by using *deaconess* Rider Meyer performed two symbolic actions: she not only linked the office to Phoebe and to ordained clergy but also communicated that it was distinct from that of deacon. The significance of the name is underscored in a *DA* article that summarily dismisses the suggestion that deaconesses should be called *sisters*, a name commonly used for any female member of a church. The article ardently defends *deaconess* as a biblical term, as a Protestant term, and as "an official title corresponding in its degree to the word 'minister'" (*DA* 3/1902:9). Essentially, the *DA* advocated the name as an accurate sign of deaconesses' position in the church. This position, along with its title, reflects careful negotiation of existing constraints: it claims authority while remaining distinct enough that it did not outright defy traditional gender roles.

ELEVATION AND SOCIALIZATION THROUGH TRAINING

To become a deaconess, women were required to complete two years of training. This emphasis on training, an intrinsic part of deaconesses' distinct group identity, functioned symbolically to shape women's attitudes toward their own sense of mission. It also performed external symbolic action by helping the Methodist Church and outside communities more readily accept women's emerging roles. The CTS, along with later deaconess training schools, became important sites for training and group identity construction. At these training schools, deaconesses learned what it meant to answer the special calling of a deaconess and how to perform these roles effectively. Deaconesses, who served as the core faculty at the schools, became models for their students. Class sizes were small, students lived together, and the practical nature of their training not only nurtured empathy and understanding for those in need but also required cooperation between students as they carried out house-to-house visitation in poor neighborhoods, taught in industrial schools, and worked in city missions.

The CTS's approach to its course work contributed to women's self-actualization by strengthening their confidence and religious convictions. In teaching the Bible, the school equipped students with knowledge and the *facilitas* that would prepare them to address any situation—proselytizing, defending, debating, counseling, or comforting. The CTS encouraged students to think critically, question and examine their beliefs, and develop and expand their skills and talents in hopes of meeting the challenges of foreign and urban mission work (Dougherty, "Methodist" 45). The CTS continually augmented and enhanced its curriculum. A 1908 ad for the school lists fourteen departments of study: Church History and Christian Missions; Ethics and Sociology; Church and City Mission Work, Public Speaking, Evangelism; Epworth League (a ministry for young adults) and Sunday-School Work; Methods in Teaching and Child-Study; Industrial Work; Elementary Medicine and Nursing; and Special Visitation and Investigation of Missions and Settlements (*DA* 7/1908:2). This curriculum also shows how the deaconess office bridged the fields of healthcare and social work. In addition to deaconess instructors, the CTS used guest lecturers including Methodist bishops, social workers, doctors, foreign missionaries, and faculty from Northwestern University. Settlement workers Jane Addams[5] and Mary McDowell also delivered lectures at the school (*DA* 3/1905:9).

Rider Meyer repeatedly stressed training as a distinguishing characteristic to elevate deaconesses as professional churchwomen. Speaking to an international Methodist conference in 1911, she linked deaconesses' authority to their training: "The character of the deaconess compels respect and confidence," asserted Rider Meyer. "She is a modern, trained woman" (*DA* 11/1911:12). An earlier *DA* article, "The Training of the Deaconesses," bemoaned the sentimental view of a deaconess as "a ministering-angel flitting in and out of the homes of the poor with material relief" or "an untiring nurse, almost superhuman in her sympathy and endurance" because these depictions failed to acknowledge deaconesses' training and skill (*DA* 4/1899:11). While the deaconess identity encompassed compassion and commitment, it eschewed the traditional view that these characteristics were somehow intrinsic to all women and provided the only requisites for effective Christian service. In fact, the article proceeds to articulate essential knowledge for deaconesses. This included biblical and theological understanding (which women should "wield [. . .] skillfully, tactfully, constantly"), as well as a thorough knowledge of other local charitable institutions, awareness of laws that may help her protect the people she serves, and an understanding of nursing and elementary medicine (*DA* 4/1899:11). The article concludes that deaconesses must continue their study to stay current (11–12). In doing so, it linked knowledge and training to the deaconess identity and elevated the deaconess office as a valid profession.

DISTINCTION THROUGH CONSECRATION, COMMITMENT, AND DRESS

Once a woman successfully completed two years of training, she applied for acceptance and licensing by the deaconess board. If approved, she was formally consecrated (*DA* 3/1911:8). Although the 1880 Methodist General Conference voted against the ordination of women, the deaconess office approved by the 1888 General Conference granted a position that required training, formal acceptance, licensing, and consecration (the laying on of hands), usually by a Methodist bishop. The deaconess consecration—the culmination of a woman's calling and preparation—sanctioned and positioned women as professionals within the church. It also held important symbolic and self-referential meaning, because these women were well aware of the similarities between a deaconess's consecration and a minister's ordination. The deaconess consecration, like clerical ordination, set these women apart from the laity through their commitment to Christ. It stipulated the following:

> Released from other cares, you give yourselves without reservation to the service of Christ. [. . .] The Church now solemnly sets you apart for her special service. You are to work for Jesus only. You are to minister to the poor, visit the sick, pray with the dying, care for the orphan, seek the wandering, comfort the sorrowing, save the sinning, and ever be ready to take up any other duty for which willing hands cannot otherwise be found.
>
> *(Book of Discipline)*

Deaconesses also confirmed their commitment through their willingness to live apart from family, often in communal deaconess homes, and to forego marriage, motherhood, and financial compensation. Each of these commitments conveyed deaconesses' sacrificial service to church leaders, parishioners, and community residents. They affirmed deaconesses' membership within a small, select group. As such, these commitments functioned as both internal and external symbolic action, legitimizing women's views of themselves and church leaders' views of deaconesses.

The most visible symbol of the deaconess identity was their distinct dress, long black or dark blue dresses with white ties at the collar. In some neighborhoods, residents referred to deaconesses as "white ties." Dr. W. H. Jordan, a pastor in Minneapolis, explained the symbolic nature of the attire: "The black bonnet and the white ties of the deaconess are not merely a costume—they are a message. They are a declaration to every observer that the religion of Jesus is not a gospel of abstract principles and precepts, but a concrete gospel of love" (*DA* 11/1905:8). Through photographs and stories, the *DA* reinforced this powerful symbolic identification between the deaconess attire and sacrificial service. One article told the story of a former CTS student who wanted to go into deaconess work but did not feel she could leave her parents. The woman pursued her own ministry, taking in eleven homeless children and educating and caring for them from her parents' home. In recognition, Rider Meyer conferred the honorary distinction of deaconess by presenting her with a bonnet and white ties (*DA* 2/1888:11). For deaconesses, dress functioned as internal symbolic action and served as a constant reminder of their Christian commitment and membership in this select group. Nathan Joseph asserts that "[w]itnessing by dress may also promote group cohesion" because it helps group members view themselves collectively and serves as a constant reminder they are not alone (51). With plain dress, deaconesses also eschewed individual pride and vanity. Moreover, they saved time and money, because they didn't have to buy or maintain a wardrobe or bother with selecting daily attire (*DA* 7/1899: 15).

For church leaders, parishioners, and members of the community, deaconesses' distinct garb underscored the group's collective identity. According to Joseph, uniforms perform this function by indicating membership, revealing and concealing status, certifying legitimacy, and suppressing individuality (67–68). In the *DA*, deaconesses confirmed that their garb provided introduction, recognition, and protection; it also inspired confidence among strangers (*DA* 7/1899:15; *DA* 6/1890:5). Deaconesses' dress distinguished them from other churchwomen and granted them access to locations where other church workers might not be allowed. It also enabled them to take advantage of positive reputations and goodwill. Even when dealing with ministers or congregants, deaconesses' dress clearly distinguished and positioned them by denoting the professional office they held.

Nevertheless, deaconess attire was a constant issue of debate. Much of the concern stemmed from prejudice toward Catholics. Asking women to remain single, to live in communal deaconess houses, and to wear such conservative attire fanned Catholic suspicions. In fact, deaconesses were often referred to as "protestant nuns" by both admirers and detractors. Defenders repeatedly emphasized that deaconesses did not take vows; women were free to leave the deaconess office if they chose to marry or for any other reason. And deaconess homes were not convents; they were open to the public (*DA* 2/1890:6). Deaconesses received letters and visitors and were encouraged to take monthlong vacations each year to rest and revitalize themselves for service. Even as it came under constant fire, deaconesses' distinct dress clearly operated as a powerful symbol of deaconesses' sacrificial Christian service and a distinguishing identifier.

TRANSFORMING WOMEN, THE CHURCH, AND SOCIETY

Together, the deaconess name, the training they received, their consecration to service, and their distinct wardrobe forged a strong deaconess group identity that functioned symbolically to transform women's perceptions of themselves and legitimize their work within the church and society. This identity helped promote and fortify the movement by attracting the first generation of deaconesses. By 1915, approximately 5,000 women had been consecrated as deaconesses (Prelinger and Keller 326). Beyond the countless lives that each of these women influenced, the deaconess movement expanded educational opportunities for women, elevated women's professional roles, expanded the church's ministries, and gave women the agency and authority to enact their own grassroots version of the social gospel.

Championing Women's Education and Training for Religious Service

By making training a requirement and core element of the deaconess identity, the deaconess movement became a powerful champion for women's education. Rider Meyer's four years working as a field secretary for the

Illinois Sunday School Association convinced her of the necessity of providing churchwomen with both intellectual and practical training. At public gatherings, young girls and women would approach her with the desire to do meaningful church work, but Rider Meyer found that most of them were ill equipped (Horton 90; Meyer 90). During this era, women were not admitted to most theological seminaries, and even though many colleges were open to women at the turn of the twentieth century, few had the preparation or means to go to college. Moreover, a college education did not guarantee the biblical knowledge or practical skills required for modern church work. This gap between adequate preparation and the professional opportunities available to women existed in both religious and secular fields.[6] Through its model and its graduates, the CTS helped establish twelve deaconess training schools in the Methodist Church, including the first training school for African American deaconesses in 1900 (Schmidt 209). Unlike the settlement house movement that attracted upper-class, college-educated women, the deaconess movement drew women with varying levels of education from all socioeconomic brackets (Dougherty, "Methodist" 50, 82). The CTS and other deaconess training schools made education affordable. Rider Meyer and other leaders leveraged the deaconess identity in speeches and in the *DA* to raise funds for scholarships and work/study programs.

The CTS also tried to make training accessible through lending libraries, correspondence courses, and intensive summer sessions for individuals who could not attend regular sessions. Through all these means, deaconess training schools transformed religious education and church work by making them available to more women. Highlighting this fact, one *DA* article boasted, "A certain great literary school states that it has sent thirty students to the mission field. It is a thing to be made public with joy and thankful pride. But the CTS [in seven years] has sent one hundred and sixty missionaries to the foreign field and six hundred more to the deaconess work of the church" (*DA* 11/1902:8). Not all women who attended the CTS became deaconesses, but Rider Meyer maintained from the school's outset that the training could also assist women who "wish to fit themselves for more efficient volunteer service in their own churches and Sunday Schools" (*DA* 1/1886:1).

Elevating Women's Roles and Expanding Church Ministries

By training women to pursue religious careers and through symbolic action such as naming and consecration, the deaconess movement distinguished deaconesses from volunteer churchwomen and closely identified them with trained clergy. Instead of arguing for female ministers, the deaconess movement carved out a space for professional churchwomen who could pursue a broad array of ministries. An 1896 editorial asserted, "the work of woman, the professional work of woman, is just as necessary to the advancement of God's cause on earth, as that of the man" (*DA* 8/1896:8). One indication of deaconesses' success in elevating women's roles in the church is the fact that many deaconesses assumed clerical duties. One deaconess in Utah reported, "I am the Superintendent of a Sunday school and teach a class also. I have Industrial school every Saturday, and to cap all, fill the pulpit regularly every two weeks" (*DA* 4/1890:5). Another in Michigan wrote, "I am helping Mr. R. on his circuit work, he preaching at one end of the circuit and I at the other. We separate Saturday and meet Monday" (*DA* 12/1890:11). And a report from the New England Deaconess Home acknowledged that one of its former students rescued a dying church in Vermont and was doing pastoral work there (*DA* 1/1902:12). Even though deaconesses performed many of the same duties as ministers, they were careful to avoid any suggestion that they had clerical ambitions. The deaconess office had created a path for women into ministry, but deaconesses navigated that path cautiously. The church had repeatedly shown that it was unwilling to accept female clergy. So, while male clergy might allow deaconesses to fill their pulpits, the women did not claim to be preachers. This careful negotiation of constraints is apparent in the exchange between a deaconess and a bishop: " 'So you are preaching. Are you!' The Bishop looked quizzically at the deaconess who, in the labors of a large country district, sometimes took a morning or evening service in the absence of the preacher. 'Oh, I don't preach,' she answered. 'I just talk.' 'Well go ahead,' said the Bishop cordially shaking her hand. 'Whatever you call it, it's all right' " (*DA* 9/1905:9).

Through identification and distinction, deaconesses claimed middle ground between male clergy and female laity, often positioning themselves as assistants to pastors. One editorial argued that deaconesses can help the church's overburdened pastors, while another characterized deaconess work as "complimentary to that of our deacons" (*DA* 6/1902:8; 3/1896:8). Nonetheless, deaconesses provided ample evidence that women could be effective ministers, and in 1956 the Methodist Church finally approved women's ordination. Just as important, deaconesses demonstrated that churches needed more ministries and trained, professional workers to pursue them. Today, it is commonplace to find individuals on church staffs responsible for youth, education, missions, community outreach, evangelism, and senior ministries, among others. These positions are filled by ordained clergy and professional church workers, many of them women. And in almost every case, these positions are recognized as important ministries and vocations within the church. Deaconesses helped transform this perception by opening church work as a career for women, providing training and support, highlighting women's success, and showing the need for more areas of ministry.

The deaconess office also gave women the training, confidence, and authority to establish new ministries and manage institutions. The range of their work and their immense responsibilities, as well as the far-reaching influence of the movement, is especially evident in World Wide Deaconess Notes (WWDN), a regular section in the *DA*. Ten years after the deaconess office was established, the WWDN included reports from numerous U.S.

cities, as well as India (*DA* 4/1898:8–12). Women became deaconesses to enact their Christian convictions and to find deeper meaning, and these reports showed orphanages, hospitals, homes for the elderly, settlements, kindergartens, refuges, Sunday schools, and industrial schools all under deaconess control. Studying and addressing pressing needs, deaconesses performed roles that secular social workers would eventually assume. However, they viewed their work and the institutions they established as Christian ministries. In addition to opening hospitals across the country, especially to care for the poor, the deaconess movement was also instrumental in training nurses and establishing nursing as a profession for women (Bullough, Sentz, and Stein 224–25; Woody 74). By 1908, there were eleven hospitals under the purview of the general deaconess board (*DA* 3/1908:2:15). Many of these included professional nursing schools, and while these schools did not require students to become deaconesses or enter missionary work, many of their students did so (*DA* 3/1905:12). Altogether, the deaconess movement helped open professional church work and other professions to women and demonstrated the need for more ministries and trained church workers.

Women's Early Enactment of the Social Gospel

The majority of early deaconesses focused their attention on conditions related to rapid urbanization in American cities; they were visible enactors of the social gospel, a subject that William Duffy takes up more fully in his chapter of this volume. Deaconesses demonstrate how group identity and their model of evangelism through service functioned as Christian symbolic action—symbolic action that is motivated by Christian motives and beliefs. Prompted by their faith, CTS faculty and students sought to address the urgent needs they saw in their city. Their response was action, not theology. According to Edwards and Gifford, men and women's social gospel efforts reflected "separate and complimentary spheres of activity" in accordance with contemporary gender ideologies (4–5). Men were more likely to focus on "oversight of industrial, political and theological concerns" and express their concerns by delivering or publishing theological and philosophical treatises (5). On the other hand, women tended to focus on social conditions affecting women, children and families. Likewise, deaconesses' Christian civic engagement came through their institutions, presence, and service. Excerpts from deaconesses' field notes were often featured along with photographs on the front page of the *DA* and repeatedly depicted deaconesses caring for residents in the poorest sections of cities.

Deaconesses were visible in the neighborhoods they served because of their distinct dress and expertise, and also because of their regular presence and witness. They canvassed door-to-door, nursed the sick, and comforted the dying. They operated missions, taught Sunday schools, opened industrial schools, and cared for the children of working mothers in their kindergartens. In earlier work, I argued that *presence* became an ethical resource for female city missionaries that enabled them to garner authority and respect in the communities they served and with audiences who later read about their efforts (Shaver, "No Cross"). Similarly, through their ongoing presence and efforts to assist residents, deaconesses earned trust and respect in these neighborhoods. Through publication of their observations, experiences, and even photographs in the *DA*, they educated readers about desperate urban conditions and urged them to help.

Persuading through their presence in urban areas, deaconesses also became a Christian conscience for the church and its parishioners, which had eagerly supported foreign missions but prior to the deaconess movement had done little to address the dire needs in its own cities. The deaconess movement persuaded church leaders and young women that Americas' cities needed Christian laborers as much as foreign lands. In urban areas where the church was often absent, deaconesses made the church present through their presence. Well-known Methodist minister Dr. William Nast Brodbeck remarked, "I believe in this work because it is the most Christ-like of all religious work. I don't depreciate the ministry, but the work of the deaconess, if properly done, is a more Christ-like service than theirs, because it is a consecration of service to the whole man. Not to the soul alone, but to body, soul, and spirit" (*DA* 3/1896:3). Whereas the church's benevolent efforts usually focused on soul-saving evangelism, deaconesses believed that addressing material needs was also an essential part of religious service. One report published in the *DA* revealed how deaconesses transformed suspicion into trust by noting that deaconesses in Baltimore, who were initially greeted with suspicion in Italian, Polish, Jewish, and Russian neighborhoods, were later warmly welcomed (*DA* 4/1908:13). Whereas residents probably assumed that the deaconesses were there for some heavy-handed evangelism, deaconesses modeled evangelism through service, "demonstrating the practical love for neighbor" (Dougherty, "Social" 207).

Other stories demonstrate the positive word-of-mouth assessments of deaconesses that passed throughout neighborhoods (*DA* 3/1905:1). One editorial explained,

> We may say, 'We are not a relief society, nor a social improvement society; our work is to bring Christ to the people,' but this is not, cannot be, wholly true. Questions of evangelization can no more be separated from questions of material conditions than our own spiritual life can be separated from its physical and intellectual manifestation.

(*DA* 3/1899:8)

Deaconesses believed that temporal relief was an essential part of their spiritual work. The deaconesses' visible presence and strong group identity helped them convey this model of evangelism through service. In response,

Methodists answered by sending donations to establish deaconess homes for outreach in urban neighborhoods, to build hospitals to serve the poor, to establish orphanages and homes for the disabled and elderly, to transport city children on trips to the country so they could breathe fresh air, and to underwrite industrial schools and kindergartens. Women across the country sent thousands of books filled with five dollars' worth of dimes they had collected. Farmers sent produce to be distributed to inner-city residents. Congregants donated houses, furniture, and books to establish deaconess homes and support deaconess-run schools. Numerous laywomen also volunteered assisting deaconesses.

CONCLUSION

Deaconesses were trained, professional churchwomen, set apart and consecrated to Christian service. They responded to and leveraged several social and cultural constraints in an effort to advance the kingdom of God. In the process, they also elevated women's roles in the church. Yet as the cultural landscape changed, so too did the office of deaconesses. Before it reached its twenty-fifth year, the heyday of the deaconess movement was at an end. Deaconesses were still in demand. They had convincingly demonstrated the value of trained, professional churchwomen and churches, hospitals, and other institutions wanted them. However, the supply was dwindling as fewer women chose to become deaconesses. In 1915, Rider Meyer retired as principal of the CTS, and in the years spanning between the two world wars, most of the deaconess training schools closed or merged with other schools (Brereton 191–92). The deaconess office was a transitional site, and much had changed for women since the deaconess office was established in 1888. More educational opportunities were available to women, who increasingly pursued nursing and social work as secular careers; some churches were already creating paid lay positions in fields such as religious education (Dougherty, "Methodist" 174; Lindley 134). That said, the deaconess office did not disappear. To this day, it remains a full-time vocation in the Methodist Church, though it looks much different. Deaconesses do not wear special garb or live in deaconess homes. They can marry, and most occupy paid positions. Moreover, with the 2004 General Conference's creation of the Home Missioner role, there is an equivalent position for men. In 2013, the 125th anniversary of the deaconess movement, there were 157 deaconesses and ten home missioners (Stephens). These individuals pursue ministries focused on prisons, the environment, immigration, peace and justice, healthcare, homelessness, senior adults, and the working poor ("Deaconess & Home"). And in an era when career women, female ministers,[7] and a wide array of church ministries are readily accepted, a distinct deaconess group identity is no longer necessary to advocate for women's professions in the church.

At the time the deaconess movement emerged, however, the group identity they developed was transformative, allowing deaconesses to elevate women's roles and promote social Christianity within the Methodist church and in society at large. Deaconesses used their position to tackle healthcare for the poor, immigration, childcare for working women, and poverty. These are issues we continue to struggle with today, yet they are they are seldom framed as Christian duties. In *Rhetoric of Motives*, Burke notes that "there is an *objective* difference in motivation between an act conceived of in the name of God and an act conceived of in the name of godless nature" (6). Deaconesses acted in the "name of God." They were compelled to address pressing social needs because they viewed them in terms of Christian mission. They were able to address those needs because they framed their actions as a Christian obligation, a rhetorical move that allowed them to negotiate social and cultural constraints that could have derailed their efforts. As such, the deaconess movement was both made possible by and functioned as a form of Christian rhetoric. To echo Brian Jackson's contribution to this volume, the deaconess movement employed "persuasive symbolic action [. . .] *that assume[d] the existence*" (this volume) of the Christian God in order to carve out space for the work deaconesses hoped to do. In the process, the group identity they constructed and the work they performed similarly functioned as Christian rhetoric. Motivated by their assumptions about God's will, the deaconesses' symbolic action in all of its manifestations served to transform the church and society. Ultimately, then, the deaconess movement was born of out of Christian conviction and functioned as Christian symbolic action that ennobled this group of women and their ministries as service to Christ.

NOTES

1 This photograph was probably taken years earlier, because Riis was living outside of New York by this time.

2 In referencing articles from the *Deaconess Advocate*, I use the abbreviation *DA* followed by the issue number, year, and page number. The *DA* was published quarterly the first year, and after that, monthly. Prior to being named the *DA* (1903–14), it was named *The Message* (1886–92), *The Message and Deaconess World* (1893), and *The Message and Deaconess Advocate* (1894–1902).

3 The Methodist Episcopal Church, commonly referred to as the Methodist Church, was officially established in the United States in 1784. Because its members have been called Methodists, I use this term throughout the chapter.

4 The Methodist General Conference is the church's highest legislative body. *The Book of Discipline* outlines the doctrine and governance of the Methodist Church.

5 In addition to lecturing at the CTS, Jane Addams delivered a graduation speech in 1906. Rider Meyer tried to get her appointed to the CTS board of trustees, but the board resisted her appointment because Hull House did not provide religious instruction (Addams 54).

6 Harris notes that the number of women receiving college degrees lagged behind the number of women entering the workforce from 1860 to 1920 (104).
7 Mountford acknowledges that while most denominations ordain women ministers, women have still struggled to gain acceptance as senior pastors by many congregations (146–47).

REFERENCES

Addams, Jane. *Twenty Years at Hull-House.* 1910. New York: Signet Classic, 1961.
Blue, Ellen. *St. Mark's and the Social Gospel: Methodist Women and Civil Rights in New Orleans, 1895–1965.* Knoxville, U of Tennessee P, 2011.
The Book of Discipline. The Methodist Episcopal Church, 1908.
Brereton, Virginia Lieson. "Preparing Women for the Lord's Work." *Women in New Worlds: Historical Perspectives on the Wesleyan Tradition.* Eds. Hilah F. Thomas and Rosemary Skinner Keller. Nashville: Abingdon, 1981. 178–99.
Bullough, Vern L., Lilli Sentz, and Alice P. Stein. *American Nursing: A Biographical Dictionary.* Vol. 2. New York: Garland, 1992.
Burke, Kenneth. *A Rhetoric of Motives.* New York: Prentice Hall, 1950.
———. "Terministic Screens." *Language as Symbolic Action.* Berkeley: U of California P, 1966: 44–62.
Cassidy, Cheryl M. "Bringing the 'New Woman' to the Mission Site: Louise Manning Hodgkins and the *Heathen Woman's Friend.*" *American Periodicals* 2.16 (2006): 172–99.
Deaconess Advocate, 1886–1914, Chicago Training School Chicago, Illinois.
"Deaconess & Home Missioner Ministry." *United Methodist Women.* Global Ministries of the United Methodist Church, n.d. Web. 1 September 2012.
Dougherty, Mary Agnes Theresa. "The Methodist Deaconess, 1885–1918: A Study in Religious Feminism." Diss. U of California Davis, 1979.
———. *My Calling to Fulfill: Deaconesses in the United Methodist Tradition.* New York: United Methodist Church, 1997.
———. "The Social Gospel According to Phoebe." *Women in New Worlds: Historical Perspectives on the Wesleyan Tradition.* Eds. Hilah F. Thomas and Rosemary Skinner Keller. Nashville: Abingdon, 1981. 200–16.
Edwards, Wendy Deichmann, and Carolyn De Swarte Gifford. "Introduction: Restoring Women and Reclaiming Gender in Social Gospel Studies." *Gender and the Social Gospel.* Eds. Wendy Deichmann Edwards and Carolyn De Swarte Gifford. Urbana: U of Illinois P, 2003. 1–17.
Gifford, Carolyn De Swarte. "Introduction." *The American Deaconess Movement in the Early Twentieth Century.* New York: Garland, 1987.
Harris, Barbara J. *Beyond Her Sphere: Women and the Professions in American History.* Westport, Conn.: Greenwood, 1978.
Henry, Kelly Bouas, Holly Arrow, and Barbara Carini. "A Tripartite Model of Group Identification: Theory and Measurement." *Small Group Research* 30.5 (1999): 558:81.
Horton, Isabelle. *High Adventure: Life of Lucy Rider Meyer.* 1928. New York: Garland, 1987.
Joseph, Nathan. *Uniforms and NonUniforms: Communicating through Clothing.* New York: Greenwood, 1986.
Konzieczka, Stephen, and Lawrence Frey. "Group Identity." *Encyclopedia of Identity.* Thousand Oaks: Sage, 2010. *Credo Reference.* Web. 22 August 2012.
Lindley, Susan Hill. *"You Have Stept Out of Your Place": A History of Women and Religion in America.* Louisville: Westminster, 1996.

Mattingly, Carol. *Appropriate[ing] Dress: Women's Rhetorical Style in Nineteenth-Century America*. Carbondale: Southern Illinois UP, 2002.

McClelland, Averil Evans. *The Education of Women in the United States*. New York: Garland, 1992.

Meyer, Lucy Rider. *Deaconesses, Biblical, Early Church, European, American with The Story of the Chicago Training School, For City, Home and Foreign Missions, and the Chicago Deaconess Home*. 2nd ed., rev. and enl. Chicago: The Message Publishing Company, 1889.

Mountford, Roxanne. *The Gendered Pulpit: Preaching in American Protestant Spaces*. Carbondale: Southern Illinois UP, 2003.

Patton, John H. "Causation and Creativity in Rhetorical Situations: Distinctions and Implications." *Quarterly Journal of Speech* 65.1 (1979): 35–55.

Pratt, Michael G. "Disentangling Collective Identities." *Identity Issues in Groups*. Ed. Jeffrey T. Polzer. Oxford: JAI, 2003. 161–88.

Prelinger, Catherine M., and Rosemary S. Keller. "The Function of Female Bonding." *Women in New Worlds: Historical Perspectives on the Wesleyan Tradition*. Vol 2. Eds. Rosemary Skinner Keller, Louise L. Queen, and Hilah F. Thomas. Nashville: Abingdon, 1982. 318–37.

Riley, Anna, and Peter J. Burke. "Identities and Self-Verification in the Small Group." *Social Psychology Quarterly* 58.2 (1995): 61–73.

Schmidt, Jean Miller. *Grace Sufficient: A History of Women in American Methodism 1760–1939*. Nashville: Abingdon, 1999.

Scott, Anne Firor. *Natural Allies: Women's Associations in American History*. Chicago: U of Illinois P, 1991.

Sharer, Wendy B. *Voice and Vote: Women's Organizations and Political Literacy, 1915–1930*. Carbondale: Southern Illinois UP, 2004.

Shaver, Lisa J. *Beyond the Pulpit: Women's Rhetorical Roles in the Antebellum Religious Press*. U of Pittsburgh P, 2012.

———. "No Cross, No Crown": An Ethos of Presence in Margaret Prior's *Walks of Usefulness*." *College English* 75.1 (2012): 61–78.

Stephens, Myka Kennedy. "Cutting-edge Ministry." *United Methodist Women*. Global Ministries of the United Methodist Church. 1 February 2013. Web. 30 May 2014.

Wade-Benzoni, Kimberly. "Intergenerational Identification and Cooperation in Organizations and Society." *Identify Issues in Groups*. Ed. Jeffrey T. Polzer. Oxford: JAI, 2003. 53–89.

Webster, J., and W. K. P. Wong. "Comparing Traditional and Virtual Group Forms: Identity, Communication and Trust in Naturally Occurring Project Teams." *Human Resource Management*. 19.1 (2008): 41–62.

Woody, Thomas. *A History of Women's Education in the United States*. Vol 2. New York: Science P, 1929.

12 Transforming Decorum
The Sophistic Appeal of Walter Rauschenbusch and the Social Gospel

William Duffy

> History is never antiquated, because humanity is always funda-
> mentally the same. It is always hungry for bread, sweaty for labor,
> struggling to wrest from nature and hostile men enough to feed its
> children. The welfare of the mass is always at odds with the self-
> ish force of the strong. The exodus of the Roman plebeians and
> the Pennsylvania coal strike, the agrarian agitation of the Gracchi
> and the rising of the Russian peasants,—it is all the same tragic
> human life.
>
> —Walter Rauschenbusch, *Christianity
> and the Social Crisis*

At the beginning of *Christianity and the Social Crisis* (CSC), Walter Rauschenbusch speculates on the value of historical reflection: "What light can
we get on the troubles of the great capitalistic republic of the West from men
who tended sheep in Judea or meddled in the petty politics of the Semitic
tribes?" (1). He answers this question in the chapter-opening epigraph, the
book's second paragraph. Thus illustrating the "tragic" continuity of human
struggle, Rauschenbusch launches into a work that popularized America's
"social gospel" movement at the turn of the twentieth century.[1]

Coterminous with the Progressive Era, the social gospel movement and
its proponents applied Christian ethics to societal ills brought about in the
wake of postwar reconstruction, including rampant poverty, poor public
health, and the increased exploitation of immigrant labor. To be accurate,
the social gospel was never a unified movement, nor did it encapsulate a
single, well-defined creed. Instead, the social gospel represented a certain
type of Christian mind-set in relation to public life, one fueled by the belief
that Jesus's message of salvation is a social imperative that can be realized
only by caring for others.

This belief was ingrained in Rauschenbusch during his time as pastor
at the Second German Baptist Church in Hell's Kitchen, where he moved
in 1886 after finishing seminary. While laboring alongside New York's
immigrant poor at the end of the nineteenth century, Rauschenbusch's faith

took on a new significance as he articulated the ethical demands of Christianity in terms that were relevant for social activists concerned with the stark social inequalities dividing the rich from the poor, especially among America's urban populations. Largely informed by his experiences in Hell's Kitchen, *CSC* was published in 1907 and quickly became a best seller, evidencing Rauschenbusch's ability to speak persuasively to a wide swath of the American public about the excesses of industrial capitalism.[2] In his warning to readers that ignoring these excesses will lead to social catastrophe, Rauschenbusch asserts that "[n]o preventives against the formation of social classes written in a paper constitution can long save us from the iron wedge which capitalism drives through society" (219). Rauschenbusch weaves such claims throughout *CSC* to craft an exigency for forwarding a Christian ethic that prioritizes social welfare over personal salvation, so that, as he puts it, "ethical conduct becomes the supreme and sufficient religious act" (7).

To appreciate fully the significance of Rauschenbusch's contribution to the social gospel requires an understanding of the rhetorical techniques he used in *CSC* to map a history of Christian ethics onto a social-scientific analysis of the economic misfortunes of America's poor and working classes. One of these techniques is the transformation of decorum, a concept that highlights occasions when rhetors use specialized discourse such as religious speech to expand how an audience is prepared to interpret that discourse. Throughout *CSC*, Rauschenbusch attempts to capture a vision of Christianity that upholds its historical message of redemption while simultaneously redefining this message in terms that equate salvation with the secular work of public welfare. As such, Rauschenbusch's work reflects John Poulakos's sophistic definition of rhetoric as "the art which seeks to capture in opportune moments that which is appropriate and to suggest that which is possible" ("Toward" 36). What Rauschenbusch achieved with *CSC* thus affirms what Poulakos describes as the practice of sophistic rhetoric itself, speech that is crafted from "concrete rhetorical situations to which situationally derived truths are the only opportune and appropriate responses" (42). In short, Rauschenbusch's social gospel rhetoric suggests the public value of religious appeals should be evaluated relative to the situation in which they are deployed.

Accordingly, I hope to further our understanding of the social gospel as a popular, historical movement and contribute to wider discussions that seek to understand better the rhetorical approaches necessary for appropriating religious discourse for civic purposes. Ronald Lee, for instance, says that rhetoricians need to offer better explanations for how religious faith supplies moral justifications for social reform (100). Such work, as this volume suggests, requires charting new avenues of inquiry for thinking about what makes Christian rhetorics resonate with social activists in the civic sphere. Studying how Rauschenbusch attempted this work might better orient rhetoricians toward an expanded understanding of "what is possible" when transforming Christian terms for addressing obstacles in the civic sphere that constrain social justice.

SOPHISTIC RHETORIC AND THE NOTION OF DECORUM

To explain how Rauschenbusch supplies readers with a framework for using Christianity as a warrant for progressive social reform, I consider sophistic rhetoric in terms of decorum. For many rhetoricians, decorum is synonymous with codes of conduct; it is the literacy of social scripts, those customs and conventions people draw on to discern appropriate from inappropriate behavior.[3] It is also the knowledge against which a speaker or writer interprets the scope of a "rhetorical situation," those occasions when discourse must be "fitting" to be effective (Bitzer 11). So what does it mean to *transform* decorum, exactly?

When a specialized set of terms circulates across publics, the meanings of these terms increase in disparity as they move from one context to another over time, making it easier to appropriate such language for a variety of ends. Nonetheless, a novel application of such specialized terminology must still make sense in the context of its proposed use. Decorum is thus "transformed" when discourse is deployed in a rhetorical situation that alters how an audience is prepared to use that discourse in similar rhetorical situations. For example, consider the growing popularity of the digital humanities in higher education. What the digital humanities actually encompass, including the criteria one should follow to determine what counts as "digital humanities" research, is actively debated. This is true even for digital humanities researchers who once identified their work under the banner of "humanities computing" in the 1980s and 1990s. What was once a small community of scholars and computer programmers has morphed into a multifaceted and increasingly complex school of practice that no longer can be claimed by any one particular group of researchers. Consequently, the term *digital humanities* is now being used in a variety of ways that don't always refer to the same thing—what counts as a decorous invocation of this critical terminology has evolved in ways that are beyond the control of those who first coined its language.

Another example engages a contested term I use in this chapter: *sophistic rhetoric*. Understanding how rhetoricians have debated this term illustrates the transformation of decorum and clarifies my use of it as a theoretical frame for studying religious discourse. Poulakos, as noted earlier, defines sophistic rhetoric by combining the notions of opportunity (*kairos*), appropriateness (decorum), and possibility. He justifies this definition by analyzing the work of those classical figures often identified as "the Sophists," such as Protagoras and Gorgias, to generate a framework for understanding sophistic rhetoric as a whole. In "Rhetoric, the Sophists, and the Possible," for instance, Poulakos distinguishes sophistic from Aristotelian rhetoric using the concepts of "actuality," which is the focus of Aristotle's philosophy of rhetoric, and "possibility," which the Sophists emphasize (215). While I do not have the space to elaborate on this distinction, the antinomy Poulakos sketches between the rhetorical approaches of Aristotle and the Sophists is heuristic and aimed at explaining sophistic rhetoric as a unique category, one that Poulakos suggests has been ignored in most histories of rhetoric (217).

For Edward Schiappa, however, the idea of sophistic rhetoric is an anachronism propelled by "incoherent historical concepts," such that "we are unlikely to come up with a historically defensible definition of 'sophistic rhetoric' that is nontrivial and uniquely valuable" ("Sophistic Rhetoric" 5). It is problematic, in other words, to use the idea of sophistic rhetoric to describe a particular kind of practice (like what I am doing in this chapter). While Schiappa points to Poulakos in particular, he is critical of all attempts to delineate "sophistic rhetoric" because he thinks it is impossible to discern in the Sophists' work a common philosophy. But Poulakos dismisses this criticism and suggests Schiappa "reads according to a narrowly conceived semanticism which holds that a given passage or fragment from the Sophists is decipherable only if we pay close attention to the meaning of each of its terms" ("Interpreting" 220). In short, Poulakos accuses his critic of narrow-mindedness—of refusing to consider, or even to acknowledge, differences of interpretation.[4] This example illustrates how specialized terminology is often contested when an audience feels it is being used inappropriately.

Here decorum is important. Schiappa challenges Poulakos on grounds that differentiate legitimate from illegitimate historiographic methods, which is to say Schiappa is primarily focused on Poulakos's definition of sophistic rhetoric as a *historical* interpretation. This is the decorum, in other words, within which Schiappa reads Poulakos. But Poulakos offers his definition not just to clarify a concept in the history of rhetoric—the context with which Schiappa is concerned—but also to offer contemporary rhetoricians an alternative approach for understanding the purpose of rhetoric itself. He is expanding, in other words, the decorum for how scholars might utilize "sophistic rhetoric" as a key term in rhetorical studies. In short, Poulakos is expanding the reach of what counts as an appropriate use of sophistic rhetoric as a critical term in rhetorical studies.

Rhetors often challenge the status quo by introducing the "possibility" of what has not yet been imagined in a rhetorical situation, and so Poulakos offers a definition that underscores what such rhetoric requires: right timing and a sense of decorum. The historical warrants Poulakos marshals to name his "sophistic" definition of rhetoric thus prove to be of little consequence in relation to the definition itself, at least in contexts where the history of sophistic rhetoric *as an idea* is not a matter of primary concern. The present study is a case in point. When investigating the role Christian rhetorics can play in progressive social movements, it is obvious that considerable rhetorical work must take place. On one hand, religious leaders must maintain their credible standing in the communities of faith they serve, but they must also develop a credible ethos for a wider public, which ostensibly includes a plurality of citizens with conflicting beliefs, whether religious or otherwise.

Such exigencies are obviously the purview of sophistic rhetoric—discourse deployed in opportune moments that is both appropriate and provocative. Such discourse reflects the rhetor's awareness of audience and "brings out in them futuristic versions of themselves, and sets before them both goals and the directions which lead to those goals" (Poulakos, "Toward" 43). In this way, if religious discourse is to spark a social movement, it requires the leadership of charismatic individuals—such as Rauschenbusch—who are able to articulate what otherwise might be indecorous speech in ways that resonate for the public at large. This observation echoes Janet Fishburn's: "A movement cannot exist unless it strikes chords of response in the public. The power of a prophetic figure is related to the ability of the prophet to verbalize a message which gives form to otherwise incoherent attitudes, reactions, and longings in the listener" (12). Within the framework of sophistic rhetoric, this is what it means to transform decorum: to expand the appeal of a discourse by illustrating its relevance in contexts that might at first appear unsuitable for such rhetoric, such as using a discussion of church membership demographics to defend legislation that outlaws real estate speculation. Rauschenbusch actually poses this latter argument in chapter 6 of *CSC*, suggesting that land speculation harms the social and spiritual well-being of a community in large, industrial centers such as New York, where corporate monopolies were buying up large tracks of land for commercial development.

But for religious discourse, the sense of urgency a prophet ignites in an audience is more important than his or her ability to verbalize (or translate) what Fishburn calls "otherwise incoherent attitudes, reactions, and longings" (12). The role of a prophet, after all, is to cast a vision of the future that inspires action in the present. For many religious orators, both in Rauschenbusch's day and our own, this means positioning their discourse as a forerunner to some momentous (if not apocalyptic) occasion, discourse that is often achieved by invoking the trope of crisis, an idea that has roots in the rhetorical concept of *kairos*, which Poulakos identifies as a moment of opportunity in his sophistic definition of rhetoric. Not surprisingly, prophetic rhetoric is often crisis rhetoric that appeals to the here and now as the fitting moment for action.

The very title of Rauschenbusch's book evidences his willingness to draw on the crisis trope to promote the social gospel, but *CSC* is not a message of apocalyptic doom and gloom. The *kairos* to which Rauschenbusch appealed was in his mind the crisis that precedes most great social revolutions, namely, instances when an exploited and disenfranchised citizenry anticipates a more just and equitable social order. One way to understand the sophistic quality of Rauschenbusch's rhetoric is to therefore consider how he uses the crisis trope to appeal to the American public at the turn of the twentieth century. Indeed, the basic argument Rauschenbusch develops in *CSC* is that one can examine the history of Christianity, beginning with the Old Testament prophets, to understand why the dawn of the twentieth century is the appropriate time to establish the kingdom of God in the industrialized world. But the book is not a work of theology; it is a treatise that sophistically outlines a vision for what Janet Nelson terms a "Christianized economic order" (443).[5] To understand this claim, and to see it as characteristic of Rauschenbusch's sophistic rhetoric, it is important to situate Rauschenbusch as a social Christian in the context of late-nineteenth-century liberal Protestantism.

THE DEVELOPMENT OF A SOCIAL GOSPEL CLASSIC

Mostly liberal Protestants, the leaders of the social gospel drew on the philosophical ethics of mid-nineteenth-century Christian socialists such as Frederick Denison Maurice to argue that Christians had a duty to care for the physical well-being of society and its spiritual health (see also Shaver, this volume). The economist Richard Ely, the well-known Congregational pastor Washington Gladden, and the writer and social organizer Josiah Strong all gained national status in the 1880s and 1890s for their efforts at engaging "the social question," the generic term they used for the myriad social and economic challenges stemming from postwar industrialization. Ely, Gladden, and Strong, as well as other social Christians such as Henry George, Shailer Matthews, Lyman Abbott, and Charles Sheldon, are all founders of the social gospel who paved avenues of thought that did not coalesce on a national scale until Rauschenbusch helped popularize the movement at the turn of the century.

It is out of this context that Rauschenbusch developed an interest in what he and his predecessors called "social Christianity." Indeed, Rauschenbusch's eventual contributions to the literature of the social gospel built upon many of the ideas these well-known pastors and Christian activists had been promoting for at least two decades. Sheldon (who coined the phrase "What would Jesus do?") revised sermons about the social responsibilities of Christians into popular works of fiction, whereas Strong's popular book *Our Country* (1885) argued for the importance of domestic missionary activity. But perhaps the most famous advocate for social Christianity before Rauschenbusch was Washington Gladden, whose many books drew on the virtues of personal piety as strategies for promoting various social reforms.

Rauschenbusch studied these works and others like them with keen interest, especially because life among the immigrant poor in Hell's Kitchen forced him to reconcile an increasingly liberal theological outlook with the pious spirituality instilled in him at seminary.[6] In other words, as much as Rauschenbusch wanted to cultivate Christian devotion among his congregants, he could not ignore the reality that his flock didn't need more piety. They needed food on the table, safe places to work, and voices of political influence advocating on their behalf. This is not to say he was willing to privilege one form of faith over another. Personal devotion to God and a commitment to the collective welfare *in the name of God* did not have to be mutually exclusive. Rauschenbusch works through these ideas in the various articles he published in the 1890s. In an *American Journal of Sociology* article, for example, he defends the efforts of progressive social reformers but warns supporters of such efforts not to water down their justifications with "a mild and sapless altruism" ("Ideals" 202). For Rauschenbusch, reconciling the "two-sided faith" of reformers who view religion and politics as separate demanded Christian warrants: "We must overhaul all the departments of our thought and work out that social Christianity which will be immeasurably more powerful and more valuable to the world than either an unsocial Christianity or an unchristian socialism" ("Ideals" 203).

Here we see Rauschenbusch arguing for a kind of reconciliation between Christian orthodoxy and political liberalism (Lasch 9). In "The Stake of the Church in the Social Movement," Rauschenbusch demonstrates his progress in achieving such reconciliation when he defends labor reform efforts by suggesting they benefit both society and church: "Churches are institutions rooted in the national life; they will flourish if their soil is fertile and good; they will decay if it is baron and parched" (18). That is, a more socialized economic system would benefit workers by giving them the resources to better serve their communities, including family and church. As Rauschenbusch asserts, "The harder it is under our social environment to do the plain righteousness demanded by the standards of everyday life, the less likely it is that Christians generally will live up to the more exacting demands of the peculiar morality of Jesus, which is theoretically the standard of the church" ("Stake" 28). Such a statement not only evidences Rauschenbusch's belief that Christians have a primary role to play in reform movements, but it also reflects his concern that as a social institution the church was failing to model the example set by Christ. Perhaps it is not surprising that his sermons during this period were marked by an emphasis on vicarious suffering, a theme that became common in social gospel advocacy thanks in large part to Rauschenbusch's example (Evans, *Kingdom* 79). Nevertheless, it was during this period in the mid-1890s that Rauschenbusch resolved to compose his own book-length treatise on social Christianity, one that would urge readers to understand that Christian asceticism rooted in individual salvation runs counter to the Gospel of Jesus, which he believed requires Christians to champion social justice.

But the book about social Christianity he intended to write in the 1890s never materialized.[7] In 1897 Rauschenbusch accepted a faculty position at his alma mater, Rochester Theological Seminary, at which point he began work on an academic treatise that would encapsulate the history of social Christianity, a piece of scholarship that reflected the institutional status he occupied as a church historian. But the more Rauschenbusch wrote, the more he seemed to be writing for a lay public who were concerned less with the fineries of academic argument than with the practical ethics of living a Christian life. Consequently, over the next decade Rauschenbusch planned, drafted, revised, and scrapped multiple manuscripts until 1905 when he finally committed to an outline for *CSC*. Historian Gary Dorrien explains that Rauschenbusch finally decided it was more important to publish a book that would promote social Christianity than was writing the opus he originally envisioned, one that would have pleased Rochester's board of trustees but would have garnered fewer readers.[8] As he writes, the book "enthralled readers with its graceful flow of short, clear sentences, its charming metaphors, and its vigorously paced argument" (Dorrien 98). But it's the argument itself that is most important. Rauschenbusch urges the creation of "a new kind of Christian" who recognizes that "a cooperative Commonwealth would give us the first chance in history to live a really Christian life without retiring from the world, and would make the Sermon on the Mount a philosophy of life feasible for all who care to try" (*CSC* 352, 341).

One early review of *CSC* notes, "[n]o one can read these pages and imagine that for the author these are only pious phrases suitable for the pulpit but not for the marketplace. His book is too earnest and too disquieting for any such suppositions" (qtd. in Evans, *Kingdom* 191). This claim—that *CSC* was "suitable for the pulpit" and the wider public—proves prescient considering that Rauschenbusch forwards a vision of Christian ethics that aligns salvation with the progressive work of social welfare. Rauschenbusch also taps into the relatively new field of evolutionary biology to develop a doctrine of the kingdom of God that is arguably post-religious; he promotes a vision for God's kingdom that exists beyond doctrinal creeds and ritualized performances. Here is where the transformation of decorum emerges. Rauschenbusch is clearly attempting to convince fellow Christians to step out from the pew and into the street to promote the social gospel, but he is also inviting secularly minded reformists to recognize their work as an extension of Jesus's social philosophy. Rauschenbusch thus constructs a rhetorical situation that will make it easier to render the social gospel's message in ways that invite wide public participation despite the "Christian" discourse animating its claims. But the sophistic quality of Rauschenbusch's rhetoric can also be demonstrated by its flexible appeal to what constitutes the "social crisis" itself as an emergent situation. Rauschenbusch, in fact, crafts opportune moments to promote the social gospel's possibilities.

HISTORY, CRISIS, AND THE KINGDOM OF GOD: MAPPING RAUSCHENBUSCH'S SOPHISTIC RHETORIC

The transformation of decorum at work in *CSC* is Rauschenbusch's articulation of evangelical theology into civic ideology, namely, by forwarding the ethics of Jesus to defend economic justice.[9] The book blends the disparate genres of history, social scientific analysis, and biblical hermeneutics into a prophetic call for what Rauschenbusch deemed an "economic and social revolution" (*CSC* xxxv). Charles Strain forwards the label "public theology" to categorize Rauschenbusch's work because it is designed to persuade committed believers and "addressed to the larger public which constitutes the social and historical contexts of the work" (24). Certainly, Rauschenbusch's book is a product of its time insofar as it mediates various intellectual controversies of the day, including debates over biblical interpretation, evolutionary theory, and Social Darwinism (Fishburn 16).

To label *CSC* "public theology" thus makes sense, but it begs a fuller description of what gives the book its sophistic appeal. Rauschenbusch triangulates historical reflection with a vision for the kingdom of God and an urgent call for economic reform. Such triangulation results in a constellation of concepts that produces a perpetual *kairos* of sorts—"opportune" moments not constrained to one specific context. Such *kairos* is sensitive to those emerging "crises" brought about by the superstructural dimensions of capitalism that render poverty and class-based oppression the result of institutional failures rather than personal shortcomings. I use the term *kairos* to name what for Rauschenbusch was a kind of open-ended warrant—the reality that in a capitalistic economy the rich will always be exploiting the poor—even though the sense of opportunity implied by the term is always relative to a particular situation. But for Rauschenbusch, appealing to God's justice *transcends* time even though enacting this justice requires action *in* time.

Thus, the *kairos* Rauschenbusch crafts—what he might describe in theological terms as the emergent reality of God's kingdom on earth—begins with his use of historical reflection. The first three chapters of *CSC*, respectively titled "The Historical Roots of Christianity: The Hebrew Prophets," "The Social Aims of Jesus," and "The Social Impetus of Primitive Christianity," establish a context out of which Rauschenbusch positions Christianity as a revolutionary social force. The history he weaves throughout these chapters lays the groundwork for one of his most provocative claims, which is that institutional religion often impedes ethical action in the world:

> Against this current [ritualized] conception of religion the prophets insisted in a right life as the true worship of God. Morality to them was not merely a prerequisite of effective ceremonial worship. They brushed sacrificial ritual aside altogether as trifling compared with righteousness, nay, as a harmful substitute and a hindrance to ethical religion.
>
> (*CSC* 5)

Rauschenbusch draws out one example after the next of prophets condemning oppressive social institutions that privilege the economic and political power of the few over the social welfare of the many.

In one example, Rauschenbusch tells the story of King Ahab and his wife Jezebel's plot to murder Naboth in order to take ownership of the latter's vineyard, a story that illustrates the righteousness of prophetic action in the face of oppressive rule. As Rauschenbusch tells it, "Ahab knew the tenacity with which the Israelite clung to his freehold, and the sanctity which attached to the ancestral inheritance, and hence, when Naboth refused to sell, the king could only fume helplessly at the failure of his pretty plans for a private park" (CSC 17). As the story goes, Ahab's wife Jezebel forges documents in Ahab's name, ordering the elders in Naboth's city to bring charges of blasphemy against Naboth. As a result, he is stoned to death. But when Ahab attempts to take possession of Naboth's land, the prophet Elijah condemns the king and proclaims God's judgment on Ahab, who then "tore his clothes, put on sackcloth and fasted" (I Kings 21:27). As Rauschenbusch explains, "Ahab had collided with the primitive land-system of Israel" and violated "the divine rights of the people" (CSC 17). The moral of this story, as with all the stories of the ancient prophets that Rauschenbusch recounts, is that faith in social justice is the faith God calls on his people to embrace. More important, these narratives of the oppressed rising up against oppressors establish a prophetic tradition in which Rauschenbusch can place the individual whom he believes is the greatest prophet of all, Jesus Christ.

For those committed to the social gospel, Jesus embodies the perfect expression of an ethical life. But in *CSC*, Rauschenbusch is careful to explain that the ethics of Jesus, while representing a continuation of those of the Hebrew prophets, were attuned to his own particular time and context. In fact, he says Jesus "was not a timeless religious teacher, philosophizing vaguely on human generalities. He spoke for his own age, about concrete conditions, responding to the stirrings of the life that surged about him" (CSC 49). What Rauschenbusch most admires about Jesus, and what he believes is most relevant for the social gospel, is that Jesus prophesied about "organic growth," how every new society is fostered "cell by cell." As Rauschenbusch explains, "[i]t takes more faith to see God in the little beginnings than in the completed results; more faith to say that God is now working than to say that he will some day work" (CSC 60). Thus, the kingdom of God is realized not by praying for a cosmic apocalypse that will initiate a new earth; it's built on the small kindnesses people show to one another when they feed the hungry, clothe the naked, and shelter the homeless. In the person of Jesus, Rauschenbusch says, we are presented with a conception of the kingdom of God that "is not a matter of getting individuals to heaven, but of transforming the life on earth into the harmony of heaven" (CSC 65).

What emerges in Rauschenbusch's thought is a decidedly egalitarian vision of the kingdom of God, one that trumps ecclesial doctrines that position it as an otherworldly heaven accessible only to believers after they die. Despite his idealistic language, Rauschenbusch's vision of the kingdom of God is not utopian. As Handy explains, "[t]he idea of the kingdom of God, so central in the thought of the social gospel, was not consciously conceived or presented merely as an idealized Christendom" (140). Like Darwin's conception of evolution, the kingdom of God in Rauschenbusch's formulation is "always but coming" and therefore never complete (*CSC* 309). It is a constant work in progress, such that "there is always but an approximation to a perfect social order" (*CSC* 421). Rauschenbusch insists the kingdom of God is a progressive reality, one that demands constant re-articulation. To echo my description of what it means to transform decorum, Rauschenbusch speaks directly to the importance of expanding the meanings of familiar terms to give them wider significance. As he says of the prophets, for example, "new occasions under the inspiration of God were able to teach them new duties and new truths. They added new terms to the synthesis of truth" (*CSC* 26). This is a sophistic claim: if the terms we have available are inadequate for the work of articulating the kingdom of God in the present, then we need new terms, or at least new ways of using old terms.

What Rauschenbusch evidences with his own discourse is that rhetorical novelty is more often than not the consequence of using old terms in new ways. Every age confronts new occasions, he tells us, so our beliefs should evolve along with the language we use to articulate these beliefs. His conception of the kingdom of God as an emergent reality relies on the religious terminology already available to Christians, but he uses this familiar vocabulary in new ways to alter what many believers envision when they hear the phrase "kingdom of God." Another example can be found in Rauschenbusch's frequent use of "Christian" in predicate form, as in "Christianizing" or "to Christianize." As Nelson explains, " 'Christianizing' for Rauschenbusch was synonymous with humanizing, democratizing and moralizing, terms he used interchangeably in his writings" (453). By using these terms interchangeably, Rauschenbusch expands their meanings; he's adding "new terms to the synthesis of truth" he intends readers to take away from the text.[10]

Rauschenbusch argues that a just social order is the only evidence of the kingdom of God at work in history. In the book's final three chapters, the crisis trope comes together; Rauschenbusch essentially posits that the future of Christianity depends on its participation in "the social movement." In short, Christians can either renew their commitment to social and economic justice or atrophy into a state of moral impotency: "If the Church tries to confine itself to theology and the Bible, and refuses its larger mission to humanity, its theology will gradually become mythology and its Bible a closed book" (*CSC* 339). This is the *kairos* Rauschenbusch invents with *CSC*, that the present moment is ripe for radical action or pregnant with possibility (Smith 47). In other words, it is not enough simply to study the prophecies of scripture to understand the present; one must study the present to understand the scriptures. The Bible, for instance, does not hold meaning outside of particular situations, and to understand the particularity of a situation requires interrogating the uniqueness of the present moment.

Herein lies the crux of Rauschenbusch's historiography: the emergent quality of the kingdom of God provides us with the imagination necessary for understanding the past while anticipating the future. As he remarks, "[t]he new present has created a new reality" (*CSC* 45).

Compare this to rhetorician Dale Sullivan's "suprarational" dimension of kairotic rhetoric and how it fosters, "under the influence of inspiration during the opportune moment, a sense of the numinous [. . .] a vision that fills the consciousness" (327). Insofar as *CSC* might be labeled prophetic, we can agree with Sullivan that it "presents a single alternative, filling the entire consciousness of the auditor, producing belief when the auditor says 'yes' instead of 'no' " (317). Accordingly, Rauschenbusch positions his readers as history's current actors who must decide whether to intervene in the fight for the oppressed, and whose decision will determine Christianity's future. Thus, the crisis at stake for Rauschenbusch is not just the social one brought about by the excesses of industrial capitalism. Christianity itself is in crisis.

Rauschenbusch's historiography also anticipates what theologian Paul Tillich describes as the "method of correlation," a kind of philosophical inquiry that links problems of existential being to the historical realities of human experience. For Tillich, *kairos* is key to understanding any historiography that uses fate or divine will to link the present to the past, because *kairos* casts time as something that is always emerging within the concrete "space" of the present. As Tillich puts it, "[t]he turning point in the struggle between space and time in history is the prophetic message" (35). In *CSC* we see this method of correlation at work in Rauschenbusch's insistence on making the "historical connection" between Jesus and the prophets in order to make the same connection between Jesus and the current "social movement." These historical connections thus function as the necessary link for realigning Christianity with prophetic or "ethical" religion.

So to label Rauschenbusch's rhetoric as sophistic is to direct attention to its timeliness, to its *kairos*. For Poulakos, and ostensibly for Rauschenbusch as well, rhetors that employ sophistic rhetoric remind their audiences that the situation is urgent and therefore significant ("Toward" 40). A newly industrialized world represented an urgent moment for Rauschenbusch, one that would test the ability of humanity to either lift one another up in the name of solidarity or maintain its current course of economic disparity. The ethics necessary for solidarity, what Rauschenbusch also calls "the spirit of Christian democracy" (*CSC* 369), are the ethics of Jesus and the kingdom of God. Thus, the kingdom of God is realized existentially to the extent that its ethics are enacted socially. But the sophistic quality of Rauschenbusch's rhetoric is also discernable in its flexible appeal to what constitutes the "social crisis" itself as an emergent situation. This is its *kairos*. The crisis Rauschenbusch proclaims, the crisis of economic exploitation and systematic poverty inhibiting the kingdom of God, is one that will be *perpetually prolonged* insofar as American democracy remains a democracy divided by class.

CONCLUSION: TRANSFORMING DECORUM

For rhetoricians interested in the public work of religious discourse, Rauschenbusch deserves our attention, and not just because he helped spark the social gospel movement. He also crafted a prophetic message about social salvation that resonated with large audiences at the turn of the twentieth century, a message that articulated Christian principles for civic ends, principles that themselves were transformed in the process. The result is nothing less than a vision for a civil religion manifested rhetorically to position the social gospel as America's best hope for maintaining the vibrancy of its democracy.[11] Indeed, Rauschenbusch and his fellow social gospel advocates supplied the discursive framework through which calls for governmental regulation and economic reform were communicated to the American public at the height of the Progressive era (Szasz 43). For these reasons, Rauschenbusch's work remains a useful model for considering the social value of religious rhetoric within a democratic public, especially if we consider how such rhetoric can be used to understand one's civic obligations in terms of his or her spiritual commitments, and vice versa.

In 2007, a trade press published a centennial edition of *CSC* featuring response essays by some of today's leading Christian social activists, including Tony Campolo, Stanley Hauerwas, Phyllis Trible, Jim Wallis, and Cornel West. While these commentators offer their own justification of the book's continued relevance, Paul Raushenbush, Walter's great-grandson, best makes this point:

> Just as Rauschenbusch awoke to the social message of the gospel through his direct experience of poverty, Christians today must not be afraid to face the most pressing issues of our day—war, terrorism, poverty, globalization, religious fanaticism, AIDS, the rights of women—and to confront these challenges first-hand. Guided by the vision of the kingdom of God, we must recognize that it is not enough to help the afflicted; we must influence the systems that cause the affliction.
>
> (xiii)

Such a claim illustrates the sophistic appeal of Rauschenbusch's rhetoric, including how appeals to the "social crisis" can be fitted to prophetic calls in the present that direct attention to the many contemporary crises, such as those noted earlier, that affect us today. In other words, Walter Rauschenbusch's positioning of the kingdom of God as an *emergent* reality is achieved only when actors *in the present* seize those opportune moments to alter whatever conditions are preventing "the social organism" from flourishing. But as Rauschenbusch himself evidences, discourse that is generated to assist in this work of transformation must be appropriate—timely and decorous—because then "it is perfectly compatible with the audience and the occasion it affirms and simultaneously seeks to alter" (Poulakos, "Toward" 41).

To ready religious discourse for civic purposes, Christian rhetors must be able to maintain their credible standing in the communities of faith where they live and work. But they must also aim their discourse toward audiences that exist beyond these communities, and in doing so render the key terms of their rhetoric in such ways that their speech remains malleable, ready to be adapted and transformed for new contexts. For religious discourse to maintain public relevancy, in other words, its terms must be deployed in such ways that their meanings remain flexible to the perplexing effects of cognitive dissonance so that multiple and perhaps even incongruous meanings can be recognized as the continually emerging (or "always becoming," to use Rauschenbusch's phrase) object of discourse. The conceptions invoked by religious terminology should therefore be presented as objects that can only be partially grasped, in part because they are in a continual state of development. For Rauschenbusch, the most important example of this is found in his articulation of the kingdom of God as more or less equivalent to an equitable social democracy, one that is built over time instead of established outright.

One other implication for rhetoricians is how Rauschenbusch creates a historical warrant for evaluating various social crises from the purview of religious ethics. That is, rather than arguing that Christianity can contribute to social movements in an auxiliary manner, Rauschenbusch contends that social movements result from religious communities transforming their spiritual commitments into social ethics that subsequently alter the social order itself. "For most of the later social gospel exponents," explains William King, "reform activity sprang not from a sense of moral obligation alone but primarily from a belief in the social nature of religious experience itself" (113). Rauschenbusch says as much in *CSC*:

> But those who hold that the flower of religion can only be raised in flowerpots will have to make their reckoning with the prophets of Israel. The very book on which they feed their private devotion and that entire religion out of which Christianity grew, took shape through a divine transformation which found its fittest and highest organs in a series of political and social preachers.

(26)

The transformation Rauschenbusch references is that of historical moments of social oppression into articulations of the kingdom of God. Rauschenbusch thus illustrates how religious creeds subsequently evolve when the discourses through which they get articulated are applied in novel ways to address novel problems.

The social gospel did have its critics, and like other popular movements, newer ones eventually subsumed it.[12] Nonetheless, Walter Rauschenbusch helped transform the decorum through which social Christians articulated their religious claims for wider publics. The claims Rauschenbusch forwards in *CSC*, especially those about salvation and the kingdom of God, remain flexible to the social crises we face today. This is why Hauerwas can declare that Rauschenbusch's book "is as desperately needed in our day as it was in his" (176). Even though we no longer live in a society that exploits child labor or lets its poor languish without the possibility of government assistance, issues such as poverty, insufficient health care, and the need for immigration reform present a new sense of urgency. The rhetorician who is attuned to the sophistic appeal of Christian rhetorics listens not just to hear *what is said* but also to hear whether what is said *could be said elsewhere*, in another time, and in another place.

NOTES

1. Rauschenbusch did not coin *social gospel*, although he did use it in the title of his last book, *A Theology for the Social Gospel*. For Rauschenbusch and other proponents of the social gospel, they mostly used "social Christianity."

2. *CSC* was "the publishing sensation of 1907" (Smucker 5). Fifty thousand copies were sold between 1907 and 1910. Evans notes that "not only was the book one of the biggest selling nonfiction books of the social gospel era, but it opened the floodgates to a variety of interpretations of modern social Christianity" (*Kingdom*, 197).

3. Harimon has surveyed how the concept of decorum has evolved in rhetorical studies: "Aristotle uses this warrant when he identifies how the appropriate style establishes credibility," whereas Cicero defines decorum as "the sensibility of an active mind attuned to its social environment" (153, 155). Harimon defines decorum as "the major stylistic code for verbal composition and the social knowledge required for political success" and thus aligns it with knowledge of social conventions (152).

4. My summary of Schiappa's criticism is cursory and elides the complexity of his argument. For a fuller appreciation of this debate, see Schiappa ("Neo-Sophistic") and Poulakos ("Interpreting").

5. Rauschenbusch critiqued capitalism because he felt it bred gross economic inequality that impedes the possibility of living in solidarity. As he writes in *CSC*, "[s]ingle cases of unhappiness are inevitable in our frail human life; but when there are millions of them, all running along well-defined grooves, reducible to certain laws, then this misery is not an individual, but a social matter, due to causes in the structure of our society and curable only by social reconstruction" (246).

6. Walter Rauschenbusch inherited the spirituality of his father, August, a prominent pastor and theologian among German Lutherans who embraced the Baptist pietistic tradition on immigrating to the United States. Pietism was a movement that stressed individual piety as the primary means of spiritual renewal (Evans, *Kingdom* 2–3). Copious prayer, scriptural study, and disciplined practices for controlling personal behavior are the hallmarks of pietism. While Walter never abandoned his pietistic leanings altogether, the poverty he encountered in Hell's Kitchen contributed to a "radical reorientation" of his Christian faith (Evans, *Kingdom* xix). Specifically, Rauschenbusch came to believe that Christians should not be concerned with saving souls for an otherworldly heaven, but with improving social conditions *to model* the perfection of heaven. Rauschenbusch thus challenged premillennial dispensationalist

eschatology that posits a forthcoming apocalypse, or "rapture," in which Jesus will carry the saved to heaven.

7 Rauschenbusch completed a manuscript in the early 1890s titled *Revolutionary Christianity*, but the book was never published. The manuscript was eventually discovered in an archive and published in 1968 as *The Righteousness of the Kingdom*.

8 Rauschenbusch worried that *CSC* would be too unorthodox for the seminary's board of trustees. As it turned out, the board did request his resignation once the book was published, but the seminary's president, Augustus Strong, came to Rauschenbusch's defense, who kept his post (see Evans, *Kingdom*, 190–91).

9 As I mentioned, Rauschenbusch's work extends many of the ideas forwarded by social Christians in the 1880s and 1890s. As a case in point, Rauschenbusch was not an economist, but he nevertheless uses *CSC* to defend a socialistic economic system. The Christian socialist Richard Ely, a well-known economist and founder of the American Economic Association, heavily influenced Rauschenbusch's thinking on socialism and is referenced in virtually all of the latter's work.

10 Kenneth Burke would call this "casuistic stretching" because Rauschenbusch is essentially offering a new set of principles to draw upon when interpreting the meaning of this language (229–32).

11 The idea of civic, or "civil," religion points to the deeply held identifications that unite a body of citizens around transcendent ideals, whether religious, political, or philosophical in nature. Roderick Hart calls "civil religion" a misnomer for what should instead be called "civic piety." While I do not have the space to consider the these concepts fully, I believe it is worthwhile to quote Hart when he explains that "[c]ivic piety in the U.S. emerges not so much from blind, momentary passion, but from a knowing, pragmatic understanding of what is required when God and country interact" (45). Rhys Williams and Susan Alexander explain that civil religious language must communicate "a transcendent moral standard and wide cultural resonance, but without the sectarian divisiveness possible in a pluralist society. It ties together understandings of God's will with national history, and projects a mandate for rightly-guided action onto all members of the national community" (4).

12 The social gospel continues to influence the ecumenical movement in American Christianity. The rise of liberation theology in the last half of the twentieth century is in many ways an extension of social gospel discourse. The Catholic Worker's movement, founded by Dorothy Day in the 1930s, remains active and echoes many of the claims first articulated by Rauschenbusch. For a collection of essays that considers the continued legacy of the social gospel, see Evans's *The Social Gospel Today*.

REFERENCES

Bitzer, Lloyd. "The Rhetorical Situation." *Philosophy and Rhetoric* 1.1 (1968): 1–14.

Burke, Kenneth. *Attitudes toward History*. 3rd ed. Berkeley: U of California P, 1984.

Dorrien, Gary. *The Making of American Liberal Theology: Idealism, Realism, and Modernity, 1900–1950*. Louisville: Westminster John Knox P, 2003.

Evans, Christopher H. *The Kingdom Is Always but Coming: A Life of Walter Rauschenbusch*. Grand Rapids: Eerdmans, 2001.

———, ed. *The Social Gospel Today*. Louisville: Westminster John Knox P, 2003.

Fishburn, Janet Forsythe. *The Fatherhood of God and the Victorian Family: The Social Gospel in America*. Philadelphia: Fortress P, 1981.

Handy, Robert T. *A Christian America: Protestant Hopes and Historical Realities*. 2nd ed. New York: Oxford UP, 1984.

Harimon, Robert. "Decorum, Power, and the Courtly Style." *Quarterly Journal of Speech* 78 (1992): 149–72.

Hart, Roderick. *The Political Pulpit*. West Lafayette, IN: Purdue UP, 1977.

Hauerwas, Stanley. "Repent. The Kingdom Is Here." *Christianity and the Social Crisis in the 21st Century*. Ed. Paul Raushenbush. New York: HaperCollins, 2007. 173–76.

King, William McGuire. " 'History as Revelation' in the Theology of the Social Gospel." *Harvard Theological Review* 76.1 (1983): 109–29.

Lasch, Christopher. "Religious Contributions to Social Movements: Walter Rauschenbusch, the Social Gospel, and Its Critics." *Journal of Religious Ethics* 18.1 (1990): 7–25.

Lee, Ronald. "The Force of Religion in the Public Sphere." *The Political Pulpit Revisited*. Ed. Roderick P. Hart and John L. Pauley II. West Lafayette: Purdue UP, 2005. 99–108.

Nelson, Janet. "Walter Rauschenbusch and the Social Gospel: A Hopeful Theology for the Twenty-First Century Economy." *CrossCurrents* 59.4 (2009): 442–56.

Poulakos, John. "Interpreting Sophistical Rhetoric: A Response to Schiappa." *Philosophy and Rhetoric* 23.3 (1990): 218–28.

———. "Rhetoric, the Sophists, and the Possible." *Communication Monographs* 51 (1984): 215–26.

———. "Toward a Sophistic Definition of Rhetoric." *Philosophy and Rhetoric* 16.1 (1983): 35–48.

Rauschenbusch, Walter. *Christianity and the Social Crisis*. 1907. Louisville: Westminster John Knox P, 1991.

———. "The Ideals of Social Reformers." *The American Journal of Sociology* 2.2 (1896): 202–19.

———. *The Righteousness of the Kingdom*. Ed. Max L. Stackhouse. Nashville: Abingdon Press, 1968.

———. "The Stake of the Church in the Social Movement." *The American Journal of Sociology* 3.1 (1897): 18–30.

———. *A Theology for the Social Gospel*. 1917. Louisville: Westminster John Knox P, 1997.

Raushenbush, Paul, ed. *Christianity and the Social Crisis in the 21st Century: The Classic that Woke Up the Church*. New York: HarperOne, 2007.

Schiappa, Edward. "Neo-Sophistic Rhetorical Criticism or the Reconstruction of Sophistic Doctrines?" *Philosophy and Rhetoric* 23.3 (1990): 192–217.

———. "Sophistic Rhetoric: Oasis or Mirage?" *Rhetoric Review* 10.1 (1991): 5–18.

Sheldon, Charles. *In His Steps: "What Would Jesus Do?"* 1896. New Spire Ed. Grand Rapids: Revell/Baker, 2012.

Smith, John E. "Time and Qualitative Time." *Rhetoric and Kairos: Essays in History, Theory, and Praxis*. Ed. Phillip Sipiora and James S. Baumlin. Albany: SUNY P, 2002. 46–57.

Smucker, Donovan E. *The Origins of Walter Rauschenbusch's Social Ethics*. Montreal: McGill Queen's UP, 1994.

Strain, Charles. "Walter Rauschenbusch: A Resource for Public Theology." *Union Seminary Quarterly Review* 34.1 (1978): 23–34.

Strong, Josiah. *Our Country: Its Possible Future and Its Present Crisis*. New York: The Baker and Taylor Company, 1885.

Sullivan, Dale L. "*Kairos* and the Rhetoric of Belief." *Quarterly Journal of Speech* 78 (1992): 317–32.

Szasz, Ferenc Morton. *The Divided Mind of Protestant America, 1880–1930.* Tuscaloosa: U of Alabama P, 1982.

Tillich, Paul. "The Struggle between Time and Space." *Theology of Culture.* Ed. Robert C. Kimball. London: Oxford UP, 1959. 30–39.

Williams, Rhys H., and Susan M. Alexander. "Religious Rhetoric in American Populism: Civil Religion as Movement Ideology." *Journal for the Scientific Study of Religion* 33.1 (1994): 1–15.

Section V

(Re)Mapping Religious Rhetorics

13 More in Heaven and Earth
Complicating the Map and Constituting Identities

Beth Daniell

When people in rhetoric and composition write about students who identify as religious, the narratives typically focus on those whose beliefs or values run counter to those of the academy in general or the teacher in particular. In these articles and chapters, teacher-writers go quickly to the most convenient label—"Christian"—often without looking at other parts of the context, such as location, socioeconomic status, race, ethnicity, denomination, educational background, and so forth. The map portrayed in such publications is a simple one: the "Christians" are one side of the territory, and "we" academics, sometimes defined as secular liberals, are on the other side (see also Vander Lei, this volume). The demarcation between the two groups is clear, with particular characteristics set up as binaries: "Christians" are narrow-minded, ignorant, oppressive, conservative, judgmental, faithful to dogma; "secular liberal academics" are open-minded; enlightened; liberating; of course, liberal; accepting; espousing critical thinking—and so on and so forth.

The bifurcated map described by rhetoric and composition excludes the possibility of the middle and ignores the complexities of human identity and thought. This map leaves no room for those who may hold liberal political views while practicing their faith or for those who, while socially conservative, experience a Christian community focused on compassion and forgiveness. My aim here is to complicate the map presented by my colleagues. To do so, I draw on a report published by the Public Religion Research Institute (PRRI) under the auspices of the Brookings Institute (Jones et al.) and on books by two New Testament scholars, Marcus Borg and John Dominic Crossan, who use rhetoric to create a space for Christian identities and to constitute Christian communities that do not show up on composition's map. The Brookings report shows that many Christians in the United States do not identify with composition's depiction of "Christian," whereas Borg and Crossan seek to interpret Christianity for modern and postmodern people who find much in traditional Christianity problematic. Both the Brookings report and Borg and Crossan reveal places on the map that may not be readily visible to those who have accepted dichotomized representations of our students and ourselves. The notion of constitutive rhetoric helps us understand not only the importance of the writings of Borg and Crossan but also the means by which these writings call into existence a Christian community that exists on newly formed ground. In short, I hope to demonstrate that there is more in heaven and earth than we have been able to see.

Because I argue for a map with more texture, I refrain as much as possible in this chapter from using such labels as evangelical, apocalyptic, and fundamentalist, terms which have precise theological meanings (and are therefore not synonymous) but which have taken on negative connotations in public discourse. But there is no escape from language, and so I try to use the terminology employed by the PRRI—conservative, moderate, liberal, progressive.[1]

THE BIFURCATED MAP: VISIBLE LOCATIONS AND THOSE NOT SO VISIBLE

The map described earlier is, for all practical purposes, the same one presented by the media, where these days every issue is portrayed as a simple pro/con argument. Following and reinforcing stereotypes, CNN, Fox, MSNBC, and other television and Internet outlets only rarely discuss the complexity of political, economic, social, religious, theological, or cultural problems: individuals and organizations are either conservative or liberal, Republican or Democrat; only rarely does a moderate appear. The world is divided between political conservatives, if not flat-out reactionaries, on one side, and political liberals, if not card-carrying Marxists, on the other. While such a simplified portrayal may be good for ratings, it is not for academic exploration. What is not presented is any middle location on this map, and what is ignored is doubt, new interpretations, complexity, contradiction, resistance. There is no room on a neatly divided map for the messiness of contemporary Christianity.

Ironically, what separates these two locations, "Christian" and "secular academics," is the shared notion that truth is factuality. As Borg explains *Reading the Bible Again for the First Time*, modernity posits truth as scientific fact; that is, science excludes propositions that cannot be verified. As a consequence, some reject religion because its narratives cannot be proved, while others "factualize" scriptural narrative, myth, poetry in order to make them true (*Reading* 16). The result is that science and religion both lose, with some people denying the validity of spiritual and religious truth and others claiming that spiritual and religious texts are scientifically or historically factual (*Reading* 16). Burke might call these two positions scientistic and dramatistic, with the former approach focusing on propositions "such as 'It *is* or It *is not*'" and latter concentrating on such "hortatory expressions as 'Thou *shalt*, or Thou *shalt not*'" found in literature, theology, and rhetoric (1340). So some Americans read the Bible "literally" even when a metaphor is staring them in the face, and others, also failing to recognize metaphor, dismiss scripture as a fantasy. What is presented between these two locations on composition's map is only desert. But as academics in the humanities and social sciences we should know that human beings are more complicated than these binaries allow.

An example of taking seriously the complicated identities of students is Sara Webb-Sunderhaus's article "A Family Affair: Competing Sponsors of Literacy in Appalachian Students' Lives." Here Webb-Sunderhaus examines the sometimes contradictory array of literacy sponsors for college students in Appalachia. Trying to maintain their Appalachian identities, these students receive inconsistent messages about the value of education—from parents, spouses and partners, other relatives, friends and classmates, professors, the college, or the university. Both economic situations and conservative forms of Christianity serve as motivators and/or obstacles. For these students, religion can serve as a sponsor of literacy and at the same time support negative cultural and familial messages about education, especially for women leaving their "place" in the home. Webb-Sunderhaus's ethnographic stance allows her to look dispassionately at the pressures and opportunities these students face, considering the conditions and contradictions in their lives. She recognizes religion and the attachment to Appalachia as strong factors but does not attribute to either the entirety of the students' identities. Webb-Sunderhaus's research participants inhabit many places on a complex map, not just one.

THE DEMOGRAPHIC CHALLENGE

Webb-Sunderhaus's description of a matrix of positions—family, economics, geography, history, religion—finds support, interestingly, in the results of the Economic Values Survey from the PRRI under the auspices of the Brookings Institute. The report on the PRRI data not only disputes a bifurcated map with religious conservatives, on one side, and nonbelievers, on the other, but also shows a map with overlays that include social, economic, theological, and political positions (Jones et al.). Released in July 2013, the report titled "Do Americans Believe Capitalism and Government Are Working? Religious Left, Religious Right & the Future of the Economic Debate" argues that the religious map of the United States is far more complicated than popular media indicate—and, I would add, more complicated than the one presented in composition studies. According to its Executive Summary, "28% of Americans are religious conservatives, 38% are religious moderates, and 19% are religious progressives; additionally, 15% of Americans are nonreligious" (Jones et al. 2). That is, there are more religious moderates and progressives in the United States (57 percent) than there are religious conservatives (28 percent). Furthermore, the summary points out that "religious progressives are significantly younger than religious conservatives" and therefore more likely to gain percentage points with time (3). The report demonstrates that religious, social, economic, and theological conservatives overlap on less than a third of the map, while the rest is occupied by complex mixtures of moderates, liberals, progressives, and the unaffiliated. For example, African Americans are the most theologically conservative, but the most economically liberal (Jones et al. 39). Younger people across a range of theological and religious positions, including conservative ones, tend to be more socially liberal than their parents and grandparents, the report points out, adding that gay marriage is gaining acceptance among Americans, even religious ones, but especially among the young (Jones et al. 40).

According to the PRRI poll, Christians in America express a variety of attitudes about politics, economics, social issues, theology, and religion. Between the conservative Christians and those who claim no religion are those Americans who see themselves as both Christian and moderate or liberal. Others call themselves progressive Christians, a term the PRRI poll uses. Some from this group, as well as from the moderate and liberal camps, might identity with the Emerging Christianity movement, a term not used in the PRRI poll (leaders claim that "emerging" is more inclusive than "progressive" because it permits a diversity of theological positions). Among these moderate, liberal, and progressive Christians—the excluded middle— are members of mainline denominations—Episcopal, Presbyterian, Methodist, Lutheran, United Church of Christ, the Society of Friends—as well as Roman Catholics and Baptists and others (denominational or not) who focus on social justice and spiritual practice.

Among our students are so-called evangelicals who speak of themselves as "Red Letter" Christians, another group not named in the PRRI data: this group believes that the true meaning of Christianity rests in the words of Jesus, often printed in red letters in the New Testament (Campolo; Pally). That is, these Christians take seriously Jesus's teachings about recognizing the sacred in each person—including the homeless, the poor, the imprisoned, the sick, the abandoned. For these young people—and some not so young— economic justice and Christianity are not opposing values. The civil rights movement, remember, was born and nourished in the black church. More recently, Pope Francis has urged Catholics to return their focus to economic rather than sexual issues. Knowing more about the diversity and complexity of our neighbors, academic writers might see that the religious landscape of America is richer, and perhaps more sympathetic, than previously thought.

In the remainder of this chapter, I examine the rhetoric of Borg and Crossan, which presents an alternative to the version of Christianity on the bifurcated map that omits Christians who identify as moderate, liberal, or progressive, as well as those who identify as members of the "church alumni association" (Spong qtd. in Stephens). The version of Christianity Borg and Crossan teach results from rhetorical readings of the Bible, chiefly the New Testament, and they present their conclusions rhetorically. In sections below, I look first at the rhetoric of their coauthored book *The First Paul: Reclaiming the Radical Visionary behind the Church's Conservative*

Icon and then at Crossan's rhetoric in *The Power of Parable: How Fiction by Jesus Became Fiction about Jesus.* In the final section, I use Maurice Charland's theory of constitutive rhetoric to assert that the rhetoric of these books does not merely persuade but actually constitutes an identity for many whose presence the bifurcated map does not account for. But first, a little background.

THE RHETORIC OF RELIGION

Borg and Crossan practice a kind of Biblical scholarship of which other disciplines—including rhetoric and composition—often seem unaware. It results from various approaches to the Bible—nineteenth-century form criticism, the study of oral forms and a forerunner of modern literary criticism; and source criticism, the search for sources such as Mark and Q for the Gospels in the New Testament and the J, E, P, and D strands in the Hebrew Testament.[2] In addition to these historical approaches, scholars also take literary approaches and put forth theological readings (Zulick 129). In the 1970s rhetorical criticism came to the fore, combining historical, literary, and theological readings, with the sociopolitical, which Margaret Zulick says is "most robust trend" in this scholarship (129–30). The rhetorical criticism practiced currently is what Zulick calls "socio-rhetorical criticism" (129–30).

New Testament scholars Borg and Crossan draw on research in many fields—history, archaeology, anthropology, ancient languages, geography, theology, and so forth—to read scripture rhetorically. They use everything they can learn from related fields to contextualize individual books (or particular passages) in a particular time, place, and setting, paying attention to theological issues or historical events in order to consider the kind of person the author might have been, describe the audience and his message to them, and examine the message for its (ideological) meaning to its ancient audience(s) and to its twentieth- or twenty-first-century readers. According to Borg in *Reading the Bible*, using these approaches "has been taught in the seminaries of mainline denominations for the better part of the last century" (ix) and is becoming "increasingly common among lay members of mainline churches" (ix). He refers to the method he uses as "historical-metaphorical" because he looks not just for the context but also for the metaphorical meaning of the narratives (37–44).

In recent decades, some of these scholars have promoted their ideas to a wider public, writing books that sell well enough to be published by major commercial presses and speaking to groups large and small in churches, on campuses, and in other settings.

Their book sales attest to their success in persuading their readers; I am told that publishers rarely have advertising budgets for these writers' books because there is no need to advertise. In addition to Borg and Crossan, a short list of other such writers-scholars and writer-preachers would include Diana Butler Bass, Walter Bruggemann, Bart Ehrmann, Richard Elliott Friedman, Amy-Jill Levine, Brian McLaren, Elaine Pagels, Richard Rohr, Barbara Brown Taylor, and Phyllis Tickle.

My reading of the work of Borg and Crossan is supported by hearing one or another of them—and sometimes both—lecture either in Atlanta or at an annual event on the East Coast. Their overall message, like that of other current mainstream scholars and theologians, is that Jesus was a Jew and his message was consistent with that of the prophets of the Hebrew Testament: social justice emanating from a love of God that inspires keeping the commandments. This may be seem obvious, but traditional Christianity has taught that Jesus was a replacement for Judaism and has regarded Old Testament prophecy primarily as the foretelling of the coming of the Messiah rather than as a critique of the dominations systems under which the prophets lived, as Walter Bruggemann explains in *The Prophetic Imagination* (xi–xvii). This bias has run through much Christian scholarship, as Bruce Herzberg points out in a recent study of Paul's use of Jewish rhetoric. Like many other Biblical scholars of our times, Borg and Crossan do not see the traditional gap between the Old and New Testaments, arguing instead for continuity between the message of the Hebrew Testament and the New. Borg and Crossan pay attention to history, especially to the occupation by various conquerors of what is called the Holy Land and to the Hebrew/Jewish response to oppression, whether foreign or homegrown. They assert that a tradition of opposing domination systems runs throughout the Bible.

As they explain the teachings of Jesus, the rhetoric of the Gospels, and the thought of Paul, these scholars take into account first-century Jewish eschatology, shaped by the Roman occupation and the cooperation of the Temple establishment with the Romans. The word eschatology is a term for "end times." Crossan explains first-century Jewish eschatology as "the Great Divine Clean-Up of the World" (125). Borg and Crossan argue that for most Jews in the first century, the end of the age did not mean the violent destruction of the world, but rather the end of the world as we know it to be, filled with cruelty, corruption, and exploitation. Certainly there were zealots in Palestine who called for a violent overthrow of Roman armies— and some who expected a divine retribution for sinners and divine rewards for the faithful. But when Jesus prayed for God's kingdom to come, Crossan argues, he was praying not for violence but for a world in which God's plan for creation would come to be (113–36).

Not only do their interpretations take a rhetorical approach to Biblical texts, assuming historically grounded writers with messages for real, historically grounded audiences, but Borg and Crossan, as I hope to demonstrate, are themselves skilled rhetoricians. While they assert the sacredness of scripture, they do not see the Bible as the infallible word of God. Rather, the Bible is viewed as multiple authors writing at different times and for different audiences. They believe that bringing various kinds of knowledge to the readings makes interpretations richer—and more believable to audiences who live the twenty-first century. Hearing them speak, one recognizes excellent classroom teachers who present well-organized lectures with humor in the right places. Years of experience teaching undergraduates has taught them to insert meta-discourse at places along the way. These skills transfer to their popular books. But, as we will see looking through Maurice Charland's theoretical lens, these scholar-rhetoricians are not just seeking to persuade; they aim, in addition, to offer a new identity and a new community to those Christians who are often invisible.

THE RHETORIC OF *THE FIRST PAUL*

Marcus Borg, for many years a professor at Oregon State University, is the quintessential Midwestern Lutheran, organized, efficient, soft-spoken. Dominic Crossan, now retired from DePaul in Chicago, is Irish Catholic, full of humor and passion. They write and speak separately and together, having become acquainted while serving as members of the "Jesus Seminar," an academic group whose purpose was to locate the authentic sayings of Jesus within the many layers of New Testament text. This work has been, as might be expected, disparaged in some Christian conservative and literalist circles but welcomed elsewhere.

Borg and Crossan begin *The First Paul* as they do several other books, by calling on popular culture for a strawman. In the first chapter "Paul: Appealing or Appalling?" Borg and Crossan cite the May 6, 2002, issue of *Newsweek*, wherein Paul's sins are recited—propagating anti-Semitism, misogyny, and heterosexism as well as defending slavery (Meacham). They describe the bad Protestant theology done in Paul's name, a doctrine that has, they say, concentrated on a set of abstract statements rather than on the precepts of Jesus. This "bad theology" has taught that faith is "theoretical assent to a proposition" rather than "*vital commitment to a program*" (168, emphasis in original). This is their main argument. Next Borg and Crossan outline the rest of their major points.

In the New Testament, they say, there are three distinct Pauls—the radical Paul, the conservative Paul, and the reactionary Paul. Only letters from the first Paul, the radical Paul, can we count on to be authentic: Romans 1, 2 Corinthians, 1 Thessalonians, Galatians, Philippians, and Philemon. Putting Paul's letters into historical context and in chronological order allows readers to see the conservative shifts across the letters. They state that their list of authentic letters is the consensus among almost all New Testament scholars. Borg and Crossan assure readers new to an historical approach to the Bible by making their main claims and arrangement clear from the outset. Readers can read on, confident that the book will proceed logically. Furthermore, these moves help establish the ethos of the writers as reasonable men and provide grounding for logos appeals that come later. As

Borg and Crossan anticipate, many readers come to this book confused by Paul's abstract language, by the contradictions in Paul's Epistles, and by the preaching they have heard about Paul. For such readers, a book with a clear logical argument and accessible language can be a welcome relief.

The second chapter "How to Read a Pauline Letter" (29–58) is a rhetorical analysis of the Letter to Philemon. Here Borg and Crossan explain how and why this letter has been misread as a defense of slavery. They argue, instead, that the message of Philemon is consistent with the overall argument they see in the authentic letters: Paul's radical vision of all human beings as equal recipients of God's grace. Crucial to Paul's theology, they assert, is this passage from his Letter to the Galatians:

> As many of you as were baptized *into Christ*
> have clothed yourselves *with Christ.*
> There is no longer Jew or Greek,
> there is no longer slave or free,
> there is no longer male and female,
> For all of you are one *in Christ Jesus.*
>
> (3:27–29, qtd. in Borg and Crossan 111)

Using this passage as a guide, Borg and Crossan read the Letter to Philemon differently from those who have seen it as a defense of slavery. In their reading, Paul argues that Philemon should accept his slave Onesimus, "whose father I have become during my imprisonment," as an equal *in Christ* (Philemon 1:10, qtd. in Borg and Crossan 37). Borg and Crossan do not claim that Paul condemns slavery in general but, rather, that Paul concludes that a Christian, Philemon, cannot own another Christian, Onesimus, as a slave. By the time readers finish this chapter, they have seen how Borg and Crossan's thesis offers a Paul who does not, in the Letter to Philemon, contradict the theology in Galatians, providing consistency in Paul's message. Readers have become familiar, as well, with Borg and Crossan's style, neither esoteric nor academic but informal and readable, accessible to readers who have found the language of Paul and the language *about* Paul impenetrable. The following chapters focus on historicizing and explaining Paul's theology, specifically in relation to what Paul means by phrases such as "Jesus Christ is Lord," "Christ Crucified," and "Justification by Faith," all three slogans that Borg and Crossan argue have been misinterpreted by Protestants. While space limitations preclude summaries that do justice to Borg and Crossan's arguments in these chapters, suffice it to say that they support their claims by redefining terms and historicizing Paul's writings.

Throughout *The First Paul* Borg and Crossan's use biblical references extensively, a major feature of their rhetoric. This has two rhetorical functions—to ground their interpretation of Paul in the scriptural texts and to enhance their ethos. Borg and Crossan not only cite particular passages but also relate those passages to similar messages in other parts of the Bible.

They quote verses they see as particularly significant. At certain points, they ask readers to read the texts for themselves. At the back of *The First Paul* is a four-page double-columned list of Biblical references the authors have quoted or paraphrased, along with the page number in the book where their discussion takes place. In addition, Borg and Crossan count the number of times Paul says X (e.g., on p. 173, they tell us that the word for creation occurs five times in Romans 8:9–23) or the number of times Paul discusses Y (on p. 58, they include a chart listing the passages where the three Pauls talk about slavery and patriarchy). Borg and Crossan are meticulous with biblical references that demonstrate that their readings are based on what Paul actually wrote because some conservative Christians dismiss work by progressive scholars as "unbiblical." But that's not a problem here, however, because both Borg and Crossan know the scriptural texts in ways only professors who have taught particular texts for forty years would know them. Thus, doubts about whether Borg and Crossan are offering idiosyncratic interpretation are allayed.

Not only does their use of scriptural texts strengthen the logos appeals of Borg and Crossan's argument, but it also augments their ethos as scholars who are masters of their subjects. Their collective ethos is further enhanced by their use of etymology—for example, how Greek shades the meaning of the Latin imperial titles elevating Augustus to divine status and how rendering that mistake into English has had theological consequences regarding the nature of Christ (100–04). Explaining the Latin terms helps contextualize Paul's language and allows for reinterpretation—but it also lets readers see another example of the authors' expertise.

At the end of the book Borg and Crossan again cite scholarly consensus to argue for their categorization of the Pauline Letters into the three categories: authentic, disputed, and almost certainly not authentic. They concede that some scholars hold divergent opinions about dating Paul's death and thus argue that conservative changes in Paul's theology across time are due to age. Borg and Crossan offer good reasons for their assertion that Paul died in 64 CE during the persecutions of Nero, too early for Paul to have written the books deemed inauthentic. Troubled by the conservative and reactionary Pauls, readers are given good reasons to see those "appalling" passages as inauthentic. Using historical and cultural research to contextualize Paul's message in the first century, Borg and Crossan argue that the eschatology Paul envisioned was not "the end of the physical world" as in the destruction of the earth but "the end of the age," the end of "the world" as it was known to be, marked as it was by injustice and violence (152).

In contrast to "this world," Paul wanted the churches to which he wrote to be "communities [that] were 'new families' in which members had the same responsibility to care for each other that biological families did. These were to be communities of caring and sharing" (187). Borg and Crossan explain Paul's repeated use of "brother" and "children of God" in the genuine letters by drawing on studies of urban life in the Roman Empire (187).

Forced from rural areas and subject to the diseases of cities, many in Paul's original audiences would have been persons literally alone, without family. Here Borg and Crossan strengthen their view of Paul's theology, but they appeal to pathos as well. For their readers who have left the church or who are now skeptical of the dogmatism of some theological position, the writers of *The First Paul* offer a reminder of the intimacy and the caring that can exist among a group of believers.

Perhaps the most important rhetorical device in *The First Paul* is definition, or to be more precise, redefinition. Often Borg and Crossan begin their redefinitions by saying something such as "[t]he common Christian understanding of X has been [. . .] but this is simply incorrect. No first-century Jew, and certainly not one of Paul's passionate belief in the goodness of God, would have thought." Here is an example: Borg and Crossan assert that seeing the crucifixion as a substitutionary sacrifice is a misunderstanding (127), tracing this theological view to Anselm of Canterbury in 1097 (128). Then they go on to explain that giving up one's life for others is not the same as taking on someone else's punishment (141). Again, they use etymology: sacrifice means that something is "made sacred." Temple sacrifices, they explain, made the gifts holy; they did not take on anyone's punishment (142–43). This explanation tells seekers that they can indeed be Christian without believing that God killed his own son as punishment for the sins of others, a doctrine that many twenty-first century people find problematic. When Borg and Crossan give an alternative interpretation, they are offering an identity that does not come with a need for believing that which seems implausible (Borg, *Reading the Bible* 50).

Because their rhetoric is effective, at least with audiences who are not Biblical literalists, Borg and Crossan cast doubt on those "appalling" teachings reported by *Newsweek*, such as defending slavery and disparaging women, passages that trouble many modern readers. Borg and Crossan ascribe those disturbing precepts to others writing in Paul's name, writers who included teachings more conservative, and then more reactionary, than those of the radical Paul. With such explanations, Borg and Crossan call the doubtful back to a Christian community different from the one in which they may have grown up. In addition, their explanation of Paul's theology helps complicate the map that compositionists use because the Christianity Borg and Crossan see in the first Paul's letters is not exclusionary but is radically inclusive.

THE RHETORIC OF PARABLES

The invitation to read Biblical texts in ways that challenge traditional teaching continues in Crossan's *The Power of Parables: How Fiction by Jesus Became Fiction about Jesus*. In this book Crossan asserts that Jesus used parables as "participatory pedagogy" (95). That is, Crossan thinks that Jesus's listeners would have interrupted the story to ask questions, to disagree about the characters' goodness or intent or social standing, to speculate on possible meanings. It would have taken Jesus far longer to tell a parable than it takes us to read one, Crossan surmises. And he tells us that would be how Jesus would have wanted it: Jesus used parables because they require audiences to think.

A parable is a metaphor combined with narrative—that is, a story that points elsewhere, Crossan explains citing the etymology of *meta + phor*, "to carry elsewhere" (8). Readers or hearers of parables should be concerned not so much with the internal relationships in the story as with its external reference, that is, what the story points to outside itself (9). Crossan lists four categorizes of parables: riddle parables (such as the Sphinx's riddle or Samson's), example parables (offering ethical admonitions), challenge parables (questioning conventional thinking), and attack parables (undermining the position of some other group; 6–7). Most of Jesus's parables, Crossan says, are challenge parables—that is, stories that ask his listeners to challenge the status quo, the tradition, and the mainstream doctrine. As in the book on Paul written with Borg, Crossan uses definition as a powerful rhetorical device:

> challenge parables humble our prejudicial absolutes, but without proposing counter absolutes in their place. They are tiny pins dangerously close to big balloons. They push or pull us into pondering whatever is taken for granted in our world—in its cultural customs, social relations, traditional politics, and religious traditions.
>
> (63)

Attack parables, which Jesus did not use, go further than challenge parables, actually criticizing some group that holds divergent opinions from the speaker's or writer's. According to Crossan, some of the Gospels contain attack parables that ask audiences to see certain characters as representatives of particular political and theological views that, for his own purposes, a particular Gospel writer wants to disparage.

Like the book about Paul, *The Power of Parable* begins with a prologue that defines the terms—metaphor, story, and metaphorical story—and describes the layout of the book. Indeed Crossan's rhetoric in this book relies primarily on arrangement. Each chapter begins with an outline of what follows; note, for example, the outline in the third chapter:

> What comes next in this chapter? I will focus, as promised, on the Good Samaritan parable of Jesus. First I cite the full text, outline its content, and add a few comments for fuller discussion later. Second I look at that text-in-context indirectly through three different interpretations: first as

a riddle parable, next as an example parable, and finally as the newly proposed category of challenge parable. Third, I look at that text-in-context directly, through both literary and social context, and argue that it is best seen as neither riddle nor example, but as challenge [. . .].

(47–48)

In each chapter Crossan follows his outline faithfully, using clear transitions—"I turn next to the Good Samaritan read as an example parable" (51)—and clear summaries—"We have just seen how this parable can be interpreted as first a riddle and then as an example parable" (53). In other words, Crossan takes up each of his points in a "bird-by-bird" kind of way with such obvious framing that a reader can hardly become lost. Because the book asks readers to consider sophisticated ways of reading unfamiliar to many, Crossan wants to make sure the steps in his argument are transparent.

Not only does Crossan reassure his audience by giving a clear outline of what is to come, but he also takes his audience from familiar, comfortable Sunday school interpretations of Jesus's parables to readings that show Jesus asking his listeners (and Crossan's readers as well) to question the religious and political power structures of their respective times. Questioning the meaning of the parables might be disconcerting to those readers who have been taught since childhood that the parables of Jesus show Christians how to think about God. But introduced subtly, Crossan's readings do not appear revolutionary. They begin, after all, with the familiar plots of Jesus's parables.

After telling his readers that challenge parables are not at all safe, but rather ask listeners to confront injustice, prejudice, and certainty, to rethink "normal," Crossan presents readings that may appeal to Americans of a certain age whose orientation has always been to "question authority." Interpretations challenging the status quo may be welcome after years and years of having the problematic parts of Jesus's parables explained away. While Jesus in his parables may not speak as directly as the Hebrew prophets, his message is the same: return to God and behave in a way that is just to all. Starting with what his readers likely know, Crossan uses clear organization to lead them step by step to another level, much as Socrates teaches Phaedrus that in making "a transition from anything to its opposite," the best way is to move forward "in small steps" (Plato 158).

For example, Crossan shows that there is far more to the parable of the Master's Money than the work ethic valued by American culture: If you invest your money, you will be blessed; if you put it under the bed, you could lose it all in a fire. In Sunday school, many little Protestants were taught, of course, that this parable really has nothing to do with money but instead with literal "talents"—calligraphy, music, math, writing, and athletics. But they knew it was really about how to thrive by investing wisely. For readers so instructed, the idea that Jesus might be asking us to look at the broader picture of poverty and oppression could be surprising (Crossan 98–106), but Crossan gets his readers to his challenge-parable interpretation gently by supplying two other readings and then providing historical background. As a challenge, the parable of the Master's Money makes sense to people who want a definition of Christianity that does not necessarily affirm the materialist culture of the United States. Putting forth a different version of the Jesus's teachings, Crossan offers twenty-first-century Christians grounding for the questions they may have asked of the American political and economic systems.

To convince readers not only to accept his intellectual argument but also to believe it, Crossan uses a conversational style that invites in readers who are neither theologians nor academics but, instead, who are Christians who work in various fields and are looking for adult ways of understanding the Bible. Crossan's style, as I previously said, owes much to his teaching undergraduates for forty years—here's this play on words, here's a joke, here's an allusion to popular culture, here's a pun, here's a memorable phrase. For example, "[i]n summary, then, and with apologies to the apostle Paul for using his phrasing, riddle parables, example parables, and challenge parables abide, these three; and the greatest of these is challenge parables" (47). In his explanation of why it is incorrect to think of "talents" as physical or mental attributes in the parable of the Master's Money, Crossan says, "[t]hat interpretation simply avoids the pointed challenge of Jesus, which is, to put it bluntly, Do you stand with the greedy or the needy?" (106).

Even when Crossan explains fine theological points, his style is memorable, using, for example, parallelism and antithesis to achieve clarity:

> Jesus proclaimed God's presence rather than God's imminence. John [the Baptist] announced . . . that God's Great Clean Up of the World was imminent, was an any-day-now event. Jesus proclaimed, on the contrary, that God's transformative advent was present, was already here and now on earth. God's kingdom was imminent, in the future, for John, but already present for Jesus.
>
> (125)

This example shows, in addition, Crossan's use of comparison and contrast to explain Jesus's eschatology by contrasting it with that of John the Baptist. Later in *The Power of Parables*, Crossan uses a number of ancient accounts of Caesar crossing the Rubicon to show how an actual historical event can be told more than one way in order to make different rhetorical points. Then, using the Caesar narratives as warrants, Crossan is able to argue by analogy that each of the Gospels presents the story of Jesus's life and ministry in a different way so that each Gospel writer can accomplish his own rhetorical purpose. This extended comparison makes Crossan's argument seem entirely reasonable: the Gospels differ from one another not just in a few details but also in rhetorical situation—written in different decades, for different audiences, under different conditions, for different purposes.

If arrangement is the most obvious rhetorical concept in *The Power of Parable*, analogy—comparison—may in fact be the most effective. Crossan's main argument is that Jesus taught in challenge parables in order to make his first-century Jewish audience think about their relationship with God and their fellow human beings, to reconsider traditional teachings about finding favor with God. But Crossan needs to allay fears that such an interpretation might be only his own idiosyncratic reading. He therefore needs to strengthen his argument by showing that it is entirely reasonable that Jesus would have used such a tactic; Crossan needs to make the backing for his warrant obvious, to use Toulmin's term (1421).

For the support he needs, Crossan discusses the books of Ruth, Jonah, and Job in the Hebrew Bible. Crossan demonstrates that these books challenge those parts of Hebrew scripture that teach ethnic purity, the exclusivity of the relationship of the Hebrews and God, and the notion of a quid pro quo relationship with God. Reading the book of Ruth as a challenge parable, Crossan asserts that the story tells readers that the ancestor of David, the hero-king of Israel, was not just a Moabite woman but was in fact an outsider, a member of a despised neighboring tribe. What does it mean when the king of God's chosen people is descended from their enemies? The book of Jonah challenges the exclusive relationship of the Jews with God by reporting that the people of Nineveh were far more obedient to God than Jonah, supposedly God's prophet. Is God only for the Jews—and by extension only for "us" (whomever the *us* happens to be)? Similarly, the holiest man in the world, Job, who is not a Jew, suffers mightily (Crossan 82). The book of Job challenges the arrogance of human beings—Job's neighbors— who think they can understand God, think for God, and explain God—a temptation not only for Job's friends but for many others as well, some living in the United States in the second decade of the twenty-first century. Ruth, Jonah, and Job call into question the traditional beliefs about finding favor with God, Crossan says.

Jesus would have been quite aware of these stories and their challenges to orthodoxy, Crossan says. This countertradition in Hebrew scripture is background for Jesus's challenges to a religious establishment that in his own time cooperated with the Roman oppressors of God's people. Here we find the point: Crossan asks twenty-first-century Christians to recognize the complexity of the tradition. In both Old and New Testaments exists religion that excludes, indulges in self-righteousness, displays its confidence in its knowledge of God's will, and judges accordingly. But Crossan demonstrates another tradition, more inclusive, humbler, less sure of its special status with God, more willing to see good in outsiders. In so doing, he offers a Christian identity unlike the one most visible on TV and on the maps of many composition scholars. The sort of certainty Crossan calls into question makes itself clear when disasters such as Hurricane Katrina or the earthquake in Haiti are seen as God's punishment, just as Job's friends believed that God was punishing Job for his sins. As Crossan puts it, "[t]he book of Job rendered foolish the absolute security of those Deuteronomic proclamations" that lay out "rules" that must be followed in order to gain favor in God's eyes (86).

Throughout *The Power of Parable*, Crossan creates an ethos for himself by both presenting a logical argument, as we have seen, but also by appealing to pathos. With the clarity of his organization and the fluency of his sentences, he calms any anxiety about reading the interpretations that differ from traditional readings. He reassures his readers by beginning with what they know and then intrigues them by presenting and explaining unfamiliar interpretations. He uses parallelism and antithesis to clarify and contrast his points in memorable ways. He amuses his readers with word play as when he paraphrases Jesus: "Do you stand with the needy or greedy?" Ending his book, Crossan heightens the emotional content by inviting his readers to assent to an at once new and very old community:

> The *power* of Jesus's parables challenged and enabled his followers to co-create with God a world of justice and love, peace and non-violence. The *power* of Jesus's historical life challenged his followers by proving at least one human being could cooperate fully with God. And if one, why not others? If some, why not all? "Ashes denote," wrote Emily Dickinson, "that fire was." And if fire ever was, fire can be again.
>
> (252)

In addition to calling forth the yearning for something better, something higher, Crossan invites readers to see themselves in these words. Without saying it directly, Crossan offers space for his readers to think, "That can be me." Clearly he is leading his audience to identify emotionally with the position he has named—that of cocreator of a just, peaceful, non-violent world. Crossan's use of pathos here serves also as an example of constitutive rhetoric.

CONSTITUTIVE RHETORIC

Beyond the rhetoric that Borg and Crossan use to counter traditional interpretations of Paul's Epistles, the Gospels, and parts of the Hebrew Bible, these writers and others like them are, I surmise, seeking to constitute a different sort of Christian community. It may already exist, though it lacks organization and visibility. The PRRI puts this loose alliance on the map by naming its members as theologically moderate, liberal, or progressive. The map being redrawn likely includes some typically labeled evangelical, usually on the conservative side of the map, especially those who call themselves Red Letter Christians. Also included on the newly configured map would be others who see themselves as part of the Emerging Christianity movement. What seems to unify these groups, the PRRI study points out, is concern about the inequality in American culture. People in these groups likely nod in agreement with Borg when he says that in scripture the word justice almost always means economic justice, which doesn't mean that everyone get the same amount, but that everyone gets enough ("What").

The audience Borg and Crossan write for and speak to includes baby boomers who came to adulthood in the 1960s and 1970s, some who left the church when it failed to take stands on significant moral and political issues and others who stayed but have found congregations and/or denominations that accept or even sponsor liberal views. Some are seekers, people who have explored many religious positions—from, for example, Baptist to agnostic to Buddhist and to the Society of Friends. Others have grown tired of increasingly intolerant views in their faith traditions and are actively looking for something else. Many are comfortable enough to afford the books and the time to attend lectures by these scholars. Some readers, like me, have heard these scholars—and similar speakers—at church retreats or at public lectures; a good number may have discussed these writers' books in reading groups or Bible studies. Others are younger people who have read texts by these scholars in religion classes or who have heard these scholars speak on campuses across the country. Still others are young people looking for a spiritual life but encountering conflicts between their social values and church doctrine—especially concerning sexual issues. Some are so-called secular liberals who want something more substantial than the Democratic Party on which to base their passionate beliefs in social justice. When Borg and Crossan—and their colleagues—speak and write, they are "hailing" these groups, "calling out" to these audiences (Charland 138).

Borg, Crossan, and others are practicing what Maurice Charland calls constitutive rhetoric. In his article "Constitutive Rhetoric: The Case of the Peuple Québécois," Charland explains not only how the term *Québécois* came to be and what it means, but how a government white paper created a "peuple" with a history and an identity from an un-united population referred to as French Canadians. The key terms in Charland's article are *interpellation* and *identification* (133). Charland explains Althusser's term interpellation by citing the French verb *interpeller*, which means "calling upon someone by name and demanding an answer" (138, 149, note 22). By employing this concept, it is easy to see Borg and Crossan as calling out to a group of people—naming them—who may then respond to that call. For instance, in *The First Paul* the critique of substitutionary atonement calls out to those readers who have been troubled by this doctrine. Using history as first principle and etymology as a second, Borg and Crossan take the position that believing this doctrine is not a requirement for counting oneself as a Christian.

The other key term, *identification*, Charland uses in the Burkean sense: "[Burke] does not posit a transcendent subject as audience member, who would exist prior to and apart from the speech to be judged, but considers audience members to participate in the very discourse by which they would be 'persuaded'" (133). That is, Borg and Crossan's audiences adopt an identity by virtue of the fact that these audience members attend the lectures and read the books: the audience "participates in the very discourse by which they would be persuaded," thus identifying with the ideas, beliefs, teachings—the very discourse which persuades them. The process of identification becomes manifest when readers write "Yes!" in the margin next to Crossan's comment, for example, that we must "hear that parable of Jesus with ancient Jewish ears attuned to Torah and not with modern American ears attuned to Wall Street" (105), or when, at lectures audience members underline passages in their Bibles and take copious notes as Borg discusses the book of Amos and its application to the American empire ("What").

Interpellation, Charland says, "occurs at the very moment one enters into a rhetorical situation, that is, as soon as an individual recognizes and acknowledges being addressed" (138). If this is true, then some readers respond to "being addressed" when Crossan explains that in the parable of the Masters Money, Jesus challenges his hearers to question an economic system that gives almost everything to an elite class and leaves others with virtually nothing. Similarly, some women in the audience—who grapple with the sexism in any tradition—"answer" when they encounter Borg and Crossan's first Paul, the radical, authentic Paul, because this first Paul almost certainly did *not* write in 1 Timothy (2:11–15) that he "permit[ted] no woman to teach or have authority over a man" (55–57). What Borg and Crossan and similar writers are doing is "hailing" those Christians in the excluded middle and inviting them to take their places on the map.

In *The First Paul* and *The Power of Parable*, Borg and Crossan speak to the contradictions with which some readers or listeners have lived for many years, the conflicts between their own values and church teachings. As Charland says, paraphrasing Stuart Hall, "we can live within many texts" (142). But the strain of living for a long time within conflicting texts allows for the possibility of a resolution, a "rearticulation," as Charland puts it (142). Borg and Crossan offer discourse that resolves these tensions, inviting their audiences—including those in the church alumni association—to find/create/take up identities within a Christian community that does not require doctrinal purity but instead challenges the domination systems of our culture and emphasizes mercy for the oppressed and disadvantaged.

I hope that my rhetoric has persuaded my readers that Borg and Crossan use rhetoric to open up scripture to nontraditional interpretations and that they use their own rhetoric to invite Christians to constitute themselves as different kinds of communities. By explaining alternative readings, they interpellate their readers with an identity that can operate in a pluralistic and technological society. Considering both the teachings of Borg and Crossan and their success with their intended audiences, those of us in rhetoric and composition might well find that our map is expanding: instead of only two locations, now other points are becoming visible. Such a map of religious rhetorics would yield new places to explore and, importantly, would broaden the view of students who identify as Christian.

NOTES

1 While the report uses the terms *conservative, moderate,* and *liberal* in its discussions of theology, politics, economics, and social values, in the section on
religious orientation, the report uses *progressive*, noting that religious leaders
prefer it over *liberal* (31, note 9).
2 One source using the term *Jehovah*, or *Yahweh*, for the name of God; another
using Elohim; another strand deemed the Priestly source; the last attributed to
the Deuternomist. In *Who Wrote the Bible?* Richard Elliot Friedman tells the
story of this scholarship. A short explanation of sources for the Gospels can
be found in chapter 3, "The Gospels as Historical Sources," in Bart Ehrman's
Did Jesus Exist? See also, Borg's *Reading the Bible*, 52, note 1.

REFERENCES

Borg, Marcus. *Reading the Bible again for the First Time: Taking the Bible Seriously
but not Literally*. San Francisco: HarperSanFrancisco, 2001.
———. "What I Wish Every Christian Knew: The Bible Is Both Personal and Political." Epworth-by-the-Sea, St. Simons Island, GA.18 January 2014. Lecture.
———, and John Dominic Crossan. *The First Paul: Reclaiming the Radical Visionary behind the Church's Conservative Icon*. New York: HarperOne, 2009.
Bruggemann, Walter. *The Prophetic Imagination*. 2nd ed. Minneapolis: Fortress P,
2001.
Burke, Kenneth. *From Language as Symbolic Action. The Rhetorical Tradition: Read-
ings from Classical Times to the Present*. 2nd ed. Eds. Patricia Bizzell and Bruce
Herzberg. Boston: Bedford/St. Martins, 2001. 1340–47.
Campolo, Tony. "What's a Red-Letter Christian?" *Beliefnet*. Web. 26 May 2014.
Charland, Maurice. "Constitutive Rhetoric: The Case of the *Peuple Quèbèçois*."
Quarterly Journal of Speech 73.2 (1987): 133–50.
Crossan, John Dominic. *The Power of Parable: How Fiction by Jesus Became Fic-
tion about Jesus*. New York: HarperOne, 2012.
Ehrman, Bart D. *Did Jesus Exist? The Historical Argument for Jesus of Nazareth*.
New York: HarperOne, 2012.
Friedman, Richard Elliot. *Who Wrote the Bible?* New York: HarperOne, 1989.
Herzberg, Bruce. "The Jewish Context of Paul's Rhetoric." *Renovating Rhetoric in
Christian Tradition*. Eds. Elizabeth Vander Lei, et al. Pittsburgh: U of Pittsburgh
P, 2014. 119–34.
Jones, Robert P. et al. *Do Americans Believe Capitalism & Government Are Work-
ing? Religious Left, Religious Right and the Future of the Economic Debate*.
Washington, D.C.: Public Religion Research Institute and the Brookings Institute,
2013. Web. 26 May 2014.
Meacham, Jon. "Sex and the Church: The Case for Change." *Newsweek* (6 May
2002): 22–32.
Pally, Marcia. "The New Evangelicals." *New York Times*. 9 December 2011. Web.
27 May 2014.
Plato. *Phaedrus. The Rhetorical Tradition: Readings from Classical Times to the
Present*. 2nd ed. Eds. Patricia Bizzell and Bruce Herzberg. Boston: Bedford, 2001.
138–68.
Stephens, Scott. "An Interview with John Shelby Spong." *Faith and Theology*. 6
September 2007. Web. 29 May 2014.

Toulmin, Stephen. From *The Uses of Argument*. *The Rhetorical Tradition: Readings from Classical Times to the Present*, 2nd ed. Eds. Patricia Bizzell and Bruce Herzberg. Boston: Bedford, 2001. 1423–28.

Webb-Sunderhaus, Sara. "A Family Affair: Competing Sponsors of Literacy in Appalachian Students' Lives." *Community Literacy Journal* 2.1 (2007): 5–24. ERIC. 26 May 2014. Web.

Zulick, Margaret D. "Rhetoric of Religion." *The SAGE Handbook of Rhetorical Studies*. Eds. Andrea Lunsford, Kirt Wilson, and Rosa Eberly. Los Angles: Sage, 2009. 125–38.

14 Charting Prospects and Possibilities for Scholarship on Religious Rhetorics

Michael-John DePalma and
Jeffrey M. Ringer

In our introduction to this collection, we noted that we use *mapping* in three ways: to *acknowledge* that which has been overlooked or ignored, to *connect* territories or domains of knowledge that may remain disconnected or under connected, and to *chart* new avenues of rhetorical inquiry that might invigorate research, teaching, and civic engagement (3–4). In this bibliographic chapter, we draw on those notions of mapping to chart scholarship on religious rhetorics. While much of what we discuss below can be classified as "Christian," we intentionally use the broader term *religious* because we cover territory beyond Christian rhetorics and hope to spur future research in non-Christian religious rhetorics. We proceed by subdividing that terrain into the same four categories we use to organize the collection itself: theory, pedagogy, methodology, and civic engagement. By discussing each in turn, we hope to provide new and seasoned scholars of religious rhetorics with a road map to understand where we have been and where we might go.

RELIGION AND RHETORICAL THEORY

The first territory we chart centers on religion and rhetorical theory. Rhetorical theory, as we employ it here, speaks to questions of how rhetoric functions and how it can be defined. We begin by acknowledging the contributions of a rhetorician who established strong theoretical groundings for understanding how religion informs rhetoric—Kenneth Burke. After discussing Burke's rhetorical theory, we explore three areas in rhetorical studies to which Christian rhetorics contribute: theories of form, theories of discourse, and theories of invention. Finally, we point to areas in the study of religious rhetorics that have potential for theory building.

One of the first rhetoricians to offer a rationale for attending to the relationship between rhetoric and religion, Burke argues that rhetoricians should examine religion because it "falls under the head of rhetoric in the sense that rhetoric is the art of persuasion, and religious cosmogonies are designed [. . .] as exceptionally thoroughgoing modes of persuasion"

(*Rhetoric of Religion* v). For Burke, the study of religious rhetoric is valuable because it provides a means by which to comprehend the functions of language for explaining human motives. In examining the relationship between religion and rhetoric through the study of religious texts, Burke offers insights regarding language as motive-laden symbolic action. The full corpus of Burke's work, for that matter, might even be understood as a religious pursuit. As Wayne Booth speculates, "Burke's lifetime project was a religious one—perhaps searching for a replacement of the childhood orthodoxies he had rejected" ("The Many" 199).

While Burke's writings are rife with examples of how religion informed his rhetorical theory, two examples stand out. The first is consubstantiality, which is central to Burke's notion of identification. Consubstantiality, which roughly translates as "of the same substance," stems from the Trinitarian understanding that the three persons of the Trinity—Father, Son, and Holy Spirit—share the same properties while remaining distinct. In Burke's estimation, identification is a chief end of rhetoric and is achieved when symbolic action results in different parties recognizing each other as consubstantial. Identification—and thus Burke's rhetorical theory—is thoroughly grounded in a religious concept. The second example is Burke's cycle of guilt, purification, and redemption. For Burke, motivation to overcome guilt rests at the center of the human drama. Guilt, which Burke links to religious concepts such as "'original sin' and sacrificial redeemer," is "intrinsic to hierarchical order" and calls for redemption through scapegoating or mortification (*Permanence* 284). Burke's rhetorical theory and his understanding of human experience are thus founded on religious concepts.

Theories of Form

A recent project that extends Burke's ideas in significant ways is William FitzGerald's *Spiritual Modalities: Prayer as Rhetoric and Performance*. FitzGerald's project uses Burke's pentad to explore the "distinct, though interrelated, elements of discursive performance" that constitute discourses of prayer (7). Specifically, FitzGerald considers prayer as *acts* of invocation made within scenes of address and motivated by attitudes of reverence. As such, FitzGerald's study examines the range of motives that shape and are shaped by discourses of prayer. One particularly significant implication of *Spiritual Modalities* is that FitzGerald models ways whereby the study of religious rhetorics might add to theoretical discussions of form. Other examples that illustrate the theoretical value of investigating forms of religious rhetoric include Russel Hirst's, James Murphy's, and Roxanne Mountford's work on the sermon; Dave Tell's work on confession; John Murphy's work on the American jeremiad; and Lisa Shaver's work on obituaries in Methodist periodicals. This payoff is also evident in several chapters of this collection (e.g., FitzGerald; Glascott; Zimmerelli). Given the essential role of written, spoken, and visual symbols in Christian traditions and practices, future studies could investigate martyr narratives, homilies, eulogies, hymns, testimonies, panegyrics, witnessing, speaking in tongues, and mystic rhetorics, among others.

Theories of Discourse

The study of religious rhetorics has also extended theories of discourse by broadening theoretical understandings of the relationship between academic and religious discourses and identity and language use. Early discussions of rhetoric and religion in composition studies construct the relationship between academic discourses and religious discourses as being at odds. Two studies working from this assumption are Chris Anderson's "The Description of an Embarrassment" and Douglas Downs's "True Believers, Real Scholars, and Real True Believing Scholars." Anderson argues that while academics should be "open to the possibility of religious discourse," students in academic settings need to write about their religious views from a social epistemic point of view (13). In asserting that the goal of rhetorical education is to challenge "foolishness that is unaware of itself, superficiality that is either/or, dogmatic, unexamined," Anderson establishes a distinction between academic discourse and religious discourse that persists in more recent scholarship. Downs, for instance, explores the discursive conflicts that university writing teachers may confront when teaching religiously committed students. He identifies several points of conflict between "Discourses of Affirmation," which are employed by "true believers" (i.e., students of faith), and "Discourses of Inquiry," which are valued and promoted by "real scholars" (i.e., academics; 41). Downs thus constructs academic and religious discourses as in opposition to one another.

Other discussions of religion and rhetoric complicate this binary. Barry Brummett posits rhetorical epistemology as a means for overcoming the perceived incommensurability between spiritual and academic epistemologies. From this perspective, spiritual epistemologies and academic ways of knowing share rhetorical persuasion as their common ground. On this basis, Brummett asserts, "[t]he question becomes not which is better or worse in any absolute or incommensurable way, but rather what is more or less persuasive about the different epistemologies" (132). Martin Medhurst, too, implicitly challenges this division in "Religious Belief and Scholarship" as he explores the possibility of a theory of Christian rhetoric. This distinction has also been complicated in recent discussions of composition teaching. Michael-John DePalma's "Re-envisioning Religious Discourses as Rhetorical Resources in Composition Teaching" provides one such example, and Jeffrey M. Ringer's "The Dogma of Inquiry: Composition and the Primacy of Faith" provides another. DePalma challenges artificial divisions between academic and religious discourses by offering Jamesian pragmatism as a framework for reenvisioning religious discourses as rhetorical resources in composition teaching. Ringer, on the other hand, draws from

Leslie Newbigin and St. Augustine to theorize "humble dogma," a terministic screen that highlights how basic beliefs motivate inquiry.

Closely related to these investigations of the relationship between academic and religious discourses are studies that examine the relationship between identity and language use. Lizabeth Rand's "Enacting Faith" has served as a critical reminder of the important place that religious beliefs hold in the lives of many students. In calling attention to the fact that students' religious identities can be "the primary kind of selfhood more than a few of them draw upon in making meaning of their lives and the world around them" (350), Rand has spurred important questions about the relationship between identity and rhetorical practice. A study that takes up such questions in significant ways is Ringer's "The Consequences of Integrating Faith into Academic Writing." Ringer asks scholars of rhetoric to consider what happens when religious students integrate their faith into their academic writing. Extending such inquiry is Amber Engelson's "The 'Hands of God' at Work," an ethnographic study that examines how two Muslim PhD students negotiate the interplay among Western capitalism, the English language, and Islamic identity. Through this study, Engelson prompts important questions about the relationship between religious identity and literacy sponsorship in increasingly globalized classroom contexts.

Theories of Invention

Investigations of religious rhetorics have also led to deeper understandings of rhetorical invention. One current running throughout Walter Jost and Wendy Olmsted's *Rhetorical Invention and Religious Inquiry*, for example, is an emphasis on rhetorical invention as existing within (or resulting from) one of numerous tensions: between the contingent and the universal, the human and the divine, the intellectual and the emotional, or the poles of Absolute Truth and sophistic relativism (11–12). James Fodor and Stanley Hauerwas speak to the tension between personal iterations of faith, on one hand, and faithfulness to a tradition or creed, on the other. They do so by discussing Christian faith in terms of performance theory and improvisation, which they define as the ability "to balance individual inventiveness with adherence to a tradition of prescribed conventions" (384). As they suggest, there is a kind of casuistry at work in shuttling between tradition and the contingent, but such casuistry is what allows for the invention of ways to address the sheer plurality of events and exigencies in human life. For Fodor and Hauerwas, rhetorical invention in terms of Christian faith is highly dynamic yet grounded in "the divine act" (387).

Other scholarship concerning Christian rhetorics similarly locates invention within similar tensions. Chris Anderson, in *Teaching as Believing*, invents ways to teach persuasively within the tensions that arise from his identity as a deacon in the Roman Catholic Church and a literature professor at Oregon State University (see also Deans, this volume). While he doesn't mention Fodor and Hauerwas specifically, how he negotiates and mines such tensions in his teaching suggests clear parallels to connections among performance theory, rhetorical invention, and agency (see also Crosby, this volume). Similarly, the Winter 2004 Special Issue of *Rhetoric & Public Affairs* (*R&PA*) takes as its starting point the religious commitments of several prominent scholars to explore how religious traditions function as a sources of rhetorical invention in public contexts (see Medhurst, *Religious*). Meanwhile, the March 2004 issue of the *Journal of Communication and Religion* (*JCR*) features the personal reflections of nine scholars of rhetoric, all of whom practice different religious traditions (see Lessl, *Civic*). Each of the contributors discusses the role of religious belief in their academic work, recognizing both tensions and inventional possibilities.

Martin Medhurst's contribution to the *JCR* special issue demonstrates the possibilities of religion for rhetorical invention. In his article, Medhurst muses on his then-recent move from a public to a Christian university. He considers how his knowledge of rhetorical theory and his religious beliefs as a Catholic might offer prospects for a "theory of Christian rhetoric" (43). While he doesn't purport to work out such a theory exhaustively, he does name values, beliefs, and principles from the Bible and other Christian writers that might inform a theory of Christian rhetoric (43–45). Medhurst thus demonstrates how mining religious traditions might lead to inventional possibilities for both critiquing and producing religious rhetorics.

Future Directions

We see significant possibilities for future theory building through the examination of religious rhetorics. Scholarship on Augustine has the potential to be particularly generative in this regard. One contribution that represents its possibility is Richard Lee Enos and Rodger Thompson's *The Rhetoric of St. Augustine of Hippo:* De Doctrina Christiana *and the Search for a Distinctly Christian Rhetoric*. This collection prompts reconsideration of the relationships between orality and literacy, wisdom and eloquence, and faith and persuasion, and it demonstrates the extent to which Augustine's rhetorical theory might enable us to reimagine contemporary notions of invention, language use, and belief. Other scholarship on Augustine (Olmsted; Ringer, "Faith"; Shuger; Yarbrough) similarly prompts rhetorical theorists to consider a range of questions: How might Augustine's works provide further insight into rhetorical concepts such as silence, ethos, memory, and discovery? How might the inclusion of Christian rhetorics in the rhetorical canon complicate how we understand other rhetorical traditions? How might Augustine's rhetorical theory complicate postmodern notions of rhetoric?

Another strand of inquiry with rich theoretical potential is research on the nature of belief. Booth and Kinneavy offer productive starting points for such research. In "Rhetoric and Religion: Are They Essentially Wedded?"

Booth asserts that "[r]hetoric, when viewed not as mere manipulation but as our entire range of resources for discoursing together when we disagree, will lead not only to a serious study of religion and of religious language [. . .] but to religion, to religious belief itself" (64). Elaborating on this point, Booth argues that

> whenever any inquirer pursues rhetoric vigorously into its true habitat, whenever anyone thinks hard not only about how to persuade to belief but about the grounds of human persuasion, whenever anyone asks honestly about how it is that minds can ever meet at all through symbol systems, sooner or later that inquirer will discover that the entire enterprise depends on belief [. . .] in a God conceived of as the Word which was God and was with God "in the beginning."
>
> (64)

Several of Booth's own works—"Systematic Wonder," "Rhetoric, Science, and Religion," and "Ending the War between Science and Religion"—provide rich models for exploring this complex dynamic between rhetoric and belief.

In *Greek Rhetorical Origins of Christian Faith*, Kinneavy also examines the relationship between belief and persuasion. He does so by demonstrating how the Greek rhetorical concept of persuasion influenced the New Testament concept of faith (*pistis*). Kinneavy's project not only displays the value of applying rhetorical principles to the interpretation of Biblical texts but also provides a means whereby to rethink Christian faith in light of classical rhetoric. More specific to the point we're developing here, Kinneavy's analysis of *pistis* opens the possibility for thinking in more nuanced ways about the relationship between rhetorical persuasion and belief formation.

A promising line of investigation that has begun moving discussions of religious rhetorics in this direction is Peter Elbow's doubting and believing games and the responses his ideas engendered in a special issue of the *Journal of the Assembly for Expanded Perspectives on Learning (JAEPL)*. In "The Believing Game or Methodological Believing," Elbow argues that in order to invent and test ideas, rhetors need to exercise doubt and belief. Assuming that all ideas have weaknesses, the doubting game encourages critique and a detached stance. The believing game, on the other hand, promotes the acceptance of ideas in order to experience their strengths.

In the *JAEPL* special issue, contributors raise important points of discussion that might serve as points of entry for future inquiry on rhetoric and belief. Elbow himself, for instance, examines the implications of "developing methodological believing as a tool that separates believing from accepting" (v). In calling for decoupling believing from temperament and commitment, he emphasizes instead the believing game as a tool for decision-making, wherein judgments are formed through rhetorics of experience (4). Building on Elbow's discussion, Nathanial Teich describes the value of believing as an ethical strategy in a broader framework that explores the complexity of emotional experiences. Mary Rose O'Reilly's contribution traces the etymology of the term *believe* to concepts of love and trust, a move she makes to challenge the Cartesian disposition toward doubt and to forward "the beloving game" as a means of creating "a space of imaginative transformation" in the classroom (28).

The final contribution to this discussion links methodological believing to questions of religious belief, identity, and discourse. In "Faith-Based Worldviews as a Challenge to the Believing Game," Bizzell complicates methodological believing by illustrating the emotional challenge students of faith pose to the use of this construct in practice. Bizzell explains how religious commitment challenges the notion of methodological believing:

> [T]o enter fully into a religious worldview, one must do much more than perform a skeptical thought experiment in which consequences are deduced from premises. One must employ the full emotional and imaginative resources that Elbow calls into play for the believing game. One must even, perhaps, engage oneself in a powerful web that seeks to impact every aspect of one's life.
>
> (32)

In critiquing the relationship between the believing game and religious commitment, Bizzell raises three questions significant to future discussions of rhetoric, religion, and belief:

1. "[W]ithout full immersion, can the believing game be practiced in good faith?" (34).
2. "As we are trying to do with diverse forms of academic discourse, will we be able to accommodate the faith-based discourses that mean so much to so many of our students—and if truth be told, to many of us as well?" (35).
3. "What if there is only work to be done by [. . .] the 'Christian mind'— or Jewish, Moslem, or Buddhist mind?" (35).

These questions should be central to future work in religious rhetorics.

RELIGION AND RHETORICAL EDUCATION

The second territory we chart is religion and rhetorical education. In doing so, we map two particularly generative areas of scholarship. First, we discuss scholarship on teaching religiously committed students, a body of work that explores the relationships between students' religious identities and rhetorical practices, along with pedagogical practices for effectively teaching faith-centered writers. Given that more than two-thirds of the world's population is religiously affiliated, rhetoricians would benefit from understanding this important dimension of students' lives. The second area of scholarship focuses on the identity formation of religiously committed graduate students in rhetorical studies. Though little research has been done in this area, such work has significant implications for the training of graduate students, the teaching of rhetoric, and studies of literacy. In what follows, we outline how using religious rhetorics in the classroom might expand twenty-first-century conceptions of rhetorical education. Finally, we call scholars to venture into territory that deserves more attention, namely how the religious commitments of teachers and scholars shape rhetorical education.

In 2005, the Higher Education Research Institute at the University of California, Los Angeles published a national study of undergraduate students' spiritual development. This multiyear project, titled "The Spiritual Life of College Students," reports that "today's college students have very high levels of spiritual interest and involvement. Many are actively engaged in a spiritual quest and are exploring the meaning and purpose of life. They also display high levels of religious commitment and involvement" (3). Despite this high level of religious involvement, many students feel the need to bracket those commitments when engaging in their academic pursuits. As Mary Buley-Meissner, Mary McCaslin Thompson, and Elizabeth Bachrach Tan note,

> [m]any students in undergraduate and graduate programs have been embarrassed, scorned, or shamed when they have acknowledged in class their religious backgrounds or faith traditions. The implicit (sometimes explicit) message from their teachers has been clear: To be educated means to be educated out of beliefs affirmed by church, temple, synagogue, or sacred circle.
>
> (2)

Such self-censorship is not limited to students of faith. Religiously committed university faculty are also often in positions that seem to require the bracketing of their religious commitments. George Marsden speaks to this point in *The Outrageous Idea of Christian Scholarship* when he writes that "our dominant academic culture trains scholars to keep quiet about their faith as the price of full acceptance in that community" (7). Elaborating on this line of argument, Marsden notes that "the process of acculturation teaches those entering the profession that concerns about faith are an intrusion that will meet with deep resentment from at least a minority of their colleagues and superiors" (7).

While the need to negotiate religious commitment and academic work is clear, feigning boundaries between religious life and academic practice is counterproductive (see Dively, "Censoring"; Marzluf). These artificial divisions unnecessarily cut off students and scholars from important ways of knowing. Along with stifling a central dimension of academic work, asking religiously committed students and scholars to bracket a primary source of invention breeds intellectual dishonesty. As several scholars have noted, religious commitments are often central to the identities of students and faculty (Barrett; Berthoff et al.; Coley; DePalma, "Re-envisioning"; Dively, "Religious"; Gere; Goodburn; Perkins; Rand; Ringer, "Consequences"; Vander Lei and kyburz). In cases where "religion is a primary source of selfhood" (Rand 350) for students and faculty, the wall of separation between one's religious devotion and academic work exists only in appearance (see Vander Lei, this volume). As Marsden notes, "[r]eligious commitments, after all, are basic to the identities and social location of many if not most human beings, and academics routinely recognize such factors as having intellectual significance" (5). For religiously committed scholars and students, setting aside values that are central to identity and worldview seems a stretch if not an impossibility.

The work of literacy scholars such as Beverly Moss, Shirley Brice Heath, Vicki Tolar Burton, Andrea Fishman, and Beth Daniell (*Communion*) have made evident the extent to which religious affiliation influences individual and communal literate identities. One critical result of this research is that educators have recognized the importance of connecting students' primary discourses to classroom settings so that the knowledge in the classroom moves on a two-way path between school and home. Where students of faith are concerned, this means learning more about how notions of literacy connect with and depart from those featured in mainstream academic settings, so that we might draw from their literate resources in our teaching (Carter; DePalma, "Re-envisioning"; Vander Lei, this volume). Such awareness is also important because students' rhetorical participation in their disciplinary communities might have significant identity implications (Ringer, "Consequences"). Our goal when working with religiously-committed students should be to "use the tension between faith [. . .] and academic inquiry as a way of learning more and learning better" (Vander Lei, "Coming" 8).

In the last decade, several scholars have made significant strides in this direction. Collections such as Buley-Meissner, Thompson, and Tan's *The Academy and Possibility of Belief*; Vander Lei and bonnie lenore kyburz's *Negotiating Religious Faith in the Composition Classroom*; and Vander Lei, Thomas Amorose, Beth Daniell, and Anne Ruggles Gere's *Renovating Rhetoric in Christian Tradition* offer valuable perspectives on the relationship between religious faith and the teaching of rhetoric. Articles published in top journals in composition studies have also provided important insights about teaching students of faith (see Vander Lei, this volume). Through this growing body of scholarship, rhetorical educators have been urged toward more informed and inclusive pedagogical practices and have developed a greater understanding of the relationship between religious beliefs and rhetorical practices.

Recent work in religion and composition has also begun to explore how students might use writing to transform religious discourses and construct alternative ways of understanding religion and religious identity. In "Unpredictable Encounters: Religious Discourse, Sexuality, and the Free Exercise of Rhetoric," TJ Geiger offers what he calls "the free exercise of rhetoric" in an effort "to assist students in developing their abilities to read, write, and speak in the mess of competing and disparate discourses that make claims on their attention and lives—discourses they might reposition themselves within and/or against" (264). As Geiger explains, "[b]y treating religion as both a personal commitment and a discursive field, we open up space for unpredictability regarding how students will reposition themselves" (263). Another scholar working toward similar ends is Mark Williams. In *Transformations: Material Terms for Writing on Religion in Composition Classrooms*, Williams forwards an approach that "might help students attend to how and why they are interested in employing [religiously inflected] resources, and how and why they might best go about re-creating and transforming their religious experiences, identities, and communities in the process of writing about them" (29). In turning attention to material conditions that influence student writing, Williams calls scholars to

> use writing to not only respect and include students' multiple personal discursive resources traditionally undervalued in the classroom, but to recognize and develop students' capacities for actively shaping and reshaping the very languages, identities, and social relations playing a key role in their writing and learning.
>
> (28)

While the current trajectory is encouraging, more work remains. One area in particular that demands more research involves the impact of religious rhetorics on twenty-first-century rhetorical education. If inquiry concerning religious rhetorics is viewed as essential to the map of rhetorical studies, then how we approach rhetorical education in undergraduate and graduate contexts must be adapted. The challenge is determining how acknowledging religious rhetorics in our field's mental maps should influence pedagogical practices in contemporary classrooms. This challenge guides many of the contributions to Cinthia Gannett and John Brereton's *Traditions of Eloquence: The Jesuits and Modern Rhetorical Studies*, a collection that illuminates how Jesuit rhetorical traditions have shaped—and might continue to shape—rhetorical education. This challenge similarly animates Thomas Dean's argument that introducing sacred texts when teaching literary and rhetorical theory can invigorate discussions of how readers filter and create meaning through the interpretive communities to which they belong (Deans; see also Deans, this volume). Patricia Bizzell's "Rationality as Rhetorical Strategy at the Barcelona Disputation, 1263: A Cautionary Tale" also provides a rich example of how the study of religious rhetorics offers a means of reimagining contemporary pedagogical practices. In this essay, Bizzell analyzes a theological debate between Rabbi Nachmanides and Friar Paul Christian. As a Jew living under oppressive Christian rule, Nachmanides was forced into this debate and was subject to the terms of disputation established by Friar Paul. As such, he faced a precarious rhetorical situation. Through her examination of the strategies that Nachmanides employed to navigate this rhetorically uneven playing field, Bizzell calls instructors to acknowledge the limits and efficacy of rational arguments, and she suggests that teachers of rhetoric should aim to help students draw from and combine appropriate discourses at hand in each particular situation. Through historical examples of religious rhetoric such as the 1263 Barcelona Disputation, Bizzell contends, students might be better prepared to do this kind of complex intellectual work.

Another area of inquiry that we view as particularly exigent is identity formation of religiously committed graduate students in rhetoric. In a 1999 exchange in *Dialogue: A Journal for Writing Specialists* called "Teaching in the Whirlwind: When Religion Becomes Visible in the Classroom," Joona Smitherman Trapp describes the persecution she faced as a Christian in a graduate English program. She writes that "English programs today are not only insensitive to the needs of the student who espouses religious beliefs, but often these students are both privately and openly persecuted for these beliefs" (15). She marvels that this is the case in a field so open to discussions of diversity and even uses the phrase "students' rights to their own beliefs" (15). Shannon Carter raises similar issues in her work with "Alex" and "Mona," two graduate students in doctoral programs in rhetoric and composition who come to realize that embracing "faith-based religious views" amounts to a kind of heresy in academic communities of practice (577, 586). Alex and Mona must thus contend with what it means to belong simultaneously to communities of practice that hold "largely irreconcilable" views (577). Finally, Toby F. Coley takes up similar questions in "Opening a Dialogue about Religious Restraint in Graduate Professionalization." Writing about his own and other graduate students' experiences as Christians in rhetoric and composition, Coley raises several critical questions for scholars of rhetoric to consider concerning the identity and enculturation of graduate students.

A related concern regarding graduate students is that of mentoring new teaching assistants (TAs). Given that TA training courses are designed to mentor new TAs in best practices and theories of teaching rhetoric, how do we prepare graduate students to work ethically with students of varied religious commitments? Though he does not deal with this issue directly, Chris Anderson alludes to it in "The Description of an Embarrassment." Anderson opens his essay by recounting an experience wherein a graduate TA encountered a student who turned in a "born-again" paper rife with "the language of the fundamentalist, of the testimonial" (14). Noting that the TA asked Anderson if he thought she should "mount" some sort of "frontal attack" against the student, Anderson admits that he was as bothered by the TA's reaction as he was by the student's use of religious language in her academic writing (14). Anderson's example raises a key question: Are graduate students being taught to teach in ways that devalues the religious subjectivities of their undergraduate students? Robert L. Brown and Michael Jon Olson address this issue when, writing about a graduate TA named "Debby," they question the degree to which they are complicit in perpetuating modernist institutional norms and epistemologies that may negatively affect undergraduate students of faith (156–59).

Related to the question of graduate student identity and professionalization is that of how scholars' religious commitments shape their work as teachers of rhetoric. We see rich possibilities for the advancement of rhetorical knowledge when scholars of rhetoric articulate the motivations and commitments that undergird their work in the classroom and the field, as is evidenced by Anderson's *Teaching as Believing* and the special issues of *R&PA* and *JCR* we mentioned earlier. Such projects provide valuable insights into the complex and often generative relationship between scholars' faith-based commitments and their lives as teachers in the academy. They also point to how tension and overlap between religion and pedagogy might open new possibilities. We see such work as vitally important to future studies of religious rhetorics.

RELIGION AND RHETORICAL METHODOLOGY

Next, we chart the discussion concerning methodologies for studying religious rhetorics. To date, scholars have employed a variety of methodologies in such research, including archival methods, interview-based case studies, pentadic cartography, ethnography, teacher-based research, rhetorical analysis, survey-based research, and discourse analysis, among others. Despite this—and despite the fact that "[m]ethodologies developed within particular disciplinary or field contexts may not travel well when moved to new places, people, and their things" (Grabill 210)—little explicit discussion of methodologies concerning religious rhetorics exists. Here, we chart the work that has been done in this area and comment on ways to open new avenues of inquiry. The core question animating such scholarly attention is this: *How might researching religious rhetorics demand new or different methodologies?*

Composition studies features a number of scholarly resources for thinking about research design. One recent example is Lee Nickoson and Mary P. Sheridan's *Writing Studies Research in Practice: Methods and Methodologies*. While this edited collection contains a number of chapters that focus on specific concerns—Grabill deals with community-based research, whereas Asao Inuoe takes up "Racial Methodologies for Composition Studies"—it features no discussion of how accounting for religious beliefs might demand new methodologies. In fact, the term *religious* only shows up once, as does *spiritual*. Both appear in Liz Rohan's "Reseeing and Redoing," which focuses on researchers' emotional attachments to their subjects. Mention of religion is simply an accident of the example she cites. We don't fault Rohan for this, but what's noteworthy is that these are the *only* mentions of religion or spirituality in this collection. At no point does the volume take up the issue of how accounting for religious rhetorics might demand new research methodologies.

There are certainly a number of ways to account for this neglect. One possible explanation is that religious rhetorics aren't central to the work of writing researchers. To put this in terms of mapping, religious rhetorics fall outside the geography of rhetorical scholarship insofar as explicit discussions about methodology are concerned. It is not essential to the map of rhetorical studies. Our response to this comes in two forms. First, from a descriptive standpoint, we would agree that the absence of explicit discussion about methodologies for studying religious rhetorics points to their marginal status within rhetorical studies. Our second response is prescriptive: we argue that explicit discussion about methodologies for studying religious rhetorics *should* be essential to the geography of rhetorical studies, and that such a state of affairs would in turn help to locate religious rhetorics more permanently on the map of rhetorical scholarship.

Another explanation is that studying religious rhetorics, whether through archival, ethnographic, or textual methodologies, is no different than studying other forms of rhetoric. For instance, the archival methods that Mike has used to research the nineteenth-century preacher Austin Phelps parallel the archival methods researchers would use to study any other historical figure: generating questions, exploring finding aids, locating archives, accessing materials, analyzing documents, mining gaps, linking archives, framing data, and so on (see DePalma, "Austin," "Rhetorical"). Similarly, the interview-based case studies Jeff employed in his research on evangelical Christian rhetoric involves many features of any other case study: sampling, recruiting participants, framing questions, analyzing data, developing coding schemes, and so forth (see Ringer, "Consequences"). And yet, as multiple scholars agree, postmodern and feminist influences on research methodologies have brought scholars' personal backgrounds and investments to the foreground (Bizzell, "Feminist"; Grabill; Rohan, "Reseeing"; Kirsch and Rohan), such that Mike cannot (and should not) separate his religious identity and upbringing from the work of researching Phelps. Neither should Jeff bracket the emotional connections he makes with participants that reflect his own background. Studying religious rhetorics, in other words, demands attention to methodology insofar as methodology entails personal connections between researcher and subject (see Cope and Ringer, this volume).

Moreover, one common refrain within scholarship about methodology is that new inquiries demand new methodologies (Grabill 210). Jan

Fernheimer's work on Jewish rhetorics is instructive here. In her introduction to *Composing Jewish Rhetorics*, Fernheimer notes that the aim of the issue is to "work through the questions" defining Jewish rhetorics and determining how to "locate" and "study them" ("Talmidae" 577–89). Fernheimer goes on to discuss how studying Jewish rhetorics poses various methodological challenges. After analyzing the sheer difficulty of what counts as "Jewish"—challenges that include questions of ethnicity, conversion, and community values—Fernheimer identifies the "place" of Jewish rhetorics as similarly troubled: Jewish rhetorics "must be approached with a 'transnational rhetorical perspective,'" one that might not always correspond well to the Western rhetorical tradition ("Talmidae" 583). Indeed, as Fernheimer and the other contributors to *Composing Jewish Rhetorics* reveal, accounting for Jewish rhetorics demands attention to its own terms, values, and beliefs (see also Bernard-Donals and Fernheimer).

One key methodological issue facing scholars of religious rhetorics in general is thus definitional: how do we define religious rhetorics? As Brian Jackson notes in this volume, defining religious rhetoric is fraught. We agree with Jackson, however, that it's a move central to our abilities as researchers to chart and name territory that we may have previously ignored. Other terms that cluster around "religious rhetorics" similarly demand careful definition. After identifying "Jewish" as a difficult term to define, Fernheimer arrives at a conclusion that could apply to many terms that name religious rhetorics: "While I wish I could offer a clear-cut and straightforward answer about which values, beliefs, rituals, and traditions are definitively Jewish, I don't think there is one; or to be more blunt, I don't think there is *only* one, or could be, or should be" ("Talmidae" 580). Such definitional diversity poses key methodological challenges to researchers of Christian and other religious rhetorics, as Emily Cope and Jeff Ringer's contribution to this volume illustrates.

In addition to the challenge of definition, researchers must also consider how to position themselves in relation to the religious discourse under investigation. Grabill recognizes that methodology as a concept includes researchers' "personal commitments and ideologies" (212). While researchers must always be wary of their own biases and perspectives, dealing with highly sensitive and deeply ingrained aspects of religious belief demands keener attention to such commitments. David Wallace, for instance, has noted that, "[w]ith the possible exception of gender/sex, religion/spirituality seems the most hardwired, the most ingrained in culture of the difference issues" (518). While Wallace's claim is certainly debatable, he does identify a possibility that, if true, highlights the methodological issue of positionality. Beth Daniell, in "An Essay on Research and Telling the Truth," came to realize the methodological necessity of revealing her interpretive "lenses" and the challenge of just "how much [. . .] to reveal" (*Communion* 176–77). While Daniell's recognition is common for post-Kuhnian researchers, she arguably must add another layer of interpretive complexity. She is not only "rhetorical, feminist, Marxist, therapeutic" but also "spiritual," specifically of the "Twelve-Step and Episcopal varieties" (177). As a result, Daniell explains "that when a participant talks about her spiritual experiences, she knows that that is a subject I, too, take seriously" (177). Central to Daniell's concerns is the role of identity and belief—both the researcher's and the participant's—in shaping or hindering identification.

Thus, the problem of definition and the question of researcher positionality raise the ever-present challenge of ethics and representation. In her foreword to *Writing Studies Research in Practice*, Gesa Kirsch notes that "[e]thics and representation [. . .] play a key role when researchers study people, places, or programs whose beliefs, values, and worldviews they might find at odds with their own" (xiv). While she's not talking specifically about *religious* beliefs and worldviews, Kirsch's statement certainly has bearing on studying religious rhetorics. Indeed, one of the methodological implications of studying religious "people, places, or programs"—or rhetorics—is that, by definition, religious beliefs must be foregrounded. Doing so certainly invites the possibility that researchers might misunderstand, reduce, or caricaturize perspectives with which they disagree. In *Toward A Civil Discourse*, for example, Sharon Crowley's impressive attention to rhetoric and rhetorical theory seems at odds with her reduction of Christianity to fundamentalism (Daniell, "Whetstones"; DePalma, Ringer, and Webber; Steiner). But while we agree that scholars researching Christian rhetorics must keep ethics and representation at the forefront when writing about perspectives "they might find at odds with their own," we would push that one step farther: researchers must be similarly cautious when writing about beliefs that *correspond* to their own. While identification can foster trust, it can also serve as a terministic screen that erases nuanced but significant differences.

What all these methodological challenges point to is the need for robust and varied methodologies for studying religious rhetorics. We would go so far as to argue that studying the complex nature of religious rhetorics not only requires methodological innovation but actually encourages it as well. Fernheimer's *Rhetoric, Race, Religion: Hatzaad Harishon and Black Jewish Identity from Civil Rights to Black Power* provides a case in point. Drawing from archival documents at the Schomburg Center in New York, Fernheimer examines black Jews' interactions with other Jews in an effort to theorize how rhetors negotiate questions of identity and authenticity. One of the central methodological issues with which Fernheimer contends is the complex nature of constructing identity categories. Given the range of factors and various combinations of qualities that might determine how groups and individuals are represented (i.e., race, religion, self-perception, history, nationality, cultural practices), Fernheimer advises scholars to make explicit how and why categories are constructed. In response to these challenges in her study of black Jews, she also brings attention to the need for the expansion of research methods by calling researchers to "clarify the definitions we use to construct" and "sharpen the methods we use to count Jews of all hues" ("Making" 48).

Our field's global turn, along with the rapid growth of religions such as Islam and Pentecostalism ("Future" 13; "Global Christianity" 9–10; "World's"), necessitates that scholars of rhetoric develop methods to understand the function of religious rhetorics that pervade Western and non-Western contexts. While it is clear that understanding the religious motivations, traditions, identities, and ideologies that have shaped rhetorical action in such settings might better enable rhetors to discover opportunities for dialogue, identification, and cooperation among various groups, designing methodologies to study such phenomena is no easy task. Such methodologies must be innovative and multifaceted. For this reason, we see great potential—and need—for methodological expansion in future studies of religious rhetoric.

RELIGION AND CIVIC ENGAGEMENT

The final territory we chart is religion and civic engagement. We first outline arguments critics have offered to create space for religious rhetorics in civic discourse. We then discuss the pervasiveness of religious voices in international public discourses and illustrate the extent to which religious discourses shape civic action and political decision making. Next, we discuss the theoretical and historical arguments that scholars have offered to show the potential of religious rhetorics to inspire and direct citizens to pursue social and political transformation, and we discuss how the prophetic tradition might aid in achieving the goals of liberatory teaching practices. In connecting these areas of inquiry, we also chart new territory for scholarly studies of religion and civic engagement and outline how religious rhetorics might lead to more ethical ways of engaging in civic action and social justice.

Floyd Anderson and Lawrence Prelli argue that a central role of rhetorical critics is to offer "expressions of alternative orientations toward social reality" or "corrective rationalizations" that aim to establish an open universe of discourse (90). A primary task for critics is to offer counterstatements to dominant discourses in order to partially reopen closed systems of discourse. An open universe is one wherein all perspectives have a legitimate seat at the democratic table, while a closed universe of discourse privileges certain perspectives above others. As we've demonstrated elsewhere with Jim Webber, discussions of public discourse in the United States tend to privilege perspectives that are grounded in scene and agency and often exclude vocabularies of motive grounded in agent, act, and purpose, thus creating a universe of discourse closed to many religious vocabularies (DePalma, Ringer, and Webber; see also Althouse, Prelli, and Anderson, this volume). In arguing for a Burkean democratic dialectic, we aimed to provide a means by which to open the universe of discourse to religious perspectives and other vocabularies of motive grounded in excluded terms.

In line with these aims, scholars of rhetoric and political theory have offered a range of arguments for the value of religious discourses in the public sphere. Though not employing Burke's terms explicitly, these critics have argued for an open universe of discourse through the inclusion of religious perspectives. One important strand of this discussion has centered on the value of epistemic diversity in a pluralistic democracy. In *The Culture of Disbelief*, Stephen Carter writes, "We do no credit to the idea of religious freedom when we talk as though religion is something of which public-spirited adults should be ashamed [. . .]. Epistemic diversity, like diversity of other kinds, should be cherished, not ignored, and certainly not abolished" (10). For Carter, honoring epistemic diversity means resisting the suggestion that religiously committed citizens should "choose a form of dialogue that liberalism accepts" (10). Instead, he argues that "liberalism develop a politics that accepts whatever form of dialogue a member of the public offers" (10). This perspective aligns with Charles Taylor's redefinition of secularism not as militating against religion but rather upholding diversity. Specifically, Taylor's ideal of secularism entails three common goals: (1) "protecting people in their belonging to and/or practice of whatever outlook they choose or find themselves in"; (2) "treating people equally whatever their choice"; and (3) "giving them all a hearing" (36). It also aligns with Michael Sandel's argument for the inclusion of religious rhetorics in public discourse. He writes that "[r]ather than avoid the moral and religious convictions that our fellow citizens bring to public life, we should attend to them more directly—sometimes by challenging and contesting them and sometimes by listening and learning from them"(268). This kind of "robust public engagement with our moral disagreements," Sandel argues, "could provide a stronger, not a weaker basis for mutual respect" (268).

Along with arguing for the inclusion of religious discourses based on epistemic diversity, theorists have also called into question the doctrine of neutrality forwarded by proponents of the liberal model. Richard John Neuhaus's position in *The Naked Public Square: Religion and Democracy in America* is representative of the kinds of arguments critics have leveled against calls for neutrality in public discourse. In an effort to challenge the liberal notion of the public square, Neuhaus writes,

> Our question can certainly not be the old one of whether religion and politics should be mixed. They inescapably do mix, like it or not. The question is whether we can devise forms for that interaction which can revive rather than destroy the liberal democracy that is required by a society that would be pluralistic and free.
>
> (9)

For Neuhaus and others, public discourse about political matters cannot be severed from a person's belief system—religious or otherwise (Hansen). Instead, religious perspectives inevitably influence deliberation and judgment about political matters. Statistical data from J. Caleb Clanton's 2008 study support this view, indicating that "nearly half of all Americans—in some cases more—allow religion to play some role in their public lives as citizens, from how they formulate political opinions to political advocacy to voting behavior" (7).

Given the importance of religion to many citizens' lives, the question rhetoricians must consider is how it can inform civic engagement. One particularly rich example of such work is the 2009 special issue of the *JCR*, "Civic Engagement from Religious Grounds." The contributors extend recent discussions of "rhetorical democracy" and publics theory (Hauser and Grim; Hauser) by focusing on functions of religious discourses in "deliberative democracy." Contributors set out to offer "a greater depth of understanding regarding how religious minds come to grips with civic concerns" (Lessl 196). A particular strength of this issue is that each of the contributors examining the role of religious rhetorics in public life does so from the perspective of a religious tradition to which they currently or have previously belonged. Their essays offer a variety of perspectives on the relationship between religion and civic engagement, ranging from Medhurst's analysis of the historical rise and emerging shifts in evangelical political activism in the United States to Anne Neville Miller's case study of the tensions between public health groups and Christian organizations who are combating the HIV epidemic in Africa. Other perspectives include Calvin Troup's historical discussion of how H. Richard Niebuhr's *Christ and Culture* offers diverse ways of engaging in religiously motivated civic action, and Mark Steiner's argument that evangelical Christians are "uniquely positioned to show the way to public discourses that are more edifying, more productive and more humane" (291). Taken together, the contributors to this issue point to Thomas Lessl's conclusion that religion is a central and significant feature of civic life for all citizens ("Innate").

David S. Gutterman also explores the civic function of religious rhetorics at length in *Prophetic Politics: Christian Social Movements and American Democracy*. He writes, "Religious revivals tend to raise awareness of, and serve to define, the breach between 'higher principles' and the lived experiences of individuals. In turn, these revivals raise similar political questions about the fissure between the nation's higher ideals and its existing social conditions" (9). Gutterman's claims are born out in several investigations into the historical uses of prophetic rhetoric, such as Margaret Zulick's "Prophecy and Providence" and John Murphy's "'A Time of Shame and Sorrow': Robert F. Kennedy and the American Jeremiad."

The potential for religious rhetorics to serve a prophetic-critical function has been explored by various scholars of the American civil rights movement. In *Rhetoric, Religion, and the Civil Rights Movement*, Davis Houck and David Dixon, for example, argue that religious rhetoric was central to the gains made during civil rights. This claim is based on their examination of the Moses Moon Collection, materials that led them to the "realization that civil rights was a fundamentally religious affair" (2). They continue, stating that

[n]o amount of Aristotelian rationalism or Enlightenment exegesis on natural rights could persuade a black Indianola, Mississippi tenant farmer to go down to the county courthouse and try to register to vote [. . . T]o 'redish,' in the Mississippi vernacular, was not primarily about political self-interest so much as it was a Divine Call to personhood, a faithful enactment of God's plan, and a fulfillment of a uniquely American promise.

(2–3)

Rhetorical studies of the civil rights movement show the extent to which religion might serve as a basis of motivation for progressive social reform. Such work also prompts questions concerning how religion might function as a catalyst for such ends in contemporary contexts. History suggests that religion can serve as a source of freedom or oppression. Thus, it is essential for rhetoricians to examine how religiously committed individuals historically have understood the relationship between religion and civic action. Work of this kind will also provide an opportunity to subject such ideas to critical reflection. This desire to understand how religious motivations—past and present—shape civic engagement lies at the center of much of the work in this collection, particularly in chapters by Will Duffy, Lisa Zimmerelli, and Lisa Shaver.

Closely tied to discussions of how religious rhetorics might inspire political transformation are conversations concerning the relationship between religious rhetorics and rhetorical education. Drawing on Cornel West's notion of "prophetic witness," Keith Gilyard discusses how religious rhetorics might extend the aims of critical pedagogies and shape thinking about issues of race and class. Following West, Gilyard defines prophetic witness as "human deeds of justice and kindness that attend to unjust sources of human hurt and misery. It calls attention to the causes of unjustified suffering and unnecessary social misery and highlights personal and institutional evil, including evil of being indifferent to personal and institutional evil" (114). Gilyard offers this definition to make a distinction between prophetic religious rhetorics that might inform critical teaching practices and private, conservative, evangelical, or fundamentalist rhetorics that undermine such goals. While Gilyard sees promise in religious rhetorics of prophetic witness for critical pedagogies and for rethinking issues of race and class, he remains unconvinced that "high-volume creativity is going to flow from fundamentalist or evangelical students" (58). His skepticism stems from the view that such students' "religiosity tends not to be of the prophetic, socially ameliorative type but the conservative, George W. Bush type" (58). For Gilyard, scholars who've argued for the inclusion of religious rhetorics in composition studies have not done enough to assess "the practical link between conservative Christianity and conservative political actions" and have failed to adequately "[h]istoricize the contrast between the fundamentalist and the prophetic" (58).

An article that provides a point of partial contrast to Gilyard's perspective is Thomas Amorose's "A Christian Rhetoric for the Public Sphere." While many of the aims Amorose articulates are consistent with those voiced by Gilyard, Amorose's notion of "public-theological rhetoric" is inclusive of a broader range of traditions and perspectives. Amorose argues for a "rhetoric-based public theology" and proposes that a "public-theological rhetoric" might serve as a basis for social justice efforts and for "building a pedagogy of public justice" (27). At the core of Amorose's essay is the assertion that "theology is an inherently rhetorical enterprise" (23). Acknowledging this provides Amorose a way to link the universal concerns of theology to a method of inquiry that deals with probable and contingent truths in particular historical contexts. Public theological discourse is not primarily about persuading citizens to adopt particular theological values on public issues. Instead, Amorose contends that "[a] true public theology must seek to reform the very basis on which that public, its notion of itself as a public, is constituted" (23). Public theological rhetoric, in other words, is an effort to reorient the public sphere. To theorize the notion of "redeemed rhetoric" aimed at cultural transformation and just social arrangements, Amorose explores how Augustine's redeemed rhetoric and Derrida's call to pursue justice faithfully could inform a "public-theological pedagogy" (43).

Another scholar who argues that theological rhetorics can be integral to the aims of liberatory pedagogies and progressive social change is Shari Stenberg. In "Liberation Theology and Liberatory Pedagogies: Renewing the Dialogue," Stenberg examines the historical divisions between liberation theology and critical pedagogy in an effort to demonstrate how the prophetic tradition of liberation theology could enrich critical approaches to composition teaching. After unpacking the reasons for the enduring split between critical pedagogy and liberation theology, Stenberg calls rhetoricians to bridge this division: "To place these traditions back in dialogue is not to espouse theology in the critical classroom, it is to return to roots that might better allow us to realize the goals of liberatory education: valuing student knowledge, enacting a reciprocal teacher-student relationship, enriching critique with both compassion and action, and participating in ongoing reflection and revision" (288–89). Stenberg adds that "[t]he prophetic tradition of liberation theology offers us visions that may not only enrich our understanding of critical pedagogy, but may also help us enact it more fully" (288).

Given the importance of religious voices in public discourse, the study of religious rhetorics ought to be a central priority for rhetorical theorists. In gaining a deeper understanding of the roles and functions of religious rhetorics in public discourse, rhetoricians will be better prepared to recognize the inventional possibilities of religious discourses, timely opportunities for counterstatements, and rhetorical appeals best suited to our present contexts. Put otherwise, through the study of religious rhetorics, scholars of

rhetoric might be better positioned to promote pathways to mutual understanding and tolerance in the public sphere.

CONCLUSION

Through the course of editing this volume, we've come to see that it is not
so much the subject of religion that has been underrepresented in rhetorical
studies, but rather perspectives that illuminate the implications of religious
rhetorics themselves. Arguments for the significance of work on religious
rhetorics are often couched in discussions of what religious figures, groups
or traditions might imply for our understanding of race, class, gender, historical periods, and so forth. There is no question that these are all highly
significant areas of inquiry, and we value scholarship that helps us understand how such issues are shaped by the presence of religious perspectives
or motives. That said, very few studies attempt to articulate the implications of such work for understanding religious rhetorics *on their own terms.*
However, as Brian Jackson's contribution to this volume makes evident,
working in this mode has the potential to open significant possibilities for
rhetorical studies. Not only will approaching the study of religious rhetorics
from this vantage help scholars "*classify* and *define* rhetorical artifacts with
more clarity," but doing so will also provide a more nuanced understanding
of the "exigencies or predicaments that drive rhetorical actors to appeal to
agencies beyond human flourishing" (28). Examining "the symbolic action
of religious *rhetors* on their own terms and with their own assumptions"
likewise allows critics to "hold[] religious *rhetors* accountable for the full
measure of what they bring to a rhetorical moment"—whether fear and
intolerance or peace and justice (Jackson 28, this volume).

Along with the possibilities such work makes available, we see foregrounding religious identity, affiliation, motivation, commitment, and influence in rhetorical scholarship as significant because it prompts a novel set of
concerns about religious rhetorics. Broadly speaking, it urges us to ask what
difference it might make when rhetorical action is motivated by religious
traditions and assumptions. Burke notes that there's an "*objective* difference" when something is said in the name of God as opposed to "godless
nature" (*Rhetoric* 6). What is that difference, and how do we account for it
as rhetorical critics, historians, theorists, activists, and educators? Additionally, the presence of religious beliefs, assumptions, motives, and identities
demands that we consider how we might understand rhetorics differently if
we examine their consequences in light of, in terms of, and in relationship
to the religious traditions and beliefs with which they are associated. What,
for example, might such an approach enable us to see or understand about
the relationship between religious rhetorics and civic action? How might it
allow us to better understand the ways religious rhetorics function across
contexts? In what ways might it lead us to rethink rhetorical history, theory,
methodology, and education? The chapters in this collection have begun to

address many of these questions, though we see much more work ahead. We hope these lines of inquiry motivate future engagement with religious rhetorics—territory that clearly has profound prospects and possibilities for rhetorical studies.

REFERENCES

Amorose, Thomas. "A Christian Rhetoric for the Public Sphere." *The Journal for Peace and Justice Studies* 20 (1999): 21–49.

Anderson, Chris. "The Description of an Embarrassment: When Students Write about Religion." *ADE Bulletin* 94 (1989): 12–15.

———. *Teaching as Believing: Faith in the University*. Waco: Baylor UP, 2004.

Anderson, Floyd D., and Lawrence J. Prelli. "Pentadic Cartography: Mapping the Universe of Discourse." *Quarterly Journal of Speech* 87.1 (2001): 73–95.

Barrett, Stephen R. *This Gonna Hurt Like Hell: A Pentecostal Student Enters the Academy*. Diss. U of New Hampshire, 1997.

Bernard-Donals, Michael, and Janice W. Fernheimer. *Jewish Rhetorics: History, Theory, Practice*. Waltham, MA: Brandeis University Press, 2014.

Berthoff, Ann E. et al. "Interchanges: Spiritual Sites of Composing." *College Composition and Communication* 45 (1994): 237–63.

Bizzell, Patricia. "Faith-Based World Views as a Challenge to the Believing Game." *JAEPL* 14 (2008–2009): 29–35.

———. "Feminist Methods of Research in the History of Rhetoric: What Difference Do They Make?" *Rhetoric Society Quarterly* 30.4 (2000): 5–17.

———. "Rationality as Rhetorical Strategy at the Barcelona Disputation, 1263: A Cautionary Tale." *College Composition and Communication* 58.1 (2006): 12–29.

Booth, Wayne C. "Ending the War between Science and Religion: Can Rhetorology Do the Job?" *Professing Rhetoric: Selected Papers from the 2000 Rhetoric Society of America Conference*. Eds. Frederick J. Antczak, Cinda Coggins, and Geoffrey D. Klinger. Mahwah: Erlbaum, 2002. 223–34.

———. "The Many Voices of Kenneth Burke, Theologian and Prophet, as Revealed in His Letters to Me." *Unending Conversations: New Writings by and about Kenneth Burke*. Eds. Greig Henderson and David Cratis Williams. Carbondale: Southern Illinois UP, 2001. 179–201.

———. "Rhetoric And Religion: Are They Essentially Wedded?" *Radical Pluralism and Truth*. New York: Crossroad, 1991. 62–80. ATLA Religion Database with ATLASerials. Web. 9 June 2013.

———. "Rhetoric, Science, and Religion." *The Essential Wayne Booth*. Ed. Walter Jost. Chicago: U of Chicago P, 2006.

———. "Systematic Wonder: The Rhetoric of Secular Religions." *The Knowing Most Worth Doing: Essays on Pluralism, Ethics, and Religion*. Ed. Walter Jost. Charlottesville: U of Virginia P, 2010.

Brown, Robert L., and Michael Jon Olson. "Storm in the Academy: Community Conflict and Spirituality in the Research University." Buley-Meissner, Thompson, and Tan 153–69.

Browning, Mark et al. "Symposium on Teaching in the Whirlwind: When Religion Becomes Visible in the Classroom." *Dialogue: A Journal for Writing Specialists* 6.1 (1999): 6–48.

Brummett, Barry. "Rhetorical Epistemology and Rhetorical Spirituality." Buley-Meissner, Thompson, and Tan 121–36.

Buley-Meissner, Mary Louise, Mary McCaslin Thompson, and Elizabeth Bachrach Tan, eds. *The Academy and the Possibility of Belief: Essays on Intellectual and Spiritual Life*. Cresskill: Hampton P, 2000.

Burke, Kenneth. *Permanence and Change: An Anatomy of Purpose*. 3rd ed. Berkeley: U of California P, 1984.

———. *A Rhetoric of Motives*. Berkeley: U of California P, 1969.

———. *The Rhetoric of Religion*. Berkeley: U of California P, 1961.

Burton, Vicki Tolar. *Spiritual Literacy in John Wesley's Methodism: Reading, Writing, and Speaking to Believe*. Waco: Baylor UP, 2008.

Carter, Shannon. "Living inside the Bible (Belt): A Critical Approach to Evangelical Rhetoric in Student Writing." *College English* 69.6 (2007): 272–95.

Carter, Stephen L. *The Culture of Disbelief: How American Law and Politics Trivialize Religion Devotion*. New York: Doubleday, 1993.

Clanton, J. Caleb. *Religion and Democratic Citizenship: Inquiry and Conviction in the American Public Square*. New York: Lexington, 2008.

Coley, Toby F. "Opening a Dialogue about Religious Restraint in Graduate Professionalization." *Rhetoric Review* 29.4 (2010): 395–413.

Crowley, Sharon. *Toward a Civil Discourse: Rhetoric and Fundamentalism*. Pittsburgh: U of Pittsburgh P, 2006.

Daniell, Beth. *A Communion of Friendship: Literacy, Spiritual Practice, and Women in Recovery*. Carbondale: Southern Illinois UP, 2003.

———. "Whetstones Provided by the World: Trying to Deal with Difference in a Pluralistic Society." *College English* 70.1 (2007): 79–88.

Deans, Thomas. "The Rhetoric of Jesus Writing in the Story of the Adulteress (John 7.53–8.11)." *College Composition and Communication* 65.3 (2014): 406–29.

DePalma, Michael-John. "Austin Phelps and the Spirit (of) Composing: An Exploration of Nineteenth-Century Sacred Rhetoric at Andover Theological Seminary." *Rhetoric Review* 27.4 (2008): 379–396.

———. "Re-envisioning Religious Discourses as Rhetorical Resources in Composition Teaching: A Pragmatic Response to the Challenge of Belief." *College Composition and Communication* 63.2 (2011): 219–43.

———. "Rhetorical Education for the Nineteenth Century Pulpit: Austin Phelps and the Influence of Christian Transcendentalism at Andover Theological Seminary." *Rhetoric Review* 31.1 (2012): 1–20.

———, Jeffrey M. Ringer, and James D. Webber. "(Re)Charting the (Dis)Courses of Faith and Politics, or Rhetoric and Democracy in the Burkean Barnyard." *Rhetoric Society Quarterly* 38.3 (2008): 311–34.

Dively, Ronda Leathers. "Censoring Religious Rhetoric in the Composition Classroom: What We and Our Students May Be Missing." *Composition Studies* 25.1 (1997): 55–66.

———. "Religious Discourse in the Academy: Creating a Space by Means of Poststructuralist Theories of Subjectivity." *Composition Studies* 21.2 (1993): 91–101.

Downs, Douglas. "True Believers, Real Scholars, and Real True Believing Scholars: Discourses of Inquiry and Affirmation in the Composition Classroom." Vander Lei and kyburz 39–55.

Elbow, Peter. "The Believing Game or Methodological Believing." *JAEPL* 14 (2008–09): 1–11.

Engelson, Amber. "The 'Hands of God' at Work: Negotiating between Western and Religious Sponsorship in Indonesia." *College English* 76.4 (2014): 292–314.

Enos, Richard Leo, and Roger Thompson, eds. *The Rhetoric of St. Augustine of Hippo: De Doctrina Christiana and the Search for a Distinctly Christian Rhetoric*. Waco: Baylor UP, 2008.

Fernheimer, Janice W., ed. *Composing Jewish Rhetorics*. Spec. issue of *College English* 72.6 (2010): 577–653.

———. "Making Klal Yisrael Count: The Difficulties of Defining Black Jewish Communities." *AJS Perspectives* (Fall 2011): 46–48.

———. *Rhetoric, Race, Religion: Hatzaad Harishon and Black Jewish Identity from Civil Rights to Black Power.* Tuscaloosa: U of Alabama P, 2013.

———. "Talmidae Rhetoricae: Drashing up Models and Methods for Jewish Rhetorical Studies." *College English* 72.6 (2010): 577–89.

Fishman, Andrea. *Amish Literacy: What and How it Means.* Portsmouth: Heinemann, 1988.

FitzGerald, William. *Spiritual Modalities: Prayer as Rhetoric and Performance.* University Park: Pennsylvania State UP, 2012.

Fodor, James, and Stanley Hauerwas. "Performing Faith: The Peaceable Rhetoric of God's Church." Jost and Olmsted 381–414.

"The Future of the Global Muslim Population: Projections for 2010–2030." *Pew Forum on Religion & Public Life.* Pew Research Center. 27 January 2011. Web. 8 June 2013.

Gannett, Cinthia, and John Brereton, eds. *Traditions of Eloquence: The Jesuits and Modern Rhetorical Studies.* New York: Fordham UP, forthcoming.

Geiger, TJ, II. "Unpredictable Encounters: Religious Discourse, Sexuality, and the Free Exercise of Rhetoric." *College English* 75.3 (2013): 250–71.

Gere, Anne Ruggles. "Revealing Silence: Rethinking Personal Writing." *College Composition and Communication* 53:2 (2001): 203–23.

Gilyard, Keith. *Composition and Cornel West: Notes toward a Deep Democracy.* Carbondale: Southern Illinois UP, 2008.

"Global Christianity: A Report on the Size and Distribution of the World's Christian Population." *Pew Forum on Religion & Public Life.* Pew Research Center. 19 Dec. 2011. Web. 8 June 2013.

Goodburn, Amy. "It's a Question of Faith: Discourses of Fundamentalism and Critical Pedagogy in the Writing Classroom." *JAC* 18.2 (1998): 333–53.

Grabill, Jeffrey T. "Community-Based Research and the Importance of a Research Stance." Nickoson and Sheridan 210–19.

Gutterman, David S. *Prophetic Politics: Christian Social Movements and American Democracy.* Ithaca: Cornell UP, 2005.

Hauser, Gerard A. *Vernacular Voices.* Columbia: U of South Carolina P, 1999.

———, and Amy Grimm. *Rhetorical Democracy: Discursive Practices of Civic Engagement.* Mahwah: Erlbaum, 2004.

Hansen, Kristine. "Religious Freedom in the Public Square and the Composition Classroom." Vander Lei and kyburz 24–38.

Heath, Shirley Brice. *Ways with Words: Language, Life, and Work in Communities and Classrooms.* 1983. Cambridge: Cambridge UP, 1998.

Hirst, Russel. "Austin Phelps's Theory of Balance in Homiletic Style." *Journal of Communication and Religion* 18 (1995): 17–27.

———. "The Sermon as Public Discourse: Austin Phelps and the Conservative Homiletic Tradition in Nineteenth-Century America." *Oratorical Culture in Nineteenth-Century America: Transformations in the Theory and Practice of Rhetoric.* Ed. Gregory Clark and S. Michael Halloran. Carbondale: Southern Illinois UP, 1993. 78–109.

———. "The Sixth Canon of Sacred Rhetoric: Inspiration in Nineteenth-Century Homiletic Theory." *Rhetoric Society Quarterly* 25 (1995): 69–89.

Houck, Davis W., and David E. Dixon, eds. *Rhetoric, Religion and the Civil Rights Movement, 1954–1965.* Waco: Baylor UP, 2006.

Inoue, Asao B. "Racial Methodologies for Composition Studies: Reflecting on Theories of Race in Writing Assessment Research." Nickoson and Sheridan 125–39.

Jost, Walter and Wendy Olmsted, eds. *Rhetorical Invention and Religious Inquiry.* New Haven: Yale UP, 2000.

Kinneavy, James L. *Greek Rhetorical Origins of Christian Faith: An Inquiry*. Oxford: Oxford UP, 1987.

Kirsch, Gesa. "Foreword: New Methodological Challenges for Writing Studies Researchers." Nickoson and Sheridan xi–xvi.

———,and Liz Rohan, ed. *Beyond the Archives: Research as Lived Process*. Carbondale: Southern Illinois UP, 2008.

Lessl, Thomas M., ed. *Civic Engagement from Religious Grounds*. Spec. issue of *Journal of Communication and Religion* 32 (2009): 195–346.

———. "Civic Engagement from Religious Grounds." *Journal of Communication and Religion* 32 (2009): 195–98.

———. "The Innate Religiosity of Public Life: An *A Fortiori* Argument." *Journal of Communication and Religion* 32 (2009): 319–46.

Marsden, George M. *The Outrageous Idea of Christian Scholarship*. New York: Oxford UP, 1997.

Marzluf, Phillip P. "Religion in U.S. Writing Classes: Challenging the Conflict Narrative." *Journal of Writing Research* 2.3 (2011): 265–97. Web. 8 June 2013.

Medhurst, Martin J. "Evangelical Christian Faith and Political Action: Mike Huckabee and the 2008 Republican Presidential Nomination." *Journal of Communication and Religion* 32 (2009): 199–239.

———. "Religious Belief and Scholarship: A Complex Relationship." *Journal of Communication and Religion* 27 (2004): 40–47.

———, ed. *Religious and Theological Traditions as Sources of Rhetorical Invention*. Spec. issue of *Rhetoric & Public Affairs* 7.4 (2004): 445–614.

Miller, Anne Neville. "Religion in the African Public [Health] Square: The Case of HIV-related Stigma." *Journal of Communication and Religion* 32 (2009): 268–88.

Moss, Beverly. *A Community Text Arises: A Literate Text and Literacy Tradition in African American Churches*. Cresskill: Hampton, 2003.

Mountford, Roxanne. *The Gendered Pulpit: Preaching in American Protestant Spaces*. Carbondale: Southern Illinois UP, 2003.

Murphy, James J. *Rhetoric in the Middle Ages*. Berkeley: U of California P, 1974.

———, ed. *Three Medieval Rhetorical Arts*. Berkeley: U of California P, 1971.

Murphy, John M. "'A Time of Shame and Sorrow': Robert F. Kennedy and the American Jeremiad." *Quarterly Journal of Speech* 76.4 (1990): 401–14. ERIC. Web. 8 June 2013.

Neuhaus, Richard John. *The Naked Public Square: Religion and Democracy in America*. 2nd ed. Grand Rapids: Eerdman's, 1986.

Newbigin, Lesslie. *The Gospel in a Pluralist Society*. Grand Rapids: Eerdmans, 1989.

Nickoson, Lee, and Mary P. Sheridan, eds. *Writing Studies Research in Practice: Methods and Methodologies*. Carbondale: Southern Illinois UP, 2012.

O'Reilly, Mary Rose. "Splitting the Cartesian Hair." *The Journal of the Assembly for Expanded Perspectives on Learning* 14 (2008–2009): 22–28.

Olmsted, Wendy. "Invention, Emotion, and Conversion in Augustine's *Confessions*." Jost and Olmsted 65–86.

Perkins, Priscilla. "'A Radical Conversion of the Mind': Fundamentalism, Hermeneutics, and the Metanoic Classroom" *College English* 63.5 (2001): 585–611.

Rand, Lizabeth A. "Enacting Faith: Evangelical Discourse and the Discipline of Composition Studies." *College Composition and Communication* 52.3 (2001): 349–67.

Ringer, Jeffrey M. "The Consequences of Integrating Faith Into Academic Writing: Casuistic Stretching and Biblical Citation." *College English* 75.3 (2013): 270–97.

———. "The Dogma of Inquiry: Composition and the Primacy of Faith." *Rhetoric Review* 32.3 (2013): 349–65.

———. "Faith and Language: Walter Hilton, St. Augustine, and Poststructural Semiotics." *Christianity and Literature* 53.1 (2003): 3–18.

Rohan, Liz. "Reseeing and Redoing: Making Historical Research at the Turn of the Millennium." Nickoson and Sheridan 2012.

Sandel, Michael J. *Justice: What's the Right Thing to Do?* New York: Farrar, Straus and Giroux, 2009.

Shaver, Lisa J. *Beyond the Pulpit: Women's Rhetorical Roles in the Antebellum Religious Press.* Pittsburgh: U of Pittsburgh P, 2012.

———. "Women's Deathbed Pulpits: From Quiet Congregants to Iconic Ministers." *Rhetoric Review* 27.1 (2008): 20–37.

Shuger, Debora K. "The Philosophical Foundations of Sacred Rhetoric." Jost and Olmsted 47–64.

"The Spiritual Life of College Students: A National Study of College Students' Search for Meaning and Purpose." *Higher Education Research Institute.* 2004. Web. 18 November 2008.

Steiner, Mark Allan. "Reconceptualizing Christian Public Engagement: 'Faithful Witness' and the American Evangelical Tradition." *Journal of Communication and Religion* 32 (2009): 289–318. *Communication and Mass Media Complete.* Web. 16 May 2011.

Stenberg, Shari J. "Liberation Theology and Liberatory Pedagogies: Renewing the Dialogue." *College English* 68.3 (2006): 271–90.

Taylor, Charles. "Why We Need a Radical Redefinition of Secularism." *The Power of Religion in the Public Sphere.* Eds. Eduardo Mendieta and Jonathan VanAntwerpen. New York: Columbia UP, 2011. 34–59.

Teich, Nathaniel. "The Rhetoric of Empathy: Ethical Foundations of Dialogic Communication." *The Journal of the Assembly for Expanded Perspectives on Learning* 14 (2008–09): 12–21.

Tell, Dave. "Jimmy Swaggart's Secular Confession." *Rhetoric Society Quarterly* 39.2 (2009): 124–46.

Trapp, Joona Smitherman. "Religious Values and the Student: A Plea for Tolerance." Browning et al. 14–22.

Troup, Calvin L. "Civic Engagement from Religious Grounds." *Journal of Communication and Religion* 32 (2009): 240–67.

Vander Lei, Elizabeth. "Coming to Terms with Religious Faith in the Composition Classroom." Vander Lei and kyburz 3–10.

———, et al., eds. *Renovating Rhetoric in Christian Tradition.* Pittsburgh: U of Pittsburgh P, 2014.

——— and bonnie lenore kyburz, eds. *Negotiating Religious Faith in the Composition Classroom.* Portsmouth: Heinemann, 2005.

Wallace, David L. "Transcending Normativity: Difference Issues in College English." *College English* 68.5 (2006): 502–30.

Williams, Mark. *Transformations: Material Terms for Writing on Religion in Composition Classrooms.* Diss., U of Louisville, 2013.

"The World's Muslims: Religion, Politics and Society." *The Pew Forum on Religion & Public Life.* Pew Research Center. 30 April 2013. Web. 8 June 2013.

Yarbrough, Stephen R. "The Love of Invention: Augustine, Davidson, and the Discourse of Unifying Belief." *Rhetoric Society Quarterly* 30.1 (2000): 29–46.

Zulick, Margaret D. "Prophecy and Providence: The Anxiety over Prophetic Authority." *Journal of Communication and Religion* 26 (2003): 195–207.

Contributors

Matthew T. Althouse is an associate professor of Communication at The College at Brockport: State University of New York, where he teaches courses in rhetoric and public address. His academic writing interests include dramatistic rhetorical theory and criticism and rhetoric and religion.

Floyd D. Anderson is a professor emeritus of Communication at The College at Brockport, State University of New York. He conducts scholarship in rhetorical theory and criticism, with special attention to the history of rhetoric, political rhetoric, and Kenneth Burke's dramatism. He has taught courses on public speaking, propaganda and persuasion, the history of rhetoric, contemporary rhetorical theory, and rhetorical criticism.

Emily Murphy Cope, a PhD candidate in English at the University of Tennessee, Knoxville, specializes in composition, the history of rhetorical education, and American religious rhetorics. She is currently completing a qualitative study of the academic writing of evangelical undergraduates at public universities and collaborating on a qualitative study of writing teacher preparation.

Richard Benjamin Crosby is an assistant professor in the English department at Iowa State University. He teaches courses in speech and rhetoric, including public speaking, persuasion, public address, rhetorical criticism, and the history of rhetoric. His research focuses on religious discourse, especially as it intersects or collides with American political culture.

Beth Daniell, a professor of English at Kennesaw State University, teaches rhetorical theory and research methods. She directs the General Education program in English and Writing across the Curriculum in the College of Humanities and Social Sciences. Beth is author of *A Communion of Friendship: Literacy, Spiritual Practice, and Women in Recovery*;

coeditor of *Women and Literacy: Local and Global Inquiries for a New Century*; and coeditor of *Renovating Rhetoric in Christian Tradition*—all taking up various permutations and intersections of literacy, rhetoric, identity, community, spirituality, religion, and women.

Thomas Deans teaches in the English Department and directs the writing center at the University of Connecticut. His is the author of *Writing Partnerships: Service-Learning in Composition* and *Writing and Community Action*, coeditor of the collection *Writing and Community Engagement: A Critical Sourcebook*, and series coeditor for the *Oxford Brief Guides to Writing in the Disciplines*. He has long been interested in how writers are depicted in literature and recently has been studying representations of literacy in religious discourses.

Michael-John DePalma is an assistant professor of English in the Professional Writing Program at Baylor University. DePalma teaches courses in rhetoric, advanced composition, technical and professional writing, composition theory, and writing pedagogy. His work has appeared in *College Composition and Communication*; *Rhetoric Society Quarterly*; *Rhetoric Review*; *Reflections: A Journal of Writing, Service Learning, and Community Literacy*; the *Journal of Second Language Writing*, and several edited collections.

William Duffy is an assistant professor of English at the University of Memphis, where he teaches courses in rhetoric and composition. His research includes work in discourse ethics, religious rhetoric, composition theory, and writing pedagogy, while his scholarship has been published in *College English*, *Composition Studies*, and *Rhetoric Review* and in various edited collections.

William T. FitzGerald is an associate professor of English at Rutgers-Camden, where he teaches courses in rhetoric, literacy, and writing studies and directs a center for teaching excellence and assessment. The author of *Spiritual Modalities: Rhetoric as Prayer and Performance* (2012), his research is centered on the intersection of prayer and rhetorical theory. His current book project analyzes prayer as a communicative practice across oral, textual, and digital media.

Brenda Glascott is an associate professor of English at California State University, San Bernardino, where she teaches courses on composition, rhetoric, literacy, and pedagogy. She is cofounder and Managing Editor of *Literacy in Composition Studies*, an open-access online peer-reviewed journal. She has published on nineteenth-century evangelical literacy narratives and embodied pedagogy. Her current research focuses on commonplaces about academic writing between 1900 and 1950.

Brian Jackson, associate professor of English at Brigham Young University, coordinates University Writing and teaches courses in rhetoric and writing studies.

Lawrence J. Prelli is a professor of Communication and affiliate professor of English and of Natural Resources at the University of New Hampshire in Durham. He conducts scholarship in rhetorical theory and criticism, with special attention to environmental rhetoric, the rhetoric of ecology, and Kenneth Burke's dramatism. Professor Prelli teaches courses on Propaganda and Persuasion, Persuasion and Public Problems, Principles of Rhetorical Criticism, and Rhetorics of Display.

Jeffrey M. Ringer is an assistant professor of English in the division of Rhetoric, Writing, and Linguistics at the University of Tennessee, Knoxville, where he teaches undergraduate and graduate courses in rhetoric, writing, and pedagogy. He has published in journals such as *College English, Rhetoric Society Quarterly, Rhetoric Review, JAC: A Journal of Rhetoric, Culture, & Politics,* and the *Journal of Second Language Writing,* as well as in several edited collections.

Lisa J. Shaver is an associate professor of English at Baylor University, where she teaches courses in rhetoric and professional writing. She is the author of *Beyond the Pulpit: Women's Rhetorical Roles in the Antebellum Religious Press* (2012). Her work has also appeared in *College English, Rhetoric Review, Pedagogy,* and the *Journal of Business and Technical Writing.*

Heather Thomson-Bunn is an assistant professor of English and a director of First-Year Writing at Pepperdine University. She teaches courses in composition, rhetorical theory, professional writing, and language theory. Her research focuses on the relationship between religious and academic discourses, as well as on the rhetorical dimensions of definition. Her work has appeared in *Composition Forum* and *Reading Research Quarterly.*

Elizabeth Vander Lei is a professor of English at Calvin College, where she directs the first-year writing program and teaches courses in writing, writing pedagogy, and linguistics. In addition to other publications, she has coedited two collections about religion and writing studies: *Renovating Rhetoric in Christian Tradition* (with Tom Amorose, Beth Daniell, and Anne Gere, 2014) and *Negotiating Religious Faith in the Composition Classroom* (with bonnie kyburz 2005).

Lisa Zimmerelli is assistant professor of Writing and Writing Center director at Loyola University Maryland. She teaches first-year writing, rhetorical and argument theory, women's rhetoric, and writing center theory and practice. Lisa's research on the history of American women's rhetorical practice has been published in *Rhetoric Society Quarterly*, *Rhetoric Review*, and *Peitho*, and she was a recipient of the 2013 *RSQ* Kneupper Award. Lisa has also published on tutor training, including *The Bedford Guide for Writing Tutors*.

Index